TREASURY OF LITERATURE

SHADES OF GOLD

SENIOR AUTHORS

ROGER C. FARR
DOROTHY S. STRICKLAND

AUTHORS

RICHARD F. ABRAHAMSON
ELLEN BOOTH CHURCH
BARBARA BOWEN COULTER
BERNICE E. CULLINAN
MARGARET A. GALLEGO
W. DORSEY HAMMOND
JUDITH L. IRVIN
KAREN KUTIPER
DONNA M. OGLE
TIMOTHY SHANAHAN
PATRICIA SMITH
JUNKO YOKOTA
HALLIE KAY YOPP

SENIOR CONSULTANTS

ASA G. HILLIARD III
JUDY M. WALLIS

CONSULTANTS

ALONZO A. CRIM
ROLANDO R. HINOJOSA-SMITH
LEE BENNETT HOPKINS
ROBERT J. STERNBERG

HARCOURT BRACE & COMPANY

Orlando Atlanta Austin Boston San Francisco Chicago Dallas New York
Toronto London

Requests for permission to make copies of any part of the work should be mailed to: Permissions Department, Harcourt Brace & Company, 6277 Sea Harbor Drive, Orlando, Florida 32887-6777.

Portions of this work were published in previous editions.

Printed in the United States of America

ISBN 0-15-301236-6

1 2 3 4 5 6 7 8 9 10   048   97 96 95 94

Acknowledgments continue on page 652, which constitutes an extension of this copyright page.

Acknowledgments
For permission to reprint copyrighted material, grateful acknowledgment is made to the following sources:
Atheneum Publishers, an imprint of Macmillan Publishing Company: Cover illustration by Zena Bernstein from *Mrs. Frisby and the Rats of NIMH* by Robert C. O'Brien. Copyright © 1971 by Robert C. O'Brien. "Mother Doesn't Want a Dog" from *If I Were in Charge of the World and Other Worries* by Judith Viorst. Text copyright © 1981 by Judith Viorst.
Avon Books: Cover illustration by Alan Daniel from *Bunnicula* by Deborah and James Howe. Illustration copyright © 1979 by Alan Daniel.
Susan Bergholz Literary Services, New York: "Name/Nombres" by Julia Alvarez. Text copyright © 1985 by Julia Alvarez. Originally published in *Nuestro,* March 1985.
Bradbury Press, an Affiliate of Macmillan Publishing Company: "The Rescue" from *Waiting to Waltz: A Childhood* by Cynthia Rylant. Text copyright © 1984 by Cynthia Rylant.
Curtis Brown, Ltd.: From pp. 7–24 in *Courage, Dana* by Susan Beth Pfeffer. Text copyright © 1983 by Susan Beth Pfeffer. Published by Dell Books.
Camden House Publishing: Cover photograph by François Gohier from *Meeting the Whales: The Equinox Guide to Giants of the Deep* by Erich Hoyt. Copyright © 1991 by Erich Hoyt.
Deborah Chandra: "Sleeping Simon" by Deborah Chandra from *Dog Poems,* selected by Myra Cohn Livingston. Text copyright © 1990 by Deborah Chandra. Published by Holiday House.
Chronicle Books: Cover photograph from *Cities in the Sand,* written and photographed by Scott Warren. Copyright © 1992 by Scott S. Warren.
Myra J. Ciardi: "The Dollar Dog" from *Doodle Soup* by John Ciardi. Text copyright © 1985 by Myra J. Ciardi. Published by Houghton Mifflin Company.
Clarion Books, a Houghton Mifflin Company imprint: From *The Princess in the Pigpen* by Jane Resh Thomas, cover illustration by Alix Berenzy. Text copyright © 1989 by Jane Resh Thomas; cover illustration © 1989 by Alix Berenzy.
Dell Books, a division of Bantam Doubleday Dell Publishing Group, Inc.: From *Make Like a Tree and Leave* by Paula Danziger, cover illustration by Joe Csatari. Text copyright © 1990 by Paula Danziger; cover illustration copyright © 1990 by Joe Csatari.
Tom Doherty Associates: From *Kid Heroes* by Neal Shusterman. Text and cover photograph copyright © 1991 by RGA Publishing Group, Inc.
Doubleday, a division of Bantam Doubleday Dell Publishing Group, Inc.: "Tides" from *Taxis and Toadstools* by Rachel Field. Text copyright 1926 by Doubleday, a division of Bantam Doubleday Dell Publishing Group, Inc.
Yvette Eastman: "At the Aquarium" from *Poems of Five Decades* by Max Eastman. Text copyright 1954 by Max Eastman.
Farrar, Straus & Giroux, Inc.: Cover illustration by Leslie W. Bowman from *El Güero* by Elizabeth Borton de Treviño. Illustration copyright © 1989 by Leslie W. Bowman.
Four Winds Press, an imprint of Macmillan Publishing Company: From pp. 1–7, with map redrawn from p. 5 in *Earth's Changing Climate* by Roy A. Gallant. Text copyright © 1979 by Roy A. Gallant.
Greenwillow Books, a division of William Morrow & Company, Inc.: Cover illustration by Peter Sis from *The Whipping Boy* by Sid Fleischman. Illustration copyright © 1986 by Peter Sis. From *Journal of a Teenage Genius* by Helen V. Griffith, cover illustration by Frank Modell. Text and cover illustration copyright © 1987 by Helen V. Griffith.
Harcourt Brace & Company: Cover illustration by Robert Steele from *Sixth-Grade Sleepover* by Eve Bunting. Copyright © 1986 by Eve Bunting. Cover illustration by Ken Durkin from *Misery Guts* by Morris Gleitzman. Illustration copyright © 1993 by Ken Durkin. Originally published in Australia by Pan Macmillan Publishers, 1991. "Sea Slant" from *Slabs of the Sunburnt West* by Carl Sandburg. Text copyright 1922 by Harcourt Brace & Company, renewed 1950 by Carl Sandburg. Cover illustration by Daniel San Souci from *Vassilisa the Wise: A Tale of Medieval Russia* by Josepha Sherman. Illustration copyright © 1988 by Daniel San Souci. "Seventh Grade" from *Baseball In April and Other Stories* by Gary Soto. Text copyright © 1990 by Gary Soto. Cover illustration by David Diaz from *Neighborhood Odes* by Gary Soto. Illustration copyright © 1992 by Harcourt Brace & Company. From *Pacific Crossing* by Gary Soto. Text copyright © 1992 by Gary Soto. "Women" from *Revolutionary Petunias and Other Poems* by Alice Walker. Text copyright © 1970 by Alice Walker. Pronunciation Key from *HBJ School Dictionary,* Third Edition. Text copyright © 1990 by Harcourt Brace & Company.

continued on page 652

TREASURY OF LITERATURE

Dear Reader,

    This gift of literature is offered to you in many golden packages, all reflecting a marvelous diversity of experience. The stories in this anthology transport you to exciting new worlds, both real and imaginary. They will introduce you to people from ancient Africa, medieval England, and the Dominican Republic, people who will enrich you with a sense of wonder and accomplishment.

    Some of the people you will read about face challenges close to home. Karana, a Native American girl, finds herself alone on her island home. Tuan Nguyen, a Vietnamese boy, must overcome the obstacle of learning a new language as he adapts to life in America. Geeder begins an exciting friendship when she meets an extraordinary woman named Zeely, who reminds her of an African princess.

    Other characters experience adventures away from home. Charlotte Doyle discovers friendship where she least expects it as she travels across the Atlantic Ocean. James and his friends make a different sort of voyage as they sail the sea on a massive golden peach. Lincoln Mendoza, a Latino exchange student spending the summer in Japan, learns something about Japanese culture and a little about himself.

    When you open this book, you open doors to discovery. You'll find stories that have been popular for generations, and you'll find contemporary favorites. All these treasures provide you with a variety of adventures; all are presented to you in many *Shades of Gold*.

Sincerely,
The Authors

SHADES OF GOLD

UNIT ONE

SURPRISES / 16

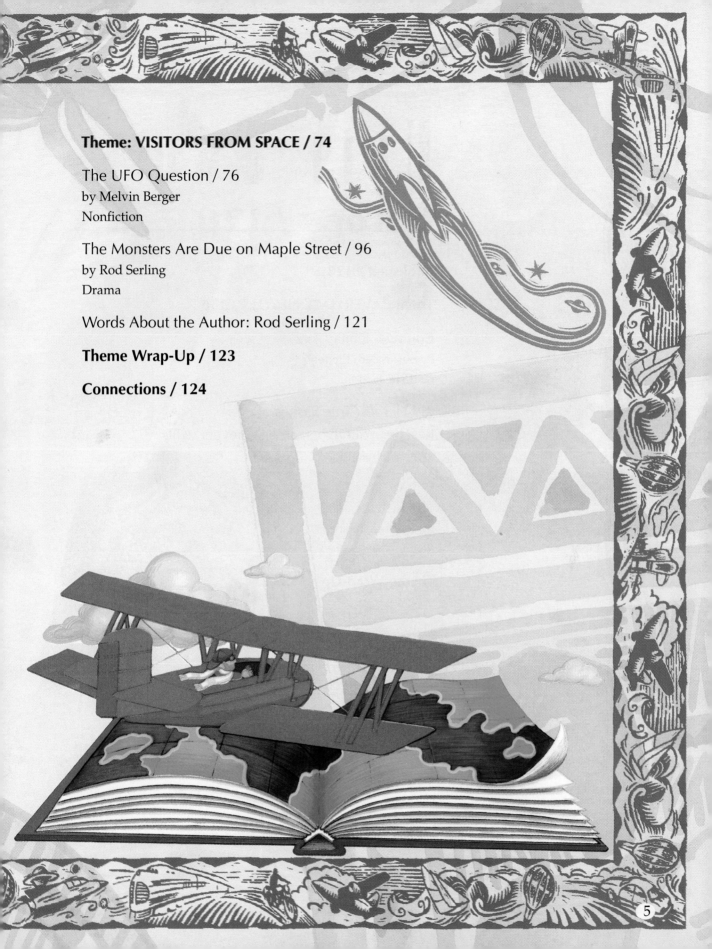

UNIT TWO
Heroes / 126

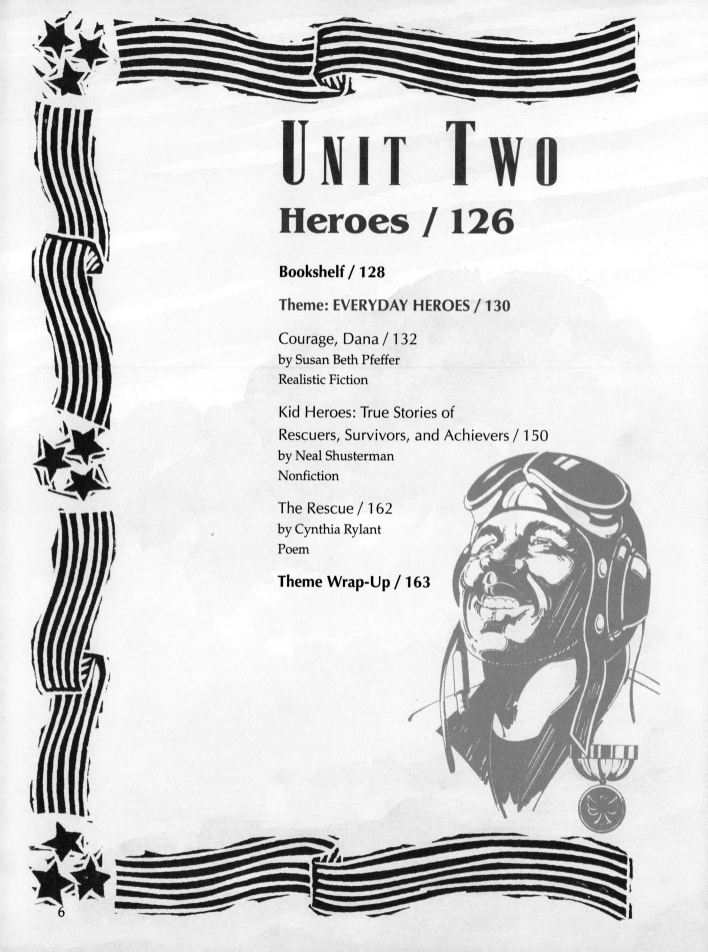

UNIT THREE
A World Away / 238

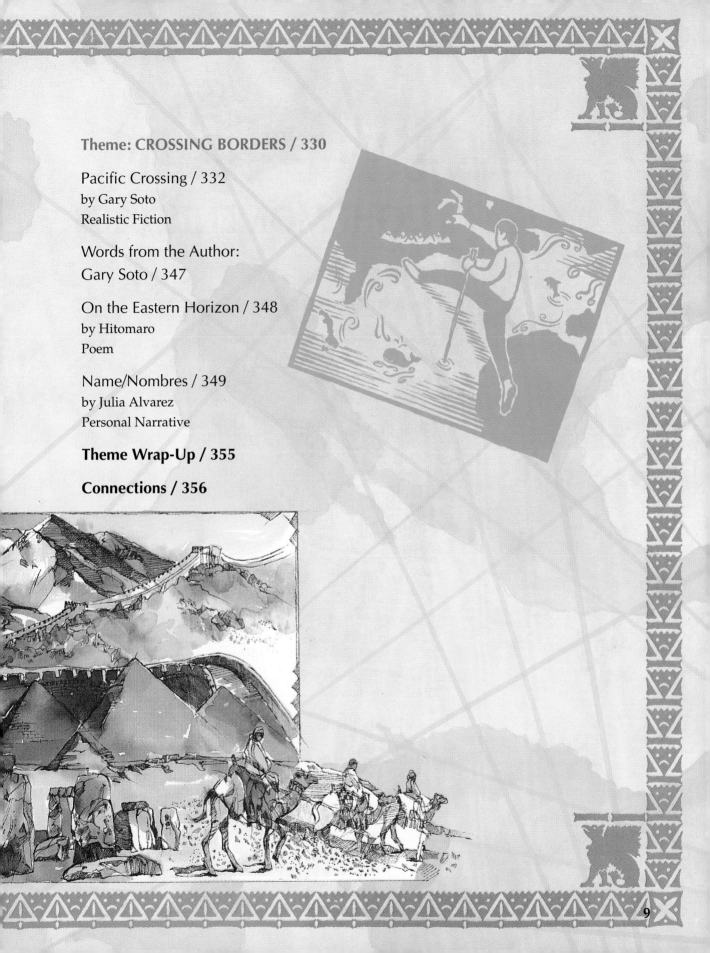

UNIT FOUR
LIGHT MOMENTS / 358

Unit Five

OCEANS / 456

UNIT SIX
OTHER PLACES/550

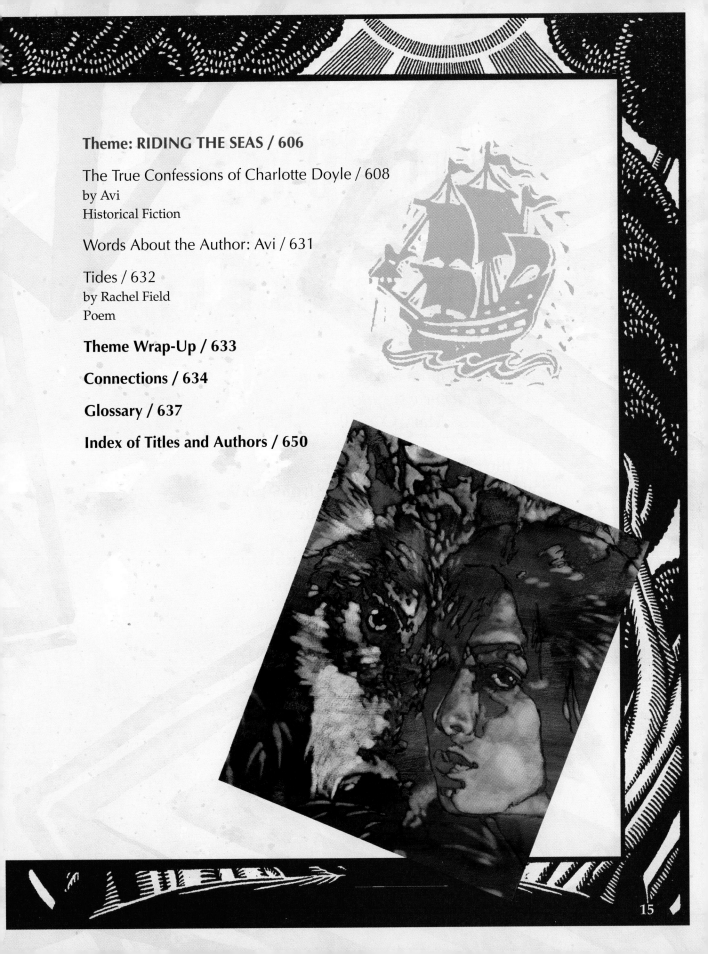

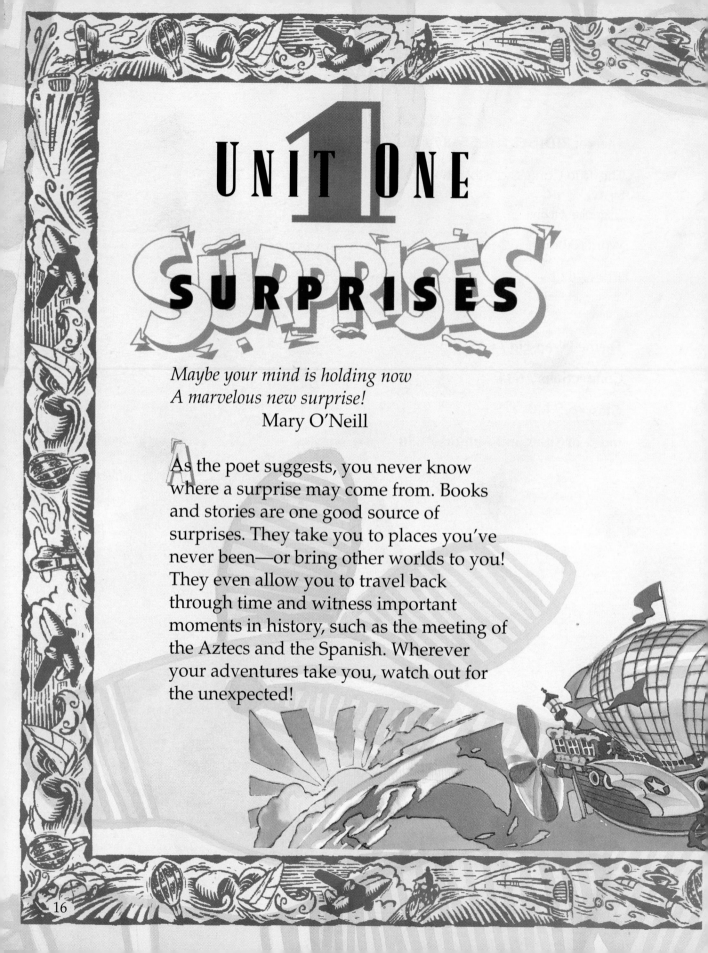

UNIT ONE
1
SURPRISES

Maybe your mind is holding now
A marvelous new surprise!
Mary O'Neill

As the poet suggests, you never know where a surprise may come from. Books and stories are one good source of surprises. They take you to places you've never been—or bring other worlds to you! They even allow you to travel back through time and witness important moments in history, such as the meeting of the Aztecs and the Spanish. Wherever your adventures take you, watch out for the unexpected!

THEMES

BOOKSHELF

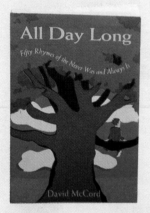

ALL DAY LONG

BY DAVID McCORD

On a range of subjects from the unusual to the common-place, David McCord's rhythmic poetry is always playful, humorous, and a pleasure to read.

Award-Winning Poet

HARCOURT BRACE LIBRARY BOOK

THE WHIPPING BOY

BY SID FLEISCHMAN

The heir to the throne, known as "Prince Brat," must not be spanked, so street boy Jemmy is hired to be punished in his place. When the bored prince runs away from home, taking Jemmy, the adventures that follow change both boys forever.

Newbery Medal, ALA Notable Book, School Library Journal Best Book

HARCOURT BRACE LIBRARY BOOK

MRS. FRISBY AND THE RATS OF NIMH

BY ROBERT C. O'BRIEN

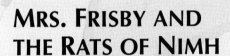

Mrs. Frisby, a widowed mouse with a sick child, seeks help from a strange group of ex-laboratory rats. Sworn to secrecy, she discovers some amazing truths, not only about the rats but also about her late husband as well.

Newbery Medal, ALA Notable Book

SIXTH-GRADE SLEEPOVER

BY EVE BUNTING

Janey discovers that sharing a problem is the first step toward solving it when she battles her fear of the dark at a slumber party.

Award-Winning Author

VASSILISA THE WISE

RETOLD BY JOSEPHA SHERMAN
ILLUSTRATED BY DANIEL SAN SOUCI

A merchant's wife comes to her husband's rescue and outwits the prince who wrongly imprisoned him.

Award-Winning Illustrator

IMAGINATIVE JOURNEYS

Books can show you things you've already seen or heard about. But they can also take you to places you can know only in your imagination. In the following selections, you'll have encounters of the imaginative kind.

C O N T E N T S

21

THE PHANTOM TOLLBOOTH

by NORTON JUSTER   illustrations by JULES FEIFFER

MILO

There was once a boy named Milo who didn't know what to do with himself—not just sometimes, but always.

When he was in school he longed to be out, and when he was out he longed to be in. On the way he thought about coming home, and coming home he thought about going. Wherever he was he wished he were somewhere else, and when he got there he wondered why he'd bothered. Nothing really interested him—least of all the things that should have.

"It seems to me that almost everything is a waste of time," he remarked one day as he walked dejectedly home from school. "I can't see the point in learning to solve useless problems, or subtracting turnips from turnips, or knowing where Ethiopia is or how to spell February." And, since no one bothered to explain otherwise, he regarded the process of seeking knowledge as the greatest waste of time of all.

As he and his unhappy thoughts hurried along (for while he was never anxious to be where he was going, he liked to get there as quickly as possible) it seemed a great wonder that the world, which was so large, could sometimes feel so small and empty.

"And worst of all," he continued sadly, "there's nothing for me to do, nowhere I'd care to go, and hardly anything worth seeing." He punctuated this last thought with such a deep sigh that a house sparrow singing nearby stopped and rushed home to be with his family.

Without stopping or looking up, he rushed past the buildings and busy shops that lined the street and in a few minutes reached home—dashed through the lobby—hopped onto the elevator—two, three, four, five, six, seven, eight, and off again—opened the apartment door—rushed into his room—flopped dejectedly into a chair, and grumbled softly, "Another long afternoon."

He looked glumly at all the things he owned. The books that were too much trouble to read, the tools he'd never learned to use, the small electric automobile he hadn't driven in months—or was it years?—and the hundreds of other games and toys, and bats and balls, and bits and pieces scattered around him. And then, to one side of the room, just next to the phonograph, he noticed something he had certainly never seen before.

Who could possibly have left such an enormous package and such a strange one? For, while it was not quite square, it was definitely not round, and for its size it was larger than almost any other big package of smaller dimension that he'd ever seen.

Attached to one side was a bright-blue envelope which said simply: "FOR MILO, WHO HAS PLENTY OF TIME."

Of course, if you've ever gotten a surprise package, you can imagine how puzzled and excited Milo was; and if you've never gotten one, pay close attention, because someday you might.

"I don't think it's my birthday," he puzzled, "and Christmas must be months away, and I haven't been outstandingly good, or even good at all." (He had to admit this even to himself.) "Most probably I won't like it anyway, but since I don't know where it came from, I can't possibly send it back." He thought about it for quite a while and then opened the envelope, but just to be polite.

"ONE GENUINE TURNPIKE TOLLBOOTH," it stated—and then it went on:

"EASILY ASSEMBLED AT HOME, AND FOR USE BY THOSE WHO HAVE NEVER TRAVELED IN LANDS BEYOND."

"Beyond what?" thought Milo as he continued to read.

"THIS PACKAGE CONTAINS THE FOLLOWING ITEMS:

"One (1) genuine turnpike tollbooth to be erected according to directions.

"Three (3) precautionary signs to be used in a precautionary fashion.

"Assorted coins for use in paying tolls.

"One (1) map, up to date and carefully drawn by master cartographers, depicting natural and man-made features.

"One (1) book of rules and traffic regulations, which may not be bent or broken."

And in smaller letters at the bottom it concluded:

"Results are not guaranteed, but if not perfectly satisfied, your wasted time will be refunded."

Following the instructions, which told him to cut here, lift there, and fold back all around, he soon had the tollbooth unpacked and set up on its stand. He fitted the windows in place and attached the roof, which extended out on both sides, and fastened on the coin box. It was very much like the tollbooths he'd seen many times on family trips, except of course it was much smaller and purple.

"What a strange present," he thought to himself. "The least they could have done was to send a highway with it, for it's terribly impractical without one." But since, at the time, there was nothing else he wanted to play with, he set up the three signs,

SLOW DOWN APPROACHING TOLLBOOTH

PLEASE HAVE YOUR FARE READY

HAVE YOUR DESTINATION IN MIND

and slowly unfolded the map.

As the announcement stated, it was a beautiful map, in many colors, showing principal roads, rivers and seas, towns and cities, mountains and valleys, intersections and detours, and sites of outstanding interest both beautiful and historic.

The only trouble was that Milo had never heard of any of the places it indicated, and even the names sounded most peculiar.

"I don't think there really is such a country," he concluded after studying it carefully. "Well, it doesn't matter anyway." And he closed his eyes and poked a finger at the map.

"Dictionopolis," read Milo slowly when he saw what his finger had chosen. "Oh, well, I might as well go there as anywhere."

He walked across the room and dusted the car off carefully. Then, taking the map and rule book with him, he hopped in and, for lack of anything better to do, drove slowly up to the tollbooth. As he deposited his coin and rolled past he remarked wistfully, "I do hope this is an interesting game, otherwise the afternoon will be so terribly dull."

BEYOND
EXPECTATIONS

Suddenly he found himself speeding along an unfamiliar country highway, and as he looked back over his shoulder neither the tollbooth nor his room nor even the house was anywhere in sight. What had started as make-believe was now very real.

"What a strange thing to have happen," he thought (just as you must be thinking right now). "This game is much more serious than I thought, for here I am riding on a road I've never seen, going to a place I've never heard of, and all because of a tollbooth which came from nowhere. I'm certainly glad that it's a nice day for a trip," he concluded hopefully, for, at the moment, this was the one thing he definitely knew.

The sun sparkled, the sky was clear, and all the colors he saw seemed to be richer and brighter than he could ever remember. The flowers shone as if they'd been cleaned and polished, and the tall trees that lined the road shimmered in silvery green.

"WELCOME TO EXPECTATIONS," said a carefully lettered sign on a small house at the side of the road.

"INFORMATION, PREDICTIONS, AND ADVICE

CHEERFULLY OFFERED.

PARK HERE AND BLOW HORN."

With the first sound from the horn a little man in a long coat came rushing from the house, speaking as fast as he could and repeating everything several times:

"My, my, my, my, my, welcome, welcome, welcome, welcome to the land of Expectations, to the land of Expectations, to the land of Expectations. We don't get many travelers these days; we certainly don't get many travelers these days. Now what can I do for you? I'm the Whether Man."

"Is this the right road for Dictionopolis?" asked Milo, a little bowled over by the effusive greeting.

"Well now, well now, well now," he began again, "I don't know of any wrong road to Dictionopolis, so if this road goes to Dictionopolis at all it must be the right road, and if it doesn't it must be the right road to somewhere else, because there are no wrong roads to anywhere. Do you think it will rain?"

"I thought you were the Weather Man," said Milo, very confused.

"Oh no," said the little man, "I'm the Whether Man, not the Weather Man, for after all it's more important to know whether there will be weather than what the weather will be." And with that he released a dozen balloons that sailed off into the sky. "Must see which way the wind is blowing," he said, chuckling over his little joke and watching them disappear in all directions.

"What kind of a place is Expectations?" inquired Milo, unable to see the humor and feeling very doubtful of the little man's sanity.

"Good question, good question," he exclaimed. "Expectations is the place you must always go to before you get to where you're going. Of course, some people never go beyond Expectations, but my job is to hurry them along whether they like it or not. Now what else can I do for you?" And before Milo could reply he rushed into the house and reappeared a moment later with a new coat and an umbrella.

"I think I can find my own way," said Milo, not at all sure that he could. But, since he didn't understand the little man at all, he decided that he might as well move on—at least until he met someone whose sentences didn't always sound as if they would make as much sense backwards as forwards.

"Splendid, splendid, splendid," exclaimed the Whether Man. "Whether or not you find your own way, you're bound to find some way. If you happen to find my way, please return it, as it was lost years ago. I imagine by now it's quite rusty. You did say it was going to rain, didn't you?" And with that he opened the umbrella and walked with Milo to the car.

"I'm glad you made your own decision. I do so hate to make up my mind about anything, whether it's good or bad, up or down, in or out, rain or shine. Expect everything, I always say, and the unexpected never happens. Now please drive carefully; good-by, good-by, good-by, good . . ." His last good-by was drowned out by an enormous clap of thunder, and as Milo drove down the road in the bright sunshine he could see the Whether Man standing in the middle of a fierce cloudburst that seemed to be raining only on him.

The road dipped now into a broad green valley and stretched toward the horizon. The little car bounced along with very little effort, and Milo had hardly to touch the accelerator to go as fast as he wanted. He was glad to be on his way again.

"It's all very well to spend time in Expectations," he thought, "but talking to that strange man all day would certainly get me nowhere. He's the most peculiar person I've ever met," continued Milo—unaware of how many peculiar people he would shortly encounter.

As he drove along the peaceful highway he soon fell to daydreaming and paid less and less attention to where he was going. In a short time he wasn't paying any attention at all, and that is why, at a fork in the road, when a sign pointed to the left, Milo went to the right, along a route which looked suspiciously like the wrong way.

Things began to change as soon as he left the main highway. The sky became quite gray and, along with it, the whole countryside seemed to lose its color and assume the same monotonous tone. Everything was quiet, and even the air hung heavily. The birds sang only gray songs and the road wound back and forth in an endless series of climbing curves.

Mile after

mile after

mile after

mile he drove, and now, gradually the car went slower and slower, until it was hardly moving at all.

"It looks as though I'm getting nowhere," yawned Milo, becoming very drowsy and dull. "I hope I haven't taken a wrong turn."

Mile after

mile after

mile after

mile, and everything became grayer and more monotonous. Finally the car just stopped altogether, and, hard as he tried, it wouldn't budge another inch.

"I wonder where I am," said Milo in a very worried tone.

"You're . . . in . . . the . . . Dol . . . drums," wailed a voice that sounded far away.

He looked around quickly to see who had spoken. No one was there, and it was as quiet and still as one could imagine.

"Yes . . . the . . . Dol . . . drums," yawned another voice, but still he saw no one.

"WHAT ARE THE DOLDRUMS?" he cried loudly, and tried very hard to see who would answer this time.

"The Doldrums, my young friend, are where nothing ever happens and nothing ever changes."

This time the voice came from so close that Milo jumped with surprise, for, sitting on his right shoulder, so lightly that he hardly noticed, was a small creature exactly the color of his shirt.

"Allow me to introduce all of us," the creature went on. "We are the Lethargarians, at your service."

Milo looked around and, for the first time, noticed dozens of them—sitting on the car, standing in the road, and lying all over the trees and bushes. They were very difficult to see, because whatever they happened to be sitting on or near was exactly the color they happened to be. Each one looked very much like the other (except for the color, of course) and some looked even more like each other than they did like themselves.

"I'm very pleased to meet you," said Milo, not sure whether or not he was pleased at all. "I think I'm lost. Can you help me please?"

"Don't say 'think,'" said one sitting on his shoe, for the one on his shoulder had fallen asleep. "It's against the law." And he yawned and fell off to sleep, too.

"No one's allowed to think in the Doldrums," continued a third, beginning to doze off. And as each one spoke, he fell off to sleep and another picked up the conversation with hardly any interruption.

"Don't you have a rule book? It's local ordinance 175389-J."

Milo quickly pulled the rule book from his pocket, opened to the page, and read, "Ordinance 175389-J: It shall be unlawful, illegal, and unethical to think, think of thinking, surmise, presume, reason, meditate, or speculate while in the Doldrums. Anyone breaking this law shall be severely punished!"

"That's a ridiculous law," said Milo, quite indignantly. "Everybody thinks."

"We don't," shouted the Lethargarians all at once.

"And most of the time *you* don't," said a yellow one sitting in a daffodil. "That's why you're here. You weren't thinking, and you weren't paying attention either. People who don't pay attention often get stuck in the Doldrums." And with that he toppled out of the flower and fell snoring into the grass.

Milo couldn't help laughing at the little creature's strange behavior, even though he knew it might be rude.

"Stop that at once," ordered the plaid one clinging to his stocking. "Laughing is against the law. Don't you have a rule book? It's local ordinance 574381-W."

Opening the book again, Milo found Ordinance 574381-W: "In the Doldrums, laughter is frowned upon and smiling is permitted only on alternate Thursdays. Violators shall be dealt with most harshly."

"Well, if you can't laugh or think, what can you do?" asked Milo.

"Anything as long as it's nothing, and everything as long as it isn't anything," explained another. "There's lots to do; we have a very busy schedule—

"At 8 o'clock we get up, and then we spend

"From 8 to 9 daydreaming.

"From 9 to 9:30 we take our early midmorning nap.

"From 9:30 to 10:30 we dawdle and delay.

"From 10:30 to 11:00 we take our late early morning nap.

"From 11:00 to 12:00 we bide our time and then eat lunch.

"From 1:00 to 2:00 we linger and loiter.

"From 2:00 to 2:30 we take our early afternoon nap.

"From 2:30 to 3:30 we put off for tomorrow what we could have done today.

"From 3:30 to 4:00 we take our early late afternoon nap.

"From 4:00 to 5:00 we loaf and lounge until dinner.

"From 6:00 to 7:00 we dillydally.

"From 7:00 to 8:00 we take our early evening nap, and then for an hour before we go to bed at 9:00 we waste time.

"As you can see, that leaves almost no time for brooding, lagging, plodding, or procrastinating, and if we stopped to think or laugh, we'd never get nothing done."

"You mean you'd never get anything done," corrected Milo.

"We don't want to get anything done," snapped another angrily; "we want to get nothing done, and we can do that without your help."

"You see," continued another in a more conciliatory tone, "it's really quite strenuous doing nothing all day, so once a week we take a holiday and go nowhere, which was just where we were going when you came along. Would you care to join us?"

"I might as well," thought Milo; "that's where I seem to be going anyway."

"Tell me," he yawned, for he felt ready for a nap now himself, "does everyone here do nothing?"

"Everyone but the terrible watchdog," said two of them, shuddering in chorus. "He's always sniffing around to see that nobody wastes time. A most unpleasant character."

"The watchdog?" said Milo quizzically.

"THE WATCHDOG," shouted another, fainting from fright, for racing down the road barking furiously and kicking up a great cloud of dust was the very dog of whom they had been speaking.

"RUN!"

"WAKE UP!"

"RUN!"

"HERE HE COMES!"

"THE WATCHDOG!"

Great shouts filled the air as the Lethargarians scattered in all directions and soon disappeared entirely.

"R-R-R-G-H-R-O-R-R-H-F-F," exclaimed the watchdog as he dashed up to the car, loudly puffing and panting.

Milo's eyes opened wide, for there in front of him was a large dog with a perfectly normal head, four feet, and a tail—and the body of a loudly ticking alarm clock.

"What are you doing here?" growled the watchdog.

"Just killing time," replied Milo apologetically. "You see—"

"KILLING TIME!" roared the dog—so furiously that his alarm went off. "It's bad enough wasting time without killing it." And he shuddered at the thought. "Why are you in the Doldrums anyway—don't you have anywhere to go?"

"I was on my way to Dictionopolis when I got stuck here," explained Milo. "Can you help me?"

"Help you! You must help yourself," the dog replied, carefully winding himself with his left hind leg. "I suppose you know why you got stuck."

"I guess I just wasn't thinking," said Milo.

"PRECISELY," shouted the dog as his alarm went off again. "Now you know what you must do."

"I'm afraid I don't," admitted Milo, feeling quite stupid.

"Well," continued the watchdog impatiently, "since you got here by not thinking, it seems reasonable to expect that, in order to get out, you must start thinking." And with that he hopped into the car.

"Do you mind if I get in? I love automobile rides."

Milo began to think as hard as he could (which was very difficult, since he wasn't used to it). He thought of birds that swim and fish that fly. He thought of yesterday's lunch and tomorrow's dinner. He thought of words that begin with J and numbers that end in 3. And, as he thought, the wheels began to turn.

"We're moving, we're moving," he shouted happily.

"Keep thinking," scolded the watchdog.

The little car started to go faster and faster as Milo's brain whirled with activity, and down the road they went. In a few moments they were out of the Doldrums and back on the main highway. All the colors had returned to their original brightness, and as they raced along the road Milo continued to think of all sorts of things; of the many detours and wrong turns that were so easy to take, of how fine it was to be moving along, and, most of all, of how much could be accomplished with just a little thought. And the dog, his nose in the wind, just sat back, watchfully ticking.

How well did this story live up to your expectations? Did it go beyond them?

What amazing things happen during Milo's drive?

"In the doldrums" is a way of saying that someone is bored, sad, or dull. Why is it appropriate for Milo to wind up in a place called the Doldrums?

Why, do you think, is it unlawful to think or laugh in the Doldrums?

Why are the Lethargarians afraid of the watchdog?

WRITE The watchdog says that wasting time is bad enough without killing it. Write two examples showing someone wasting time and two examples showing someone killing it.

Books Fall Open

from *All Day Long*

by David McCord

illustrated by Laura Freeman

Books fall open,
you fall in,
delighted where
you've never been;
hear voices not once
heard before,
reach world on world
through door on door;
find unexpected
keys to things
locked up beyond
imaginings.
What *might* you be,
perhaps *become*,
because one book
is somewhere? Some
wise delver into
wisdom, wit,
and wherewithal
has written it.
True books will venture,
dare you out,
whisper secrets,
maybe shout
across the gloom
to you in need,
who hanker for
a book to read.

IMAGINATIVE JOURNEYS

Does "Books Fall Open" describe the adventure of reading a story like "The Phantom Tollbooth"? Explain your answer.

WRITER'S WORKSHOP

Milo travels to some unusual places after going through the tollbooth. Think of an interesting place you have been. Write a personal narrative to describe your visit, and tell why it was memorable.

Writer's Choice   Stories or poems might take you on a journey. Dreams can too. What do the words *imaginative journeys* make you think of? Choose an idea and write about it. Share your response with a friend.

THEME

FANTASTIC HAPPENINGS

What do you enjoy most about reading stories? Meeting unique characters? Visiting fantastic places? In reading the following selections, you may find that one of the most delightful things about reading stories is that anything can happen.

CONTENTS

JAMES
And The
GIANT
PEACH

written by Roald Dahl
illustrated by Francisco X. Mora

Through a series of peculiar incidents, James finds himself inside a giant peach with gigantic friendly insects. The peach is as huge as a house, and the room in which James meets his new friends contains several pieces of furniture. Suddenly, the peach household rolls down a hill and into the sea, beginning the first of many marvelous adventures.

The sun was shining brightly out of a soft blue sky and the day was calm. The giant peach, with the sunlight glinting on its side, was like a massive golden ball sailing upon a silver sea.

"Look!" cried the Centipede just as they were finishing their meal. "Look at that funny thin black thing gliding through the water over there!"

They all swung around to look.

"There are two of them," said Miss Spider.

"There are *lots* of them!" said the Ladybug.

"What are they?" asked the Earthworm, getting worried.

"They must be some kind of fish," said the Old-Green-Grasshopper. "Perhaps they have come along to say hello."

"They are sharks!" cried the Earthworm. "I'll bet you anything you like that they are sharks and they have come along to eat us up!"

"What absolute rot!" the Centipede said, but his voice seemed suddenly to have become a little shaky, and he wasn't laughing.

"I am *positive* they are sharks!" said the Earthworm. "I just *know* they are sharks!"

And so, in actual fact, did everybody else, but they were too frightened to admit it.

There was a short silence. They all peered down anxiously at the sharks who were cruising slowly round and round the peach.

"Just assuming that they *are* sharks," the Centipede said, "there still can't possibly be any danger if we stay up here."

But even as he spoke, one of those thin black fins suddenly changed direction and came cutting swiftly through the water right up to the side of the peach itself. The shark paused and stared up at the company with small evil eyes.

"Go away!" they shouted. "Go away, you filthy beast!"

Slowly, almost lazily, the shark opened his mouth (which was big enough to have swallowed a perambulator) and made a lunge at the peach.

They all watched, aghast.

And now, as though at a signal from the leader, all the other sharks came swimming in toward the peach, and they clustered around it and began to attack it furiously. There must have been twenty or thirty of them at least, all pushing and fighting and lashing their tails and churning the water into a froth.

Panic and pandemonium broke out immediately on top of the peach.

"Oh, we are finished now!" cried Miss Spider, wringing her feet. "They

will eat up the whole peach and then there'll be nothing left for us to stand on and they'll start on us!"

"She is right!" shouted the Ladybug. "We are lost forever!"

"Oh, I don't want to be eaten!" wailed the Earthworm. "But they will take me first of all because I am so fat and juicy and I have no bones!"

"Is there *nothing* we can do?" asked the Ladybug, appealing to James. "Surely *you* can think of a way out of this."

Suddenly they were all looking at James.

"Think!" begged Miss Spider. "*Think,* James, *think*!"

"Come on," said the Centipede.

"Come on, James. There *must* be *something* we can do."

Their eyes waited upon him, tense, anxious, pathetically hopeful.

"There *is something* that I believe we might try," James Henry Trotter said slowly. "I'm not saying it'll work . . ."

"Tell us!" cried the Earthworm. "Tell us quick!"

"We'll try anything you say!" said the Centipede. "But hurry, hurry, hurry!"

"Be quiet and let the boy speak!" said the Ladybug. "Go on, James."

They all moved a little closer to him. There was a longish pause.

"*Go on!*" they cried frantically. "*Go on!*"

And all the time while they were waiting they could hear the sharks threshing around in the water below them. It was enough to make anyone frantic.

"Come on, James," the Ladybug said, coaxing him.

"I . . . I . . . I'm afraid it's no good after all," James murmured, shaking his head. "I'm terribly sorry. I forgot. We don't have any string. We'd need hundreds of yards of string to make this work."

"What sort of string?" asked the Old-Green-Grasshopper sharply.

"Any sort, just so long as it's strong."

"But my dear boy, that's exactly what we do have! We've got all you want!"

"How? Where?"

"The Silkworm!" cried the Old-Green-Grasshopper. "Didn't you ever notice the Silkworm? He's still downstairs! He never moves! He just lies there sleeping all day long, but we can easily wake him up and make him spin!"

"And what about me, may I ask?" asked Miss Spider. "I can spin *just* as well as any Silkworm. What's more, *I* can spin patterns."

"Can you make enough between you?" asked James.

"As much as you want."

"And quickly?"

"Of course! Of course!"

"And would it be strong?"

"The strongest there is! It's as thick as your finger! But why? What are you going to do?"

"I'm going to lift this peach clear out of the water!" James announced firmly.

"You're mad!" cried the Earthworm.

"It's our only chance."

"The boy's crazy!"

"He's joking!"

"Go on, James," the Ladybug said gently. "How are you going to do it?"

"Skyhooks, I suppose," jeered the Centipede.

"Seagulls," James answered calmly. "The place is full of them. Look up there!"

They all looked up and saw a great mass of seagulls wheeling round and round in the sky.

"I'm going to take a long silk string," James went on, "and I'm going to loop one end of it around a seagull's neck. And then I'm going to tie the other end to the stem of the peach." He pointed to the peach stem, which was standing up like a short thick mast in the middle of the deck.

"Then I'm going to get another seagull and do the same thing again, then another and another—"

"Ridiculous!" they shouted.

"Absurd!"

"Poppycock!"

"Balderdash!"

"Madness!"

And the Old-Green-Grasshopper said, "How can a few seagulls lift an enormous thing like this up into the air, and all of us as well? It would take hundreds . . . thousands . . ."

"There is no shortage of seagulls," James answered. "Look for yourself. We'll probably need four hundred, five hundred, six hundred . . . maybe even a thousand . . . I don't know . . . I shall simply go on hooking them up to the stem until we have enough to lift us. They'll be bound to lift us in the end. It's like balloons. You give someone enough balloons to hold, I mean *really* enough, then up he goes. And a seagull has far more lifting power than a balloon. If only we have the *time* to do it. If only we are not sunk first by those awful sharks. . . ."

"You're absolutely off your head!" said the Earthworm. "How on earth do you propose to get a loop of string around a seagull's neck? I suppose you're going to fly up there yourself and catch it!"

"The boy's dotty!" said the Centipede.

"Let him finish," said the Ladybug. "Go on, James. How *would* you do it?"

"With bait."

"Bait! What sort of bait?"

"With a worm, of course. Seagulls love worms, didn't you know that? And luckily for us, we have here the biggest, fattest, pinkest, juiciest Earthworm in the world."

"You can stop right there!" the Earthworm said sharply. "That's quite enough!"

"Go on," the others said, beginning to grow interested. "Go on!"

"The seagulls have already spotted him," James continued. "That's why there are so many of them circling around. But they daren't come down to get him while all the rest of us are standing here. So this is what—"

"Stop!" cried the Earthworm. "Stop, stop, stop! I won't have it! I refuse! I—I—I—I—"

"Be quiet!" said the Centipede. "Mind your own business!"

"I *like* that!"

"My dear Earthworm, you're going to be eaten anyway, so what difference does it make whether it's sharks or seagulls?"

"I won't do it!"

"Why don't we hear what the plan is first?" said the Old-Green-Grasshopper.

"I don't give a hoot what the plan is!" cried the Earthworm. "I am not going to be pecked to death by a bunch of seagulls!"

"You will be a martyr," said the Centipede. "I shall respect you for the rest of my life."

"So will I," said Miss Spider. "And your name will be in all the news-papers. Earthworm gives life to save friends . . ."

"But he won't *have* to give his life," James told them. "Now listen to me. This is what we'll do . . ."

53

"Why, it's absolutely brilliant!" cried the Old-Green-Grasshopper when James had explained his plan.

"The boy's a genius!" the Centipede announced. "Now I can keep my boots on after all."

"Oh, I shall be pecked to death!" wailed the poor Earthworm.

"Of course you won't."

"I will, I know I will! And I won't even be able to see them coming at me because I have no eyes!"

James went over and put an arm gently around the Earthworm's shoulders. "I won't let them *touch* you," he said. "I promise I won't. But we've *got* to hurry! Look down there!"

There were more sharks than ever now around the peach. The water was boiling with them. There must have been ninety or a hundred at least. And to the travelers up on top, it certainly seemed as though the peach were sinking lower and lower into the water.

"Action stations!" James shouted. "Jump to it! There's not a moment to lose!" He was the captain now, and everyone knew it. They would do whatever he told them.

"All hands below deck except Earthworm!" he ordered.

"Yes, yes!" they said eagerly as they scuttled into the tunnel entrance. "Come on! Let's hurry!"

"And you—Centipede!" James shouted. "Hop downstairs and get that Silkworm to work at once! Tell him to spin as he's never spun before! Our lives depend upon it! And the same applies to you, Miss Spider! Hurry on down! Start spinning!"

In a few minutes everything was ready.

It was very quiet now on the top of the peach. There was nobody in sight—nobody except the Earthworm.

One half of the Earthworm, looking like a great, thick, juicy, pink sausage, lay innocently in the sun for all the seagulls to see.

The other half of him was dangling down the tunnel.

James was crouching close beside the Earthworm in the tunnel entrance, just below the entrance, waiting for the first seagull. He had a loop of silk string in his hands.

The Old-Green-Grasshopper and the Ladybug were further down the tunnel, holding onto the Earthworm's tail, ready to pull him quickly in out of danger as soon as James gave the word.

And far below, in the great hollow stone of the peach, the Glow-worm was lighting up the room so that the two spinners, the Silkworm and Miss Spider, could see what they were doing. The Centipede was down there, too, exhorting them both frantically to greater efforts, and every now and again James could hear his voice coming up faintly from the depths, shouting, "Spin, Silkworm, spin, you great fat lazy brute! Faster, faster, or we'll throw you to the sharks!"

"Here comes the first seagull!" whispered James. "Keep still now, Earthworm. Keep still. The rest of you get ready to pull."

"Please don't let it spike me," begged the Earthworm.

"I won't, I won't. Ssshhh . . ."

Out of the corner of one eye, James watched the seagull as it came swooping down toward the Earthworm. And then suddenly it was so close that he could see its small black eyes and its curved beak, and the beak was open, ready to grab a nice piece of flesh out of the Earthworm's back.

"Pull!" shouted James.

The Old-Green-Grasshopper and the Ladybug gave the Earthworm's tail an enormous tug, and like magic the Earthworm disappeared into the tunnel. At the same time, up went James's hand and the seagull flew right into the loop of silk that he was holding out. The loop, which had been cleverly made, tightened just the right amount (but not too much) around its neck, and the seagull was captured.

"Hooray!" shouted the Old-Green-Grasshopper, peering out of the tunnel. "Well done, James!"

Up flew the seagull with James paying out the silk string as it went. He gave it about fifty yards and then tied the string to the stem of the peach.

"Next one!" he shouted, jumping back into the tunnel. "Up you get again, Earthworm! Bring up some more silk, Centipede!"

"Oh, I don't like this at all," wailed the Earthworm. "It only just missed me! I even felt the wind on my back as it went swishing past!"

"Ssshh!" whispered James. "Keep still! Here comes another one!"

So they did it again.

And again, and again, and again.

And the seagulls kept coming, and James caught them one after the other and tethered them to the peach stem.

"One hundred seagulls!" he shouted, wiping the sweat from his face.

"Keep going!" they cried. "Keep going, James!"

"Two hundred seagulls!"

"Three hundred seagulls!"

"Four hundred seagulls!"

The sharks, as though sensing that they were in danger of losing their prey, were hurling themselves at the peach more furiously than ever, and the peach was sinking lower and lower still in the water.

"Five hundred seagulls!" James shouted.

"Silkworm says he's running out of silk!" yelled the Centipede from below. "He says he can't keep it up much longer. Nor can Miss Spider!"

"Tell them they've *got* to!" James answered. "They can't stop now!"

"We're lifting!" somebody shouted.

"No, we're not!"

"I felt it!"

"Put on another seagull, quick!"

"Quiet, everybody! Quiet! Here's one coming now!"

This was the five hundred and first seagull, and the moment that James caught it and tethered it to the stem with all the others, the whole enormous peach suddenly started rising up slowly out of the water.

"Look out! Here we go! Hold on, boys!"

But then it stopped.

And there it hung.

It hovered and swayed, but it went no higher.

The bottom of it was just touching the water. It was like a delicately balanced scale that needed only the tiniest push to tip it one way or the other.

"One more will do it!" shouted the Old-Green-Grasshopper, looking out of the tunnel. "We're almost there!"

And now came the big moment. Quickly, the five hundred and second seagull was caught and harnessed to the peach-stem . . .

And then suddenly . . .

But slowly . . .

Majestically . . .

Like some fabulous golden balloon . . .

With all the seagulls straining at the strings above . . .

The giant peach rose up dripping out of the water and began climbing toward the heavens.

In a flash, everybody was up on top.

"Oh, isn't it beautiful!" they cried.

"What a marvelous feeling!"

"Good-by, sharks!"

"Oh, boy, this is the way to travel!"

Miss Spider, who was literally squealing with excitement, grabbed the Centipede by the waist and the two of them started dancing around and around the peach stem together. The Earthworm stood up on his tail and did a sort of wriggle of joy all by himself. The Old-Green-Grasshopper kept hopping higher and higher in the air. The Ladybug rushed over and shook James warmly by the hand. The Glow-worm, who at the best of times was a very shy and silent creature, sat glowing with pleasure near the tunnel entrance. Even the Silkworm, looking white and thin and completely exhausted, came creeping out of the tunnel to watch this miraculous ascent.

Up and up they went, and soon they were as high as the top of a church steeple above the ocean.

"I'm a bit worried about the peach," James said to the others as soon as all the dancing and the shouting had stopped. "I wonder how much damage those sharks have done to it underneath. It's quite impossible to tell from up here."

"Why don't I go over the side and make an inspection?" Miss Spider said. "It'll be no trouble at all, I assure you." And without waiting for an answer, she quickly produced a length of silk thread and attached the end of it to the peach stem. "I'll be back in a jiffy," she said, and then she walked calmly over to the edge of the peach and jumped off, paying out the thread behind her as she fell.

The others crowded anxiously around the place where she had gone over.

"Wouldn't it be dreadful if the thread broke," the Ladybug said.

There was a rather long silence.

"Are you all right, Miss Spider?" shouted the Old-Green-Grasshopper.

"Yes, thank you!" her voice answered from below. "I'm coming up now!"

And up she came, climbing foot over foot up the silk thread, and at the same time tucking the thread back cleverly into her body as she climbed past it.

"Is it *awful?*" they asked her. "Is it all eaten away? Are there great holes in it everywhere?"

Miss Spider clambered back onto the deck with a pleased but also a rather puzzled look on her face. "You won't believe this," she said, "but actually there's hardly any damage down there at all! The peach is almost untouched! There are just a few tiny pieces out of it here and there, but nothing more."

"You must be mistaken," James told her.

"Of course she's mistaken!" the Centipede said.

"I promise you I'm not," Miss Spider answered.

"But there were hundreds of sharks around us!"

"They churned the water into a froth!"

"We saw their great mouths opening and shutting!"

"I don't care what you saw," Miss Spider answered. "They certainly didn't do much damage to the peach."

"Then why did we start sinking?" the Centipede asked.

"Perhaps we *didn't* start sinking," the Old-Green-Grasshopper suggested.

"Perhaps we were all so frightened that we simply imagined it."

This, in point of fact, was closer to the truth than any of them knew. A shark, you see, has an extremely long sharp nose, and its mouth is set very awkwardly underneath its face and a long way back. This makes it more or less impossible for it to get its teeth into a vast smooth curving surface such as the side of a peach. Even if the creature turns onto its back it still can't do it, because the nose always gets in the way. If you have ever seen a small dog trying to get its teeth into an enormous ball, then you will be able to imagine roughly how it was with the sharks and the peach.

"It must have been some kind of magic," the Ladybug said.

What did you think was the funniest part of the story? Give reasons for your choice.

What was James's plan for saving his friends and himself from the sharks?

If James's plan had not worked, what would have happened to the passengers on the peach? Explain your answer.

WRITE Imagine you are James. Write about another way you might save yourself and your friends from the sharks.

AWARD-WINNING
AUTHOR

Roald Dahl

Roald Dahl had no plans to be a writer. After graduating from an English public school in 1931, he wanted to find a job that would take him to "wonderful faraway places like Africa or China." His wish came true, as he first worked for the Shell Oil Company in Tanganyika (now Tanzania) and, later, as a fighter pilot in North Africa during World War II. After his plane was shot down by German machine-gun fire, Dahl, who was seriously injured in the crash, was transferred to a noncombat post in Washington, D.C. One day, over lunch, he was interviewed for a magazine article in the *Saturday Evening Post,* but the interviewer was too busy eating to take notes. Dahl took the notes instead, and the writer, as a gesture of thanks, sent the story to the magazine with Dahl's name on it. That was the beginning of his career as a writer.

From 1940 through 1960, Dahl wrote many magazine articles and short stories for adults. He also wrote one children's story, "The Gremlins," in 1943, but it wasn't until 1961 when *James and the Giant Peach* was published that his career as a children's book author really took off. Dahl has said that the ideas for *James* and for many of his other children's books came from the bedtime stories he made up each night to tell his five children. Making up these stories also taught Dahl lessons about how to write for children: "If you think a child is getting bored, you must think of something that jolts [the story] back. Something that tickles."

"The writer for children," Dahl wrote, "must be a jokey sort of fellow. He must like simple tricks and jokes and riddles and other childish things. He must be unconventional and inventive." A giant peach that transports a small English boy across the ocean certainly qualifies as inventive.

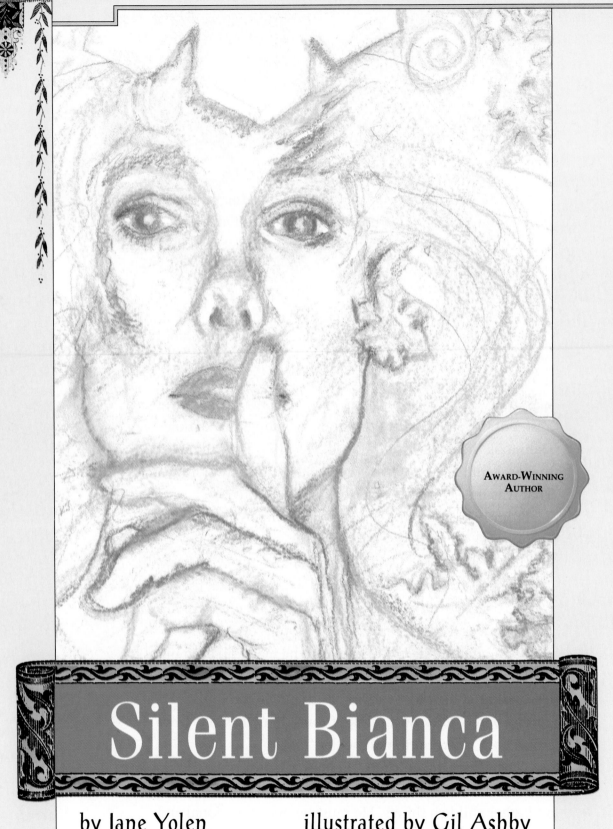

AWARD-WINNING
AUTHOR

Silent Bianca

by Jane Yolen   illustrated by Gil Ashby

from *The Girl Who Cried Flowers and Other Tales*

Once far to the North, where the world is lighted only by the softly flickering snow, a strange and beautiful child was born.

Her face was like crystal with the features etched in. And she was called Bianca, a name that means "white," for her face was pale as snow and her hair was white as a moonbeam.

As Bianca grew to be a young woman, she never spoke as others speak. Instead her words were formed soundlessly into tiny slivers of ice. And if a person wanted to know what she was saying, he had to pluck her sentences out of the air before they fell to the ground or were blown away by the chilling wind. Then each separate word had to be warmed by the hearthfire until at last the room was filled with the delicate sounds of Bianca's voice. They were strange sounds and as fragile as glass.

At first many people came to see the maiden and to catch her words. For it was said that she was not only beautiful but wise as well.

But the paths to her hut were few. For the frost cut cruelly at every step. And it took so long to talk with Bianca that after a while, no one came to visit her at all.

Now it happened that the king of the vast country where Bianca lived was seeking a wife who was both beautiful and wise. But when he asked his council how to find such a bride, the councilors scratched their heads and stroked their beards and managed to look full of questions and answers at the same time.

"Can you do such a thing?" asked one. "Can you not do such a thing?" asked another. "How is it possible?" asked a third. And they spent a full day looking up to the ceiling and down to the floor and answering each question with another.

At last the king said, "Enough of this useless noise. I will find a way and I will find a woman. And the one who will be my bride will be filled with silence and still speak more wisdom than any of you."

At that the councilors left off talking and began to laugh. For it was well known that wisdom was to be found in things said, not in silence. And it was also known that no one—not even the king—was as wise as the members of the king's council.

But the king sent his most trusted servant, a gentle old painter named Piers, to the corners of the kingdom. Piers was to talk with all the maidens of noble birth. Then he was to bring back portraits of the most beautiful of these from which the king might choose a bride.

Piers traveled many days and weeks. He wearied himself in the great halls and draughty palaces listening to the chattering, nattering maidens who wanted to marry the king. At last, his saddlebags filled with their portraits and his mind packed with their prattle, he started for home.

On his way home from the cold lands, Piers became lost in a fierce snowstorm. He was forced to seek shelter in a nearby hut. It was the hut where Bianca made her home. Piers meant to stay but a single day. But one day whitened into a second and then a third. It was soon a week that the old man had remained there, talking to Bianca and warming her few words by the fire. He never told her who he was or what his mission. If she guessed, she never said. Indeed, in *not* saying lay much of her wisdom.

At last the storm subsided and Piers returned to the king's castle. In his saddlebags he carried large portraits of the most beautiful noble maidens in the kingdom. But the old man carried on a chain around his neck a miniature portrait of Bianca. She had become like a daughter to him. The thought of her was like a calm, cool breeze in the warmer lands where he lived.

When the day came for the king to make his choice, all of

the king's council assembled in the Great Hall. Piers drew the large portraits from his saddlebags one by one and recalled what the maidens had spoken. The king and his council looked at the pictures and heard the words. And one by one they shook their heads.

As Piers bent to put the final portrait back into his pack, the chain with the miniature slipped out of his doublet. The king reached over and touched it. Then he held it up to the light and looked at the picture.

"Who is this?" he asked. "And why is this portrait smaller and set apart from the rest?"

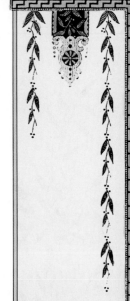

Piers answered, "It is a maiden known as Bianca. She lives in the cold lands far to the North. She speaks in slivers that cut through lies." And he told them about the storm and how he had met the beautiful, silent girl and discovered her great wisdom.

"This is the one I shall marry," said the king.

"It would be most improper," said the councilors together. "She is not noble-born."

"How does one judge nobility?" asked the king. "How does one measure it?"

The councilors scratched their heads and looked puzzled. "Can you do such a thing?" asked one. "Can you not do such a thing?" said another. "How is it possible?" asked a third. And they continued this way for some time.

At last the king silenced them with his hand. "Enough of this noise. I will make a measure. I will test the wisdom of this Silent Bianca," he said. And under his breath, he added, "And I will test *your* wisdom as well."

Then the king sent his council, with Piers to guide them, off to the cold lands to bring Bianca back to the throne.

Piers and the councilors traveled twenty days and nights until the stars fell like snow behind them and at last they came to the chilly land where Bianca made her home. There they packed up Bianca and her few belongings and immediately started back to the king.

But when they reached the road that ran around the castle, strange to say, they found their way blocked by soldiers. Campfires blossomed like flowers on the plain. At every turning and every straightaway stood a guard. It seemed there was no place where they could pass.

"This is very odd," said Piers. "There have never been soldiers here before. Could some unknown enemy have captured the castle while we were away?"

The councilors tried to question the guards, but none would answer. Not even a single question. Unused to silence, the councilors fell to puzzling among themselves. Some said one thing and some said another. They talked until the sun burned out behind them, but they could figure out no way to get beyond the guards and so bring Bianca to the king.

The air grew cold. The dark drew close. The councilors, weary with wondering, slept.

Only Bianca, who had said nothing all this time, remained awake. When she was certain that all the councilors were asleep, and even Piers was snoring gently, Bianca arose. Slowly she walked along the road that circled around the castle. Now and then she opened her mouth as if to scream or speak or sigh. But of course no sounds came out of her mouth at all. Then she would close it again, kneeling humbly when challenged by a silent guard's upraised spear. For the guards still spoke not a word but remained closemouthed at their posts.

And so from path to path, from guard to guard, from

campfire to campfire, Bianca walked.

Just at dawn, she returned to the place where the councilors and Piers slept leaning on one another's shoulders like sticks stacked up ready for a fire.

As the sun flamed into the sky, a sudden strange babble was heard. At first it was like a single woman crying, calling, sobbing. Then, as the sun grew hotter and the morning cookfires were lit, it was as though a thousand women called to their men, wailing and sighing at each campfire and at every turning. It was the slivers of Bianca's voice which she had so carefully placed during her long night's walk; the slivers warmed and melted by the rising sun and the burning coals.

But the guards did not know this. And they looked around one way and another. Yet the only woman near them was Bianca, sitting silently, smiling, surrounded by Piers and the puzzled councilors.

And then, from somewhere beyond the guards, a chorus of women cried out. It was a cry like a single clear voice. "Come home, come home," called the women. "Leave off your soldiering. You need no arms but ours. Leave off your soldiering. No arms . . . no arms but ours."

The guards hesitantly at first, by ones and twos, and then joyfully by twenties and hundreds, threw down their weapons. Then they raced back home to their wives and sweethearts. For they were not really an unknown enemy at all but townsmen hired by the king to try the wisdom of the councilors and of Bianca.

When the councilors realized what Bianca had done, they brought her swiftly to the king. Instead of scratching their heads and looking puzzled, they spoke right out and said, "She is most certainly wise and more than fit for a king to marry."

The king, when he heard how Bianca had fooled the guards, laughed and laughed for he thought it a grand joke. And when he stopped laughing and considered the meaning of her words, he agreed she was indeed even wiser than old Piers had said.

So the king and Bianca were married.

And if the king had any problems thereafter, and his council could give him only questions instead of answers, he might be found at the royal hearthstone. There he could be seen warming his hands. But he was doing something more besides: He would be listening to the words that came from the fire and from the wise and loving heart of Silent Bianca, his queen.

What did you like about Bianca? What didn't you like?

In what ways are the king's councilors and Bianca different?

How does Bianca get the guards to return to their homes?

WRITE   Do you think Bianca is happy to be the queen? Write a few paragraphs explaining your answer.

FANTASTIC HAPPENINGS

In what ways are James and Bianca clever in solving their problems?

WRITER'S WORKSHOP

Poets sometimes write narrative poems to tell about fantastic happenings. Retell the story of either James or Bianca in a short narrative poem. Be sure to tell the story from beginning to end.

Writer's Choice

Both selections tell about fantastic happenings. Can you think of a fantastic happening, imaginary or real? Choose an idea and write your response. Think of a way to share it with others.

T H E M E

VISITORS FROM SPACE

Is that object in the sky a plane, a meteor, a very bright planet? Or is it something more surprising? The following selections explore our continuing fascination with unexplained flying objects.

C O N T E N T S

75

The UFO Question

by Melvin Berger
illustrations by Rick Garcia

The radio announcer on the evening news program of October 31, 1938, kept telling his listeners to remain calm. He assured them that the authorities were on the scene. They were taking all steps necessary to prevent a catastrophe.

Although he tried to sound calm, there was a note of panic in his voice. His fright was not hard to understand. He was reporting that a spaceship from Mars had just landed in New Jersey. In vivid details he described how the Martians were spreading throughout the countryside, capturing or killing any humans who tried to stop them.

Terror spread like wildfire among those in New Jersey and nearby states who were tuned in to the program. As people learned what was happening, they bolted their doors and locked their windows. Others hid beneath beds or crawled into cellars. Nearly everyone wanted to escape the alien invaders. While thousands threw their most valuable belongings into bags and fled their homes by foot or car, many others, too frightened to move, stayed glued to their radio sets.

But very soon the facts came out. The newscast about the landing of Martians on Earth was nothing more than fiction—a realistic dramatization of H. G. Wells's book *War of the Worlds.* What was very real—and totally unexpected—was the reaction of the public. Almost everyone was fully prepared to believe in an invasion from Mars!

THE BELIEF IN LIFE ELSEWHERE

In our own day, with men on the moon and spaceships on Mars, the belief in life elsewhere is perhaps greater than ever. But what facts do we actually have about intelligent beings in space? Do they exist? If so, what are they like? And what are our chances of communicating or visiting with them?

For the longest time, writers of science fiction and fantasy were the only ones seeking answers to these questions. But more recently, scientists have begun researching the possibility of life on planets that revolve around other suns. Using the tools and methods of modern science, highly trained researchers are shedding new light on an old subject—one that has long been hidden behind a screen of rumors, half-truths and unreliable observations.

TWO FABLES FOR OUR TIME

One day, a newly hatched crow was looking at his feathers. "Are

all crows black like me?" he asked his mother.

"Of course they are," his mother answered. "Every crow in our flock is black. All the crows in the fields and forests for miles around are black. Everyone knows that every crow is black."

When he was a little bigger, the young crow went flying off by himself. After a while he saw another bird. It looked like a crow. It said "Caw, caw" like a

But I'm white."

The young crow quickly flew back to his mother. "I just saw a white crow!" he shouted in great excitement.

"You made a mistake," she said very firmly. "It was probably a dove."

"I'm sure it was a crow," he insisted.

His mother grew angry. "I've seen hundreds and hundreds of crows. They're all black. Crows are black. And that's final!"

The young crow just smiled.

Moral: It takes just one exception to prove that there are exceptions.

crow. But it wasn't black. It was white!

The young crow flew over to the other bird. "Are you a crow?" he asked.

"Yes, I am," the white bird answered.

"But you're white instead of black," said the young crow.

"I know," replied the white crow. "The other crows in my flock are black. My parents are black crows. So I'm a crow, too.

Suzy Owl and Billy Owl were the two young children of the Owl family. One Christmas morning Suzy and Billy were opening their presents. "Here's a pretty skirt from Aunt Nancy!" Suzy cried.

"And here's a great book about monsters from Grandma Eleanor," Billy said.

They kept on unwrapping their presents and calling out the name of the person who had given them each gift. Then suddenly Suzy said, "Here's a doll. But I don't know who gave it to me."

A minute later Billy said, "And I don't know who gave me this baseball mitt."

The two children looked at each other. "It must be Santa Claus," Suzy decided.

"Of course!" Billy agreed. "After all, we know who gave us all the other presents. This proves there is a Santa Claus!"

Mom and Dad Owl started to laugh. "We bought you the doll and mitt," they confessed. "We didn't put cards in the boxes as a joke. But neither of us is Santa Claus!"

Moral: When something happens that seems hard to figure out, look first for a simple explanation.

These fables have two very different morals. They also illustrate two different ways of thinking about UFOs and ETs.

The first fable suggests that even one unexplained UFO sighting or ET contact is proof enough that such things exist. According to the second fable, though, even happenings that are surprising and unexpected may have simple explanations.

Over the years there have been thousands of reports of UFO sightings and ET contacts. Almost all the incidents have been explained in ordinary ways. Still, a few remain unaccounted for. That leaves it up to each of us to decide what to think. Do you believe that only one unexplained UFO or ET incident proves that UFOs and ETs exist? Or do you believe that even though a few incidents are hard to figure out, they offer no

real proof of life in other worlds?

It was three o'clock on the afternoon of June 24, 1947. Kenneth Arnold, a 32-year-old salesman, was flying his private

plane from Chehalis to Yakima, Washington, to call on a customer. Suddenly, off to his left, Ken saw a bright flash of light. He noticed nine strange-looking aircraft flying toward Mount Rainier.

"I could see their outline quite plainly against the snow as they approached the mountain," he later said. "They flew very close to the mountaintops, directly south to southeast, down the hog's back of the range, flying like geese in a diagonal line, as if they were linked together.

"They were approximately 20 or 25 miles away," Arnold also reported, "and I couldn't see a tail on them. I watched for about three minutes . . . a chain of saucerlike things at least 5 miles long, swerving in and out of the high mountain peaks. They were flat like a pie pan and so shiny they reflected the sun like a mirror."

The startled pilot estimated that each silvery craft was 45 to 50 feet long. They seemed to be flying at a height of about 9,500 feet. And he put their speed at 1,700 miles an hour—about three times swifter than any existing plane! "I never saw anything so fast," he said later.

As Arnold watched in amazement, the strange-looking aircraft dove, soared and scooted this way and that before disappearing out of sight. After locating the point on his map, he continued his flight to the Yakima airport.

Arnold's account of the mysterious sightings created an absolute sensation. Newspapers and magazines around the world rushed to print stories about what he had seen. Using the pilot's words, they reported that the unidentified craft looked "like a saucer would if you skipped it across the water." That name caught on, and soon everyone was talking about "flying saucers."

The news reached the ears of officials in the U.S. Air Force. Since it is their job to protect the United States from air attack, they decided to investigate. After

all, the craft that Arnold saw might threaten the nation's security.

An expert in military intelligence questioned Arnold at great length. He reported: "It is the personal opinion of the interviewer that Mr. Arnold actually saw what he stated that he saw. It is difficult to believe that a man of Mr. Arnold's character and apparent integrity would state that he saw objects and write up a report to the extent that he did if he did not see them."

In the little town of Maysville, Kentucky, on January 7, 1948, a number of people noted a strange-looking object in the sky overhead. Someone called the State Police. Several officers rushed out to look, and they, too, noticed something moving across the sky that they could not recognize. The police called the Godman Air Force Base near Louisville, Kentucky, for more

information. The control tower could offer no explanation. But they agreed to help identify the flying object.

Meanwhile, other reports of the same craft began pouring in. People from many different locations described it in similar terms: It was round, between 250 and 300 feet in diameter, metallic in color and glowing brightly. Everyone also said that it was heading westward at great speed.

By now the top commanders at Godman were at the control tower. None of them could identify the object. But while they were trying to decide what to do next, a flight of four F–51 jets from the Air National Guard passed nearby on a routine training flight. Since these very fast planes were already in the air, the officers at Godman asked the lead pilot, Captain Thomas Mantell, to investigate.

Captain Mantell banked his plane south to look for the object. Very soon he radioed the control tower, "Object traveling at half my speed and directly ahead of me and above. I'm going to take a closer look. It appears metallic and tremendous

in size. I'm going to 20,000 feet." Then silence.

At 3:20 P.M. the Godman control tower got word that Captain Mantell's plane had crashed. Based on first reports, some said that he had made contact with the mysterious object. Others suspected that the unidentified object had somehow caused his plane to go down.

On December 13, 1961, George E. Weber was walking across the parking lot of George

shining from the bottom of the object. Meyer told of an orange-brown glow from the center area. The craft had neither wings nor propellers and left no vapor trail in the air. The two men in the parking lot had it in view for about three minutes. Meyer could watch only for a minute before the beeping horns of the cars he was blocking forced him to move along with the traffic.

Launched on July 16, 1969, the Apollo 11 space shot had three astronauts on board—Neil Armstrong, Edwin Aldrin and Michael Collins. The historic flight was the first to place a human being on the moon.

After their return, certain stories began circulating about bizarre happenings on their trip. On the second day, when they were about halfway to the moon, it was said, the crew observed some shiny white objects flying alongside their ship and keeping pace with them. They supposedly photographed the objects. Two days later, they again saw the objects and again recorded the sighting on film.

Washington University in Washington, D.C., when a guard pointed out a strange-looking object in the sky. Mean-while, William John Meyer, Jr., who was driving his car and waiting for a traffic light to change, also noted the same object overhead.

All three descriptions of the object were similar—dark gray in color, diamond-shaped, about 20 feet long and moving silently at a height of about 1,500 feet.

Weber mentioned a light

According to some reports, the astronauts noted two objects flying together in close formation. At times they would come close together. Then they would separate. Both appeared to be emitting some sort of liquid. After watching their movements in space, the astronauts decided the objects were under intelligent control.

The report of astronaut sightings of unidentified objects was taken very seriously. Because astronauts are highly trained as pilots and scientists, they are considered very reliable observers. In this case, not only had they presumably sighted the objects, but they had also taken photos of them. It had long been expected that if there are intelligent beings elsewhere in the universe, they would be very interested in our space shots.

Colonel Osires Silva is a trained aeronautical engineer as well as the head of Brazil's state-owned oil company. Because of his background and position everyone listened very carefully to what he had to say when his private plane landed at the airport at São José dos Campos on May 19, 1986.

Silva told how he and his pilot had seen a strange light in the air. He described "a dancing point in the sky." The two observers estimated the object's speed at about 900 miles per hour.

On checking with the control tower, it was learned that some unidentified objects were also being picked up on the radar screen. The airport authorities quickly called the Brazilian Defense Center. They sent up six

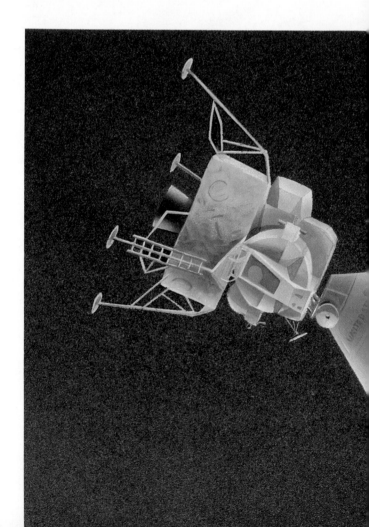

of their fastest jets to locate and identify these mysterious lights.

Although all the pilots saw the lights, the planes they were flying could not catch up with the objects emitting them. After some three hours, the pilots lost sight of the lights entirely. They also disappeared from the radar screen. Even though the Brazilian Air Force investigated the incident, they never released their findings.

These have been among the best-known sightings of UFOs in recent years. At first, the accounts were generally accepted to be true. Like the black crow's finding the white crow in our first fable, many people believed it takes just one UFO sighting to prove that UFOs exist.

Later, however, a number of investigators tried to discover whether or not these reports were accurate. Like Suzy and Billy Owl in the second fable, they wanted to see if there were simple explanations of events that were hard to understand. Very often what they found was completely different from the original reports.

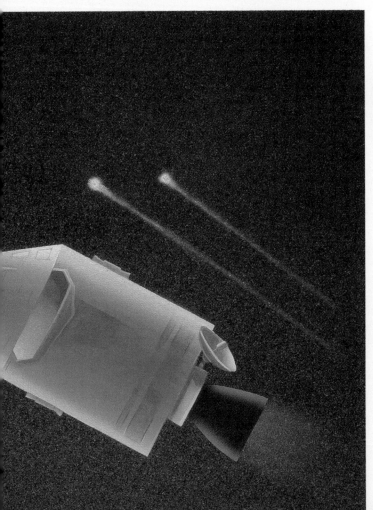

THE KENNETH ARNOLD CASE

This case proved to be one of the simplest to understand. Bright sunlight shining on clouds among mountain peaks frequently creates optical illusions, making things seem real that are not. One effect that has been noted often is the optical illusion of disks of light that seem to be floating in the air. There is every reason to believe that such round, flat, thin objects are what Arnold saw. The nine disks were merely a false impression of "flying saucers" caused by the particular relationship of the sun, clouds and mountains at the time.

THE CAPTAIN MANTELL CASE

Investigators of the Mantell incident found that the captain had been chasing a Skyhook balloon. The incident occurred, however, at a time when the Skyhook balloon was still a military secret. No one outside the program knew that it even existed.

The balloon, it was discovered, had a metallic surface, measured 100 feet across and carried various scientific measuring instruments. Captain Mantell did not crash

because of any encounter with a UFO. The Air Force authorities said that he flew too high without oxygen and blacked out.

THE WEBER-MEYER SIGHTINGS

The 1961 Weber-Meyer sighting in Washington, D.C., is still listed as an unsolved case. After nearly thirty years, no one has been able to confirm it either as a known object, a natural event or a true encounter with a UFO.

THE APOLLO 11 INCIDENT

The Apollo 11 incident proved to be an out-and-out fake. When Neil Armstrong was asked about seeing UFOs, he answered, "We didn't see them, and with what we . . . are doing in space, that's a real wonder."

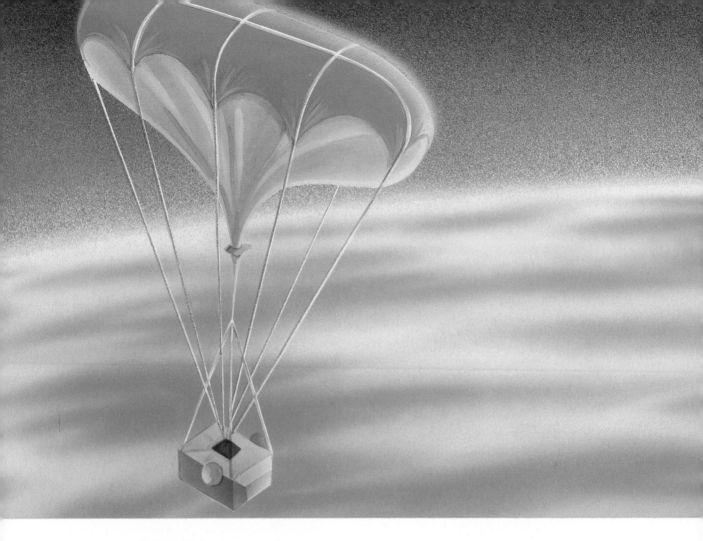

NASA official Charles Redmond adds, "We don't have any UFO secrets."

One photograph of Earth taken from Apollo 11 did, however, show a bright white object floating in the air. But upon further investigation, it proved to be nothing more than a piece of metal that had broken off when the lunar module was released. In the same way, movie film shot from inside the spacecraft reveals a number of strange lights and shapes. All the experts agree, however, that they are simply reflections and glares in the window.

It now seems clear that the early reports of UFOs involving Apollo 11 were based on false quotes and transcripts of conversations between the crew and Mission Control. Also, it was discovered that someone had retouched the photos to make them look as though UFOs were present. Nevertheless, the desire

to believe in UFOs is very strong in some people. Even when NASA released the original transcripts and the original photos, which did not show UFOs, some Americans continued to think that the Apollo 11 crew had seen UFOs. A few even charged that NASA was hiding the truth!

THE COLONEL SILVA SIGHTING

The results of the Brazilian Air Force investigation of the "dancing point of light" that Colonel Silva watched have never been made public. Nor have any other scientists been able to explain what the colonel, his pilot and the six pilots of the Air Force jets observed or what the radar screen showed that night.

James Oberg, a leading UFO researcher, points out that radar can be fooled by birds, insects or certain weather conditions. But neither he nor any of the others who have looked into the case has succeeded in identifying the mysterious lights. Colonel Silva's sighting, therefore, remains another significant case of an unsolved UFO encounter.

UFOs IN PERSPECTIVE

Sightings of UFOs are nothing new. As long ago as A.D. 98, a number of ancient Romans reported seeing a round burning shield flashing across the sky. Another sighting from around that time was of a giant globe, brighter than the sun, coming down to Earth and then flying off again. In fact, all through the Middle Ages people related tales about strange objects and unexplained lights that they saw in the sky—and sometimes on land as well.

What *is* new are the efforts of scientists to study UFOs. Soon after Kenneth Arnold reported seeing flying saucers in 1947, the U.S. Air Force set up an office to investigate all such sightings to make sure they were not part of a military attack or invasion. The inquiry was later given the name Project Blue Book. In 1969 the project was brought to a close when the Air Force concluded that UFOs did not threaten the nation's security.

Besides the Air Force, many private organizations set up UFO investigations. Some of them are still in operation. Worldwide, reports on UFO sightings still pour in at the rate of about 100 a day!

To help in the study of UFOs, scientist J. Allen Hynek divided UFO sightings into six types.

The first three are distant observations:

1. Bright lights seen in the night sky.
2. Bright ovals or disks seen in the daytime sky.
3. Objects detected only by radar.

The final three are much closer and thus more exciting:

4. Close encounters of the first kind—sighting an unidentified object on Earth.
5. Close encounters of the second kind—sighting an

unidentified object on Earth and tracing its physical effects on things or beings.

6. Close encounters of the third kind—sighting an unidentified object on Earth and making physical contact with the object or its occupants.

Most UFO reports fall into one of the first three of Dr. Hynek's categories. But experts find eventually that most of them, perhaps 90 percent or more, are not true UFOs. They are really IFOs—Identified Flying Objects.

According to these experts, people may be fooled into thinking they are making a Type One sighting when they catch an unusual or unexpected view of a plane, a meteor, the very bright planet Venus or one of the other planets. Weather balloons, particular cloud formations, artificial satellites, and blimps account for a large percentage of Type Two observations. False radar signals can come either from flocks of birds, swarms of insects or unexplained radar waves called "angels."

When Project Blue Book stopped operating, it had studied over 12,000 UFO sightings. Of the total number, the experts were able to explain well over 90 percent of the reported incidents. In over 2,000 of the cases, the observers were found to be seeing Venus or another planet, a particularly bright star or some other natural astronomical body or event. In another 1,500 cases, the object sighted proved to be an airplane. Nearly 800 more were glimpses of artificial satellites, and about 500 were balloons. A total of about 6,500 were false reports, posed or retouched photos, strange cloud formations, birds, insects and just plain human error.

When all was said and done, however, there remained about 700 events for which no explanation could be found, either natural or man-made. What do the experts say about these?

Major Hector Quintanilla, former director of Project Blue Book, insists that there are no UFOs. He cites the absence of even one fully confirmed report of a UFO sighting. Astronomer Carl Sagan concurs. A true sighting, he expects, would have many reliable witnesses all coming forward at the same time.

Other experts make these points: UFOs could not land and then take off without leaving significant evidence of the tremendous force needed to launch or slow down a spaceship. Since a spaceship would have to travel an immense distance to arrive on Earth, it would not just appear in a remote area, stay for a few minutes and then quickly fly away. Most likely it would stay for a period of time and make better contact with the Earth's inhabitants. And with all the military air defense and civilian air traffic systems now operating, it is virtually impossible for any aircraft to enter the earth's air space without being detected.

Still, in a February 1987 Gallup poll, almost half of all Americans said they believe in UFOs. Some had had UFO experiences themselves and don't accept the scientists' explanations. Many more had read or seen very dramatic accounts of the most exciting of these encounters. For all these people, the unsolved, unexplained UFO events are enough to convince them that there are living beings that have come to Earth from the outer reaches of space in what we call UFOs.

After you read the explanations, what did you think about the UFO stories?

Why do the experts feel that there are no "real" UFOs?

Which of the five sightings described in the article are UFOs and which are IFOs? Support your answers.

Do you think the people who reported the sightings that were later explained believed the explanations? Consider each case.

According to Carl Sagan, a true sighting of a UFO would have many reliable witnesses. How does his statement apply to the sightings described in the selection?

WRITE Do you think Project Blue Book should be started again? Write a paragraph explaining your opinion.

THE MONSTERS ARE DUE ON

by Rod Serling
illustrated by
John Nickle

EMMY
AWARD

CHARACTERS

Narrator
Tommy
Steve Brand
Don Martin
Myra Brand, *Steve's wife*
Woman
Voice One
Voice Two
Voice Three
Voice Four
Voice Five
Pete Van Horn
Sally, *Tommy's mother*

Charlie
Man One
Les Goodman
Ethel Goodman, *Les's wife*
Man Two
Figure One
Figure Two
Ice-cream vendor
Second Boy buying ice cream
Charlie's wife
Other Residents of Maple Street

ACT ONE

(Fade in on a shot of the night sky. . . the various heavenly bodies stand out in sharp, sparkling relief.)

Narrator. There is a fifth dimension beyond that which is known to man. It is a dimension as vast as space, and as timeless as infinity. It is the middle ground between light and shadow—between science and superstition. And it lies between the pit of a man's fears and the summit of his knowledge. It is the dimension of imagination. It is an area which we call The Twilight Zone.

The camera moves slowly across the heavens until it passes the horizon and stops on a sign that reads "Maple Street." It is a tree-lined, quiet small-town American street. The houses have front porches on which people sit and swing on gliders, conversing across from house to house. Steve Brand polishes his car parked in front of his house. His neighbor, Don Martin, leans against the fender watching him. A Good Humor man rides a bicycle and is just in the process of stopping to sell some ice cream to a couple of kids. Two women gossip on the front lawn. Another man waters his lawn.

Narrator. Maple Street, U.S.A., late summer. A tree-lined little world of front-porch gliders, hopscotch, the laughter of children, and the bell of an ice-cream vendor.

(There is a pause, and the camera moves over to a shot of the Good Humor man and two small boys who are standing alongside, just buying ice cream.)

Narrator. At the sound of the roar and the flash of the light, it will be precisely six-forty-three P.M. on Maple Street.

(At this moment one of the little boys, Tommy, looks up to listen to a sound of a tremendous screeching roar from overhead. A flash of light plays on both boys' faces and then moves down the street past lawns and porches and rooftops and then disappears.

Various people leave their porches and stop what they are doing to stare up at the sky.

Steve Brand, *the man who has been polishing his car, stands there transfixed, staring upwards. He looks at* Don Martin, *his neighbor from across the street.)*

Steve. What was that? A meteor?

Don *(nods).* That's what it looked like. I didn't hear any crash, though, did you?

Steve *(shakes his head)*. Nope. I didn't hear anything except a roar.

Myra *(from her porch)*. Steve? What was that?

Steve *(raising his voice and looking toward the porch)*. Guess it was a meteor, honey. Came awful close, didn't it?

Myra. Too close for my money! Much too close.

(The camera moves slowly across the various porches to people who stand there watching and talking in low conversing tones.)

Narrator. Maple Street. Six-forty-four P.M., on a late September evening. *(a pause)* Maple Street in the last calm and reflective moment . . . before the monsters came!

(The camera takes us across the porches again. A man is replacing a light bulb on a

front porch. He gets down off his stool to flick the switch and finds that nothing happens.

Another man is working on an electric power mower. He plugs in the plug, flicks the switch of the power mower off and on, but nothing happens.

Through a window we see a woman pushing her finger up and down on the dial hook of a telephone. Her voice sounds far away.)

Woman. Operator, operator, something's wrong on the phone, operator! (Myra Brand *comes out on the porch and calls to* Steve.)

Myra (*calling*). Steve, the power's off. I had the soup on the stove, and the stove just stopped working.

Woman. Same thing over here. I can't get anybody on the phone either. The phone seems to be dead.

(We look down the street. Small, mildly disturbed voices are heard coming from below.)

Voice One. Electricity's off.

Voice Two. Phone won't work.

Voice Three. Can't get a thing on the radio.

Voice Four. My power mower won't move, won't work at all.

Voice Five. Radio's gone dead.

(Pete Van Horn, a tall, thin man, is seen standing in front of his house.)

Pete. I'll cut through the back yard . . . . See if the power's still on on Floral Street. I'll be right back.

(He walks past the side of his house and disappears into the back yard.

The camera pans down slowly until we are looking at ten or eleven people standing around the street and overflowing to the curb and sidewalk. In the background is Steve Brand's car.)

Steve. Doesn't make sense. Why should the power go off all of a sudden, and the phone line?

Don. Maybe some kind of an electrical storm or something.

Charlie. That don't seem likely. Sky's just as blue as anything. Not a cloud. No lightning. No thunder. No nothing. How could it be a storm?

Woman. I can't get a thing on the radio. Not even the portable.

(The people again begin to murmur softly in wonderment and question.)

Charlie. Well, why don't you go downtown and check with the police, though they'll probably think we're crazy or something. A little power failure and right away we get all flustered and everything—

Steve. It isn't just the power failure, Charlie. If it was, we'd still be able to get a broadcast on the portable.

(There is a murmur of reaction to this. Steve looks from face to face and then over to his car.)

Steve. I'll run downtown. We'll get this all straightened out.

(He walks over to the car, gets in it, and turns the key.

Looking through the open car door, we see the crowd watching him from the other side. Steve starts the engine. It turns over sluggishly and then just stops dead. He tries it again, and this time he can't get it to turn over. Then, very slowly and reflectively, he turns the key back to "off" and gets out of the car.

The people stare at Steve. He stands for a moment by the car and then walks toward the group.)

Steve. I don't understand it. It was working fine before . . .

Don. Out of gas?

Steve *(shakes his head).* I just had it filled up.

Woman. What's it mean?

Charlie. It's just as if . . . as if everything had stopped. . . . *(Then he turns toward Steve.)* We'd better walk downtown.

(Another murmur of assent at this.)

Steve. The two of us can go, Charlie. *(He turns to look back at the car.)* It couldn't be the meteor. A meteor couldn't do *this.*

(He and Charlie exchange a look. Then they start to walk away from the group.

Tommy, a serious-faced young boy in spectacles, stands halfway between the group and the two men, who start to walk down the sidewalk.)

Tommy. Mr. Brand—you'd better not!

Steve. Why not?

Tommy. They don't want you to.

(Steve and Charlie exchange a grin, and Steve looks back toward the boy.)

Steve. *Who* doesn't want us to?

Tommy *(jerks his head in the general direction of the distant horizon).* Them!

Steve. Them?

Charlie. Who are them?

Tommy *(intently).* Whoever was in that thing that came by overhead.

(Steve knits his brows for a moment, cocking his head questioningly. His voice is intense.)

Steve. What?

Tommy. Whoever was in that thing that came over. I don't think they want us to leave here.

(Steve leaves Charlie, walks over to the boy. He forces his voice to remain gentle.)

Steve. What do you mean? What are you talking about?

Tommy. They don't want us to leave. That's why they shut everything off.

Steve. What makes you say that? Whatever gave you that idea?

Woman (*from the crowd*). Now isn't that the craziest thing you ever heard?

Tommy (*persistently, but a little intimidated by the crowd*). It's always that way, in every story I ever read about a ship landing from outer space.

Woman (*to the boy's mother, Sally, who stands on the fringe of the crowd*). From outer space, yet! Sally, you better get that boy of yours up to bed. He's been reading too many comic books or seeing too many movies or something!

Sally. Tommy, come over here and stop that kind of talk.

Steve. Go ahead, Tommy. We'll be right back. And you'll see. That wasn't any ship or anything like it. That was just a . . . a meteor or something. Likely as not—(*He turns to the group, now trying*

to weight his words with an optimism he *obviously doesn't feel but is desperately trying to instill in himself as well as the others.)* No doubt it did have something to do with all this power failure and the rest of it. Meteors can do some crazy things. Like sunspots.

Don *(picking up the cue).* Sure. That's the kind of thing—like sunspots. They raise Cain with radio reception all over the world. And this thing being so close—why, there's no telling the sort of stuff it can do. *(He wets his lips and smiles nervously.)* Go ahead, Charlie. You and Steve go into town and see if that isn't what's causing it all.

(Steve and Charlie walk away from the group down the sidewalk as the people watch silently.

Tommy *stares at them, biting his lips, and finally calls out again.)*

Tommy. Mr. Brand!

(The two men stop. Tommy *takes a step toward them.)*

Tommy. Mr. Brand . . . please don't leave here.

(Steve *and* Charlie *stop once again and turn toward the boy. There is a murmur in the crowd, a murmur of irritation and concern, as if the boy were bringing up fears that shouldn't be brought up; words which carried with them a strange kind of truth that came without logic. Again comes a murmur of reaction from the crowd.*

Tommy *is partly frightened and partly defiant as well.*)

Tommy. You might not even be able to get to town. It was that way in the story. Nobody could leave. Nobody except—

Steve. Except who?

Tommy. Except the people they'd sent down ahead of them. They looked just like humans. And it wasn't until the ship landed that—(*The boy suddenly stops, conscious of the parents staring at them and the sudden hush of the crowd.*)

Sally (*in a whisper, sensing the antagonism of the crowd*). Tommy, please son . . . honey, don't talk that way—

Man One. That kid shouldn't talk that way . . . and we shouldn't stand here

106

listening to him. Why this is the craziest thing I ever heard of. The kid tells us a comic book plot, and here we stand listening—

(Steve *walks toward the camera and stops beside the boy.*)

Steve. Go ahead, Tommy. What kind of story was this? What about the people they sent out ahead?

Tommy. That was the way they prepared things for the landing. They sent four people. A mother and a father and two kids who looked just like humans . . . but they weren't.

(*There is another silence as* Steve *looks toward the crowd and then toward* Tommy. *He wears a tight grin.*)

Steve. Well, I guess what we'd better do then is to run a check on the neighborhood and see which ones of us are really human.

(*There is laughter at this, but it's a laughter that comes from a desperate attempt to lighten the atmosphere. The people look at one another in the middle of their laughter.*)

Charlie. There must be something better to do than stand around makin' bum jokes about it. (*rubs his jaw nervously*)

I wonder if Floral Street's got the same deal we got. (*He looks past the houses.*) Where is Pete Van Horn anyway? Didn't he get back yet?

(*Suddenly there is the sound of a car's engine starting to turn over.*

We look across the street toward the driveway of Les Goodman's *house. He is at the wheel trying to start the car.*)

Sally. Can you get it started, Les?

(Les Goodman *gets out of the car, shaking his head.*)

Les. No dice.

(*He walks toward the group. He stops suddenly as, behind him, inexplicably and with a noise that inserts itself into the silence, the car engine starts up all by itself. Les whirls around to stare toward it.*

The car idles roughly, smoke coming from the exhaust, the frame shaking gently.

Les's eyes go wide, and he runs over to his car.

The people stare toward the car.)

Man One. He got the car started somehow. He got *his* car started!

(*The people continue to stare, caught up by this revelation and wildly frightened.*)

Woman. How come his car just up and started like that?

Sally. All by itself. He wasn't anywheres near it. It started all by itself.

(Don Martin *approaches the group and stops a few feet away to look toward* Les's *car and then back toward the group.*)

Don. And he never did come out to look at that thing that flew overhead. He wasn't even interested. (*He turns to the group, his face taut and serious.*) Why? Why didn't he come out with the rest of us to look?

Charlie. He always was an oddball. Him and his whole family. Real oddball.

Don. What do you say we ask him?

(*The group suddenly starts toward the house. In this brief fraction of a moment, they take the first step toward changing from a group into a mob. They begin to head purposefully across the street toward the house at the end. Steve stands in front of them. For a moment their fear almost turns their walk into a wild stampede, but Steve's voice, loud, incisive, and commanding, makes them stop.*)

Steve. Wait a minute . . . wait a minute! Let's not be a mob!

(*The people stop, seem to pause for a moment, and then much more quietly and slowly start to walk across the street. Les stands alone facing the people.*)

Les. I just don't understand it. I tried to start it, and it wouldn't start. You saw me. All of you saw me.

(*And now, just as suddenly as the engine started, it stops, and there is a long silence that is gradually intruded upon by the frightened murmuring of the people.*)

Les. I don't understand. I swear . . . I don't understand. What's happening?

Don. Maybe you better tell us. Nothing's working on this street. Nothing. No lights, no power, no radio. (*then meaningfully*) Nothing except one car—yours!

(*The people pick this up and now their murmuring becomes a loud chant filling the air with accusations and demands for action. Two of the men pass Don and head toward Les, who backs away, backing into his car and now at bay.*)

Les. Wait a minute now. You keep your distance—all of you. So I've got a car that starts by itself—well, that's a freak thing, I admit it. But does that make

me a criminal or something? I don't know why the car works—it just does!

(This stops the crowd momentarily, and now Les, *still backing away, goes toward his front porch. He goes up the steps and then stops to stand facing the mob.)*

Steve *(quietly)*. We're all on a monster kick, Les. Seems that the general impression holds that maybe one family isn't what we think they are. Monsters from outer space or something. Different from us. Aliens from the vast beyond. *(He chuckles.)* You know anybody that might fit that description around here on Maple Street?

Les. What is this, a gag or something? *(He looks around the group again.)* This a practical joke or something?

(Suddenly the porch light goes on and then off. There's a murmur from the group.)

Les. Now, I suppose that's supposed to incriminate me! The light goes on and off. That really does it, doesn't it? *(He looks around at the faces of the people.)* I just don't understand this—*(He wets his*

lips, looking from face to face.) Look, you all know me. We've lived here five years. Right in this house. We're no different from any of the rest of you! We're no different at all. Really . . . this whole thing is just . . . just weird—

Woman. Well, if that's the case, Les Goodman, explain why—*(She stops suddenly, clamping her mouth shut.)*

Les *(softly)*. Explain what?

Steve *(interjecting)*. Look, let's forget this—

Charlie *(overlapping him)*. Go ahead, let her talk. What about it? Explain what?

Woman *(a little reluctantly)*. Well . . . sometimes I go to bed late at night. A couple of times . . . a couple of times I'd come out on the porch, and I'd see Mr. Goodman here in the wee hours of the morning standing out in front of his house . . . looking up at the sky. *(She looks around the circle of faces.)* That's right, looking up at the sky as if . . . as if he were waiting for something, *(pauses)* as if he were looking for something.

(There's a murmur of reaction from the crowd again. As Les starts toward them, they back away frightened.)

Les. You know really . . . this is for laughs. You know what I'm guilty of?

(He laughs.) I'm guilty of insomnia. Now what's the penalty for insomnia?

(At this point the laugh, the humor, leaves his voice.)

Les. Did you hear what I said? I said it was insomnia. (a pause as he looks around, then shouts) I said it was insomnia! You fools. You scared, frightened rabbits, you. You're sick people, do you know that? You're sick people—all of you! And you don't even know what you're starting because let me tell you . . . let me tell you—this thing you're starting—that should frighten you. As God is my witness . . . you're letting something begin here that's a nightmare.

ACT TWO

Scene 1.

(Fade in on Maple Street at night. On the sidewalk, little knots of people stand around talking in low voices. At the end of each conversation they look toward Les Goodman's house. From the various houses, we can see candlelight but no electricity. There is an all-pervading quiet that blankets the whole area, disturbed only by the almost whispered voices of the people standing around. In one group Charlie stands staring across at the Goodmans' house. Two men stand across the street from it in almost sentrylike poses.)

111

Sally *(a little timorously).* It just doesn't seem right, though, keeping watch on them. Why . . . he was right when he said he was one of our neighbors. Why, I've known Ethel Goodman ever since they moved in. We've been good friends—

Charlie. That don't prove a thing. Any guy who'd spend his time lookin' up at the sky early in the morning—well,

there's something wrong with that kind of a person. There's something that ain't legitimate. Maybe under normal circumstances we could let it go by, but these aren't normal circumstances. Why, look at this street! Nothin' but candles. Why, it's like goin' back into the Dark Ages or somethin'!

(Steve walks down the steps of his porch, down the street over to *Les's house, and*

112

then stops at the foot of the steps. Les stands there, his wife behind him, very frightened.)

Les. Just stay right where you are, Steve. We don't want any trouble, but this time if anybody sets foot on my porch, that's what they're going to get—trouble!

Steve. Look, Les—

Les. I've already explained to you people. I don't sleep very well at night sometimes. I get up and I take a walk and I look up at the sky. I look at the stars!

Ethel. That's exactly what he does. Why this whole thing, it's . . . it's some kind of madness or something.

Steve *(nods grimly).* That's exactly what it is—some kind of madness.

Charlie's Voice *(shrill, from across the street).* You best watch who you're seen with, Steve! Until we get this all straightened out, you ain't exactly above suspicion yourself.

Steve *(whirling around toward him).* Or you, Charlie. Or any of us, it seems. From age eight on up!

Woman. What I'd like to know is, what are we gonna do? Just stand around here all night?

Charlie. There's nothin' else we can do! *(He turns back, looking toward* Steve *and* Les *again.)* One of 'em'll tip their hand. They got to.

Steve *(raising his voice).* There's something you can do, Charlie. You could go home and keep your mouth shut. You could quit strutting around like a self-appointed hanging judge and just climb into bed and forget it.

Charlie. You sound real anxious to have that happen, Steve. I think we better keep our eye on you too!

Don *(as if he were taking the bit in his teeth, takes a hesitant step to the front).* I think everything might as well come out now. *(He turns toward* Steve.) Your wife's done plenty of talking, Steve, about how odd you are!

Charlie *(picking this up, his eyes widening).* Go ahead, tell us what she's said.

(Steve walks toward them from across the street.)

Steve. Go ahead, what's my wife said? Let's get it all out. Let's pick out every idiosyncrasy of every single man, woman, and child on the street. And then we might as well set up some kind of a kangaroo court. How about a firing squad at dawn, Charlie, so we can get rid of all the suspects? Narrow them down. Make it easier for you.

Don. There's no need gettin' so upset, Steve. It's just that . . . well . . . Myra's talked about how there's been plenty of nights you spent hours down in your basement workin' on some kind of radio or something. Well, none of us have ever seen that radio—

(By this time Steve *has reached the group. He stands there defiantly close to them.)*

Charlie. Go ahead, Steve. What kind of "radio set" you workin' on? I never seen it. Neither has anyone else. Who do you talk to on that radio set? And who talks to you?

Steve. I'm surprised at you, Charlie. How come you're so dense all of a sudden? *(He pauses.)* Who do I talk to? I talk to monsters from outer space. I talk to three-headed green men who fly over here in what look like meteors.

(Myra Brand steps down from the porch, bites her lip, calls out.)*

Myra. Steve! Steve, please. *(Then looking around, frightened, she walks toward the group.)* It's just a ham radio set, that's all. I bought him a book on it myself. It's just a ham radio set. A lot of people have them. I can show it to you. It's right down in the basement.

Steve *(whirls around toward her).* Show them nothing! If they want to look inside our house—let them get a search warrant.

Charlie. Look, buddy, you can't afford to—

Steve *(interrupting him).* Charlie, don't tell me what I can afford. And stop telling me who's dangerous and who isn't and who's safe and who's a menace. *(He turns to the group and shouts.)* And you're with him, too—all of you! You're standing here all set to crucify—all set to find a scapegoat—all desperate to point some kind of a finger at a neighbor! Well now, look, friends, the only thing that's gonna happen is that we'll eat each other up alive—

(He stops abruptly as Charlie *suddenly grabs his arm.)*

Charlie *(in a hushed voice).* That's not the only thing that can happen to us.

(Down the street, a figure has suddenly materialized in the gloom. In the silence we can hear the clickety-clack of slow, measured footsteps on concrete as the figure walks slowly toward them. One of the women lets out a stifled cry. The young mother grabs her boy, as do a couple of others.)

Tommy (shouting, frightened). It's the monster! It's the monster!

(Another woman lets out a wail, and the people fall back in a group, staring toward the darkness and the approaching figure. The people stand in the shadows watching. Don Martin joins them, carrying a shot gun. He holds it up.)

Don. We may need this.

Steve. A shotgun? (He pulls it out of Don's hand.) Good Lord—will anybody think a thought around here! Will you people wise up. What good would a shotgun do against—

(Charlie pulls the gun from Steve's hand.)

Charlie. No more talk, Steve. You're going to talk us into a grave! You'd let whatever's out there walk right over us, wouldn't yuh? Well, some of us won't!

(Charlie *swings the gun around to point it toward the sidewalk. The dark figure continues to walk toward them. Charlie slowly raises the gun. As the figure gets closer and closer, he suddenly pulls the trigger. The sound of the shot explodes in the stillness.*

   The figure suddenly lets out a small cry, stumbles forward onto his knees, and then falls forward on his face. Don, Charlie, and Steve *race forward to him.* Steve *is there first and turns the man over. The crowd gathers around them.*)

Steve (*slowly looks up*). It's Pete Van Horn.

Don (*in a hushed voice*). Pete Van Horn! He was just gonna go over to the next block to see if the power was on—

Woman. You killed him, Charlie. You shot him dead!

Charlie (*looks around at the circle of faces, his eyes frightened, his face contorted*). But . . . but I didn't know who he was. I certainly didn't know who he was. He comes walkin' out of the darkness—how am I supposed to know who he was? (*He grabs* Steve.) Steve—you know why I shot! How was I supposed to know he wasn't a monster or something? (*He grabs* Don *now.*) We're all scared of the same thing. I was just tryin' to . . . tryin' to protect my home, that's all! Look, all of you, that's all I was tryin' to do. (*He looks down wildly at the body.*) I didn't know it was somebody we knew! I didn't know—

(*There's a sudden hush and then an intake of breath. Across the street all the lights go on in one of the houses.*)

Woman (*in a very hushed voice*). Charlie . . . Charlie . . . the lights just went on in your house. Why did the lights just go on?

Don. What about it, Charlie? How come you're the only one with lights now?

Les. That's what I'd like to know. (*A pause as they all stare toward* Charlie.)

Les. You were so quick to kill, Charlie, and you were so quick to tell us who we had to be careful of. Well, maybe you had to kill. Maybe Peter there was trying to tell us something. Maybe he'd found out something and came back to tell us who there was amongst us we should watch out for—

(*Charlie* backs away from the group, his eyes wide with fright.)

Charlie. No . . . no . . . it's nothing of the sort! I don't know why the lights are on. I swear I don't. Somebody's pulling a gag or something.

(*He bumps against* Steve, *who grabs him and whirls him around.*)

Steve. A gag? A gag? Charlie, there's a dead man on the sidewalk, and you killed him! Does this thing look like a gag to you?

(*Charlie* breaks away and screams as he runs toward his house.)

Charlie. No! No! Please!

(*A man breaks away from the crowd to chase* Charlie. *As the man tackles him and lands on top of him, the other people start to run toward them.* Charlie *gets up, breaks away from the other man's grasp, and lands a couple of desperate punches that push the man aside. Then he forces his way, fighting, through the crowd and jumps up on his front porch.*)

Charlie *is on his porch as a rock thrown from the group smashes a window alongside of him, the broken glass flying past him. A couple of pieces cut him. He stands there perspiring, rumpled, blood running down from a cut on the cheek. His wife breaks away from the group to throw herself into his arms. He buries his face against her. We can see the crowd converging on the porch.)*

Voice One. It must have been him.

Voice Two. He's the one.

Voice Three. We got to get Charlie.

(Another rock lands on the porch. Charlie pushes his wife behind him, facing the group.)

Charlie. Look, look I swear to you . . . it isn't me . . . but I do know who it is . . . I swear to you, I do know who it is. I know who the monster is here. I know who it is that doesn't belong. I swear to you I know.

Les *(shouting).* What are you waiting for?

Woman *(shouting).* Come on, Charlie, come on!

Man One *(shouting).* Who is it, Charlie, tell us!

Don *(pushing his way to the front of the crowd).* All right, Charlie, let's hear it!

(Charlie's eyes dart around wildly.)

Charlie. It's . . . it's . . .

Man Two *(screaming).* Go ahead, Charlie.

Charlie. It's . . . it's the kid. It's Tommy. He's the one!

(There's a gasp from the crowd as we see Sally holding the boy. Tommy at first doesn't understand and then, realizing the eyes are all on him, buries his face against his mother.)

Sally *(backs away).* That's crazy. That's crazy. He's a little boy.

Woman. But he knew! He was the only one who knew! He told us all about it. Well, how did he know? How *could* he have known?

(Various people take this up and repeat the question.)

Voice One. How could he know?

Voice Two. Who told him?

Voice Three. Make the kid answer.

Man One. What about Les's car?

Don. It was Charlie who killed old man Van Horn.

Woman. But it was the kid here who knew what was going to happen all the time. He was the one who knew!

Steve (*shouts at his hysterical neighbors*). Are you all gone crazy? (*pause as he looks about*) Stop!

(*A fist smashes* Steve's *face, staggering him. The next few lines are spoken wildly, suggesting the coming of violence.*)

Don. Charlie has to be the one—where's my rifle—

Woman. Les Goodman's the one. His car started! Let's wreck it—

Ethel. What about Steve's radio—he's the one that called them—

Les. Smash the radio. Get me a hammer. Get me something.

Steve. Stop—Stop—

Charlie. Where's that kid—let's get him.

Man One. Get Steve—get Charlie—they're working together.

(*The crowd starts to converge around the mother, who grabs* Tommy *and starts to run with him. The crowd starts to follow, at first walking fast, and then running after him. Suddenly* Charlie's *lights go off and the lights in other houses go on, then off.*)

Man One (*shouting*). It isn't the kid . . . it's Bob Weaver's house.

Woman. It isn't Bob Weaver's house; it's Don Martin's place.

Charlie. I tell you it's the kid.

Don. It's Charlie. He's the one.

(*People shout, accuse, and scream as the lights go on and off. Then, slowly, in the middle of this nightmarish morass of sight and sound, the camera starts to pull away until, once again, we have reached the opening shot looking at the Maple Street sign from high above.*)

Scene 2.
(*The metal side of a spacecraft sits shrouded in darkness. An open door throws out a beam of light from the illuminated interior. Two figures appear, silhouetted against the bright lights. We get only a vague feeling of form.*)

Figure One. Understand the procedure now? Just stop a few of their machines and radios and telephones and lawn mowers . . . throw them into darkness for a few hours, and then just sit back and watch the pattern.

Figure Two. And this pattern is always the same?

Figure One. With few variations. They pick the most dangerous enemy they can find . . . and it's themselves. And all we need do is sit back . . . and watch.

Figure Two. Then I take it this place . . . this Maple Street . . . is not unique.

Figure One (*shaking his head*). By no means. Their world is full of Maple Streets. And we'll go from one to the other and let them destroy themselves. One to the other . . . one to the other . . . one to the other—

Scene 3.

(*The camera moves up for a shot of the starry sky, and over this we hear the Narrator's voice.*)

Narrator. The tools of conquest do not necessarily come with bombs and explosions and fallout. There are weapons that are simply thoughts, attitudes, prejudices—to be found only in the minds of men. For the record, prejudices can kill and suspicion can destroy. A thoughtless, frightened search for a scapegoat has a fallout all its own for the children . . . and the children yet unborn. (*a pause*) And the pity of it is . . . that these things cannot be confined to . . . The Twilight Zone!

(*Fade to black. The end.*)

Who are the monsters on Maple Street? Explain your answer.

Why do people begin accusing neighbors of being monsters?

Name the people suspected of being monsters and tell why they were accused.

What do you think will happen during the night on Maple Street?

At the end, the narrator says "prejudices can kill and suspicion can destroy." Explain what is meant.

WRITE   Write a headline and a lead sentence for a newspaper story about the incident on Maple Street. The lead sentence should give facts about *who*, *what*, *when*, and *where*.

Words About the Author:

Rod Serling

As a boy growing up in Binghamton, New York, Rod
Serling enjoyed listening to stories on the radio. He could
see the characters come alive in his imagination. It isn't
surprising that he decided to make his career writing for

radio and later for television and the movies. His first 43 freelance scripts were rejected. His breakthrough came in 1951 when he sold his first television drama. His critically acclaimed show *Patterns*, broadcast in 1955, was called a high point in television's evolution. In that era of live television, it was the first time a show was ever telecast more than once.

His best-known television series, *The Twilight Zone*, aired from 1959 to 1965 and can be seen now on reruns and videotape. Serling, who created, produced, and hosted the program, liked to deal with issues such as intolerance, fear, and prejudice on the show. "I think prejudice is a waste," he said, "and its normal end is violence." Serling received an Emmy Award in 1959 for his work on *The Twilight Zone*.

VISITORS FROM SPACE

Compare the experiences with UFOs in the selections "The UFO Question" and "The Monsters Are Due on Maple Street." How are they the same? How are they different?

WRITER'S WORKSHOP

In "The UFO Question," the author says that about one hundred UFO sightings are reported each day worldwide. Imagine that you are part of the team that handles these reports. Refer to the examples from the selection as you make up a case in which someone reports seeing a UFO. Write a description of the sighting, including all important details. Then use your scientific understanding of UFOs to write a possible explanation for the sighting.

Writer's Choice
In these selections people react in different ways to visitors from space. What do you think about visitors from space? Write a story or give your opinion about the possibility of space visitors. Share your ideas with your classmates.

CONNECTIONS

MULTICULTURAL CONNECTION

THE VALLEY OF MEXICO

Imagine how surprised you would be to encounter a civilization unlike any you had ever seen before. That's what happened in 1519, when Spanish troops under Hernando Cortés landed in Mexico.

For native Mexicans, it was almost as if aliens from space had arrived. The Spaniards had pale skin, wore suits of armor, and carried guns. They also rode horses, animals that were unknown in the Americas.

The Spaniards were equally surprised when they crossed a mountain pass and looked down on the Valley of Mexico. Below them lay the Aztec capital of Tenochtitlán, set on an island in a shimmering lake. Tenochtitlán was larger and more splendid than any European city of the time. One Spaniard wrote, "The soldiers asked whether it was not all a dream."

Imagine that you have come upon a fabulous city and civilization. Where is it located, and what is it like? Share your ideas in a class brainstorming session.

ART/MATH CONNECTION

DESIGN A CITY

Working with a partner, design a city based on ideas from your brainstorming session. Make a drawing of the city (top view and side view), and give your city a name. Display your drawings, and discuss them with classmates.

SOCIAL STUDIES CONNECTION

ANCIENT MODERN CITIES

Mexico City is built on the site of old Tenochtitlán [tä•nôch'tē•tlän'], and signs of its ancient past can still be seen. Research Mexico City or another modern city with an ancient history, such as Cuzco, Peru; Athens, Greece; or Beijing, China. Write a report on that city.

Clockwise from top: ancient Tenochtitlán, Spanish soldier, ruins in ancient Greece, pagoda from old Beijing, Aztec calendar

MEXICO CITY

UNIT TWO

HEROES

In my opinion, those who turn out to be heroes are people who respond in particular ways to their circumstances.

Lois Lowry

How do you recognize a hero? True heroes come in all sizes and shapes and from every land. Heroes such as Mohandas Gandhi and Martin Luther King, Jr., though leaders in their own countries, belong to the world. What makes someone a hero? Is it courage? Determination? Action? Consider what makes a hero as you read the next selections.

THEMES

BOOKSHELF

ZEELY

BY VIRGINIA HAMILTON

Elizabeth changes her name to Geeder for the summer and is ready for something unusual to happen. When she meets the elegant Zeely, Geeder is sure she is in the presence of royalty.

ALA Notable Book

HARCOURT BRACE LIBRARY BOOK

THE WRIGHT BROTHERS: HOW THEY INVENTED THE AIRPLANE

BY RUSSELL FREEDMAN

Orville and Wilbur were two bicycle mechanics who changed the course of history by inventing the world's first powered airplane. Letters and other eyewitness accounts show how the Wright Brothers worked as a team and shared equal credit for their invention.

Newbery Honor, Outstanding Science Trade Book

HARCOURT BRACE LIBRARY BOOK

COLIN POWELL: STRAIGHT TO THE TOP

BY ROSE BLUE AND CORINNE NADEN

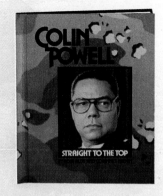

This biography describes General Colin Powell's childhood, his meteoric rise through the military, and his service as chairman of the Joint Chiefs of Staff during the Persian Gulf War.

LAST SUMMER WITH MAIZON

BY JACQUELINE WOODSON

Eleven-year-old Margaret idolizes her best friend, Maizon, but learns to get along without her when Maizon leaves their neighborhood to attend a private boarding school.

Award-Winning Author

THE SUMMER OF THE SWANS

BY BETSY BYARS

Sara is having a difficult summer dealing with the emotions involved in growing up. When her younger brother disappears, Sara is called on to find him.

Newbery Medal, ALA Notable Book

THEME

EVERYDAY HEROES

★ - - - - - ★

When you think of a hero, who comes to mind? Do you think of your best friend, a stranger who saves a life, or someone in your own family? The next selections may make you reconsider your ideas about heroes.

CONTENTS

131

Dana Parker is busy enough just trying to adjust to life at junior high. Imagine her surprise when she becomes a heroine!

132

COURAGE, Dana

by **Susan Beth Pfeffer**

illustrated by **Phil Cheung**

I got to the corner of Main and North streets, just in time to miss the traffic light. I swear they run that thing just for pedestrians to have to stand there. It's a busy corner, and unless you're really feeling daring, you don't cross against the light. That's the sort of dumb thing Charlie might do, but not me. I wasn't in that big a hurry to get home and work on my book report.

I half noticed the people who were waiting for the light with me, the way you half notice things when you really aren't thinking about anything special, just waiting to cross the street. There was a woman carrying a bag from Woolworth's, and a man in a business suit who looked a little like my father, and a mother with a half dozen packages in one hand, trying to control her little kid with the other. The kid was two or maybe three. I don't have that much experience with little kids, so it's hard for me to tell how old they are, or if they're boys or girls. This one was just a wriggling kid in overalls and a blue shirt.

But then the kid managed to wriggle away from its mother. And before she even had a chance to notice, the kid had run smack into the middle of Main and North streets, with a big blue car coming right at it.

The funny thing is I didn't even think. If I'd taken one second to think, I never would have moved. I would have stood there frozen and watched the car hit the kid. It couldn't possibly have stopped in time. I couldn't even be sure if the driver would see the kid, it was so little.

Not that any of that really registered. Instead, I ran into the street, right into the path of that big blue car, and pushed the kid out of the way. The momentum of pushing kept me going, and I stumbled along, half holding the hysterical kid and half holding my school books.

I knew the car could hit us. It was roaring at us like a blue giant. But the funny thing was I felt like a giant too, an all-powerful one, like even if the car hit us, it wouldn't hurt us because I was made of steel, too. Like Superman. And as long as I was there, the kid was safe. I moved my giant steel legs and lifted the kid with my giant steel arms, and in what couldn't have been more than ten seconds, but felt more like ten years, I pushed both of us out of the path of the car.

By the time I'd gotten to the other side of the street with the kid, the blue car's brakes were screeching it to a halt. But over that noise, and the noise of the kid crying, I could hear its mother screaming from way across the street. It was amazing how far off she looked.

I really wanted to lean against the lamppost, but I wasn't going to let go of that kid. I'd already lost most of my books, since I wasn't about to go to the middle of the street and pick them up where I'd dropped them. So I stood there, holding on to the kid with my grip getting weaker and weaker as I started to realize just what I'd done, and just what the car could have done to the kid and me.

The man in the business suit stood in the middle of the street, holding his hand up to stop the cars, and picked up my books for me. The kid's mother, still screaming, crossed the street, walked over to where we were, and started weeping. She was shaking pretty hard, too, but nowhere near as hard as I was. The kid ran to its mother, and the two of them hugged and sobbed. That left me free to grab onto the lamppost, which I did, with both arms.

"I couldn't see, I didn't see," the driver of the blue car cried at us. I guess she pulled her car over to the side of the street, because I watched her join us. She seemed like a nice lady, too, not the sort that drove blue giant monster cars and aimed them at kids. "I have two of my own. I never would have . . ."

"He just got away from me," the kid's mother said. "I was holding his hand, and then he just broke away from me. . . ."

"Here are your books," the businessman said, handing them to me. That meant I had to give up the lamppost, which I did reluctantly. That car could have killed me. I risked my life for some little kid—I didn't even know if it was a boy or a girl. I could have been killed trying to save some strange kid's life.

"I have to go home now," I said, trying to sound conversational. Nobody was paying any attention to me anyway. I grabbed my books and took about a half dozen steps away from the corner of Main and North streets before my legs gave way, and I practically sank onto the sidewalk.

"I'll drive you home," the woman with the Woolworth's bag said. "My car is right here."

I ignored all the warnings about taking lifts from strangers, and gratefully followed the woman into her car. She didn't say anything to me, except to ask where I lived. A couple of times, though, she patted me on the hand, as if to say things were going to be all right.

"Here," I said when we got to our house. What a beautiful house, too. I'd never noticed just how beautiful it was before. The grass was mowed, and there were marigolds blooming in the front garden. Marigolds. If that car had hit me, I might never have seen marigolds again.

"There's no car in the driveway," the woman said. "Are you sure your parents are home?"

"Oh, no, they aren't," I said. "They both work."

"I won't leave you here alone," she said.

"That's okay," I said. "My older sister should be in." I fumbled around, got the key from my pocket and unlocked the front door. The woman followed me in, to make sure Jean really was there.

She was in the living room, sprawled on the sofa, watching TV and eating an apple. I wanted to hug her.

"You see?" I said instead. "She's here."

"If you want, I'll stay until your parents come," the woman said.

"No, really," I said. "I'm okay."

"Dana?" Jean asked, turning around to face us. "What's the matter? What's going on?"

"You should be very proud of your younger sister," the woman said. "She saved a little boy's life. She's quite a heroine."

And that was the first I realized that I really was one.

The next morning at the breakfast table, I was trying to finish my math homework. I hadn't felt like working the night before, and I'd had to tell the story of what happened with the kid to Jean and Mom and Dad so often that I almost believed it had happened. But I didn't think the math teacher would accept it as an excuse for my homework not being done. Jean was nibbling on her toast, and Mom was drinking her orange juice and reading the paper. Dad was upstairs shaving.

"Good grief!" Mom exclaimed, and nearly choked on her juice.

"What?" Jean asked. I didn't even look up.

"There's an article here about Dana," she said.

That was enough to arouse my attention. So I put aside the math, and got up to see what Mom was talking about.

Sure enough, the *Herald* had an article on page 28, all about what had happened. "Mystery Girl Saves Tot's Life" the headline read.

I tried skimming the article, but it wasn't easy with Mom calling to Dad to come downstairs, and Jean reading it out loud.

"Listen to this," Jean said. "'I'd know her anywhere. She was about fourteen years old, and she was wearing a red shirt.' Fourteen."

"Do I really look fourteen?" I asked.

"No," Mom said. "The woman was in a state of shock. Bill! Come down here!"

"If Dana looks fourteen, I must look sixteen," Jean said. "That's only fair."

"I wasn't wearing a red shirt," I said. "But it's got to be me."

"Of course it's you," Mom said.

"What's all the excitement?" Dad asked. He still had lather over half his face.

"Look at this," Mom said, and she took the paper away from me before I had a chance to finish it. I didn't think that was fair, since it was about me, but Dad started reading the article before I had a chance to protest. "Would you look at that," he said. "You're famous, Dana."

"She isn't famous yet," Jean said. "Nobody knows Dana's the one who saved that kid."

"Can I tell the lady?" I asked.

"I don't see why not," Mom said. "I'm sure she wants to thank you in person."

"That's what the article says," Jean said. "I owe my child's life to this girl. I won't be happy until I can thank her personally."

"We wouldn't want her to be unhappy forever," Dad said. "I think Dana should go to the paper after school and let them know. They can contact this woman."

"Why can't I go before school?" I asked. What a great excuse not to finish my math.

"Because school is more important," Mom said. "This can wait. Now, finish your homework, and then you'd better get going."

"Do you think they'll put my picture in the paper?" I asked.

"They might," Dad said. "I guess we'd better prepare ourselves for life with a celebrity."

"All I did was . . ." I started to say. But then I realized what I did was save that kid's life. Who knows? The kid might grow up to be president. Or cure cancer. And it would all be thanks to me. I smiled.

"I think the next few days are going to be absolutely unbearable," Jean said, looking at me. "Anybody mind if I change my name?"

"No teasing," Dad said. "Face it, Jean, you're as proud of Dana as the rest of us."

"I guess," she said, and then she smiled at me. "Sure, why not? My sister, the heroine."

I have to admit I liked the sound of it.

It wasn't easy making it to lunch without telling Sharon the whole story, but every spare minute I had until then I spent on my homework. It was hard concentrating on homework when I knew I was going to go to the paper after school and become famous. The little Dutch boy with his finger in the dike probably didn't have to do his homework for a week after he'd saved Holland. But there were no such breaks for me.

"Did you see that article in the paper?" I asked Sharon as soon as we sat down with our trays.

"What article?" Sharon asked.

"This one," I said, pulling it out of my schoolbag. It hadn't been easy getting Mom and Dad to agree that I should have the one copy of it. But they decided they could buy more on their way to work, so they let me take mine to school.

Sharon skimmed the article. I practically knew it by heart. Another reason my homework hadn't gotten done. "What about it?" she asked.

"That's me," I said. "I'm the fourteen-year-old who saved that kid's life."

"What are you talking about?" she asked, and then she read the article more carefully. "You're not fourteen, Dana. And you were wearing an orange shirt yesterday, not red. How can it be you?"

"It was me," I said, grabbing the article back from her. "It was after we had our ice cream cones. There are witnesses and everything."

Sharon looked at me and laughed. "You're crazy," she said.

"I am not crazy!" I cried. "That's me they're writing about. And Mom and Dad said I could go to the paper after school and let them know it was me. They might even run my picture in the paper."

"Dana, you're my best friend," Sharon said. "I've known you forever. You would never do anything that brave. I'm sorry, but you just wouldn't."

"What are you talking about?" I asked. I was too upset to start eating lunch, even though it was chili, my favorite. Instead, I fingered the article and tried not to pout.

"Dana, you're afraid of your own shadow," Sharon said. "I remember when you wet your pants just because of a little lightning."

"I was in kindergarten then," I said. "And it wasn't just the lightning. I was too scared to ask where the bathroom was."

"See what I mean?" she said. "You were too scared to ask where a bathroom was, and you expect me to believe you ran in front of a car and saved some kid's life? Really, Dana."

"But I did," I said. "Besides, I wasn't scared to ask about the bathroom. More like shy. Embarrassed. And I really did save the kid's life. I didn't think about it. I just did it. And if that kid cures cancer someday, it's going to be because of me."

"I think you've gone crazy," Sharon said, then started eating her chili. "So did you work on your book report?"

"I didn't work on anything!" I shouted. "Listen to me, Sharon. I'm the person they're looking for. I saved that kid's life. That seemed a little more important than some dumb book report. And I don't understand why you won't believe me. Have I ever lied to you before?"

"No," Sharon said. She stopped eating her chili and looked me over thoughtfully. "You're not a liar."

"Thank you," I said.

"It's just hard to believe, that's all," Sharon said, and went back to her chili.

"I'm going to the paper after school," I said. "I was going to ask you if you wanted to come with me, but since you don't believe me, I guess there isn't any point."

"You're really going?" Sharon asked.

"Of course I am," I said. "I told you my parents said I could."

"That's an awfully long walk for a practical joke," she said.

"Don't come," I said. "Don't see a mother's grateful tears." That had been my favorite phrase in the whole article.

"If I go with you, will you really go through with it?" Sharon asked.

"If it isn't true, I'll treat you to ice cream," I said. "A sundae. Deal?"

"Deal," Sharon said.

I didn't much like the idea that Sharon believed in ice cream more than she believed in me, but I was glad to have company when I went to the paper. I could have asked Jean, but she was fourteen, and looked enough like me that I was afraid the woman might think Jean was the one who saved the kid's life. Sharon doesn't look anything like me.

School that afternoon was even harder to concentrate on than school that morning. I thought I would scream when the clock only moved one second at a time. Fortunately none of my teachers called on me, so I didn't have to let everybody know I didn't have the slightest idea what was going on. If Sharon hadn't believed me, I doubted anybody else would accept my explanation.

When the final bell rang, I jumped up, grabbed my books and Sharon, and practically pushed her out of the building.

"What's the hurry?" she asked. "You'll be just as much a heroine three minutes from now."

"I want to get it over with," I said. The truth was, the longer the day had gone, the more uncertain I'd gotten. Maybe two kids' lives had been saved the day before. Maybe the lady wouldn't recognize me. The longer I waited, the more her memory would fade. I just wanted to have it done with.

So I forced Sharon to keep pace with me, and I half ran to the paper. I knew where it was, but hadn't been inside it since our class trip in second grade.

"We're going to die of heart attacks before we ever get there," Sharon said, puffing by my side. I'm in better shape than she is.

144

"It's only four blocks more," I said. "Come on, you can do it."

"I want to live!" she screeched at me, but I ignored her. I had my moment of destiny waiting for me four blocks away. If she couldn't make it, that was her problem.

We were both panting pretty hard by the time we got to the newspaper building. I didn't protest when Sharon raised her hand up to stop me from going in until we both caught our breath. She took out a comb and combed her hair, then offered it to me. I combed mine as well. If they were going to take a picture of me, I wanted to look neat.

"Come on," I said, and walked into the building. I straightened myself as best I could and tried to look fourteen. But my stomach was hurting and my heart was beating, and all of a sudden I started worrying that I'd dreamed the whole thing up.

"Yes?" the receptionist asked.

"I'm the person in the paper," I said. "I mean that article about the mystery girl who saved the tot's life. That's me."

"Oh," the receptionist said, raising her eyebrows. She didn't look like she believed me, and she didn't even know me.

"She really is," Sharon said. "Honest."

I turned around to face her. "Why do you believe me now?" I whispered at her.

"You're not crazy enough to do this if you didn't really do it," she whispered back.

The receptionist looked at both of us, but then she pressed a few buttons and said, "Mrs. Marsh, there's a girl here who claims she's the one who saved that child's life."

I stood there, not even breathing.

"All right," the receptionist said, and hung up. "Girls, Mrs. Marsh would like you to go to the city room and talk with her. She's waiting for you. Straight down the hallway and then it's the first left."

"Okay," I said, and Sharon and I started walking that way. Sure enough, the city room was easy enough to recognize, and Mrs. Marsh was standing there by the door. She'd written the article about me. I'd never met a reporter before, and I felt even more nervous. But Mrs. Marsh didn't look scary. Actually, she sort of looked like my mother.

"Which one of you?" she asked.

"Me," I said. "I mean I. My name is Dana Alison Parker, and I saved that kid's life."

"Come on over here," Mrs. Marsh said, leading Sharon and me to her desk. "Could you tell me a few details about what happened yesterday, Dana? Just to make sure we're talking about the same thing."

"Sure," I said, and I told her the whole story. I'd told it often enough the day before. I made sure to mention the businessman who picked up my books from the street, and the woman who'd been driving the car and had two of her own, and the woman with the Woolworth's bag who'd taken me home. "The kid was wearing overalls," I said. "And a blue shirt, but I didn't know if it was a boy or a girl. It's hard to tell sometimes."

"You certainly sound like you were there," Mrs. Marsh said. "A lot of what you told me wasn't in my article."

"Dana wouldn't lie," Sharon said. "Are you going to call the lady and let her know?"

"Yes, I think I will," Mrs. Marsh said, and sure enough, she dialed a number. Before I knew it, Mrs. Marsh was saying, "Mrs. McKay, I think we've found your heroine. Would you like to come down to the paper and meet her? Fine. We'll expect you here in ten minutes." She hung up the phone and smiled at me. "Can I get you something?" she asked us. "A soft drink, maybe?"

"No, thank you," I said, and Sharon shook her head.

"Wait here," Mrs. Marsh said. "We're going to want some photographs." She got up and went to the other end of the room.

"Do you think there'll be a reward?" Sharon asked me.

"A reward?" I asked.

"Well, you did save that kid's life," she said. "And he might cure cancer, just like you said."

"A reward," I said. What would I do with a reward? And how much might it be?

But I didn't like the way my mind was going. I didn't save that kid's life just to get some money. I didn't even do it to get my name in the paper, or to earn the respect of everybody I knew. I still wasn't sure why I did it, but it wasn't for any sort of profit.

Of course thinking about a reward made the minutes go a lot faster. Mrs. Marsh came back with a photographer, who was holding an awfully big camera with a huge flash attachment. He winked at me, but I started getting nervous again. Mrs. McKay might not recognize me. I couldn't be sure I'd recognize her, and I'd been a lot less upset than she was.

But then Mrs. Marsh started walking toward the door, and I recognized Mrs. McKay all right, and her little boy. Sharon and I both stood up, and I had this horrible thought that Mrs. McKay would walk over to Sharon and thank her by mistake.

But I didn't have to worry. With the photographer clicking and flashing away, Mrs. McKay swooped up her boy and ran to me. "It's her!" she cried as she got closer to me. "Oh, how can I ever thank you?" And soon she was hugging me and the little boy, and the photographer was going crazy, and Mrs. Marsh was taking notes, and Sharon was looking at me almost respectfully. "Oh, thank you, thank you, thank you."

And I swear she cried grateful tears right on me.

Do you think Dana should have been celebrated as a hero for rescuing the boy? Explain your answer.

About saving the boy, Dana says, "I still wasn't sure why I did it, but it wasn't for any sort of profit." Why do you think she saved the boy?

Dana's friend Sharon doesn't think Dana is brave. What kind of person do you think Dana is? Use examples from the story to support your ideas.

Compare the way Dana feels the day she rescues the boy with the way she feels the following day. How do her feelings change?

WRITE   Write your own definition for the word hero. Then write a paragraph explaining whether or not Dana fits your definition.

KID HEROES

True

Stories of

Rescuers,

Survivors,

and

Achievers

by Neal Shusterman
Illustrations by John Patrick

The dictionary defines hero as a person whose courage, strength, or achievement is outstanding—courage enough to perform a rescue, strength enough to overcome and survive adversity, or the achievement of someone determined to make a mark on the world.

Keep reading to find out what amazing things an everyday, normal kid can do.

AWARD-WINNING AUTHOR

Anyone can be a hero... even a kid!

KID HEROES

True Stories of Rescuers, Survivors, and Achievers

NEAL SHUSTERMAN

author of *The Shadow Club*

KID HEROES

Night Fire

It's a quiet February night in Greenwood, South Carolina. Ten-year-old Leatrice Harrison is spending the night at her grandmother's house, along with her three-year-old sister, Jametta, and two young cousins.

In the middle of the night, Leatrice awakens, catching a trace of smoke in the air. When she opens her bedroom door, heavy smoke pours in from the direction of the kitchen. Something in the kitchen had caught on fire, and the flames had spread so quickly that the entire room had been consumed. The entire house would be in flames in a matter of seconds.

Leatrice quickly wakes her baby sister. By now the smoke is so thick their eyes sting, and they can barely breathe. Keeping low to the ground, where the air is better, Leatrice tells Jametta to follow her, then rouses her cousins, bringing them through the smoke and out into the safety of the cool night.

By now the entire house is aflame. Windows shatter, walls buckle, sparks and huge cinders are cast into the sky by the force of the blaze . . .

. . . And that's when Leatrice realizes that Jametta isn't there. Jametta had been so scared that she hadn't followed her sister out of the house!

Leatrice races back into the burning building, and finds Jametta still in the bedroom, surrounded by flames. As Leatrice grabs Jametta, their clothes ignite, and Leatrice tries to protect her baby sister from the flames.

They barely escape from the inferno with their lives.

Both Leatrice and Jametta are hospitalized for second- and third-degree burns. Leatrice's burns are so bad that she has to stay in the hospital for almost a month, but in the end, both she and her sister recover from that awful night, thanks to Leatrice's fast action.

Newsflash!

SAN MANUEL, ARIZONA—Twelve-year-old Hector Sierra made an electrifying rescue today.

Hector was climbing a tree with his friend Andrew when all of a sudden Andrew slipped, lost his grip on a tree-limb, and began a twenty-foot fall.

Andrew reached for whatever he could get his hands on and found himself grabbing a live high-voltage wire! Hector reached out to grab his friend and save him, but when he did, Hector became the ground for the electrical current—that is, the electricity passed through Andrew and Hector, and into the tree.

Hector was able to break Andrew's fall and get him free from the wire, but both boys were rushed to the hospital, nearly electrocuted. Their condition was listed as serious.

Both boys survived. Since the incident last year, Hector has needed three operations to recover from the electrical burns he received, but the knowledge of having saved his friend's life has kept him cheerful and brave through it all.

Brent Meldrum

The "Time-Life Remover"

Susan Meldrum says her five-year-old son Brent is a very confident boy. She also says he's very strong for his age. Perhaps his strength and confidence comes from the karate classes he takes, but wherever they come from, they saved Tanya Branden's life!

Brent and Tanya were playing together when Tanya began to choke on a piece of hard candy.

"I heard about this thing called the 'Time-Life Remover,' or something like that," says Brent. "I saw it on this TV show called *Benson*. Benson was choking and this guy goes behind him, then puts both arms around him, squeezes him real hard, and saves him.

"I could see Tanya was turning blue—really blue. My mother was going crazy, yelling at me to get away, but I didn't listen, because I knew what I had to do. Tanya could barely talk, so I went behind her and gave her the Time-Life Remover—I squeezed and

lifted her up. She weighed forty pounds, but I did it. Then I banged her down on her feet. Finally she coughed and the candy flew out. Tanya was really glad. She says I'm her hero. She didn't kiss me or anything, though. I mean, I'm just her boyfriend!"

What Brent did is not the Time-Life Remover, but the *Heimlich maneuver*, developed in 1974 by a man named Henry Heimlich. If someone is choking on a piece of food or other small object, the Heimlich maneuver can save his or her life. You put your arms around the victim from behind, clasping your hands together in front. Then with the lower knuckle of your thumb, you thrust sharply right beneath the rib cage. That will cause whatever is stuck in the victim's windpipe (or *trachea*) to pop out with a rush of air. It might not seem so difficult, but before the Heimlich maneuver was invented, many people choked to death because

no one knew how to save them. Now thousands of people's lives are saved each year by the Heimlich maneuver—and it's so easy, even a five-year-old child can do it!

Brent's not the only kid who's saved someone with the Heimlich maneuver—Amy Barbee saved two people at a retirement center she worked at, and eight-year-old Freddie Self saved his friend's life.

"Now I'm this big hero," says Brent, who got a lot of publicity from his life-saving episode. "People just keep calling all day—the news and people like that. I wouldn't mind it so much, but they always call me in the middle of cartoons, you know?"

WEST SENECA, NEW YORK—Twelve-year-old James Bliemeister used quick thinking and even quicker gum chewing today to ward off a disaster.

James was baby-sitting at a neighbor's house when the three-year-old child he was staying with rammed his pedal fire engine into a gas pipe. Gas began to hiss out of a hole in the pipe. If James didn't stop the leak quickly, there could have been an explosion!

James remembered he had seen a pack of chewing gum upstairs. Holding his finger in the hole, he sent the three-year-old to get the gum, but the little boy didn't understand. He brought James some toy cars instead. James sent the boy off again. Finally the child returned with the gum. James popped several pieces into his mouth, chewing until the gum was soft enough, then used the wad to plug the hole. After he tied the gum in place with a sock, James called his father, and his father called the gas company.

When the gas company arrived, James was commended for saving the day, and acting very responsibly in a dangerous situation.

KID HEROES

On an Icy Lake...

Eleven-year-old Michelle Lampert does not know how to swim. Of course, there are lots of people who can't swim, but how many nonswimmers do you know who have saved two people from drowning?

Cheney Lake is located on the eastern side of Anchorage, Alaska. It's a deep, icy lake with banks of thick mud.

Two boys were playing on a piece of land that jutted out into the lake. It took only a moment for them to lose their footing and find themselves up to their necks in water, sinking into mud as thick as tar.

The boys panicked and screamed at the top of their lungs for help. The only person to hear them was Michelle. By the time Michelle got to the scene, only one boy was screaming; the other was floating in the lake, unconscious. Michelle threw a rope to the conscious boy and dragged him to safety, but saving the other boy was not going to be as easy. He was floating face down, and had probably been sent into shock by the frigid forty-degree water of the lake. As far as Michelle knew, he was already dead.

Even though Michelle could not swim, she made her way out into the icy water. She grabbed the boy and pulled him toward shore, ignoring the sting of the water as it drained the heat from her shivering body.

Back on shore, Michelle pumped the boy's stomach, using a technique she had learned in school. Finally the boy coughed up water and began to breathe again.

Had it not been for Michelle's bravery, the two boys would have suffered an icy death in the cruel waters of Cheney Lake.

KID
HEROES

Which of these stories do you like the most? Explain why.

Which of these kid heroes do you think is the bravest? The smartest? Explain your answers.

What personality trait or traits do these heroes have in common? Give examples from the stories to support your answer.

WRITE   Think of a time when you or someone you know did something heroic. Briefly describe what happened.

THE RESCUE

Running down the tracks one day,
thunder and lightning coming up on me,
and there a little girl crying
and walking,
looking at the sky.
Me scared to death of storms
crossing over:
You going home? Want me to walk with you?
And turning away from my house to walk her
through Beaver
to hers.
Lightning and thunder strong now.
So there's her mother on the porch, waving,
and she says bye to me then runs.
I turn around
and walk in the storm
slow and straight,
but inside,
a little girl crying.

BY CYNTHIA RYLANT

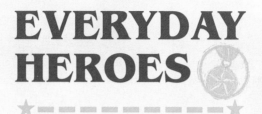

EVERYDAY HEROES

Would you say that Dana is an everyday hero just like the kid heroes? Explain what you think.

WRITER'S WORKSHOP

Although Dana says she didn't contact the newspaper to claim a reward, imagine that she or one of the kid heroes is given a medal or some recognition. Write a speech in which you tell what one of the characters did, praise his or her actions, and present an award.

Writer's Choice

Do you know someone you would call an everyday hero? You could write about your hero, or you could write him or her a letter. Respond in some way, and share your writing.

THEME

COURAGE AND KINDNESS

Both of the following selections were written by the same author, Lois Lowry. But the stories are about very different heroes.

CONTENTS

The One
Hundredth Thing
About Caroline

LOIS LOWRY

ALA Notable
Book

The One Hundredth Thing About Caroline

by Lois Lowry ◙ illustrated by Charles Pyle

> *Eleven-year-old Caroline Tate lives with her mother and J.P., her older brother, in New York City. J.P., who loves taking apart toasters, alarm clocks, and mixers, is an electronics genius. Caroline's best friend, Stacy, is a future investigative reporter. Ever since becoming a member of the Museum of Natural History, Caroline has wanted to be a paleontologist. On a rainy Saturday she pays a visit to her favorite museum.*

The museum wasn't a long walk. Caroline headed east to Central Park, and then south to 79th Street, where the enormous building covered the entire block.

In front of the museum, next to the huge statue of Theodore Roosevelt, a boy was unwrapping a candy bar. He dropped the wrapper on the museum steps.

"Excuse me," Caroline said to him politely and pointed to the nearby sign: LITTERING IS FILTHY AND SELFISH. SO DON'T DO IT.

The boy looked at her for a moment. Then very carefully he reached into his pocket, removed a wadded-up tissue, and dropped it ostentatiously next to his candy wrapper. He grinned nastily and sauntered off.

Caroline looked around for a policeman. But there were only two nuns, a taxi driver leaning against his parked cab, and a couple of mothers with a troop of Brownies.

She thought about making a citizen's arrest. But the boy was bigger than she—he looked at least fifteen—and besides, he was already down at the corner of 78th Street.

She sighed and picked up his trash with two fingers. It was almost as bad as touching parsnips. She dropped it into a trash can angrily and headed up the steps into the museum.

"Hello, Mr. Erwitt," she called into the office inside the front door. Mr. Erwitt looked up from his desk and waved.

"Hello there, Caroline," he called back. "Great exhibit in Meteorites, Minerals, and Gems this afternoon!"

"Thanks anyway, Mr. Erwitt," she said. "I have work to do on the fourth floor."

She showed her membership card to the woman at the admissions booth, took the little blue button that indicated she hadn't sneaked in, and attached it to her raincoat. Then she walked past the postcard counter and the gift shop, down the hall to the elevator.

The fourth floor was absolutely her favorite place in the entire museum. No question. Biology of Invertebrates, on the first floor, was okay; and so was Small Mammals. On the second floor, African Mammals was kind of interesting because of the stuffed elephants and the gorilla who looked like King Kong and had a leaf sticking out of his mouth to indicate that he was a harmless plant-eater. Primates, on the third floor, wasn't too bad.

But the fourth floor was heaven. The Hall of Early Dinosaurs even had blue walls, which was what Caroline had always supposed heaven had.

She went into the blue-walled Early Dinosaur room and stood there, awed, as she always was. There, in the center, were the Stegosaurus, the Allosaurus, and the gigantic Brontosaurus—only their bones, of course—standing in their huge, awkward poses.

"Hi, you guys," said Caroline. She thought of them as old buddies. She always came in to say "Hi," even when she was going to the Late Dinosaur exhibit, as she was today.

They all smiled their toothy smiles at her. Even Allosaurus, a fierce flesh-eater, looked sweet and happy and a little embarrassed, standing there without his skin, quite helpless.

Then she went over to say "Hi" to the mummified Anatosaurus in his glass case. They had found him in Wyoming, of all places, with his skin still on. Sometimes Caroline wished her father had moved to Wyoming instead of Des Moines; she would be tempted to visit him more often if he had. There might be a mummified Anatosaurus buried in his backyard.

Finally, she walked to the end of the huge room and said, "Greetings, Jaws," to the jaws of the giant extinct shark that hung at the entrance to the room of Fossil Fishes.

The jaws just hung there, wide open, as if they were waiting for a dentist to say "Spit."

Caroline wasn't all that crazy about the shark jaws. They gave her the creeps. But she always said "Greetings" to them, politely, before she left the Hall of Early Dinosaurs. She did it for the same reason that she was always very nice to Marcia-Anne Hennessy, the worst bully in her class at school.

She didn't want the giant shark jaws, or Marcia-Anne Hennessy, ever to take a dislike to her.

Then Caroline took out her notebook and headed to her destination: Late Dinosaurs. That room was just as big, though the walls were green. And in the center, dominating the Triceratops and the two Trachodonts next to him, stood the hideous, monstrous Tyrannosaurus Rex. Even without his skin, quite naked and with all his bones exposed, he was horrifying. It made Caroline shiver just to look at him. It also gave her a stiff neck, because he was so tall that she almost had to do a backbend to see his face towering above her, looking down, with his sharp teeth exposed. If ever, by magic, he should come to life, Caroline thought a little nervously, he would only have to bend his mammoth neck, snap his jaws, and in one bite he could consume a whole Scout troop.

"Boo!"

Caroline jumped and dropped her pencil.

"Sorry, Caroline," said the man behind her. "I didn't mean to scare you, really."

Caroline smiled sheepishly. "That's okay, Mr. Keretsky. You just startled me. How are you?"

Gregor Keretsky was Caroline's hero. Stacy had two heroes:

Woodward and Bernstein, the journalists who had broken the Watergate story in the *Washington Post*. And J.P.'s hero was Guglielmo Marconi, the Italian electrical engineer who had invented the wireless receiver. Caroline could drive her brother into a screaming rage whenever she wanted to just by referring to Goo-goo Macaroni.

But she did that only when she was driven to desperation, because she knew how sacred people's heroes were. She was lucky that her hero was right here, in the Museum of Natural History, and that he was one of her best friends. Gregor Keretsky was a vertebrate paleontologist, one of the world's experts on dinosaurs. His office was on the fourth floor of the museum, and sometimes he invited Caroline to have a cup of tea with him. She loved his office; it had bookcases filled with every book that had ever been written about dinosaurs, and some of them had been written by Gregor Keretsky himself.

"I'm fine"—her hero grinned—"and I've been looking for you. I knew my little paleontologist friend would be here, because it is Saturday. And I need your help once again, Caroline."

Caroline sighed. Poor Mr. Keretsky. He had this problem that she helped him with from time to time.

"Neckties?" she asked.

He nodded, embarrassed. "Tomorrow I fly to London. There is a conference there on Monday morning."

"Let's take a look," said Caroline, and she followed him to his office.

He closed the door, because this was a very private consultation. Then he took a bag marked "Brooks Brothers" out of a desk drawer. He took three neckties out of the bag and laid them on the top of the desk.

"What do you think?" he asked helplessly.

Poor Mr. Keretsky was colorblind. No one knew, not even his secretary. And he had no wife. Caroline was the only person in the world to whom he had confided his secret problem since 1946. In 1946, when he had left Europe and come to live in the United States, the Department of Motor Vehicles had refused him a driver's license because he couldn't tell a red light from a green.

His suits were all gray, and his shirts were all white. So those were not a problem. But neckties, he said, made him crazy. He desperately needed help with neckties.

"These two," said Caroline decisively after looking them over. "Keep these two. But take this one back." She wrinkled her nose and handed him the third tie. "It's purple and brown. Really ugly, Mr. Keretsky. Very severely ugly."

"Are you sure?" he asked sadly. "I do like the pattern on this one. It has a—what would you say?—a pleasant geometric order to it."

"Nope," said Caroline firmly. "Take it back."

"The woman at the store said that it was very, very attractive," Mr. Keretsky pointed out.

"What did it cost?"

He turned it over and looked at the price tag. "$22.50," he said.

Caroline groaned. "No *wonder* she said it was very, very attractive. She conned you, Mr. Keretsky. She sold you the ugliest necktie in New York City, for a ridiculously high price. Don't trust her again, under any circumstances."

"All right," he said, sighing, and put the tie back into the bag. "But the others, they are not ugly? You are certain?"

"The others are fine. The striped one's gray and dark green, with a little yellow. And the paisley's some nice shades of blue. They'll look nice on you."

"Caroline," said Gregor Keretsky, "you have once again preserved my dignity. Come to the cafeteria with me and I will buy you a big ice cream."

Caroline fingered her notebook. She really didn't want to miss a chance to talk to one of the world's most famous vertebrate paleontologists. But she had planned to work on a drawing of Tyrannosaurus Rex.

She compromised. "Okay," she said. "I'll go to the cafeteria. But would you do me a favor? Would you tell me everything you know about Tyrannosaurus Rex?"

Gregor Keretsky began to laugh. "Caroline," he said, "that would take me days, I think!"

She laughed, too. She knew he was right. "Well," she said, "tell me a *little* about him, then, over some ice cream."

"By the way," she whispered, as they waited for the elevator. "I wouldn't wear those cuff links to London if I were you."

"These?" Mr. Keretsky held up one wrist. "Why not? These I just bought. There is something wrong with them?"

"Mr. Keretsky," Caroline said as tactfully as she could, "they're *pink*."

Do you agree with Caroline that people's heroes are sacred? Explain your answer.

Are you surprised at Caroline's choice of a hero? Explain your answer.

WRITE Caroline has been to the museum many times, but she is still awed by what she sees in the Hall of Early Dinosaurs. Write a few sentences telling why.

An Interview with
Lois Lowry

Writer Ilene Cooper spoke with Lois Lowry about how she came to write her Newbery Award–winning novel, **Number the Stars.** *This interview tells how Lois Lowry thinks people become heroes and how Mr. Keretsky in* **The One Hundredth Thing About Caroline** *is a different kind of hero from the Danish heroes in* **Number the Stars.**

AWARD-WINNING
AUTHOR

COOPER: *Many people, children and adults, who read* Number the Stars *come away from it wondering if they could be heroes. What do you think makes a hero?*

LOWRY: Although we can't pick the circumstances in which we find ourselves, we can and do choose the way we respond to situations. In my opinion, those who turn out to be heroes are people who respond in particular ways to their circumstances. They respond in a way that may put them at personal risk or call upon them to make sacrifices, without any idea of personal gain.

COOPER: *Who are some of today's heroes?*

LOWRY: First let me say I think the word *hero* is often misused. What we often call a hero today is really an idol. Sports figures or movie stars aren't heroes. They are idols and that's okay, but different. They are successful, and kids admire and respect them, but a baseball player or a rock singer doesn't take any risks or make any sacrifices or set aside any ambitions. My personal heroes are

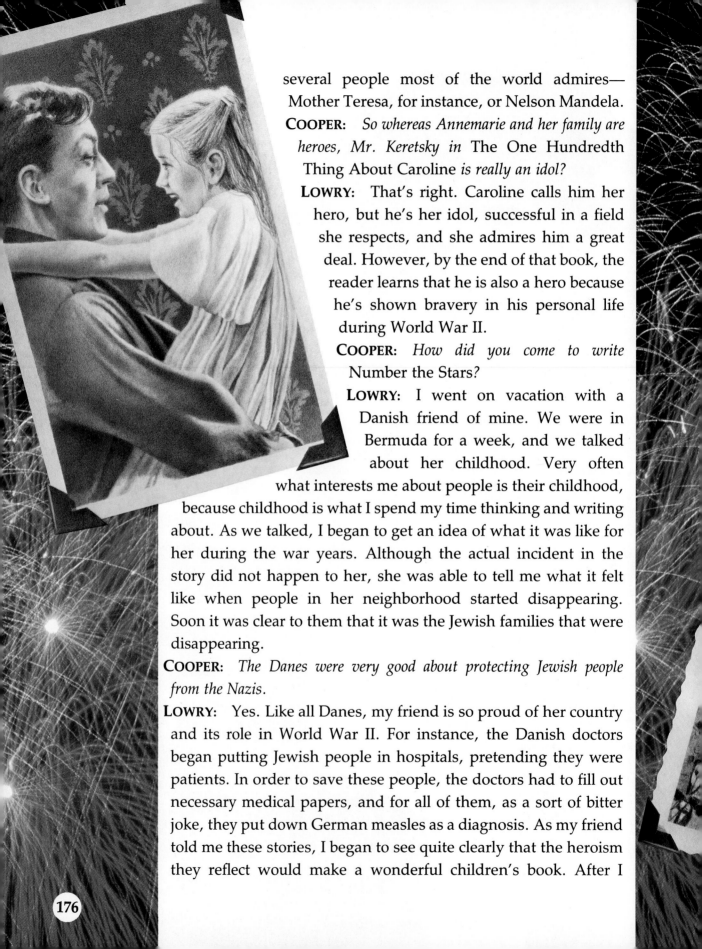

several people most of the world admires—Mother Teresa, for instance, or Nelson Mandela.

COOPER: *So whereas Annemarie and her family are heroes, Mr. Keretsky in* The One Hundredth Thing About Caroline *is really an idol?*

LOWRY: That's right. Caroline calls him her hero, but he's her idol, successful in a field she respects, and she admires him a great deal. However, by the end of that book, the reader learns that he is also a hero because he's shown bravery in his personal life during World War II.

COOPER: *How did you come to write* Number the Stars?

LOWRY: I went on vacation with a Danish friend of mine. We were in Bermuda for a week, and we talked about her childhood. Very often what interests me about people is their childhood, because childhood is what I spend my time thinking and writing about. As we talked, I began to get an idea of what it was like for her during the war years. Although the actual incident in the story did not happen to her, she was able to tell me what it felt like when people in her neighborhood started disappearing. Soon it was clear to them that it was the Jewish families that were disappearing.

COOPER: *The Danes were very good about protecting Jewish people from the Nazis.*

LOWRY: Yes. Like all Danes, my friend is so proud of her country and its role in World War II. For instance, the Danish doctors began putting Jewish people in hospitals, pretending they were patients. In order to save these people, the doctors had to fill out necessary medical papers, and for all of them, as a sort of bitter joke, they put down German measles as a diagnosis. As my friend told me these stories, I began to see quite clearly that the heroism they reflect would make a wonderful children's book. After I started writing, I saw that I would need to do a great deal of research on the story, and I eventually went to Denmark. I spoke to people who had been alive during the war. I went to the Holocaust Museum, which is dedicated to the role of Denmark during the Holocaust. That was where I saw the shoes of fish skin that I used in my story.

COOPER: *Unlike* Number the Stars, *most of your stories take place today. Your Anastasia Krupnik books are especially popular. Why do you keep coming back to her?*

LOWRY: I hadn't intended to write books about the same character, but I did because kids liked them so well. Anastasia is an old friend by now. I know her family, their neighborhood. I can see them in my head so clearly. There's a familiarity about the Krupniks that makes them easy to write about.

COOPER: *Is it more difficult to find heroes today because the newspapers and television tell us so much about people's everyday lives?*

LOWRY: It's true that we do find out more about our heroes than we ever did in the past, but that doesn't have to deter us from having heroes. After all, heroes are human too. It's in those extraordinary circumstances that I spoke of where they rise to more than human stature.

177

NUMBER
the Stars

by Lois Lowry

illustrated by David Wilgus

By 1943, German troops had occupied Denmark for about
a year. Annemarie Johansen; her little sister, Kirsti; and her
best friend, Ellen, could remember when there was plenty
of food and when the tall German soldier, "the Giraffe," and
his partner didn't stand watch on the street corner near the
school. These soldiers had stopped the three girls one day
when they were running home from school. Annemarie's older
sister, Lise, had died in an accident two weeks before she was
to be married; but Peter, her sister's fiancé, still visited the
Johansens to bring news of the Danish Resistance and to offer
gifts to the family. Ellen's family, the Rosens, lived in the
same building as the Johansens. On many afternoons,
Mrs. Rosen would have "coffee," hot water with herbs,
with Annemarie's mother.

The days of September passed, one after the other, much the same. Annemarie and Ellen walked to school together, and home again, always now taking the longer way, avoiding the tall soldier and his partner. Kirsti dawdled just behind them or scampered ahead, never out of their sight.

The two mothers still had their "coffee" together in the afternoons. They began to knit mittens as the days grew slightly shorter and the first leaves began to fall from the trees, because another winter was coming. Everyone remembered the last one. There was no fuel now for the homes and apartments in Copenhagen, and the winter nights were terribly cold.

Like the other families in their building, the Johansens had opened the old chimney and installed a little stove to use for heat when they could find coal to burn. Mama used it too, sometimes, for cooking, because electricity was rationed now. At night they used candles for light. Sometimes Ellen's father, a teacher, complained in frustration because he couldn't see in the dim light to correct his students' papers.

"Soon we will have to add another blanket to your bed," Mama said one morning as she and Annemarie tidied the bedroom.

"Kirsti and I are lucky to have each other for warmth in the winter," Annemarie said. "Poor Ellen, to have no sisters."

"She will have to snuggle in with her mama and papa when it gets cold," Mama said, smiling.

"I remember when Kirsti slept between you and Papa. She was supposed to stay in her crib, but in the middle of the night she would climb out and get in with you," Annemarie said, smoothing the pillows on the bed. Then she hesitated and glanced at her mother, fearful that she had said the wrong thing, the thing that would bring the pained look to her mother's face. The days when little Kirsti slept in Mama and Papa's room were the days when Lise and Annemarie shared this bed.

But Mama was laughing quietly. "I remember, too," she said. "Sometimes she wet the bed in the middle of the night!"

"I did not!" Kirsti said haughtily from the bedroom doorway. "I never, *ever* did that!"

Mama, still laughing, knelt and kissed Kirsti on the cheek. "Time to leave for school, girls," she said. She began to button Kirsti's jacket. "Oh, dear," she said, suddenly. "Look. This button has broken right in half. Annemarie, take Kirsti with you, after school, to the little shop where Mrs. Hirsch sells thread and buttons. See if you can buy just one, to match the others on her jacket. I'll give you some kroner—it shouldn't cost very much."

But after school, when the girls stopped at the shop, which had been there as long as Annemarie could remember, they found it closed. There was a new padlock on the door, and a sign. But the sign was in German. They couldn't read the words.

"I wonder if Mrs. Hirsch is sick," Annemarie said as they walked away.

"I saw her Saturday," Ellen said. "She was with her husband and their son. They all looked just fine. Or at least the *parents* looked just fine—the son *always* looks like a horror." She giggled.

Annemarie made a face. The Hirsch family lived in the neighborhood, so they had seen the boy, Samuel, often. He was a tall teenager with thick glasses, stooped shoulders, and unruly hair. He rode a bicycle to school, leaning forward and squinting, wrinkling his nose to nudge his glasses into place. His bicycle had wooden wheels, now that rubber tires weren't available, and it creaked and clattered on the street.

"I think the Hirsches all went on a vacation to the seashore," Kirsti announced.

"And I suppose they took a big basket of pink-frosted cupcakes with them," Annemarie said sarcastically to her sister.

"Yes, I suppose they did," Kirsti replied.

Annemarie and Ellen exchanged looks that meant: Kirsti is so *dumb*. No one in Copenhagen had taken a vacation at the seashore since the war began. There *were* no pink-frosted cupcakes; there hadn't been for months.

Still, Annemarie thought, looking back at the shop before they turned the corner, where was Mrs. Hirsch? The Hirsch family had gone *somewhere*. Why else would they close the shop?

Mama was troubled when she heard the news. "Are you sure?" she asked several times.

"We can find another button someplace," Annemarie reassured her. "Or we can take one from the bottom of the jacket and move it up. It won't show very much."

But it didn't seem to be the jacket that worried Mama. "Are you sure the sign was in German?" she asked. "Maybe you didn't look carefully."

"Mama, it had a swastika on it."

Her mother turned away with a distracted look. "Annemarie, watch your sister for a few moments. And begin to peel the potatoes for dinner. I'll be right back."

"Where are you going?" Annemarie asked as her mother started for the door.

"I want to talk to Mrs. Rosen."

Puzzled, Annemarie watched her mother leave the apartment. She went to the kitchen and opened the door to the cupboard where the potatoes were kept. Every night, now, it seemed, they had potatoes for dinner. And very little else.

Annemarie was almost asleep when there was a light knock on the bedroom door. Candlelight appeared as the door opened, and her mother stepped in.

"Are you asleep, Annemarie?"

"No. Why? Is something wrong?"

"Nothing's wrong. But I'd like you to get up and come out to the living room. Peter's here. Papa and I want to talk to you."

Annemarie jumped out of bed, and Kirsti grunted in her sleep. Peter! She hadn't seen him in a long time. There was something frightening about his being here at night. Copenhagen had a curfew, and no citizens were allowed out after eight o'clock. It was very dangerous, she knew, for Peter to visit at this time. But she was delighted that he was here. Though his visits were always hurried—they almost seemed secret, somehow, in a way she couldn't quite put her finger on—still, it was a treat to see Peter. It brought back memories of happier times. And her parents loved Peter, too. They said he was like a son.

Barefoot, she ran to the living room and into Peter's arms. He grinned, kissed her cheek, and ruffled her hair.

"You've grown taller since I saw you last," he told her. "You're all legs!"

Annemarie laughed. "I won the girls' footrace last Friday at school," she told him proudly. "Where have you been? We've missed you!"

"My work takes me all over," Peter explained. "Look, I brought you something. One for Kirsti, too." He reached into his pocket and handed her two seashells.

Annemarie put the smaller one on the table to save it for her sister. She held the other in her hands, turning it in the light, looking at the ridged, pearly surface. It was so like Peter, to bring just the right gift.

Papa became more serious. "Annemarie," he said, "Peter tells us that the Germans have issued orders closing many stores run by Jews."

"Jews?" Annemarie repeated. "Is Mrs. Hirsch Jewish? Is that why the button shop is closed? Why have they done that?"

Peter leaned forward. "It is their way of tormenting. For some reason, they want to torment Jewish people. It has happened in other countries. They have taken their time here—have let us relax a little. But now it seems to be starting."

"But why the button shop? What harm is a button shop? Mrs. Hirsch is such a nice lady. Even Samuel—he's a dope, but he would never harm anyone. How could he—he can't even see, with his thick glasses!"

Then Annemarie thought of something else. "If they can't sell their buttons, how will they earn a living?"

"Friends will take care of them," Mama said gently. "That's what friends do."

Annemarie nodded. Mama was right, of course. Friends and neighbors would go to the home of the Hirsch family, would take them fish and potatoes and bread and herbs for making tea. They would be comfortable until their shop was allowed to open again.

Then, suddenly, she sat upright, her eyes wide. "Mama!" she said. "Papa! The Rosens are Jewish, too!"

Her parents nodded, their faces serious and drawn. "I talked to Sophy Rosen this afternoon, after you told me about the button shop," Mama said. "She knows what is happening. But she doesn't think that it will affect them."

Annemarie thought, and understood. She relaxed. "Mr. Rosen doesn't have a shop. He's a teacher. They can't close a whole school!" She looked at Peter with the question in her eyes. "Can they?"

"I think the Rosens will be all right," he said. "But you keep an eye on your friend Ellen. And stay away from the soldiers. Your mother told me what happened on Østerbrogade."

Annemarie shrugged. She had almost forgotten the incident. "It was nothing. They were only bored and looking for someone to talk to, I think."

She turned to her father. "Papa, do you remember what you heard the boy say to the soldier? That all of Denmark would be the king's bodyguard?"

Her father smiled. "I have never forgotten it," he said.

"Well," Annemarie said slowly, "now I think that all of Denmark must be bodyguard for the Jews, as well."

"So we shall be," Papa replied.

Peter stood. "I must go," he said. "And you, Longlegs, it is way past your bedtime now." He hugged Annemarie again.

Later, once more in her bed beside the warm cocoon of her sister, Annemarie remembered how her father had said, three years before, that he would die to protect the king. That her mother would, too. And Annemarie, seven years old, had announced proudly that she also would.

Now she was ten, with long legs and no more silly dreams of pink-frosted cupcakes. And now she—and all the Danes—were to be bodyguard for Ellen, and Ellen's parents, and all of Denmark's Jews.

Would she die to protect them? *Truly?* Annemarie was honest enough to admit, there in the darkness, to herself, that she wasn't sure.

For a moment she felt frightened. But she pulled the blanket up higher around her neck and relaxed. It was all imaginary, anyway—not real. It was only in the fairy tales that people were called upon to be so brave, to die for one another. Not in real-life Denmark. Oh, there were the soldiers; that was true. And the courageous Resistance leaders, who sometimes lost their lives; that was true, too.

But ordinary people like the Rosens and the Johansens? Annemarie admitted to herself, snuggling there in the quiet dark, that she was glad to be an ordinary person who would never be called upon for courage.

Alone in the apartment while Mama was out shopping with Kirsti, Annemarie and Ellen were sprawled on the living room floor playing with paper dolls. They had cut the dolls from Mama's magazines, old ones she had saved from past years. The paper ladies had old-fashioned hair styles and clothes, and the girls had given them names from Mama's favorite book. Mama had told Annemarie and Ellen the entire story of *Gone With the Wind*, and the girls thought it much more interesting and romantic than the king-and-queen tales that Kirsti loved.

"Come, Melanie," Annemarie said, walking her doll across the edge of the rug. "Let's dress for the ball."

"All right, Scarlett, I'm coming," Ellen replied in a sophisticated voice. She was a talented performer; she often played the leading roles in school dramatics. Games of the imagination were always fun when Ellen played.

The door opened and Kirsti stomped in, her face tear-stained and glowering. Mama followed her with an exasperated look and set a package down on the table.

"I won't!" Kirsti sputtered. "I won't ever, *ever* wear them! Not if you chain me in a prison and beat me with sticks!"

Annemarie giggled and looked questioningly at her mother. Mrs. Johansen sighed. "I bought Kirsti some new shoes," she explained. "She's outgrown her old ones."

"Goodness, Kirsti," Ellen said, "I wish my mother would get *me* some new shoes. I love new things, and it's so hard to find them in the stores."

"Not if you go to a *fish* store!" Kirsti bellowed. "But most mothers wouldn't make their daughters wear ugly *fish* shoes!"

"Kirsten," Mama said soothingly, "you know it wasn't a fish store. And we were lucky to find shoes at all."

Kirsti sniffed. "Show them," she commanded. "Show Annemarie and Ellen how ugly they are."

Mama opened the package and took out a pair of little girl's shoes. She held them up, and Kirsti looked away in disgust.

"You know there's no leather anymore," Mama explained. "But they've found a way to make shoes out of fish skin. I don't think these are too ugly."

Annemarie and Ellen looked at the fish skin shoes. Annemarie took one in her hand and examined it. It was odd-looking; the fish scales were visible. But it was a shoe, and her sister needed shoes.

"It's not so bad, Kirsti," she said, lying a little.

Ellen turned the other one over in her hand. "You know," she said, "it's only the color that's ugly."

"Green!" Kirsti wailed. "I will never, *ever* wear green shoes!"

"In our apartment," Ellen told her, "my father has a jar of black, black ink. Would you like these shoes better if they were black?"

Kirsti frowned. "Maybe I would," she said, finally.

"Well, then," Ellen told her, "tonight, if your mama doesn't mind, I'll take the shoes home and ask my father to make them black for you, with his ink."

Mama laughed. "I think that would be a fine improvement. What do you think, Kirsti?"

Kirsti pondered. "Could he make them shiny?" she asked. "I want them shiny."

Ellen nodded. "I think he could. I think they'll be quite pretty, black and shiny."

Kirsti nodded. "All right, then," she said. "But you mustn't tell anyone that they're *fish*. I don't want anyone to know." She took her new shoes, holding them disdainfully, and put them on a chair. Then she looked with interest at the paper dolls.

"Can I play, too?" Kirsti asked. "Can I have a doll?" She squatted beside Annemarie and Ellen on the floor.

Sometimes, Annemarie thought, Kirsti was such a pest, always butting in. But the apartment was small. There was no other place for Kirsti to play. And if they told her to go away, Mama would scold.

"Here," Annemarie said, and handed her sister a cut-out little girl doll. "We're playing *Gone With the Wind*. Melanie and Scarlett are going to a ball. You can be Bonnie. She's Scarlett's daughter."

Kirsti danced her doll up and down happily. "I'm going to the ball!" she announced in a high, pretend voice.

Ellen giggled. "A little girl wouldn't go to a ball. Let's make them go someplace else. Let's make them go to Tivoli!"

"Tivoli!" Annemarie began to laugh. "That's in Copenhagen! *Gone With the Wind* is in America!"

"Tivoli, Tivoli, Tivoli," little Kirsti sang, twirling her doll in a circle.

"It doesn't matter, because it's only a game anyway," Ellen pointed out. "Tivoli can be over there, by that chair. 'Come, Scarlett,'" she said, using her doll voice, "'we shall go to Tivoli to dance and watch the fireworks, and maybe there will be some handsome men there! Bring your silly daughter, Bonnie, and she can ride on the carousel.'"

Annemarie grinned and walked her Scarlett toward the chair that Ellen had designated as Tivoli. She loved Tivoli Gardens, in the heart of Copenhagen; her parents had taken her there, often, when she was a little girl. She remembered the music and the brightly colored lights, the carousel and ice cream and especially the magnificent fireworks in the evenings; the huge colored splashes and bursts of lights in the evening sky.

"I remember the fireworks best of all," she commented to Ellen.

"Me too," Kirsti said. "I remember the fireworks."

"Silly," Annemarie scoffed. "You never saw the fireworks." Tivoli Gardens was closed now. The German occupation forces had burned part of it, perhaps as a way of punishing the fun-loving Danes for their lighthearted pleasures.

Kirsti drew herself up, her small shoulders stiff. "I did too," she said belligerently. "It was my birthday. I woke up in the night and I could hear the booms. And there were lights in the sky. Mama said it was fireworks for my birthday!"

Then Annemarie remembered. Kirsti's birthday was late in August. And that night, only a month before, she, too, had been awakened and frightened by the sound of explosions. Kirsti was right—the sky in the southeast had been ablaze, and Mama had comforted her by calling it a birthday celebration. "Imagine, such fireworks for a little girl five years old!" Mama had said, sitting on their bed, holding the dark curtain aside to look through the window at the lighted sky.

The next evening's newspaper had told the sad truth. The Danes had destroyed their own naval fleet, blowing up the vessels one by one, as the Germans approached to take over the ships for their own use.

"How sad the king must be," Annemarie had heard Mama say to Papa when they read the news.

"How proud," Papa had replied.

It had made Annemarie feel sad and proud, too, to picture the tall, aging king, perhaps with tears in his blue eyes, as he looked at the remains of his small navy, which now lay submerged and broken in the harbor.

"I don't want to play anymore, Ellen," she said suddenly, and put her paper doll on the table.

"I have to go home, anyway," Ellen said. "I have to help Mama with the housecleaning. Thursday is our New Year. Did you know that?"

"Why is it yours?" asked Kirsti. "Isn't it our New Year, too?"

"No. It's the Jewish New Year. That's just for us. But if you want, Kirsti, you can come that night and watch Mama light the candles."

Annemarie and Kirsti had often been invited to watch Mrs. Rosen light the Sabbath candles on Friday evenings. She covered her head with a cloth and said a special prayer in Hebrew as she did so. Annemarie always stood very quietly, awed, to watch; even Kirsti, usually such a chatterbox, was always still at that time. They didn't understand the words or the meaning, but they could feel what a special time it was for the Rosens.

"Yes," Kirsti agreed happily. "I'll come and watch your mama light the candles, and I'll wear my new black shoes."

But this time was to be different. Leaving for school on Thursday with her sister, Annemarie saw the Rosens walking to the synagogue early in the morning, dressed in their best clothes. She waved to Ellen, who waved happily back.

"Lucky Ellen," Annemarie said to Kirsti. "She doesn't have to go to school today."

"But she probably has to sit very, very still, like we do in church," Kirsti pointed out. "*That's* no fun."

That afternoon, Mrs. Rosen knocked at their door but didn't come inside. Instead, she spoke for a long time in a hurried, tense voice to Annemarie's mother in the hall. When Mama returned, her face was worried, but her voice was cheerful.

"Girls," she said, "we have a nice surprise. Tonight Ellen will be coming to stay overnight and to be our guest for a few days! It isn't often we have a visitor."

Kirsti clapped her hands in delight.

"But, Mama," Annemarie said, in dismay, "it's their New Year. They were going to have a celebration at home! Ellen told me that her mother managed to get a chicken someplace, and she was going to roast it—their first roast chicken in a year or more!"

"Their plans have changed," Mama said briskly. "Mr. and Mrs. Rosen have been called away to visit some relatives. So Ellen will stay with us. Now, let's get busy and put clean sheets on your bed. Kirsti, you may sleep with Mama and Papa tonight, and we'll let the big girls giggle together by themselves."

Kirsti pouted, and it was clear that she was about to argue. "Mama will tell you a special story tonight," her mother said. "One just for you."

"About a king?" Kirsti asked dubiously.

"About a king, if you wish," Mama replied.

"All right, then. But there must be a queen, too," Kirsti said.

Though Mrs. Rosen had sent her chicken to the Johansens, and Mama made a lovely dinner large enough for second helpings all around, it was not an evening of laughter and talk. Ellen was silent at dinner. She looked frightened. Mama and Papa tried to speak of cheerful things, but it was clear that they were worried, and it made Annemarie worry, too. Only Kirsti was unaware of the quiet tension in the room. Swinging her feet in their newly blackened and shiny shoes, she chattered and giggled during dinner.

"Early bedtime tonight, little one," Mama announced after the dishes were washed. "We need extra time for the long story I promised, about the king and queen." She disappeared with Kirsti into the bedroom.

"What's happening?" Annemarie asked when she and Ellen were alone with Papa in the living room. "Something's wrong. What is it?"

Papa's face was troubled. "I wish that I could protect you children from this knowledge," he said quietly. "Ellen, you already know. Now we must tell Annemarie."

He turned to her and stroked her hair with his gentle hand. "This morning, at the synagogue, the rabbi told his congregation that the Nazis have taken the synagogue lists of all the Jews. Where they live, what their names are. Of course the Rosens were on that list, along with many others."

"Why? Why did they want those names?"

"They plan to arrest all the Danish Jews. They plan to take them away. And we have been told that they may come tonight."

"I don't understand! Take them where?"

Her father shook his head. "We don't know where, and we don't really know why. They call it 'relocation.' We don't even know what that means. We only know that it is wrong, and it is dangerous, and we must help."

Annemarie was stunned. She looked at Ellen and saw that her best friend was crying silently.

"Where are Ellen's parents? We must help them, too!"

"We couldn't take all three of them. If the Germans came to search our apartment, it would be clear that the Rosens were here. One person we can hide. Not three. So Peter has helped Ellen's parents to go elsewhere. We don't know where. Ellen doesn't know either. But they are safe."

Ellen sobbed aloud, and put her face in her hands. Papa put his arm around her. "They are safe, Ellen. I promise you that. You will see them again quite soon. Can you try hard to believe my promise?"

Ellen hesitated, nodded, and wiped her eyes with her hand.

"But, Papa," Annemarie said, looking around the small apartment, with its few pieces of furniture: the fat stuffed sofa, the table and chairs, the small bookcase against the wall. "You said that we would hide her. How can we do that? Where can she hide?"

Papa smiled. "That part is easy. It will be as your mama said: you two will sleep together in your bed, and you may giggle and talk and tell secrets to each other. And if anyone comes—"

Ellen interrupted him. "Who might come? Will it be soldiers? Like the ones on the corners?" Annemarie remembered how terrified Ellen had looked the day when the soldier had questioned them on the corner.

"I really don't think anyone will. But it never hurts to be prepared. If anyone should come, even soldiers, you two will be sisters. You are together so much, it will be easy for you to pretend that you are sisters."

He rose and walked to the window. He pulled the lace curtain aside and looked down into the street. Outside, it was beginning to grow dark. Soon they would have to draw the black curtains that all Danes had on their windows; the entire city had to be completely darkened at night. In a nearby tree, a bird was singing; otherwise it was quiet. It was the last night of September.

"Go, now, and get into your nightgowns. It will be a long night."

Annemarie and Ellen got to their feet. Papa suddenly crossed the room and put his arms around them both. He kissed the top of each head: Annemarie's blond one, which reached to his shoulder, and Ellen's dark hair, the thick curls braided as always into pigtails.

"Don't be frightened," he said to them softly. "Once I had three daughters. Tonight I am proud to have three daughters again."

"Do you really think anyone will come?" Ellen asked nervously, turning to Annemarie in the bedroom. "Your father doesn't think so."

"Of course not. They're always threatening stuff. They just like to scare people." Annemarie took her nightgown from a hook in the closet.

"Anyway, if they did, it would give me a chance to practice acting. I'd just pretend to be Lise. I wish I were taller, though." Ellen stood on tiptoe, trying to make herself tall. She laughed at herself, and her voice was more relaxed.

"You were great as the Dark Queen in the school play last year," Annemarie told her. "You should be an actress when you grow up."

"My father wants me to be a teacher. He wants *everyone* to be a teacher, like him. But maybe I could convince him that I should go to acting school." Ellen stood on tiptoe again, and made an imperious gesture with her arm. "I am the Dark Queen," she intoned dramatically. "I have come to command the night!"

"You should try saying, 'I am Lise Johansen!'" Annemarie said, grinning. "If you told the Nazis that you were the Dark Queen, they'd haul you off to a mental institution."

Ellen dropped her actress pose and sat down, with her legs curled under her, on the bed. "They won't really come here, do you think?" she asked again.

Annemarie shook her head. "Not in a million years." She picked up her hairbrush.

The girls found themselves whispering as they got ready for bed. There was no need, really, to whisper; they were, after all, supposed to be normal sisters, and Papa had said they could giggle and talk. The bedroom door was closed.

But the night did seem, somehow, different from a normal night. And so they whispered.

"How did your sister die, Annemarie?" Ellen asked suddenly. "I remember when it happened. And I remember the funeral—it was the only time I have ever been in a Lutheran church. But I never knew just what happened."

"I don't know *exactly*," Annemarie confessed. "She and Peter were out somewhere together, and then there was a telephone call, that there had been an accident. Mama and Papa rushed to the hospital—remember, your mother came and stayed with me and Kirsti? Kirsti was already asleep and she slept right through everything, she was so little then. But I stayed up, and I was with your mother in the living room when my parents came home in the middle of the night. And they told me Lise had died."

"I remember it was raining," Ellen said sadly. "It was still raining the next morning when Mama told me. Mama was crying, and the rain made it seem as if the whole *world* was crying."

Annemarie finished brushing her long hair and handed her hairbrush to her best friend. Ellen undid her braids, lifted her dark hair away from the thin gold chain she wore around her neck—the chain that held the Star of David—and began to brush her thick curls.

"I think it was partly because of the rain. They said she was hit by a car. I suppose the streets were slippery, and it was getting dark, and maybe the driver just couldn't see," Annemarie went on, remembering. "Papa looked so angry. He made one hand into a fist, and he kept pounding it into the other hand. I remember the noise of it: slam, slam, slam."

Together they got into the wide bed and pulled up the covers. Annemarie blew out the candle and drew the dark curtains aside so that the open window near the bed let in some air. "See that blue trunk in the corner?" she said, pointing through the darkness. "Lots of Lise's things are in there. Even her wedding dress. Mama and Papa have never looked at those things, not since the day they packed them away."

Ellen sighed. "She would have looked so beautiful in her wedding dress. She had such a pretty smile. I used to pretend that she was *my* sister, too."

"She would have liked that," Annemarie told her. "She loved you."

"That's the worst thing in the world," Ellen whispered. "To be dead so young. I wouldn't want the Germans to take my family away—to make us live someplace else. But still, it wouldn't be as bad as being dead."

Annemarie leaned over and hugged her. "They won't take you away," she said. "Not your parents, either. Papa promised that they were safe, and he always keeps his promises. And you are quite safe, here with us."

For a while they continued to murmur in the dark, but the murmurs were interrupted by yawns. Then Ellen's voice stopped, she turned over, and in a minute her breathing was quiet and slow.

Annemarie stared at the window where the sky was outlined and a tree branch moved slightly in the breeze. Everything seemed very familiar, very comforting. Dangers were no more than odd imaginings, like ghost stories that children made up to frighten one another: things that couldn't possibly happen. Annemarie felt completely safe here in her own home, with her parents in the next room and her best friend asleep beside her. She yawned contentedly and closed her eyes.

It was hours later, but still dark, when she was awakened abruptly by the pounding on the apartment door.

Annemarie eased the bedroom door open quietly, only a crack, and peeked out. Behind her, Ellen was sitting up, her eyes wide.

She could see Mama and Papa in their nightclothes, moving about. Mama held a lighted candle, but as Annemarie watched, she went to a lamp and switched it on. It was so long a time since they had dared to use the strictly rationed electricity after dark that the light in the room seemed startling to Annemarie, watching through the slightly opened bedroom door. She saw her mother look automatically to the blackout curtains, making certain that they were tightly drawn.

Papa opened the front door to the soldiers.

"This is the Johansen apartment?" A deep voice asked the question loudly, in terribly accented Danish.

"Our name is on the door, and I see you have a flashlight," Papa answered. "What do you want? Is something wrong?"

"I understand you are a friend of your neighbors the Rosens, Mrs. Johansen," the soldier said angrily.

"Sophy Rosen is my friend, that is true," Mama said quietly. "Please, could you speak more softly? My children are asleep."

"Then you will be so kind as to tell me where the Rosens are." He made no effort to lower his voice.

"I assume they are at home, sleeping. It is four in the morning, after all," Mama said.

Annemarie heard the soldier stalk across the living room toward the kitchen. From her hiding place in the narrow sliver of open doorway, she could see the heavy uniformed man, a holstered pistol at his waist, in the entrance to the kitchen, peering in toward the sink.

Another German voice said, "The Rosens' apartment is empty. We are wondering if they might be visiting their good friends the Johansens."

"Well," said Papa, moving slightly so that he was standing in front of Annemarie's bedroom door, and she could see nothing except the dark blur of his back, "as you see, you are mistaken. There is no one here but my family."

"You will not object if we look around." The voice was harsh, and it was not a question.

"It seems we have no choice," Papa replied.

"Please don't wake my children," Mama requested again. "There is no need to frighten little ones."

The heavy, booted feet moved across the floor again and into the other bedroom. A closet door opened and closed with a bang.

Annemarie eased her bedroom door closed silently. She stumbled through the darkness to the bed.

"Ellen," she whispered urgently, "take your necklace off!"

Ellen's hands flew to her neck. Desperately she began trying to unhook the tiny clasp. Outside the bedroom door, the harsh voices and heavy footsteps continued.

"I can't get it open!" Ellen said frantically. "I never take it off—I can't even remember how to open it!"

Annemarie heard a voice just outside the door. "What is here?"

"Shhh," her mother replied. "My daughters' bedroom. They are sound asleep."

"Hold still," Annemarie commanded. "This will hurt." She grabbed the little gold chain, yanked with all her strength, and broke it. As the door opened and light flooded into the bedroom, she crumpled it into her hand and closed her fingers tightly.

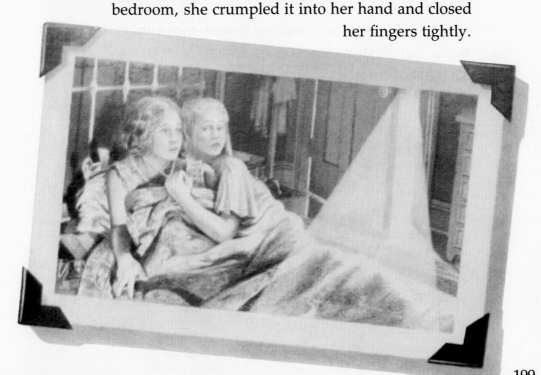

Terrified, both girls looked up at the three Nazi officers who entered the room.

One of the men aimed a flashlight around the bedroom. He went to the closet and looked inside. Then with a sweep of his gloved hand he pushed to the floor several coats and a bathrobe that hung from pegs on the wall.

There was nothing else in the room except a chest of drawers, the blue decorated trunk in the corner, and a heap of Kirsti's dolls piled in a small rocking chair. The flashlight beam touched each thing in turn. Angrily the officer turned toward the bed.

"Get up!" he ordered. "Come out here!"

Trembling, the two girls rose from the bed and followed him, brushing past the two remaining officers in the doorway, to the living room.

Annemarie looked around. These three uniformed men were different from the ones on the street corners. The street soldiers were often young, sometimes ill at ease, and Annemarie remembered how the Giraffe had, for a moment, let his harsh pose slip and had smiled at Kirsti.

But these men were older and their faces were set with anger.

Her parents were standing beside each other, their faces tense, but Kirsti was nowhere in sight. Thank goodness that Kirsti slept through almost everything. If they had wakened her, she would be wailing—or worse, she would be angry, and her fists would fly.

"Your names?" the officer barked.

"Annemarie Johansen. And this is my sister—"

"Quiet! Let her speak for herself. Your name?" He was glaring at Ellen.

Ellen swallowed. "Lise," she said, and cleared her throat. "Lise Johansen."

The officer stared at them grimly.

"Now," Mama said in a strong voice, "you have seen that we are not hiding anything. May my children go back to bed?"

The officer ignored her. Suddenly he grabbed a handful of Ellen's hair. Ellen winced.

He laughed scornfully. "You have a blond child sleeping in the other room. And you have this blond daughter—" He gestured towards Annemarie with his head. "Where did you get the dark-haired one?" He twisted the lock of Ellen's hair. "From a different father? From the milkman?"

Papa stepped forward. "Don't speak to my wife in such a way. Let go of my daughter or I will report you for such treatment."

"Or maybe you got her someplace else?" the officer continued with a sneer. "From the Rosens?"

For a moment no one spoke. Then Annemarie, watching in panic, saw her father move swiftly to the small bookcase and take out a book. She saw that he was holding the family photograph album. Very quickly he searched through its pages, found what he was looking for, and tore out three pictures from three separate pages.

He handed them to the German officer, who released Ellen's hair.

"You will see each of my daughters, each with her name written on the photograph," Papa said.

Annemarie knew instantly which photographs he had chosen. The album had many snapshots—all the poorly focused pictures of school events and birthday parties. But it also contained a portrait, taken by a photographer, of each girl as a tiny infant. Mama had written, in her delicate handwriting, the name of each baby daughter across the bottom of those photographs.

She realized too, with an icy feeling, why Papa had torn them from the book. At the bottom of each page, below the photograph itself, was written the date. And the real Lise Johansen had been born twenty-one years earlier.

"Kirsten Elisabeth," the officer read, looking at Kirsti's baby picture. He let the photograph fall to the floor.

"Annemarie," he read next, glanced at her, and dropped the second photograph.

"Lise Margrete," he read finally, and stared at Ellen for a long, unwavering moment. In her mind, Annemarie pictured the photograph that he held: the baby, wide-eyed, propped against a pillow, her tiny hand holding a silver teething ring, her bare feet visible against the hem of an embroidered dress. The wispy curls. Dark.

The officer tore the photograph in half and dropped the pieces on the floor. Then he turned, the heels of his shiny boots grinding into the pictures, and left the apartment. Without a word, the other two officers followed. Papa stepped forward and closed the door behind him.

Annemarie relaxed the clenched fingers of her right hand, which still clutched Ellen's necklace. She looked down, and saw that she had imprinted the Star of David into her palm.

Would you call Annemarie and her family heroes? Explain your answer.

Why do the Johansens help the Rosens by hiding Ellen?

Why does Mr. Johansen show baby pictures of his daughters rather than a later family photograph?

The characters in this story face many hardships. Which hardship do you think would be the most difficult to face? Explain your answer.

Why does Annemarie yank the Star of David necklace off Ellen's neck?

WRITE   Annemarie says that all of Denmark must be bodyguard for the Jews. Write a paragraph explaining how the characters in the story act as bodyguards.

COURAGE AND KINDNESS

Compare the heroes in the two stories. How are they similar? How are they different?

WRITER'S WORKSHOP

Heroes can be quiet like Gregor Keretsky or brave in the face of danger like Papa Johansen and his family. Write a realistic story that includes a character who is a hero. Include details that show your character's qualities.

Writer's Choice
What does the theme Courage and Kindness mean to you now that you have read "Number the Stars" and "The One Hundredth Thing About Caroline"? Write your response to the theme. Share your writing with your classmates.

T H E M E

EXTRAORDINARY PEOPLE

What makes some people fascinating? The things they can do? The way they look or behave? You will read about two characters with special talents and qualities that set them apart.

C O N T E N T S

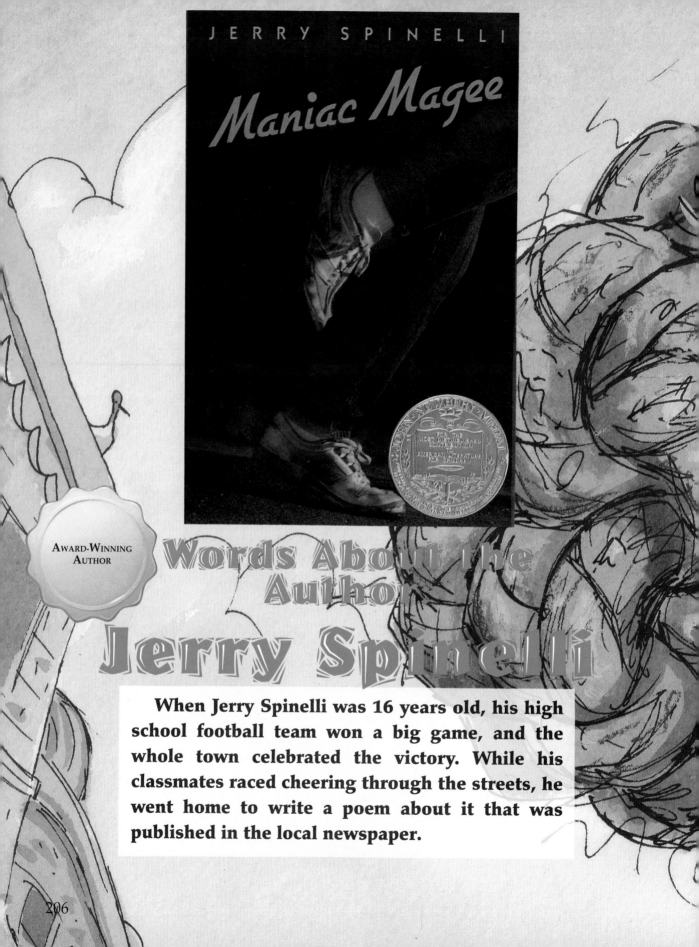

JERRY SPINELLI

Maniac Magee

Words About the Author

Jerry Spinelli

When Jerry Spinelli was 16 years old, his high school football team won a big game, and the whole town celebrated the victory. While his classmates raced cheering through the streets, he went home to write a poem about it that was published in the local newspaper.

It wasn't quite so easy for him to find things to write about as an adult. Not until he was married and had his own children did he find his niche, writing books for children. He gets his ideas from his family, and from his own memories. Reflecting on the power of childhood memories he says, "Isn't it a magical, wonderful thing that our childhoods are not irretrievably lost to us, like the juice squeezed forever from an orange?"

Oh yes, there's one more place Spinelli gets his ideas. As he told some school kids, he gets them "from you. You're the funny ones. You're the fascinating ones."

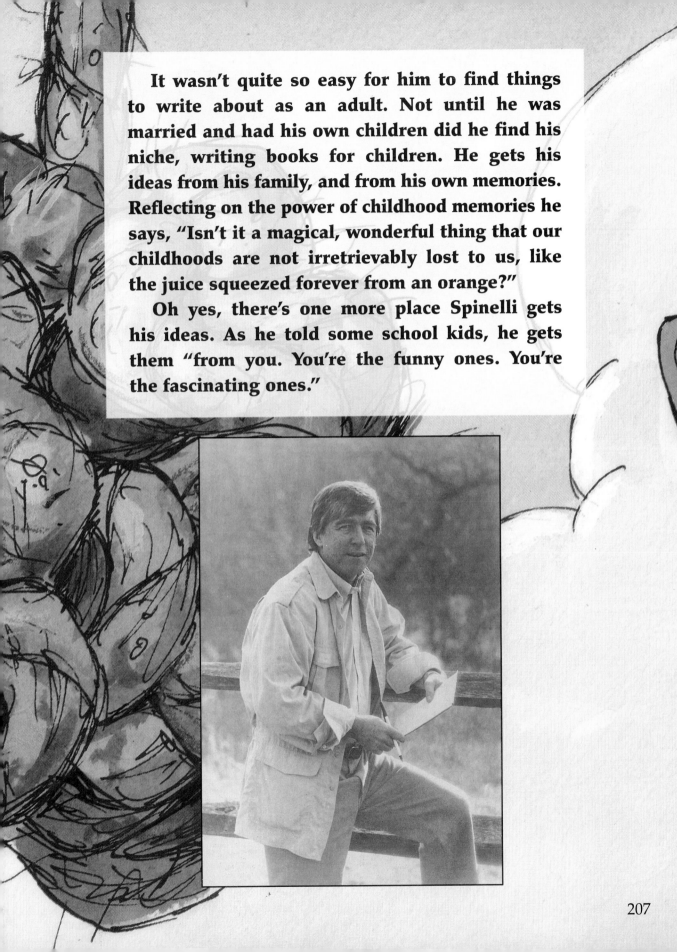

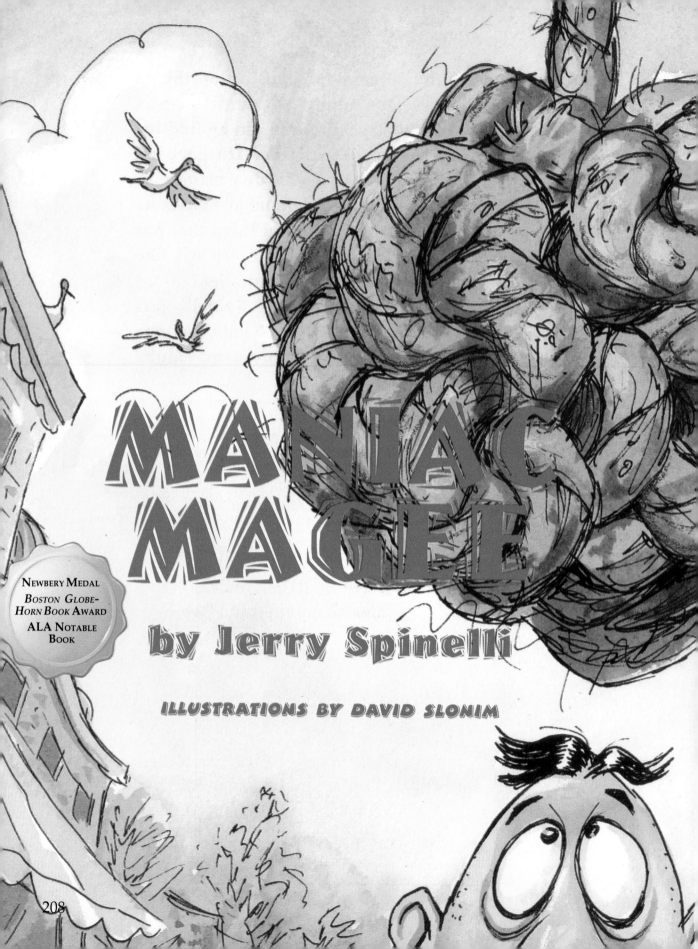

MANIAC MAGEE

by Jerry Spinelli

ILLUSTRATIONS BY DAVID SLONIM

If the Wonders of the World hadn't stopped at seven, Cobble's Knot would have been number eight.

Nobody knew how it got there. As the story goes, the original Mr. Cobble wasn't doing too well with the original Cobble's Corner Grocery at the corner of Hector and Birch. In his first two weeks, all he sold was some Quaker Oats and penny candy.

Then one morning, as he unlocked the front door for business, he saw the Knot. It was dangling from the flagpole that hung over the big picture window, the one that said FROSTED FOODS in icy blue-and-white letters. He got out a pair of scissors and was about to snip it off, when he noticed what an unusual and incredible knot it was.

And then he got an idea. He could offer a prize to anyone who untangled the Knot. Publicize it. Call the newspaper. Winner's picture on the front page, Cobble's Corner in the background. Business would boom.

Well, he went ahead and did it, and if business didn't exactly boom, it must have at least peeped a little, because eons later, when Maniac Magee came to town, Cobble's Corner was still there. Only now it sold pizza instead of groceries. And the prize was different. It had started out being sixty seconds alone with the candy counter; now it was one large pizza per week for a whole year.

Which, in time, made the Knot practically priceless. Which is why, after leaving it outside for a year, Mr. Cobble took it down and kept it in a secret place inside the store and brought it out only to meet a challenger.

If you look at old pictures in the *Two Mills Times,* you see that the Knot was about the size and shape of a lopsided volleyball. It was made of string, but it had more contortions, ins and outs, twists and turns and dips and doodles than the brain of Albert Einstein himself. It had defeated all comers for years, including J.J. Thorndike, who grew up to be a magician, and Fingers Halloway, who grew up to be a pickpocket.

Hardly a week went by without somebody taking a shot at the Knot, and losing. And each loser added to the glory that awaited someone who could untie it.

"So you see," said Amanda, "if you go up there and untie Cobble's Knot—which I *know* you can—you'll get your picture in the paper and you'll be the biggest hero ever around here and *nooo*-body'll mess with you then."

Maniac listened and thought about it and finally gave a little grin. "Maybe you're just after the pizza, since you know I can't eat it."

Amanda screeched. "Jeff-*freee*! The pizza's not the point." She started to hit him. He laughed and grabbed her wrists. And he said okay, he'd give it a try.

They brought out the Knot and hung it from the flagpole. They brought out the official square wooden table for the challenger to stand on, and from the moment Maniac climbed up, you could tell the Knot was in big trouble.

To the ordinary person, Cobble's Knot was about as friendly as a nest of yellowjackets. Besides the tangle itself, there was the weathering of that first year, when the Knot hung outside and became hard as a rock. You could barely make out the individual strands. It was grimy, moldy, crusted over. Here and there a loop stuck out, maybe big enough to stick your pinky finger through, pitiful testimony to the challengers who had tried and failed.

And there stood Maniac, turning the Knot, checking it out. Some say there was a faint grin on his face, kind of playful, as though the Knot wasn't his enemy at all, but an old pal just playing a little trick on him. Others say his mouth was more grim than grin, that his eyes lit up like flashbulbs, because he knew he was finally facing a knot that would stand up and fight, a worthy opponent.

He lifted it in his hands to feel the weight of it. He touched it here and touched it there, gently, daintily. He scraped a patch of crust off with his fingernail. He laid his fingertips on it, as though feeling for a pulse.

Only a few people were watching at first, and half of them were Heck's Angels, a roving tricycle gang of four- and five-year-olds. Most of them had had sneaker-lace or yo-yo knots untied by Maniac, and they expected this would only take a couple of seconds longer. When the seconds became minutes, they started to get antsy, and before ten minutes had passed, they were zooming off in search of somebody to terrorize.

The rest of the spectators watched Maniac poke and tug and pick at the knot. Never a big pull or yank, just his fingertips touching and grazing and peck-pecking away, like some little bird.

"What's he doin'?" somebody said.

"What's taking so long?"

"He gonna do it or not?"

After an hour, except for a few more finger-size loops, all Maniac had to show for his trouble were the flakes of knot crust that covered the table.

"He ain't even found the end of the string yet," somebody grumbled, and almost everybody but Amanda took off.

Maniac never noticed. He just went on working.

By lunchtime they were all back, and more kept coming. Not only kids, but grownups, too, black and white, because Cobble's Corner was on Hector, and word was racing through the neighborhoods on both the east and west sides of the street.

What people saw they didn't believe.

The knot had grown, swelled, exploded. It was a frizzy globe—the newspaper the next day described it as a "gigantic hairball." Now, except for a packed-in clump at the center, it was practically all loops. You could look through it and see Maniac calmly working on the other side.

"He found the end!" somebody gasped, and the corner burst into applause.

Meanwhile, inside, Cobble's was selling pizza left and right, not to mention zeps (a Two Mills type of hoagie), steak sandwiches, strombolis, and gallons of soda. Mr. Cobble himself came out to offer Maniac some pizza, which Maniac of course politely turned down. He did accept an orange soda, though, and then a little kid, whose sneaker laces Maniac had untied many a time, handed up to him a three-pack of Tastykake butterscotch Krimpets.

After polishing off the Krimpets, Maniac did the last thing anybody expected: he lay down and took a nap right there on the table, the knot hanging above him like a small hairy planet, the mob buzzing all around him. Maniac knew what the rest of them didn't: the hardest part was yet to come. He had to find the right routes to untangle the mess, or it would just close up again like a rock and probably stay that way forever. He would need the touch of a surgeon, the alertness of an owl, the cunning of three foxes, and the foresight of a grand master in chess. To accomplish that, he needed to clear his head, to flush away all distraction, especially the memory of the butterscotch Krimpets, which had already hooked him.

In exactly fifteen minutes, he woke up and started back in.

Like some fairytale tailor, he threaded the end through the maze, dipping and doodling through openings the way he squiggled a football through a defense. As the long August afternoon boiled along, the exploded knot-hairball would cave in here, cave in there. It got lumpy, out of shape, saggy. The *Times* photographer made starbursts with his camera. The people munched on Cobble's pizza and spilled across Hector from sidewalk to sidewalk and said "Ouuuu!" and "Ahhhh!"

And then, around dinnertime, a huge roar went up, a volcano of cheers. Cobble's Knot was dead. Undone. Gone. It was nothing but string.

Would you have tried to untie Cobble's Knot? Why or why not?

Why do people wander away and then come back to watch Maniac?

What kind of person is Maniac? Give examples from the story to support your ideas.

In your opinion, why does Maniac try to untie the knot?

WRITE   Maniac has a special talent that makes him a hero. Write a paragraph about a situation in which a special talent you have might make you a hero.

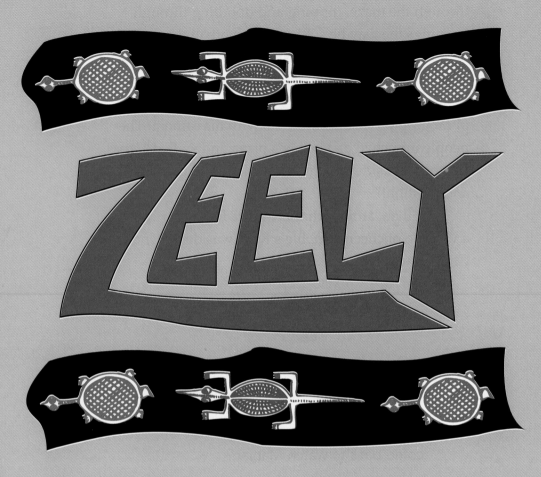

ZEELY

ALA Notable
Book

by Virginia Hamilton

Illustrations by Lonnie Knabel

Geeder and her younger brother, Toeboy, are spending the summer on their Uncle Ross's farm. One night, they decide to sleep outside. Geeder scares Toeboy by telling him a story about night travellers, mysterious figures that walk in the dark. That night, Geeder actually sees a figure on the road. A few weeks later, when the children from the town gather at a bonfire, Geeder tells them about Zeely Tayber, a woman unlike anyone she has ever seen before.

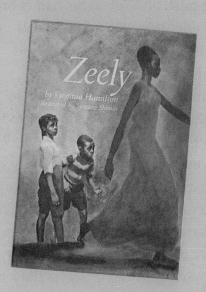

Geeder and Toeboy lay under a dark sky that night. The moon went away and the stars seemed hard and far off. Toeboy slept fitfully and Geeder stared into the night. Under the covers with her lay Uncle Ross' flashlight. She did not touch it; she hardly realized it was beside her. Any thought of the night traveller had drifted far back in her mind. She slipped into a sound sleep.

Geeder did not dream or speak out in the night, nor did she witness the passing of the night traveller down Leadback Road. But Toeboy did. Perhaps it was the excitement of the bonfire that caused him to turn and toss in his sleep. He awoke several times, turned, saw that Geeder was asleep and went back to sleep himself. Maybe it was the fact that the night traveller did not only walk down Leadback Road this night. Before it passed the hedge in front of the house, it paused for as much as thirty seconds. It seemed to listen; perhaps it waited. Whatever its reason for stopping there in the road, it did so when Toeboy had awakened from a dream of bright fires.

He couldn't have said why he crawled all the way out of the lilac bush and sat there with his toes touching the wet grass. It wasn't just to see if Geeder was still asleep. Maybe he had heard some sound or maybe he thought he was still at the bonfire, for the bright, clear faces of his friends, the smell of smoke and the shape of the flames were with him still. Toeboy saw the thing at the hedge right away. It stood where the hedge parted, at the foot of the path leading to the house. It had no arms or legs. He knew at once what he saw, and he wasn't afraid.

"Good evening, Miss Zeely," he said, softly. "How do you do?"

Zeely Tayber turned slightly toward the place where Geeder slept. She made a movement as though to silence Toeboy. Then, she glided on down Leadback Road and the darkness of the night was all there was.

Before daybreak, a fog rose from the hollows and fanned out through the catalpa trees. It lay like smoke over swimming holes. When Geeder and Toeboy awoke at six-thirty, it covered all the land. The whole town and countryside was trapped in a thick fog, too warm and wet to be anything other than strange. They found their bedding soaked. Even their clothing, which they had slept in in order to save time in the morning, was uncomfortably damp.

Toeboy was about to tell Geeder that he had seen Zeely Tayber come down the road in the night when she whispered excitedly, "Toeboy, it's begun!"

And so it had begun. Nat Tayber had started his prize animals down Leadback Road. Toeboy forgot to tell how Zeely looked in the darkness and Geeder forgot to feed Uncle Ross' chickens. They ran to the elm tree near the road and climbed to the top. There, they could see perfectly and not be seen. They saw Uncle Ross hurry out of the house, look around for them and then wait by the road. From their vantage point they could see above the mist. Suddenly, the sun broke through and the top of the mist was spread with gold.

It was seven o'clock by the time Nat Tayber and his hogs reached the elm tree. Uncle Ross stood nearby, hoping, perhaps, that Nat would need him to help move the animals. Nat didn't, of course. He had hired strong, husky lads from the village.

"The mood he's in," Geeder whispered, "he won't ask Uncle Ross for anything."

"He's got mud all over him," Toeboy said.

"I bet he fell chasing one of his hogs. Oh, does he look mean!" Geeder said.

Nat Tayber was covered with mud from the chest down. In one hand, he carried a long prodding pole. All the boys he had hired were equipped with the same sort of poles.

"I don't see Zeely," said Geeder. "She ought to be right in front." All she could see through the mist was the trail of animals and Nat Tayber and his boys. Suddenly, Geeder found Zeely far back at the end of the line of animals.

"Why, what's she doing way back there?" Geeder whispered. Zeely moved slowly in and out of the mist, never once hurrying and never speaking. She wore a long, white smock that reached to her feet.

Toeboy recognized the smock Zeely wore. It was what had made her appear to have no arms or feet or head the night before. The smock was streaked with mud.

"She's got herself all dirty," he said. "She's about as muddy as old Nat."

"Hush, Toeboy!" Geeder whispered. "I don't care if she is dirty. Just look at

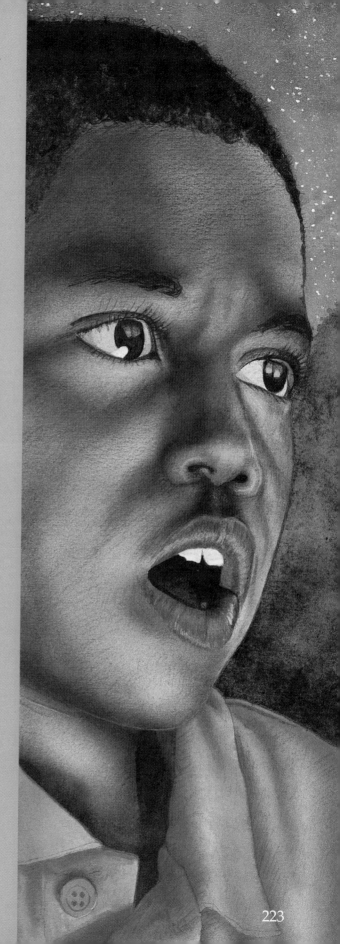

223

her! Oh, she's pretty, with all that mist around her!"

Zeely Tayber carried a pail of feed instead of a prodding pole. Whenever one of the huge razorbacks stopped for too long, she held the pail under its snout. As it ate, she walked forward again until the animal was moving. It was a slow process but it worked well. Still, the hogs took their time.

"I bet Nat thinks he's going to get those hogs through town before it's full of trucks and cars," Geeder said to Toeboy.

"He won't make it," Toeboy said, "not the rate he's going."

"It'll serve him right for not letting Zeely lead," Geeder said. "Can't you just see the street packed with folks and those animals and Nat and all those boys trying to get through?"

On Leadback Road, some of Nat Tayber's hogs got going in the wrong direction; others lay down by Uncle Ross' hedge to rest. The boys he had hired rushed to the hedge, hitting the tired animals with their poles. When the first blow was struck, Geeder held her breath. Finally, she had to turn her face away.

"That's no way to treat hogs," Uncle Ross hollered. "Those are prize animals—that's no way!"

Nat Tayber ignored him. "Hit them! Hit them!" he yelled to the boys. "That will make them move!"

The animals rose, squealing frantically, and lumbered away down the road toward the village. The rest of the hogs followed as fast as their great bulk would let them. Nat and the boys ran after the hogs.

Through it all, Geeder had watched silently. She felt sick when the animals were hit so hard and sorry when they were forced to run down Leadback Road. And now, she was left with a sour taste on her tongue.

"Goodness knows, animals shouldn't be hurt by anyone," she whispered to herself.

She felt like not going into town, fearing to see the animals beaten again. Then, Zeely passed by the tree. She did not seem to be a part of what had happened, nor to be aware of the press of smelling, dirty animals around her. Geeder whistled so Zeely would look up and see her.

Once she sees me, Geeder thought, I know she'll want me to help.

Zeely Tayber paused. But then she went on, as silent and serene as ever. Toeboy and Geeder watched her disappear into the mist.

Geeder guessed Zeely hadn't heard her. "Maybe when she gets into town and sees me there . . .," she whispered, not quite able to finish the wish, even to herself. She and Toeboy climbed down the tree and raced for the catalpa trees.

There was a shorter route through the forest to town.

They were more than halfway along, running fast, when Toeboy thought about seeing Zeely Tayber.

"I saw Miss Zeely last night," he began. "And Geeder, it was very late, I know it was because I was so sleepy. She looked just as funny, like she didn't have any arms or anything. That was because the night was so dark."

Geeder stopped dead in her tracks. She was panting hard and her eyes were too wide, as though she hadn't enough light to see. "What did you say?" she whispered.

"I just said that Miss Zeely came down the road last night," Toeboy said, catching his breath.

Geeder stared at him and slowly nodded her head. "The other part," she said softly, "how did you say she looked?"

"She looked funny, that's all," Toeboy said. He fidgeted uncomfortably under Geeder's gaze. "See, she had on that long dress she was wearing today and it made her seem to glide. I couldn't see her face. And that bucket she carried floated with her." He laughed. "That was because I couldn't see her arms."

"Bucket?" Geeder said. Her voice made hardly a sound.

"The feed pail," Toeboy said. "I guess she was coming from feeding the hogs. Geeder, what's the matter?"

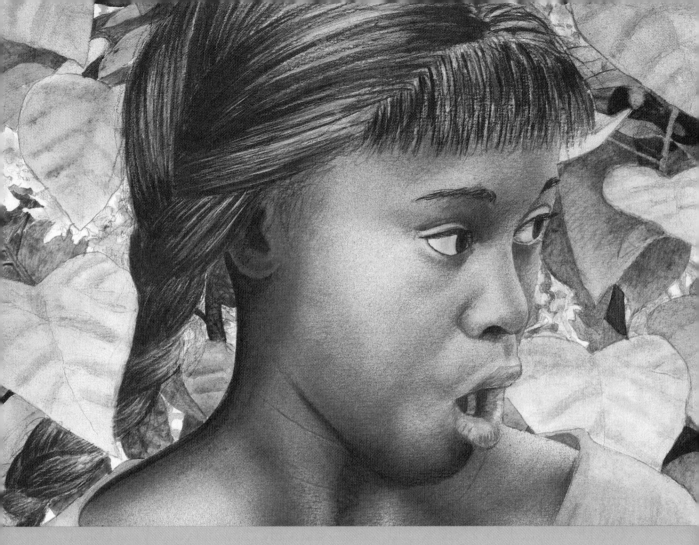

Geeder sat down, hard, on the ground. "Oh, Toeboy!" she said. She covered her face with her hands and rocked back and forth. "Oh, my goodness, Toeboy! That wasn't Zeely Tayber you saw. That was the night traveller!"

As soon as she said the words, Geeder had a clear vision of the night traveller, the time she had seen it. It had had no arms or legs, no head. It was a thing that moved right on the air and Toeboy had seen it. A shiver ran up her spine.

"Toeboy!" she said, "You saw a night traveller and no one is ever supposed to see one!"

Geeder looked so terrified that all of a sudden Toeboy was aware of the wet, misty trees surrounding them. The catalpas were so dense they could have been a solid wall. Anything could hide within them, just there, where it was as dark as night. He felt his back grow cold.

"I thought it was just Zeely Tayber," he said.

"No," Geeder said.

"It stopped right by the path to the house," Toeboy said.

"Toeboy, did it do anything?" Geeder asked.

Toeboy nodded, watching the trees. He crouched next to Geeder and his voice began to tremble as he spoke. "I thought it was going to say something," he said. "I was sitting right out in front of the lilac bush and it was looking at me. And you know what it did, Geeder?"

"What?" she said. She put one hand on his shoulder, pulling him closer.

"It moved real funny," he said, "and I got the feeling it didn't want me to say anything. I guess it didn't like noise."

"Oh, Toeboy!" Geeder said. "Can you just think what it would have done if you had made a sound!"

Toeboy tried to swallow but he couldn't. He remembered he had said good evening to what he thought was Miss Zeely Tayber. "What do you think it would have done?" he asked.

"Why, it would come back some night," Geeder said. "It would wait until you were asleep!"

An awful fear welled inside Toeboy. The night traveller was sure to get him because he had talked to it. He wanted to get away from the old trees around him and Geeder. He wanted to be as close to Uncle Ross as he could get.

All at once, Geeder jumped to her feet and started to run. Toeboy fell flat on the ground and covered his head with his arms. His eyes were closed tight and Geeder, seeing him, had to laugh.

"Silly!" she called. "Nothing's going to get you in broad daylight. It's the hog drive—did you forget?"

Toeboy lifted his head.

"There's Zeely to see," Geeder said. "And don't you worry about the night traveller. You just stay close to me."

"Just look at all the people!" Geeder had not thought so many folks could fit on the main street. The mood was right for a parade. The children were all there, the ones who had been at the bonfire the night before and still others who had heard the story of Zeely.

"Let's get closer!" Geeder grabbed Toeboy by the arm and pushed her way through the children at the curbs until she was right in front. Now she could see all the folks talking in small groups at the corners. They would glance curiously at the children and then quickly away.

"They don't want us to know why they're here," she said, "but I know why. They've come to see Zeely just like we have!"

Before Nat Tayber reached the center of the village, the air held the smell of hogs. The scent caught in the mist not yet evaporated by the sun. Wild, piercing squeals cut through the musky odor as Nat and his boys used their poles. Geeder shivered and crossed her fingers so the animals would not get hurt badly. People poured forth from stores and shops, taking up positions on both sides of the street. There were women in bonnets against the mist, with loaded shopping bags and baskets. There were farm people in their coveralls and wide-brim hats. There were all kinds of people there—townspeople, country folk and hordes of near-hysterical boys and girls, unable to speak for fear they might spoil what was to come.

"Geeder, I'm going," Toeboy said. "I want to go back to Uncle Ross."

"Toeboy, what's wrong with you?" Geeder said. She couldn't believe she had heard him right.

"I don't *like* it here," he said, "and I don't want to see those animals hurt."

He was thinking about the night traveller and wondering what it would do when it caught up with him.

"Oh, don't be dumb, Toeboy! They won't get hurt," Geeder said. "Zeely won't let them get hurt. You stay right where you are."

"How will she keep them from getting hurt?" Toeboy asked.

"She won't let them, that's all," Geeder said. "Don't you worry."

"Let me go," Toeboy pleaded. "I don't want to see the hogs run any more."

Geeder ignored him, holding on to him tightly as the hogs came on in a mass.

"There's the mist over everything," she whispered to herself. "It makes the street all wet and shining. Look how the sun comes through in patches. There's not a thing to say about it, it's a special day to the stars. Zeely Tayber is the brightest star of all!"

The hogs looked as if they were half crazed from fear. Many of them frothed at the mouth and staggered blindly in circles. Nat Tayber and his boys managed to get in front of them to slow the lead animals down. It was a wonder the boys and Nat didn't get bitten, for the hogs snapped at and fought anything that got in their path.

All the time, Toeboy struggled to free himself, but Geeder grimly held him.

The odor and sight of the frightened, exhausted animals sickened her.

"They'll be all right," she said softly to Toeboy. "You'll see, nobody will hurt them."

Through the street passed Zeely Tayber, her long smock brilliant in the mist. She moved straight and tall. Often, a fresh gust of breeze billowed the smock, causing her to appear to rise above the animals. She was taller than any of the men along the curbs and taller than the young trees lining the street. Through all the terrific noise and brutal movement, she made no sudden motion, nor did her face change from its serenity.

"Oh, she's just wonderful!" Geeder whispered. "She's just the most beautiful lady!"

And so Zeely was. She was beautiful and tall and unlike anyone else in the whole town.

Suddenly an enormous sow fell. She frothed at the mouth and grunted, as though something hurt her. Other hogs trampled her and still she was unable to move.

"That's awful!" Geeder said. "Oh, somebody do something!"

Toeboy jerked free from Geeder and instantly disappeared back in the crowd.

"Well, you just go home then," Geeder muttered.

Someone was shouting, "A sow's fallen! A sow's fallen!" The injured sow still lay grunting in the street. Other folks began shouting the same thing, and in a while, Nat Tayber raced back through the animals.

Something happened to Geeder when she saw Nat heading for the sow. Her face grew burning hot and her arms felt cold. She was in the street before she knew it. She was going away from Nat toward Zeely, who was still at the rear of the line of animals.

Geeder could hear people shouting at her to get out of the way before she was trampled. Once, somebody reached for her. She felt the sharp prick of fingernails as she pulled away. All of them, the people shouting and the one person who had tried to hold her back, seemed far away. She didn't think about anything except hurrying.

She was running. She got in the way of a hog. Some animals snapped at her, knocking into her; she was crying a little, from somewhere in her throat. There was pain in her left foot where a big boar had stepped on her. The stench of the animals made her legs weak. She almost fell, but then Zeely was just ahead. Geeder had to step between two sows to get to her. She placed her hand as lightly as she could on the back of one animal in order to get around it.

The heat of the hog shot up her arm and she gasped in terror.

The crowd roared in Geeder's mind. She couldn't think what they were saying because the sound ebbed and rose, like many voices over the radio when there is too much static.

Miss Zeely was standing still. Miss Zeely was staring at her.

Zeely Tayber moved to shield Geeder from the hogs. She didn't touch Geeder, but leaned over her. Geeder started talking before Zeely had a chance to warn her out of the way of the hogs.

"It's a sow," Geeder said. She rested one hand on her knee, trying to catch her breath. "It's all sick in the street, just lying down. Nat . . . your father. He's got his pole!"

Geeder straightened up too quickly. There was a stitch in her side that took her breath away. She had to bend down and come up slowly before the pain eased. Then, Zeely had Geeder by the arm.

Zeely was walking fast. She leaned forward like a young tree bent in a storm. She walked as though she had made a path through the animals and not one animal touched her, nor Geeder, either. Not more than a half minute had passed since the time Geeder had begun to run and Zeely had started back with her through the hogs. In no time, they saw Nat Tayber prodding the

stricken sow hard with his pole. Zeely stopped a few feet from Nat. She let go of Geeder, gently, one finger at a time. Geeder watched Zeely's eyes empty of strain and fill with something that glinted and flared.

The sow lay grunting under Nat's prodding. She could not move. Then, his face frozen in an awful grimace, Nat Tayber raised the prodding pole high above his head. Before he could bring it down on the sow, Zeely was there beside him.

Zeely grabbed Nat's wrist. The pole stood poised and trembling in the air and mist. Zeely looked long and hard at Nat. Her lips moved as she spoke softly to him. Nat twisted the pole. It jerked toward Zeely's head and then, slowly, came down to rest at Nat's side. In a second, Nat had turned on his heel. He was gone to lead the animals, not once glancing at the crowd.

The crowd hushed. At once, the stench of the hogs was overpowering. Geeder felt sick and dizzy. She dug her nails in her palms and breathed in short, quick gasps.

Zeely Tayber bent down beside the stricken sow. As if on a string, the people lining the street bent down at the same moment. Up and down the sidewalks, people were squatting or kneeling. They could have been praying there, they were so quiet, watching Zeely.

Geeder knelt down beside Zeely. She took Zeely's feed pail on her lap and held it at an angle so Zeely could reach into it. Geeder forgot the hog smell and all the people watching, so close was she to Zeely Tayber.

Zeely took a bit of feed from the pail and held it in her hand out to the sow. The sow feebly lifted her head and ate from Zeely's hand.

A soft murmur passed along the street. It reached Geeder and went through her, in and out of her, draining her of her strength. She felt weak.

Now, the sow struggled to get up. Soon, it was able to walk. Zeely took the feed pail from Geeder without a word. She did so carefully, graciously, and walked away.

"It's all right," Geeder murmured, as if Zeely had thanked her. "I thought you might need me to help."

The sow followed along at Zeely's heels like a pet of some kind. Zeely no longer needed to hold out her hand with the feed. She simply lowered the pail, allowing the sow to eat. All the way to Red Barn, the sow tagged along behind Zeely. She waited while Zeely got other hogs up and moving, for many more had fallen. She stumbled close behind when Zeely moved quickly along.

The people watching couldn't believe what they saw happen in front of their eyes. Geeder stood among them, listening to what was said and watching Zeely and the hogs move out of sight.

"That Tayber girl has bewitched the sow," some people said.

"It is because she is animal, like those hogs." People snickered and laughed.

Many voices caught and whirled in Geeder's mind. She grew angry and pushed her way out of the crowd.

Geeder trotted, limping, to Uncle Ross' farm. She was still weak, bruised and slightly sick to her stomach. But the air had cleared. The mist, thick as smoke, had risen and gone. By the time she passed through the catalpa trees, the smell and danger of hogs had left her. Zeely Tayber was with her still, deep in her thoughts.

"I helped her," Geeder whispered. "I knew she'd want me to."

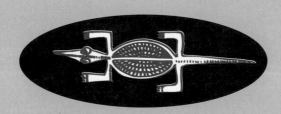

Would you like to have Geeder as a friend? Explain your answer.

What happens the night Geeder and Toeboy sleep outside? Explain what you think Toeboy sees.

What does Zeely do that makes her seem extraordinary to the townspeople and to Geeder?

If Geeder talked to Zeely, what questions might she ask?

WRITE   Write a brief character description of a person who has impressed you. Describe his or her actions and appearance. Tell why you were impressed.

AWARD-WINNING AUTHOR

WOMEN

by Alice Walker

They were women then.
My mama's generation
Husky of voice—Stout of
Step
With fists as well as
Hands
How they battered down
Doors
And ironed
Starched white
Shirts
How they led
Armies
Headragged Generals
Across mined
Fields
Booby-trapped
Ditches
To discover books
Desks
A place for us
How they knew what we
Must know
Without knowing a page
of it
Themselves.

EXTRAORDINARY PEOPLE

How do other people influence the characters and their decisions to act in "Maniac Magee" and "Zeely"?

WRITER'S WORKSHOP

Imagine that you know Maniac Magee or Zeely and that you think he or she is extraordinary. Write a letter to a friend persuading him or her that Maniac or Zeely is extraordinary. Include details from the story to support your argument.

Writer's Choice

You have just read about two extraordinary people. Think about what makes a person extraordinary. Write about what you think. Then share what you've written with others.

235

Connections
CONNECTIONS

MULTICULTURAL CONNECTION

HERO OF INDIA—AND THE WORLD

One of the great heroes of the twentieth century was Mohandas Gandhi (1869–1948) of India. Gandhi was the father of Indian independence. The story of his life continues to inspire people everywhere who are struggling for human rights and freedom.

Gandhi gained fame for his use of nonviolent protest in the movement to free India from British rule. Under Gandhi's leadership, millions of Indians simply refused to obey their British rulers. Gandhi was jailed repeatedly, but his popular support was so great that the British always released him. Finally, after three decades of struggle, India won its independence in 1947. Gandhi's ideas about nonviolence influenced Dr. Martin Luther King, Jr., and other leaders in all parts of the world.

Have a "great heroes" discussion with your classmates. Think of women and men who have worked to improve conditions for people. Compare and contrast these heroes and their achievements.

SOCIAL STUDIES/LANGUAGE ARTS CONNECTION

GREAT HERO PROFILE

Write a biographical sketch of one of the heroes mentioned in your discussion. Be sure to explain what it was that made that man or woman a hero. Include a picture of your subject, if possible, and present an oral report to your classmates.

LANGUAGE ARTS CONNECTION

DRAMATIC MOMENTS

With a partner or a group of classmates, write a scene for a play about one of the heroes you have studied. Your scene should capture an important moment in that hero's life. Be sure to use correct play format. Add stage directions where they are necessary. You might enjoy rehearsing the scene and presenting it to your classmates.

Clockwise from top: Mohandas Gandhi; Lech Walesa; Dr. Martin Luther King, Jr., on Selma march, 1965; Rosa Parks (left)

UNIT 3 THREE

A WORLD AWAY

Our culture includes not only traditions from within our borders but also those brought here by people from around the world. How important is it to preserve all those traditions? The griots of West Africa, whom you will read about later, thought their history important enough to memorize in songs. Think about their dedication as you read about cultures from near and far.

THEMES

BOOKSHELF

THE PRINCESS IN THE PIGPEN

BY JANE RESH THOMAS

Elizabeth falls asleep in seventeenth-century England and awakens in twentieth-century Iowa. Befriended by a farming family, Elizabeth works to convince them that she is of another era and must return to her home.

Award-Winning Author

HARCOURT BRACE LIBRARY BOOK

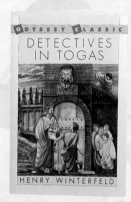

DETECTIVES IN TOGAS

BY HENRY WINTERFELD

Set in the days of the Roman Empire, this novel tells the story of six students who must solve a crime for which their friend Rufus has been blamed. With the help of their teacher, the boys follow clues that often lead to danger, but in the end justice is served.

HARCOURT BRACE LIBRARY BOOK

Kon-Tiki and I

BY ERIK HESSELBERG

The author recounts his hair-raising adventures aboard a balsa-wood raft en route from Peru to Polynesia.

Cities in the Sand

BY SCOTT WARREN

Using information gleaned from archaeological digs, the author describes the life-style, development, and eventual demise of the prehistoric settlers of the southwestern United States.

Award-Winning Author

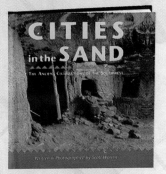

A Jar of Dreams

BY YOSHIKO UCHIDA

When Rinko is snubbed at school and in the street, she almost wishes she were not Japanese. Then Aunt Waka visits from Japan, and all the family members find new strength from learning about their heritage.

Notable Children's Trade Book in the Field of Social Studies

THEME

EXPLORING AFRICA

Egypt . . . Mummy . . . Treasures . . . Yes, as these words tell you, you are going to read about ancient Egyptians — but perhaps not exactly in the way you think.

CONTENTS

BEHIND THE
SEALED
DOOR

BY IRENE AND LAURENCE SWINBURNE

ALA NOTABLE
BOOK

Sarcophagus
of King Tut

The great kings of Egypt built large tombs and piled them high with treasures. Jewels, precious oils, gold chairs and thrones, bracelets, rings, statues—all this and much more was stored in these final resting places. Why did the kings hoard so much wealth in their tombs? It was because of their religion. Someday, they firmly believed, the gods would raise them from the dead. Also, they believed that they themselves were gods and would be welcomed into the land of the dead by their fellow gods. When that happened, they would need the things they had used in this world.

Wall painting in the tomb of Sen-Nefer

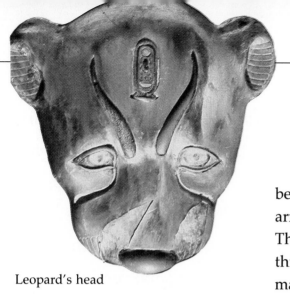

Leopard's head

But, in fact, the kings would be very poor indeed when they arrived in the other world. Through the centuries, grave thieves upset the royal plans and made off with the valuables buried in the tombs.

The thieves had no respect for the dead kings. They did not care if the rulers got to the land of the gods or not. They only cared about looting the riches in the tombs.

To get to the treasures, they had to dig through rock, break down huge doors, puzzle out mazes of passages that were found in the pyramids, and avoid traps that had been made to catch them. Often they bribed the guards to look the other way. The robbers did all this knowing that if they were caught, they would be horribly tortured and then put to death. Because of their greed, many priceless objects have been lost forever—golden statues melted down and sold, jewels removed from their settings, works of art destroyed.

Earring from King Tut's tomb

Between the years 2600 and 1529 B.C., the kings built enormous pyramids for their tombs. When a king died, his body would be

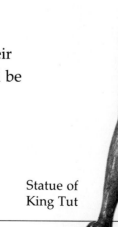

Statue of King Tut

Statue of
King Tut

carried into the tomb as high priests wailed funeral chants. But the dead king would not rest in peace for long. In a few years or even months, thieves would find their way to the heart of the pyramid where the king lay and carry off anything they could get their hands on. Even though probably many of the robbers were caught, just the sight of those massive tombs would remind others of the riches that lay within them, and a new gang would try its luck.

Finally, Tuthmosis I, who ruled from 1505 to 1493 B.C., realized a new way must be found to keep the royal graves from being looted. He decided to break with that long tradition and be buried in the valley that would be known as the Valley of the Kings. From this time on, the kings would be buried in tombs cut out of the rocky soil of the Valley.

Scarab bracelet
from King Tut's tomb

Queen Hatshepsot's Temple in the Valley of the Kings

You might think that the Valley would be a beautiful area, with shady trees, sparkling brooks, and flowers of every color. But you would be wrong. The Valley of the Kings is one of the most deserted and uninviting places in the world. Its landscape consists of brown rocks and brown sand. It has no trees, no streams, and no flowers. Few birds fly into this forbidding cemetery. However, it was much easier to protect than the pyramids.

Hundreds lived or worked in the Valley. There were men who did the heavy work of digging into the rock. There were craftsmen who performed such jobs as painting the walls of the tombs. There were the priests who were in charge of all activity in the Valley. And, of course, there were the soldiers, whose duty it was to keep out the thieves. The most important work was that of the mummifiers, people who made the kings' bodies into mummies. Mummifying is a process that can preserve bodies for hundreds, sometimes even thousands, of years.

The ancient Egyptian skill of mummifying has fascinated people up to our time. After the body had been specially treated, it was dried, a process that took seventy days. Then it was washed with special sweet-smelling oils. The body was carefully wrapped in linen. The linen had been soaked in gum, a sticky substance that came from a gum tree. Metal charms and special prayers on papyrus were enfolded in the wrappings. There was plenty of room for these items, for the linen was wound around the body many times.

The exact location of a king's tomb was usually kept a secret—though, of course, some people had to know about it. Tuthmosis I assigned a trusted official, Ineni, to prepare his tomb. Ineni carried out his duty faithfully. As he wrote later, "I alone supervised the construction of His Majesty's cliff tomb. No one saw it, no one heard it."

But nothing stopped the tomb robbers. In fact, the thieves became so successful that sometimes the priests, hoping to fool them, would have the royal mummies moved from cave to cave. Several mummies might be stored in one tomb for a time while other tombs were empty. This created puzzles for archaeologists much later, who might find the tomb of one king occupied by a different king's mummy.

The ancient Egyptian civilization lasted for over 3,000 years. Yet finally it too came to an end. At various times after that, other nations conquered the country, but the work of the tomb robbers continued as before. It was as if they had discovered an unending goldmine in the Valley of the Kings, and through the centuries they searched for undiscovered graves of kings.

By the late 1800s the Valley had been gone over carefully, and many archaeologists believed that nothing more would be found. However, in 1871 they were surprised to learn that objects of great value were being sold by people who lived on a hill near the Valley of the Kings. Experts agreed that these objects could only have come from the tombs of kings.

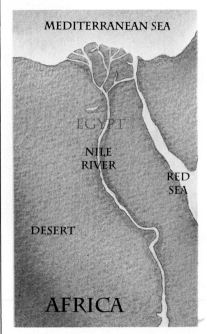

After some very clever detective work, it was found that most of the objects had been sold by a man named Abd-el-Rasul.

Abd-el-Rasul was arrested, and he confessed that he had been the seller of the valuable relics. Even more amazing was his statement that for years the entire income of the village of Qurna had been derived from selling such relics. What's more, his family had been in this business for six centuries!

Recently his people had found a tomb high on the face of a cliff. It could be entered only through a small hole, into which a thin man could squeeze. Hoping to please the officials and avoid a long jail sentence, he offered to lead the way to the grave.

Forty mummies were found in the small tomb! The mummies were taken to the Cairo Museum. As the boat carrying the remains of the kings passed down the Nile, hundreds of thousands of Egyptians lined the banks of the great river. They threw dust upon themselves, a sign of mourning. People fired rifles in the air in salute. All this was done to honor these dead kings who had ruled some 3,000 years before.

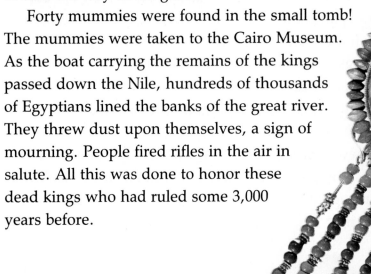

Earring from King Tut's tomb

Painting of King Sennedjem and his wife working in a field

Only in recent years have people begun to treat the tombs of the ancient Egyptian kings with respect. In your opinion, why did people's attitudes change from disrespect to respect?

What did Abd-el-Rasul do with the objects he stole?

King Tuthmosis I was buried in a tomb cut out of the rocky soil. Was he better protected than the kings who were buried in the pyramids? Explain your answer.

WRITE   How do you feel about the thefts from the Egyptian kings' tombs? Write a few paragraphs explaining your answer.

PAULA DANZIGER
Make Like a Tree and Leave

EGYPTIAN PROJECT

Make Like a Tree
AND
LEAVE

by Paula Danziger

Matthew Martin and his friends only wanted to make the best Egyptian project for their sixth-grade class. Instead they made a big mistake.

"The suspense builds." Matthew, holding up a baseball cap, looks at the three classmates, who are sitting on his bedroom floor. "Inside this very hat are four small blank, folded pieces of paper. The fifth has an X on it. One of us and only one will get that X. Who, I ask you, who will get that paper?"

*illustrated by
Deborah Nourse Lattimore*

253

"If you'd cut out the drama and let us pick, we could answer that question very quickly." Brian Bruno looks like he's ready to grab the cap out of Matthew's hands.

Holding the cap behind his back, Matthew says, "How can the suspense build if we pick right away?"

"I don't want suspense. I want to find out now," Billy Kellerman says. "Why do you always have to turn everything into a major production?"

"Because it's more fun that way." Matthew grins. "Anyway, Mrs. Stanton made me the chairman of the Mummy Committee, so I get to do it my way."

"Baloney," Billy says. "I overheard Mrs. Stanton tell Ms. Wagner that she only made you the chairman of the Mummy Committee because she's 'trying to get you to use your leadership qualities in a more positive way.'"

"Baloney to you. . . . I don't believe it." Matthew glares.

"It's true. I was in the bathroom in the nurse's office and the nurse had gone out for a minute, and the two of them came in and didn't know I was there. I also found out that Ms. Wagner is going out with Mr. King. You can learn a lot hanging out in the nurse's office." Billy grins. "And Ms. Wagner told her about the time she made you the chairman of the fourth-grade Volcano Committee."

"That explosion was NOT my fault!" Matthew protests.

"We only have two weeks to finish. . . . We better get started," Joshua Jackson reminds them. "Come on, Matthew. Let's not start fighting and instead of letting the suspense build, let's build the mummy."

"Oh, okay." Matthew relents, holding out the baseball cap. "Hurry up and pick, then. See if I care."

Joshua closes his eyes and selects a piece of paper.

Billy Kellerman keeps his open and stares at the papers, wishing that he had X-ray vision, and then he chooses.

Brian Bruno crosses his fingers and then picks a piece of paper.

The paper falls to the ground because Brian Bruno is not good at holding on to paper with crossed fingers.

Matthew takes the last one out of the cap, puts the cap back on his head with the visor facing backward, and says, "At the count of three, everyone open his paper. . . . One . . . two . . . three . . . go."

Matthew looks down at his paper. There is no X.

He's not sure whether he's sad or happy . . . or relieved.

There's no question that Joshua is happy. He's waving his paper and yelling, "No X. No X."

For a minute Matthew thinks that he should have put an L on the paper instead of an X so that Joshua could have yelled out "No L. No L," since he's acting like it's Christmas even though it's only October.

Then he looks around.

Billy's smiling.

Brian says, "How about if we make it the first person who gets two X's? Isn't that a great idea?"

"Come on. It'll be fun. All we have to do is turn you into a mummy like the Egyptians used to do," Matthew reminds him. "It'll be easy. Billy got all the stuff to do it from his father's supply cabinet. It took the Egyptians seventy days to prepare a body. We'll be done today."

"The Egyptians only did it to dead people," Brian reminds him.

"Dead animals too." Joshua has been doing a lot of research.

"I'm still alive." Brian gets up and starts pacing around. "I'm not a dead person. I'm not a dead animal. I'm not sure that this is a good idea."

"You thought it was a great idea until you got the X." Matthew gets up too. "It'll be fun. We'll use the plaster gauze stuff that Dr. Kellerman uses all the time on his patients. Remember, we used that stuff in third grade to make face masks."

"That was just our faces. You're going to do it to my whole body. What if I get claustrophobia?" Brian looks less than overjoyed.

"Claustrophobia." Matthew grins. "Isn't that fear of a little old fat man in a red suit who shows up at Christmas?"

"That's so funny I forgot to laugh." Brian scowls. "You know that means fear of being closed in."

"Look." Billy starts taking out the boxes of plaster gauze that they've been storing at the bottom of Matthew's already messy closet. "I'm planning to be an orthopedist just like my dad and I've watched him work before. It'll be a breeze . . . and the plaster dries very quickly and then we'll cut it off of you. Nothing to it. Nothing at all."

"And I'll teach you how to win at Super Gonzorga, that new computer game. You'll be able to beat everyone but me," Matthew says.

"Everyone but you and Chloe Fulton," Billy reminds him. "You know she's almost as good as you are . . . sometimes she even beats you."

Matthew chooses to ignore Billy. "And Brian, I'll do the hieroglyphics poster with you. We'll do a poster about a guy named Hy Roglifics, who invents the Egyptian alphabet."

"Let's not and say we did." Brian shakes his head.

Joshua puts his hand on Brian's shoulder to stop him from pacing. "I'll ask my father to make you the peanut butter cookies that you like so much."

"It's a deal." Brian smiles for the first time since he's picked the X.

The boys hear a door slam downstairs as Amanda Martin enters the house.

"Matthew? Are you home, you little creepling?"

Matthew helps Billy take out more boxes of plaster.

"Aren't you going to answer her?" Billy asks.

"Not when she calls me names. I bet that one of her dumb friends is with her. She always acts like a big shot when that happens." Matthew makes a face. "Maybe we should tie her up and put this stuff around her, but not leave the mouth, eye, and nose openings for her, and put her in the bottom of my closet for seventy days and use her for our school project."

"Sisters." Joshua says, knowing what it feels like to have an older sister, since he has one who is Amanda's best friend.

There's a pounding on Matthew's door, and Amanda flings the door open.

She's wearing a Hard Rock Café sweatshirt and a pair of old blue jeans. Blonde-haired, with blue eyes, Amanda squints as she glares at the boys, since she has given up wearing her glasses, except for when she absolutely needs to see. She is wearing at least one ring on each of her fingers, dozens of silver bangle bracelets on her right arm, and earrings. The one on the right side has stars and moons on it. The earring in her left earlobe is a heart that is engraved "Amanda and Danny Forever."

"Privacy." Matthew yells, thinking that every time he looks at his sister, she seems to be getting much older . . . and much meaner.

"You didn't answer. I needed to know if you were here, since Mom and Dad said that I have to check on you. It's not my fault that they both work and I have to check." She looks around the room at all the boxes. "What are you guys planning to do . . . make face masks like they do in third grade? You better do it downstairs, on the back porch, so it doesn't make a mess. You know that our parents will kill you if you ruin the new wall-to-wall carpeting."

Matthew realizes she's right but still doesn't answer.

Amanda stares at him. "Cindy's with me and we're going to be upstairs in my room discussing private stuff. So don't bother me."

Matthew is getting sick of the way that she acts toward him in front of his friends but knows that if he says something, it will get worse.

It's not fair that one kid gets to be older and the boss all the time.

Amanda leaves.

Matthew looks at his friends and says, "Let's go downstairs and get as far away from the dweeb as possible."

"And as close to the refrigerator as possible." Joshua is getting hungry until he remembers how Mrs. Martin believes in health food. "Is there anything good in there . . . anything edible?"

Matthew grins widely, showing his dimples. "My dad and I made a deal with her. We can have one box of stuff in the freezer and one thing in the refrigerator that she isn't allowed to complain about. We have a large bottle of soda and a box of frozen Milky Ways."

"Great. Let's get these boxes downstairs and then do some serious snacking before we get to work," Joshua suggests.

As the boys head down the steps carrying the plaster gauze, Matthew thinks about how this is going to be the best sixth-grade project ever. Mrs. Stanton is NOT going to be sorry that she picked him to be chairman.

*   *   *   *   *

Brian Bruno stands on the porch wondering why he didn't join the Pyramid Committee instead.

A giant garbage bag with a hole in the middle for his head has been placed over his body so that only his feet, neck, and head show.

A bathing cap covers his ears and red hair.

Vaseline is smeared over his freckled face.

Joshua Jackson is holding a Milky Way bar to his mouth so he can nibble on it.

"We're going to have to stop feeding you soon," Matthew informs him. "We're almost up to your chest area and what if you start to choke? We won't be able to do the Heimlich maneuver on you because you'll be all covered up with plaster."

Matthew is trying to be the most responsible chairman of a Mummy Committee that ever was.

Continuing to wind the bandages around, while Billy wets the gauze so that it turns almost instantly into a plaster cast, Matthew says, "Brian, how about letting us do some of the real stuff that the Egyptians used to do? We can cut a slit in the left side of your body and take out your liver, lungs, stomach, and intestines."

"Forget it," Brian mumbles, his mouth full of Milky Way.

Matthew does not care to forget it. "Then we can embalm them and place them in a jar."

"Cut it out." Brian is getting very unamused.

"That's what I was just suggesting." Matthew smiles and continues. "Did you know that the Egyptians used to remove the brain through the nostrils, using metal hooks? That would be a cinch. I'd just have to look up in the attic for one of the hooks we used to use when we made pot holders. Don't you think that's a great idea?"

Brian looks like he does not think it's a great idea. He thinks that Matthew may not be the best head of the Mummy Committee of all time.

The other guys look at each other and think that it's time to change the subject.

Billy looks at the mummy/Brian and says, "We should use the three-inch tape for his face, not the four-, five-, or six-."

"Let's do another layer or two first on the rest of the body," Matthew says. "We have to make sure that it'll be strong enough not to break after we cut it off Brian, put the two sides back together, and plaster it together."

"Fair deal." Billy is really enjoying pretending to be a doctor.

As they work, Joshua holds up a glass of soda and a straw so that Brian can sip.

He keeps talking to Brian to help him keep his mind off what's happening. "It's a shame that Amanda and Cindy are so rotten that they'd never give us any old jewelry even if we asked them. Did you know that there should be magic amulets tucked between the wrappings? That would make it more accurate."

Brian doesn't want a history lesson. "Would you guys please hurry up? I'm beginning to have trouble standing here. This is getting heavy . . . and I think I'm going to have to go to the bathroom soon."

Joshua immediately puts the soda away.

"We're almost done." Matthew starts putting the gauze on Brian's face, careful to leave large holes for his eyes, nose, and mouth. "Billy, stop working on the body. Help me with Brian's face."

As Billy starts working on the face, Joshua helps to prop up Brian.

Matthew goes for his mother's biggest pair of scissors.

He returns just as Billy is finishing up.

It looks great.

"Get me out of here, you guys." Brian's voice sounds a little muffled.

Checking, Matthew sees that Brian is getting enough air.

Looking, he can see how Brian just might be getting a little tired.

"No sweat," Matthew says, to reassure him.

"Easy for you to say. You're not covered by a plastic garbage bag and a ton of cement." Brian does not sound happy.

Matthew sits down on the floor, ready to cut Brian out of the mummy cast.

It doesn't take him very long to realize that the scissors are not going to cut through the cast.

"Why don't *you* try this, Billy?" He hands the scissors over, trying to look and feel calm.

It takes Billy an equally short period to discover the limitations of the scissors. "This always worked in third grade."

"I don't think we had as many layers," Matthew says softly, knowing that he is in deep trouble, deep deep deep trouble.

"What's going on out there?" Brian begins to sound panicky.

Matthew goes up to his mummy/friend and says, "I don't know how to tell you this, but we've run into a minor problem."

"My father's going to kill me if he finds out," Billy says. "I asked if I could take just a few rolls. He thought that we were making masks again."

Joshua says, "Someone give me a hand supporting this. He's getting heavy."

Matthew makes a decision, one that he doesn't like but knows is necessary. "I'll be right back. I'm going to get Amanda."

"Hurry," everyone else says at once.

Rushing out of the room and racing up the steps, Matthew realizes that while Brian Bruno is in heavy-duty plaster, he, Matthew Martin, is in heavy-duty trouble.

And it's not going to be easy to get either of them out.

*   *   *   *   *

Matthew knocks at the bedroom door, yelling, "Amanda. Amanda. Open up."

"What do you want? I told you not to bother me." Her voice comes out loud and clear through the closed door.

Matthew opens it anyway.

Amanda and Cindy are sitting on the bed, using the machine that Amanda got for her birthday . . . the Crimper.

Their hair looks like it's been caught in a waffle iron. Cindy's is totally wrinkly. Amanda's is half-finished.

"I told you—" Amanda starts to scream.

"Emergency. It's an emergency. You've got to come immediately." Matthew is almost out of breath. "And you can't tell on me, promise."

Amanda and Cindy jump off the bed.

As they run downstairs, Cindy remembers that the Crimper is still on and runs back up the stairs.

Matthew explains to Amanda as they rush into the kitchen.

Amanda looks at Joshua and Billy, who are holding up the mummy and looking very scared.

The mummy doesn't look like it has much emotion, but it's obvious that Brian does.

He's yelling, "Get me out of here. I want to go home."

Amanda tries the scissors.

Cindy walks in and says, "We've got an electric carving knife at home, but that would be too dangerous, right?"

"Right." Amanda nods, knowing that she is going to have to be in charge of this situation and wishing this time that she were not the oldest.

"I'm calling Mom." She picks up the phone and dials.

Asking for her mother, she listens for a minute and then says, "Please have her call the second she gets back. Tell her it's an emergency. . . . No . . . Everything is all right . . . sort of . . . but please have her call."

Amanda informs everyone. "One of the gorillas called in sick. Mom had to put on the costume and go deliver the message."

Picking up the phone again and mumbling, "I've begged her . . . absolutely begged her to get a normal job . . . but did she listen? . . . no . . . and she's even bought the company and has to spend more time there."

"Hurry," Matthew pleads. "Do something."

"I'm thirsty," Brian says softly.

Rushing over to get the glass, Matthew realizes that the problem could get even worse . . . if that was possible to imagine.

Going back to Brian, he says, "Which is worse? Thirst . . . or having to go to the bathroom? Because if I give this to you . . . you know what's going to have to happen sooner or later. You're going to have to go."

Amanda is on the phone explaining the situation to her father. "And hurry, Dad, hurry."

Amanda hangs up and looks at Cindy as if to say, "Do you believe this?"

Then she looks at Matthew.

"Don't say 'I told you so,' because you didn't," he says. "When's Dad coming home?"

"He's on his way immediately . . . and he's going to call Dr. Kellerman from the car phone to find out what we should do," Amanda explains.

The boys look terrified.

All they wanted to do was make the best project.

"I can't stand up anymore." Brian sounds like he's going to cry. "And I want to talk to my parents and I can't because they went away on a vacation and my grandmother's watching us and she's going to have a heart attack if she finds out about this."

Amanda walks over and pats the cast. "Brian. It'll be all right. I promise you. . . . Just hang in there."

"Where else am I going to go?" Brian asks and for some reason finds what she's said very funny and starts to laugh . . . and laugh . . . and laugh.

"Hysteria." Amanda, who has been reading psychology magazines, thinks, What should I do? . . . Should I do what they always do in the pictures? . . . slap him and say, "Get a hold of yourself"? But how can that help? . . . I'd only be hitting the cast . . . and breaking one of my nails . . . and how can he get a hold of himself? . . . He's in a full-length body cast.

Amanda is beginning to feel a little hysterical herself.

Mr. Martin rushes into the house and looks at the situation. "Okay. Everyone stay calm. I've talked with Dr. Kellerman and here are the possibilities."

"I want to go home." Brian has stopped laughing and is very upset. "I want to get out of here."

"Okay. I promise that we will get you out of there as quickly as possible, in the best way possible." Mr. Martin looks over at the scissors and quickly realizes they are not going to work. "Dr. Kellerman says that we can put you in a warm tub of water and the cast will become soft enough to take off in about half an hour."

"He won't fit into the bathtub. He's too tall and standing too straight." Amanda is calming down, now that she is not the oldest person in the room.

"Then we're going to have to get you over to Dr. Kellerman's right away," Mr. Martin decides. "But he won't fit into my car. . . . We just may have to call an ambulance."

Brian starts to cry.

Actually no one in the room is feeling very good either.

There's a moment of silence, and then as Mr. Martin picks up the phone to call the emergency number, Mrs. Martin rushes in, wearing a gorilla costume.

"I just stopped by on my way back to work to see if you needed anything and . . ." She looks at everyone. "What's going on?"

Quickly Mr. Martin explains.

Mrs. Martin says, "Amanda. Cindy. Come with me. I want you to help me empty out the station wagon, Amanda. First, though, I want you to put your glasses back on. You know that you must wear them."

As the females rush out, Mr. Martin says, "Brian. Everything's going to be all right. I'll be back in a minute. I'm going to get something out of the garage."

"Don't leave us alone." Billy is afraid that he's getting too tired to help keep Brian from falling.

"Just for a minute." Mr. Martin rushes out, returning in a few minutes with a piece of equipment that is used to move heavy things. "I just remembered this dolly. We haven't used it in years."

Mrs. Martin and the girls return.

Mr. Martin continues. "Honey, I want you to help the boys support Brian while he hops onto this dolly."

It takes a few minutes but finally Brian is on the dolly, and Mrs. Martin and the kids make sure that he stays on while Mr. Martin wheels the dolly over to the car.

Mrs. Martin works her way into the front of the back section of the station wagon. It is not an easy task for a person wearing a gorilla suit, but there is no time to change.

Everyone helps lift and slide Brian into the back section of the car.

"I want someone to hold my hand," he cries out.

"I'll get in and pat on the cast." Amanda crawls into the back, her hated glasses back on her face. "Cindy, could you wait here until we get back? If Danny calls, don't tell him about this. I want to . . . later."

"Okay." Cindy nods.

"I'll drive this car," Mrs. Martin says. "Honey, you take your car."

"I want to go. Please," Matthew pleads. "I want to help."

Mrs. Martin quickly says, "Billy. Matthew. You come with me. Joshua and Cindy, would you please put this stuff in the garage?"

She points to some of the things that are used by her message-delivery company . . . a chicken suit, boxes of balloons, mouse outfits, confetti, and heart-shaped boxes.

"Sure." The Jacksons immediately get to work.

Mrs. Martin talks quickly. "Just let your mother know what's going on. And we'll call Brian's family as soon as we get to the doctor's."

While they're driving along, Matthew looks at his mother, who has taken the gorilla head off but is still wearing the gorilla body. "Mom, I'm sorry. We didn't mean to do anything wrong. I promise. Is Brian going to be all right?"

Mrs. Martin nods. "I think so. Just stay calm. We'll discuss this later. The important thing right now is to get him out of there and never do anything like this again."

"I promise." Matthew sits quietly for the rest of the drive.

Amanda also sits quietly, hoping that no one she knows sees them. A mother in a gorilla suit and her own half-crimped hair are just too embarrassing for words.

Billy Kellerman sits in the backseat wondering what his father is going to do. He knows what he's going to do to Brian . . . help him. . . . He's not so sure what his father is going to do to him, his son.

Everyone gets to the office at the same time. Dr. Kellerman is waiting at the door with a stretcher. He and his nurses and the Martins, as well as some of the relatives of waiting patients, lift Brian onto the stretcher and get him into the office.

Once Brian is on the examining table, everyone except the medical staff and Mr. and Mrs. Martin go back into the waiting room.

Matthew and Billy explain to everyone how it was all a mistake, how they were just trying to do the best sixth-grade project, that they had no idea that it would all end like this, that they hope that Brian is going to be okay.

"He'll be fine, boys. Don't worry." An older woman tries to comfort them. "Dr. Kellerman is a wonderful doctor."

Her husband looks at Amanda and says, "Is she also part of your Egypt unit, or did she just stick her hand in an electric socket?"

Amanda puts one hand up to her half-crimped hair, puts her other hand over her face, and tries to think of the best way to get back at Matthew.

"Don't listen to him," the old woman says. "My husband is quite a kidder. He just likes to joke around."

Amanda is all ready to say, "Yeah. He's about as funny as a rubber crutch," until she remembers where she is, in an orthopedic doctor's office. She says nothing.

The old man continues. "I guess your little mummy friend is all wrapped up in his problems. . . . But don't worry . . . there's really no gauze for concern. . . . Get it? No *gauze* for concern."

"Melvin, that's enough." His wife pats him on the hand. "Remember, there is a little boy in the office who needs help. This is not the time for your corny jokes."

Everyone in the office quiets down and thinks about Brian, who is at that moment being talked to by Dr. Kellerman.

"Brian, there is nothing to worry about. In a little while we will have you out of there." Dr. Kellerman speaks softly, calming down not only Brian but also Mrs. and Mr. Martin, who are standing nearby.

In a very muffled voice, Brian says something.

Leaning over, Dr. Kellerman asks him to repeat it and then tells the Martins, "Brian says that as long as it's gone this far, I should try to save the cast so that they can still use it for the mummy project."

"What a guy." Mr. Martin pats the cast. "Brian. Don't worry. We'll do whatever is best for YOU."

"What is best?" he asks the doctor.

Dr. Kellerman smiles. "We can do both. Get him out quickly and save the cast."

Leaning over, he explains. "Okay, Brian. I'm going to use the cast cutter. Don't worry. I know that it looks like a pizza cutter and sounds like a buzz saw . . . but it's not. It'll be a little noisy because attached to the saw is a vacuum cleaner, which sucks up the dust from the cut cast. Brian, don't worry. The saw doesn't even turn around and around. It vibrates quickly. First I'm going to take the face mask off to give you more breathing room and then I'll take off the rest."

The Martins stand there and watch the doctor work.

Dr. Kellerman cuts through the plaster around Brian's face, uses a cast spreader, and then lifts off the face mask.

Everyone looks down at Brian's face, which is all scrunched up and covered with dust.

As Dr. Kellerman brushes off the dust, he says, "See, I told you it would get better. How are you feeling?"

Brian nods. "Better."

Dr. Kellerman continues working.

Mrs. Martin strokes Brian's face and talks to him.

Dr. Kellerman and his nurse lift the front of the cast off.

Taking it, Mr. Martin leans it against the wall.

The doctor asks the nurse for a pair of scissors.

"No." Brian yells. "Don't cut me. You promised."

"I'm only going to cut off the garbage bag," Dr. Kellerman explains. "It's not good for you to be in it, and it's covered with plaster."

"But I only have underpants on under this." Brian looks up at everyone.

"I'll loan you one of my doctor jackets," Dr. Kellerman says.

"Now, let's get you up and out of there."

Mr. Martin and Dr. Kellerman help Brian sit up.

Brian looks at Mrs. Martin. "You're dressed like a gorilla." And then he starts laughing.

Everyone begins to laugh.

Dr. Kellerman and Mr. Martin help Brian get out of the plastic bag.

The nurse and Mrs. Martin look the other way, since that was the only way that Brian would agree to get out of the garbage bag.

Then Mr. Martin helps Brian to rush to the bathroom.

When they come back, Dr. Kellerman gives Brian an examination to make sure that everything is okay.

It is and Brian stands up to get a hug from Mrs. Martin.

Brian, dressed in a doctor's coat that is about five times too large for him, gets a hug from Mrs. Martin, dressed in her gorilla suit.

Dr. Kellerman takes a Polaroid picture and then looks at Mr. Martin. "I believe that there are several young men in my waiting room, one related to you, one related to me. Something tells me that these young men should have a talking to."

"I agree." Mr. Martin nods.

"I'll take Brian to his house and meet you at home soon," Mrs. Martin says and leads Brian out into the waiting room, where all the waiting patients, their families, their friends, and Amanda applaud the release of Brian from his plaster prison.

The two people cheering the most are extremely happy, even though they know that they are due for the lecture of their young lifetimes.

Nurse Payne sticks her head out the door. "William. Matthew. Please come in. The doctor and Mr. Martin will see you now."

If you were a member of the Mummy Committee, who would you rather be, Matthew or Brian? Explain your answer.

In what ways is this story both humorous and serious?

What is each of the boys worried about once they finish putting on the wrappings?

Is Matthew's decision to ask for Amanda's help a good one? Explain your answer.

WRITE If you had to do an Egyptian project, how would you do it differently from the way Matthew and his friends do theirs? Write a description of your project.

WORDS
ABOUT THE
AUTHOR

PAULA DANZIGER

AWARD-WINNING
AUTHOR

Born in Washington, D.C., in 1944, Paula Danziger grew up in Virginia and New Jersey. After studying English in college, she became a teacher.

She decided to write a book to tell students about survival and "learning to like oneself, dealing with school systems, and being able to celebrate one's own uniqueness." The result was *The Cat Ate My Gymsuit*, her first novel.

After the success of her first book, Danziger continued to write about the problems of growing up. She still thinks of writing as the center of her life. She likes writing because it lets her use her sense of humor. "Writing is an exciting, often frustrating process," she says. "It's filled with change, pain, joy, revision, and refinement. It's life."

EXPLORING AFRICA

What information from the first selection helped you to better understand the mummy project in the second selection?

WRITER'S WORKSHOP

The process of mummifying was described in both selections. Choose one selection and write a how-to paragraph presenting the steps that the Egyptians followed for real mummifying or that the boys followed for their project.

Writer's Choice   What do the words *exploring Africa* make you think of now that you have read these two selections? Choose an idea to write about. After you write, share your idea with others.

THEME

ACROSS TIME

+ + + + + + + 🏰 + + + + + + +

Imagine being plucked out of the twentieth century
and waking up in a medieval castle. Do you think
you'd enjoy being transported back in time? Read
on to find out what it might be like to live in the
distant past or future.

CONTENTS

The PRINCESS *in the* PIGPEN

by JANE RESH THOMAS
Illustrations by Mark Brought

THE PRINCESS
IN THE PIGPEN
JANE RESH THOMAS

Elizabeth and her mother, who live in seventeenth-century London, are sick with a terrible fever. Suddenly Elizabeth is mysteriously transported to a pigpen in twentieth-century Iowa. Her porcelain doll Mariah, and her music box have been transported with her. Elizabeth tries to convince Joe and Kathy McCormick, their daughter Ann, and the sheriff that she is the daughter of the Duke and Duchess of Umberland. They think the fever is affecting her mind. Elizabeth is given a shot of penicillin, and then she rests.

FITFUL DREAMS DISTURBED Elizabeth's sleep all afternoon. When at last she opened her eyes, she saw Ann standing in a pool of dazzling sunlight beside her bed, looking at her gravely.

"I am glad you have come back," said Elizabeth.

"I'm sorry I was so cross this morning," Ann said. "Who did you say you were?"

"I was and am yet Lady Elizabeth, daughter of the Duke and Duchess of Umberland," she said, for what seemed like the hundredth time.

"Where do you live?" Ann's manner was intense, as if she could not wait for answers. "And what's the name of your house? And your parents' names?"

"Most of the year, we live in London, at Charington. In summer, and when the plague is raging, we go to the country. And my parents are Michael and Margaret." Elizabeth sighed. These fools still did not believe her. "Why are you asking me these questions again?"

"Mom helped me find the right history books in the study before I left for school this morning." Ann visibly curbed her excitement. "I still don't know whether to believe you, but you can help me check out your story if you want to. We can prove it, one way or the other."

"Anything to find my parents again. But why does everyone here insist upon talking about history? My parents were alive one day ago, in the year of our Lord, 1600."

Elizabeth sat up with an effort. "The sheriff talks of the eighteenth century as if it were long ago. That pamphlet bears the date 1988." She gestured in despair at the *Time* magazine she had thrown across the room in confusion. "And now you speak of finding me in histories. 'Tis too fantastic."

"I know." Ann's voice was softer. "But this year really is 1988. Cross my heart and hope to die, stick a needle in my eye." She drew an "X" on her chest with her finger. "You swear, too."

"'Sblood!" Elizabeth touched her forehead, her chest, and each shoulder with the tips of her fingers. "Cross my heart and hope to die."

"If you're honest, we'll find you in the books." Ann held her robe for Elizabeth. "Are you well enough to go downstairs to the study?"

"Yes. And you will see I am honest." Elizabeth would humor Ann and her talk of histories. It was nice to have her company, even though she spoke such foolishness, and they might stumble on a clue to the way home from Iowa.

"Bring your doll," said Ann, snatching her rag doll from under the quilt. She led the way downstairs, through a hallway off the kitchen, to the study. She blustered into the room, just as she did everything, chattering. "Here are the books, on Mom's desk."

She tucked her doll high up under her arm and picked up several volumes from the stacks of books piled amid papers and

beach stones and feathers on one of the two large desks. "That's
Dad's desk over there," she said, settling down against the
puffed cushions of a flowered sofa that was arranged with two
big, soft chairs before a broad stone fireplace.

She propped the doll against a pillow embroidered with
stags and leaves. "Come on in." Ann looked up and beckoned
to Elizabeth. "We can sit together on the couch."

But Elizabeth stood in the doorway with Mariah in her arm,
looking with amazement at the walls lined from floor to ceiling
with books. "Can you read?" Elizabeth asked. Although she
knew Ann attended school, she was shocked that these peasants
could afford a library that rivaled Father's own, and still
amazed that they could even read at all. Father said that before
Mr. Caxton brought the printing press to England, books had
been copied by hand; even now, they were very expensive.

"Of course I can read. Can't you?" Not waiting for an

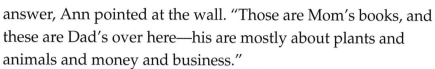

answer, Ann pointed at the wall. "Those are Mom's books, and these are Dad's over here—his are mostly about plants and animals and money and business."

Ann walked to the far end of the room. "These are mine." Taking a book down, she held up her doll. "Raggedy Ann was born in this story about her. You can read it if you want to." She put the book back in its place and searched until she found another. "Here's the one for you—*A Wrinkle in Time.* The kids in this one are lost in space and time."

Ann went back to the sofa and beckoned again. "Come on."

Elizabeth did not answer. She was staring at a box that stood on a table beside the fireplace. Inside the box, flickering images of tiny human beings danced. A child no bigger than Elizabeth's hand was coaxing a shepherd dog like those that herded sheep and kept the wolves away from the flocks on the English moors.

"Oh, that's only the TV. You must have TV in England," said Ann.

The boy in the box was saying, "Come on, Lassie. Come." Elizabeth obeyed his command, mesmerized. She walked across the room toward Ann, her arm outstretched, to touch the boy and the dog with her pointed finger. Her manicured fingernail struck the hard surface of the box, and the boy and the dog ran across the moor, just as if Elizabeth did not exist and had not this moment struck them without meaning to. Jolly music arose from the box while the boy and the dog played. It was as if a sorcerer had breathed life into a perfectly natural painting and hidden elfin musicians behind the canvas.

"Haven't you ever seen TV?"

Elizabeth was speechless with wonder. She looked at the back of the box, but found only a tangle of wires and a grille. When she looked again at the moving picture, the boy and his dog had disappeared, and the music was gone. Now another boy sat eating at a table, while an invisible man talked about something he called "cornflakes."

"If it distracts you," said Ann, dismissing the magic as if it were nothing, "let's turn it off for now." She touched a small knob at the side. With a click, the boy and his bowl of porridge disappeared. The front of the box was no longer brightly lit, but gray and blank and lifeless.

"It's only TV," said Ann, as if repeating the word could explain the wonderful box.

"What happened to the tiny boy and the tiny dog? Where did they go when you touched the knob?"

"I don't know. I guess they went into the air." Ann didn't seem worried or even curious. "It works on electricity, but I don't understand how."

Electricity again. More magic spells. Feeling as if she were a walking dreamer, Elizabeth sat down beside Ann and settled Mariah on a pillow worked in a needlepoint unicorn design. It was a coarse copy of a tapestry Elizabeth had seen hanging in the Queen's palace. She picked up the heavy blue book.

"Mom said that the quickest way to find information about the Umberlands is to check the index." Ann showed Elizabeth the finely printed lists in the back of the book that more than covered her lap. "Look up 'Umberland.'"

Elizabeth turned to a similar index in the blue book, but her gaze returned again and again to the silent box. Perhaps she could surprise the boy when he came back to life.

"Here's Michael, Duke of Umberland." Ann turned quickly to a page inside and read for a moment as Elizabeth anxiously looked over her shoulder. "It only mentions him," she said with disappointment, turning the page. "But here's a picture. Look at the fancy clothes." She showed Elizabeth the portrait of a man in doublet and long hose, leaning against a tree, reading a book.

"'Tis Essex!" Elizabeth felt stunned. Here was her friend in a history of England. She struggled to comprehend the proof

that she had somehow come to a time when her friend's life, and her own, was past.

"Do you really know that guy?" Ann asked.

"I do." As in a dream, Elizabeth searched the index of her own blue book. "Here is Father again!"

She quickly located the page and began to read. "How Father would laugh to hear about the so-called 'quarrel' between him and Essex! Father has tried to distance himself in public, but really they are the best of friends." Father always said that he valued his head, so he did his best to stay out of political schemes, but he loved his friends almost as much as his head. Elizabeth knew more than the author of the book she was reading.

She raced through the story of her friend and Father's, the charming, energetic Essex, and the crystal ball of Kathy's history book revealed his future to her. She gasped at what she saw,

read on again, then clapped the book shut and threw it across
the cold hearth.

"What's the matter?"

Elizabeth stared at the book and the ashes that had risen
in a cloud around it and now sifted down to bury its blue
cover.

"What is it?"

Elizabeth counted months on her fingers. "Four." She
dropped her hand into her lap, too shocked to cry. "In four
months' time, Rob Devereux, my dear Essex, will be dead. In
February, the Queen will execute him for rebellion and treason."
Elizabeth shut her eyes. "And in three more years, my sweet old
Queen will join him in the grave."

But of course this was foolishness. The Queen might be
angry at her old friend, but the Queen had been angry at others
and forgiven them. Surely she would command Essex to speak
to her on his knees. She would banish him from court. But
surely she would never behead him. Surely. She would never.

"*HERE'S THE BOX* of tissues." Ann pushed something into Elizabeth's lap. "You know. Like handkerchiefs. To blow your nose."

Elizabeth wiped her eyes and stared at the cold ashes on the hearth.

"Is it really true that they cut off people's heads?"

Elizabeth nodded. "Too true." She went to the hearth, weighed down by her new knowledge. Silently she fished out the book with one finger and her thumb, blew away ashes that clung to the blue cover, and brushed it with tissues.

She sat down again with Ann's garish pink robe pulled snug around her and her hands clasped on the book in her lap. "Essex. He would call me Poppet." She remembered Essex tousling her hair, bringing her sweetmeats, lifting her up in his arms, as affectionate as he had always been since she was a baby. "I feel I have, of a sudden, grown old."

Ann patted Elizabeth's knee.

"I do not think I like knowing the future." Elizabeth brushed at the ashes left on the book. "Can it be that I really have come through time so far from home? How can I look at Rob Devereux again, knowing what will befall him? Go back I must, of course. I must take the blessed medicine to my mother."

Suddenly frantic, she turned again to the index in the blue book. "U." Her finger moved down the page, and she muttered at what she saw there. "Umberland, Andrew. John, Duke of. Michael." She clapped the book shut again. "No Margaret! No Catherine! No Elizabeth! This foolish scribe hardly mentions Father, and he thinks Margaret too inconsequential for his book! Perhaps he is wrong about Rob Devereux as well." She heard her shrill voice echo in the fireplace and trail off up the chimney.

The girls sat quietly, stunned into silence by Elizabeth's passion. Then Ann asked, "Did you hear what you said a minute ago? That you would take the medicine back to your mother?"

"Yes," said Elizabeth firmly. "That is what I intend to do."

"But how will you go back?"

Elizabeth shut her eyes. "I do not know, but I must find a way. My mother needs my help."

Very gently, no longer blustering and chattering, Ann took the blue book away and put another larger volume in Elizabeth's lap. "Try this one. Maybe a different historian is wiser. Besides, this book has colored pictures."

Ann and Elizabeth read first in one book and then in another. Once Ann held up a picture of the majestic Queen for Elizabeth to see. "Nothing! Nothing here about Charington House or you. Nothing but portraits of this stern Queen of yours. And boring paintings of the English ships that fought

against the Spanish Armada." She flipped the book shut. "I never even heard of the Armada before. Now I don't ever want to hear about it again."

Elizabeth nodded. "Your historians seem to think that the Armada and the Queen and Shakespeare's plays are the only things that matter in my time." Elizabeth stroked Prissy from head to tail, enjoying the purr that vibrated under her hand.

"Same thing in books about America," said Ann. "Who ever heard whether Columbus or George Washington had kids?" She took the next book from the stack and read the title aloud. "'*Daily Life in Queen Elizabeth's Court.*"

Ann paused and turned to her friend. "Tell the truth, Elizabeth. Do you really know the Queen? Do you really go to fancy balls and wear velvet dresses all the time?"

"I do speak the truth, with all my heart. I know the Queen very well, indeed. But not even she wears velvet all the time."

Ann stared at the fireplace.

"What is it?" asked Elizabeth.

"I can see myself dancing with a prince," said Ann dreamily. Then she suddenly laughed. "Me, dancing with a prince!" She turned a page in the book on her lap. "I hope we find something soon. Mom'll be coming home, and we'll have to help with dinner."

The girls read quietly again until Ann broke the silence. "Elizabeth!" She pointed at the page. "Here it is!" She slammed the book shut on her fingers to save her place.

Holding the book in her arms, Ann hurried to her mother's desk and rummaged with one hand through a drawer until she found a pad of paper and a pencil.

Back on the sofa, Ann picked up Raggedy Ann and opened the book, keeping the open page secret. "Describe your coat of arms," she commanded.

"'Tis a rampant stag and a panther, with a cluster of acorns and oak leaves. You saw it on the back of my music box." Elizabeth found the music box in the pocket of the robe and held up the carved walnut case for Ann to see. "I keep it with me, and Mariah, in case I should find my way suddenly back to Charington." She patted her other pocket. "And the medicine is here."

"Shut your eyes and tell me what the stag looks like."

"One branch of his antlers is broken."

"And the colors?"

"A banner of blue and gold, with oak leaves traced in red."

Ann looked at Elizabeth with wonder. "I know it's farfetched, just as Mom and Dad said, but sometimes I almost believe you. Here." She handed the paper and pen across Prissy. "Here's another test. We'll prove once and for all whether or not you're a princess."

"I am no princess." Elizabeth spoke with a newly felt calm. At that moment, it didn't matter what anyone else believed; Elizabeth herself knew the truth. "Only the daughter of a duke."

"Well, whatever you are. Can you draw a picture of your house? Charington House." Ann paged through the book and found her place again.

With the skill of a trained artist, Elizabeth began to draw the long front of Charington. "There are thirty windows on the second story," she said, "and four fewer on the bottom, because of the entryway. I counted them last summer." With a hand guided surely by memory, she penciled in the windows and then began work on the roof. "Although the house has sixty chimneys, one may see only twelve of those from the front. They are located . . . about here . . . and here."

She drew rapidly, a small smile on her face, with the
pleasure anyone might feel who had come upon a photograph
of a beloved place.

"Your house is huge," said Ann, as she watched the drawing
come to life. "Where did you learn to draw like that?"

"My tutor gives me drawing lessons. Here is the gravel
drive," Elizabeth went on. "And here the staircase down to the
lagoon, which Father built last year." She looked at Ann for a
moment. "The workmen diverted a sluice of water from the
Thames," she explained. "Everybody told him that it couldn't
be done, but that only made Father more determined to design
a way."

"Why in the world do you need so many chimneys?" Ann
opened the book to the place she had marked with her finger,
and looked at something inside. "I can see how big your house
is, but a few furnaces should be enough to heat it."

"Furnaces?" said Elizabeth. "Charington is very modern.
Each room is heated by its own fireplace."

Ann nodded, and looked at the book again. She began to count something under her breath. "Right again. Twelve." She stared at Elizabeth in silence. Then she held the book up dramatically for Elizabeth to see. "Look!" she said, as if Elizabeth were not already wide-eyed.

For there on the page was a painting in black and white of her own dear Charington. And there beneath the picture of her house was a colored portrait of Michael and Margaret and their daughter. Margaret held a little baby in her arms, a baby dressed in a christening gown that hung almost to the floor.

Elizabeth gasped, and she thought her heart had stopped as she struggled for composure. "Those are certainly my parents, looking a little older than they really are. And this girl resembles me. But who is the baby?"

"Look on the chair beside the girl."

Elizabeth looked closely at the picture. "The music box," she said, but she was looking at something else in the shadow of the chair. It seemed to be a doll, one with a blue dress and striped stockings and a shock of red hair.

Elizabeth looked again at the girl in the portrait. "See how tall she stands. 'Tis as if she had put aside childish things and become a young woman."

"Yes," said Ann excitedly. "That's exactly what I thought. But look at the date painted at the bottom of the portrait."

"1605. Why, in 1605, I shall be fourteen years old. I shall be a young woman." Elizabeth read the caption under the portrait. "'Michael and Margaret, Duke and Duchess of Umberland, and their children, John and Elizabeth.'" Then the sheriff had been right. Her mother would indeed survive the illness Elizabeth had left her with. And if Margaret should bear a son, the family line would continue, just as the sheriff said it had until "it petered out in the eighteenth century."

"In your time, everything was so beautiful," Ann said. She smoothed her sweatshirt with the palms of her hands. "Are the gold and pearls on your dresses real?"

"Yes, all real." Elizabeth looked in wonderment at the portrait of her own future, remembering the day when she broke her mother's most precious vase. She had left a note of apology that said, "I am nothing like I will be when I grow up."

She had written those words with a confidence she had not felt; she had not been sure what she would be. She imagined herself beautiful and calm and responsible enough not to break her mother's treasures, but how could anyone know what she would be in the secret, dim future? Now she looked at a portrait that was like a strange mirror reflecting back the years ahead, and saw herself beautiful and self-possessed. Perhaps she would be responsible too.

"1605." Ann interrupted Elizabeth's thoughts and began quickly to search the page for something. "Listen! This is the part I read first. It's terrible, but it tells you for sure that you returned to your own time.

"'Charington,'" Ann read, "'was one of the finest houses owned by Elizabethan courtiers. It unfortunately burned to

the ground in 1607 when a candle fell into a bundle of tinder, setting the wood paneling and the carpets and draperies alight.'"

"Burned to the ground?" Elizabeth exclaimed. "Everything? Everything gone in smoke?"

"Not everything. The portrait survived, and something better too."

"Oh, do go on!"

Ann pointed to the line she was reading, and Elizabeth's voice joined Ann's. "'The Duke's fabulous collection of classical literature was a total loss, except for two volumes which his daughter Elizabeth rescued, Plutarch's *Lives* and Homer's *Odyssey*, books now held by the British Museum.'"

Ann looked at Elizabeth with triumph in her eyes. "Now listen to the best part. 'Elizabeth saved more than books that day. It was she who spread the alarm and who led her injured parents and young brother through the smoke to safety.'"

Elizabeth was silent as she tried to take in this strange story about her future and the world's past. She knew these events had not happened to her yet, but if they hadn't happened, how could they be in a book?

"Oh, Elizabeth. You were telling the truth!" Ann embraced her. "After supper," she said, "we'll figure out a way for you to go back home again so you can be there when the fire starts."

At last, someone believed all that Elizabeth knew of herself, and more. She took Ann's hand and clung to it, her relief at finding an ally mixed with disbelief of her own about Essex and the fire and the baby named John.

Elizabeth looked out the window, far across the Iowa cornfields. It was not corn she saw, but Charington in flames. She saw her mother, as she had been when Elizabeth last kissed her, lying ill in the great canopied bed.

"Medicine," she said. "I must take the tonic back with me."

If you were Elizabeth, would you try to return to Charington or remain with Ann? Explain your choice.

What things in Ann's life amaze Elizabeth? What does Ann learn about Elizabeth that amazes her?

What does Ann believe about Elizabeth in the beginning of the selection? What convinces Ann to change her mind?

In the portrait of Elizabeth's family, Elizabeth sees a doll. What does its description tell you?

WRITE Write three questions you would have asked Elizabeth if you had met her.

David Macaulay

Making the complicated understandable is David Macaulay's great gift. He has done it in his many books that look at structures, from the pyramids to cathedrals. He has shown audiences how buildings are built and how they are unbuilt—in *Unbuilding*, he takes apart the Empire State Building. He has looked beneath the earth in *Underground*. He's been called "a born teacher with an interest in things nobody before had the skill or the courage to try to explain." Macaulay himself has said, "I consider myself first and foremost an illustrator, in the broadest sense, someone who makes things clear through pictures and teaches through pictures."

David Macaulay was born in England, and he remembers his early years there very happily. He liked to take his time getting to school and let his mind wander. "Whenever the opportunity to daydream presented itself, I did." At age 11, Macaulay moved to America with his family: "It was an incredible shock." The kids seemed older, more mature. Macaulay feels he left childhood behind when he got to the States, but he kept his imagination in reserve, coming back to it when he needed it.

Although Macaulay had always enjoyed watching his mother draw scenes from family tales, it wasn't until Macaulay was a teenager that he discovered his own talent. He began drawing portraits of the Beatles, much to his classmates' delight. But when it was time to go to college, he thought it would be more practical to study architecture. That helped Macaulay learn a way of thinking that allowed him to understand how things worked.

After a year of teaching and working in an interior design studio, Macaulay became interested in book illustration. He also began writing stories. Although he admits they weren't very good, the illustrations that accompanied the stories were good enough to interest a publisher. There was a gargoyle in one of his stories, and it was that creature that made an editor suggest he write a book about cathedrals.

Since then, Macaulay has traveled to exotic places to research his books. He's been to France, visited Rome, climbed the Great Pyramid, all the while making sketches for his books. Macaulay is most interested in making his books realistic. He says, "One of the things I always try to do in a picture is to make the reader more of a participant than a spectator. I want him up on the roof of the building, and I want him to feel slightly sick because it's a long way up. If a reader can share that experience of being involved in a process, he will remember it. If I have any expertise at all, it is in that kind of communication."

Castle

by David Macaulay

CASTLE

DAVID MACAULAY

L ord Kevin's castle, although imaginary, is based in concept, structural process, and physical appearance on several castles built to aid in the conquest of Wales between 1277 and 1305. Their planning and construction epitomized over two centuries of military engineering accomplishments throughout Europe and the Holy Land.

The town of Aberwyvern, also imaginary, is based in concept and physical appearance on towns founded in conjunction with castles in Wales during the same twenty-eight-year period. This combination of castle and town in a military program displays both superior strategical skill and the farsightedness required for truly successful conquest.

On March 27, 1283, King Edward I of England named Kevin le Strange to be Lord of Aberwyvern—a rich but rebellious area of northwest Wales. Although the title was bestowed out of gratitude for loyal service, the accompanying lands were not granted without a more significant royal motive. In an attempt to dominate the Welsh once and for all, Edward had embarked on an ambitious and very expensive program to build a series of castles and towns in strategic locations throughout the land. Whenever possible he encouraged loyal noblemen like Kevin to undertake, at their own expense, similar projects which would fit into his master plan.

Both castle and town were intended as tools of conquest but each had its own distinct function. The castle and the wall which was built around the town were primarily defensive structures.

Whatever offensive use they had stemmed from their placement along important supply and communication routes and to some extent from their intimidating appearance. Their most important function was to protect the new town. Once established and prosperous, the town would provide a variety of previously unavailable social and economic opportunities, not only to the English settlers who would first occupy it, but eventually to the Welsh as well. By gradually eliminating the need and desire for military confrontation a town, unlike a castle, would contribute to both conquest and peace.

In order to protect his newly acquired land, Lord Kevin immediately began making preparations to build both a castle and a town. He hired James of Babbington, a master engineer of great skill, to design the project and supervise the work. At King Edward's suggestion a site was to be selected along the coast near the mouth of the river Wyvern, a vital link between the mountainous interior and the sea. After considering several possibilities, Master James and his staff settled on the exact location.

The castle was to be built on a high limestone outcrop, which extended into the water. This took advantage of the natural defensive properties of the river and, at the same time, because of the height of the outcrop, assured an unbroken view of the adjacent land. At the foot of the outcrop, where the castle site was accessible from the land, he located the town. It would act as a landward barrier and together with the river would create the castle's first ring of defense.

In addition to his staff, Master James had brought with him diggers, carpenters, laborers, and several boatloads of timber, tools, and hardware.

The carpenters were immediately put to work erecting barracks and workshops for themselves and for the soldiers who would protect the site. They also constructed a large but still temporary building to house Master James and staff, as well as Lord Kevin and his family, who were expected sometime the following month.

Once the approximate perimeter of the town had been established, the diggers enclosed the area with a wide ditch. Carpenters then erected a sturdy wooden fence called a palisade along the inside edge of the ditch to secure the site until a more permanent stone wall could be constructed.

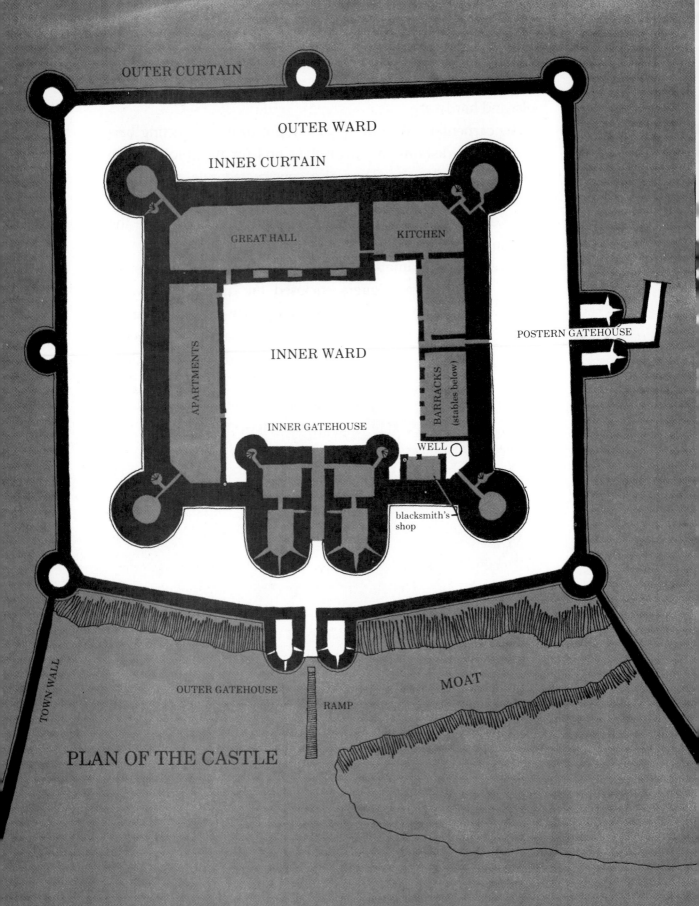

OUTER CURTAIN

OUTER WARD

INNER CURTAIN

GREAT HALL

KITCHEN

POSTERN GATEHOUSE

APARTMENTS

INNER WARD

BARRACKS
(stables below)

INNER GATEHOUSE

WELL

blacksmith's
shop

TOWN WALL

OUTER GATEHOUSE

RAMP

MOAT

PLAN OF THE CASTLE

As soon as the preliminary work was under way, Master James and his staff began planning the entire complex. The castle was designed first. The most important considerations were that it be able to resist direct attack and withstand a siege. This increasingly popular and often successful tactic involved surrounding both castle and town completely, cutting off all access to the outside. The strategy was simply to wait until all food and drink within the walls were gone, leaving the defenders with two equally unpleasant alternatives—starvation or surrender.

In planning the castle defenses, Master James combined several ideas developed in other castles, on which he had served as apprentice to the master engineer. The castle was laid out as a series of progressively smaller yet stronger defensive rings, one inside the other.

The space in the center of the castle was called the inner ward. It was enclosed by a high wall called the inner curtain. The area around the outside of the inner curtain was called the outer ward and it was enclosed by a lower wall called the outer curtain. Rounded towers were located along both walls, making it possible for soldiers to observe the entire perimeter of the structure.

Whenever a large doorway was required in either wall it was flanked by a pair of U-shaped towers. The opening itself was fortified by an elaborate system of bridges, gates, and barriers. The whole unit was called a gatehouse. A small gatehouse was located on one side of the outer curtain to protect the postern gate. This gate led to a fortified path running down the side of the outcrop between the castle and the river.

Besides housing Lord Kevin, his family, staff, and servants, when they were in Wales, the castle was to be the permanent home of the steward and his family, their staff and servants, and a garrison of soldiers.

The apartments of both the lord and the steward, along with a chapel, several offices, and a dungeon, were located in the towers of the inner curtain. The rest of the castle's residents lived and worked in buildings in the inner ward.

In planning for the possibility of siege, Master James protected the all important well by locating it in the inner ward. This reduced the danger that the castle's main water supply would ever be poisoned by the enemy—an act which would virtually ensure the castle's defeat. He also included a number of large food-storage rooms throughout the castle, many of which were kept filled at all times.

Inner curtain

The outer curtain, which measured about three hundred feet along each of the four sides, was to be twenty feet high and eight feet thick. The walls of the towers would be of the same thickness, but ten feet higher to provide a good view of the curtain on either side. The inner curtain, which measured about two hundred feet to a side, was to be thirty-five feet high and twelve feet thick, and its towers would be fifty feet tall. The increased height of the inner curtain would enable soldiers on top of it to fire over and reinforce those soldiers guarding the outer curtain.

The tops of all walls and towers within each curtain were connected by walks. This gave the soldiers on one part of the wall immediate access to any other part that might be under attack. The walk along the tops of the outer curtain was reached by staircases located against its inner face. The walk around the top of the inner curtain was reached by one of the spiral staircases built into each tower. Once on the walk, soldiers were protected by a narrow wall called a battlement, which was built along its outer edge.

Outer curtain

Both curtain walls and towers were perfectly vertical, except along the bottom of the outer face, where they spread out at a sharp angle. The sloping base, called a batter, had two main functions. First, it strengthened the structure and, second, it created a surface off which stones and other missiles dropped from the tops of the walls would bounce toward the enemy.

As the height of the walls increased, a temporary wooden framework, called scaffolding, was required to support both workers and materials. The poles were lashed together and secured to the wall by horizontal pieces set into holes, called putlog holes, which were intentionally left between the stones. The putlog holes along the outer face of both walls and towers rose on a gradual incline. Planks were nailed to the scaffolding inserted in these holes to create ramps up which heavy material could be dragged or carried.

Hoists and pulleys were attached to the scaffolding for lifting lighter materials and tools.

When a section of castle or town wall reached walk level, its battlement, or crenelation, was constructed. This was a wall

consisting of alternating high and low segments. The high segments, called merlons, each contained an arrow loop—a narrow vertical slit through which a soldier could shoot his arrows and remain completely protected. The lower segments, called embrasures, created openings from which missiles could be dropped on the enemy.

Every merlon was capped by three vertical stone spikes called finials, and immediately below each arrow loop was a square putlog hole. In time of battle, beams or logs were extended through these holes to support a temporary wooden balcony, or hoarding, from which missiles and arrows could be dropped and fired more accurately toward the base of the walls.

TOWN GATEHOUSE SECTION

The last major pieces of construction in both castle and town defense were the gatehouses. Because these were the most vulnerable parts of the walls, they were designed and built with great care.

Between the two towers of each gatehouse, a row of parallel stone arches supported a room above the road. From this room a heavy timber grille called a portcullis could be lowered to block the opening. The portcullis slid up and down in grooves cut into the walls on both sides. The bottom of each vertical piece of the portcullis was pointed and capped with iron. The face of the portcullis was also clad with iron for additional strength. Beyond the portcullis was a set of heavy wooden doors also reinforced with iron straps.

Immediately behind the doors were two holes opposite each other in the walls. A heavy piece of timber called a drawbar was pulled from the basement through one of the two holes, across the roadway, and set into the other hole to further secure the doors.

Arrow loops in the basements of the towers gave the soldiers complete control of the entry area.

If any part of an enemy force was careless enough to get caught in the space between the towers, it was showered with a variety of missiles and arrows. These would be dropped or fired through openings in the floor above called murder holes.

During the summer of 1287 work was completed on the gatehouses leading into the castle. The inner gatehouse had two portcullises, two sets of doors, and two drawbars. The outer gatehouse was equally well equipped and had the additional advantage of a drawbridge.

This flat timber platform was designed to pivot on an axle like a seesaw. The axle was set into holes cut in the base of each tower on both sides of the opening. The bridge was then fastened to the top of the axle—one end extending in through the gateway toward the outer ward, the other end spanning the moat. The inner end of the bridge was weighted and when the supports were removed it swung down into a specially designed pit cut into the rock between the towers. At the same time the other end swung upward, breaking the connection across the moat and blocking the entrance. To allow entry, the bridge would then be hoisted back into a horizontal position and the supports replaced underneath the weighted end.

OUTER GATEHOUSE SECTION

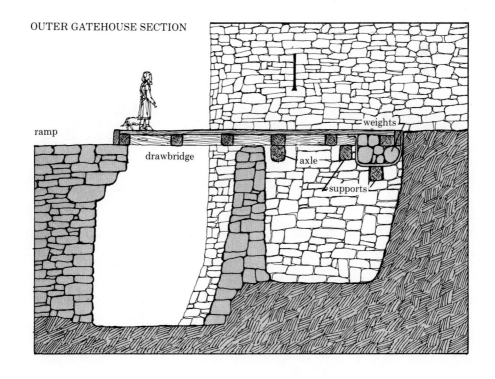

ramp

drawbridge

weights

axle

supports

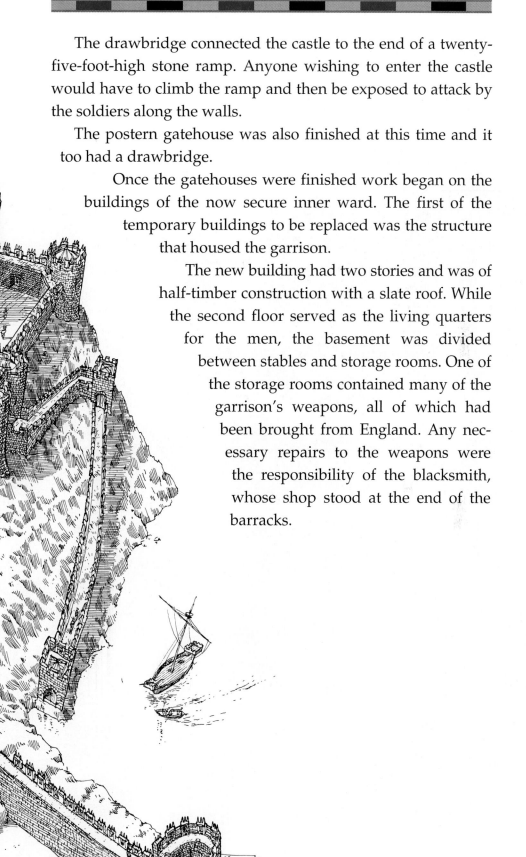

The drawbridge connected the castle to the end of a twenty-five-foot-high stone ramp. Anyone wishing to enter the castle would have to climb the ramp and then be exposed to attack by the soldiers along the walls.

The postern gatehouse was also finished at this time and it too had a drawbridge.

Once the gatehouses were finished work began on the buildings of the now secure inner ward. The first of the temporary buildings to be replaced was the structure that housed the garrison.

The new building had two stories and was of half-timber construction with a slate roof. While the second floor served as the living quarters for the men, the basement was divided between stables and storage rooms. One of the storage rooms contained many of the garrison's weapons, all of which had been brought from England. Any necessary repairs to the weapons were the responsibility of the blacksmith, whose shop stood at the end of the barracks.

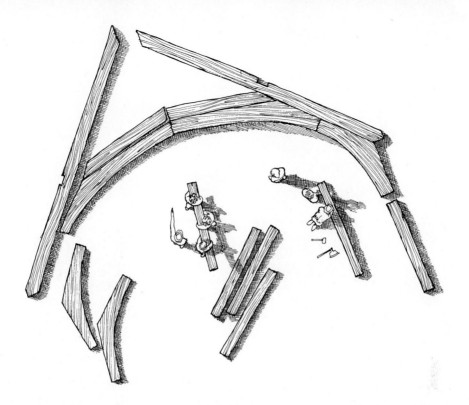

The largest new building in the ward was to be the great hall. It would serve as the general gathering and dining area for the entire population of the castle, it would be thirty-five feet wide and over one hundred feet long.

Master James located the hall in one corner of the inner ward so that only two new walls would be needed to enclose the space. They were both built of stone and capped with battlements. The longer of the two ran parallel to the rear curtain wall and contained three large windows and a door. The new wall at the end of the hall contained a large fireplace and a doorway to the kitchen. Two other fireplaces were already built into the curtain walls. The masons had set a row of corbels into the rear curtain wall about eight feet off the floor. This was repeated in the longer of the new walls.

As soon as the walls were finished, the carpenters began work on the roof. It was to rest on a row of parallel timber frames called trusses, which would span the width of the hall. Each truss was arched on the bottom for additional strength and built to form a peak on top.

First a vertical wooden post was set on each corbel and secured to the wall. Next, the carefully cut pieces of timber were assembled and hoisted into place with the ends of each truss resting on opposite wall posts. The tops of the trusses were then connected to each other and covered with wood planks and lead sheets. Once the roof was watertight the interior walls were plastered and painted and the windows were filled with glass.

Next to the hall and in the other rear corner of the inner ward was the kitchen. It contained ovens for baking bread, special fireplaces for cooking and smoking meat, and a large storage area for wine and ale barrels. Set into the rear curtain wall was a large stone sink. Water was piped directly into the sink from a stone tank called a cistern located at the top of the corner tower. The flat sloping roof over the kitchen was supported on beams set into a row of holes in the rear curtain.

New half-timber buildings were eventually constructed around the edge of the entire inner ward, replacing the last of the laborers' housing and workshops built almost four years earlier. They contained not only additional living space for Lord Kevin, Lady Catherine, and their closest attendants, but also a number of guest rooms and private quarters for members of the staff, including Walter the bailiff, Robert the Chaplain, and Lionel the barber and doctor.

Smaller rooms on the ground floors of all the buildings were allotted to servants, laborers, and general storage. Master John, the castle cook, lived in a small apartment close to the kitchen with his family and two assistants. In another corner of the ward kennels were built, along with a special shed called a mew, in which Lord Kevin's hunting birds were housed.

Although a number of dogs and cats were allowed to roam at will throughout the castle in hopes of controlling the rodent population, one small area of the inner ward was intentionally fenced off. Here Lady Catherine had insisted that a lawn of imported English turf be laid and a garden for flowers and herbs be planted.

In October of 1288, when the walls and towers of the castle were finished, the exterior of the entire structure was white-washed with lime, giving it the appearance of having been carved from a single enormous piece of stone and greatly enhancing its already powerful image.

The following spring saw only a handful of laborers returning to Aberwyvern. There was very little to do, and the

day-to-day maintenance of castle and town wall could now be managed by the craftsmen who had settled permanently in the town. At this point Lady Catherine considered the castle ready for occupation and, on April 29, arrived with her ladies in waiting, children, and servants to join Lord Kevin in their Welsh home.

What did you learn about castles that you didn't know before?

Where were the main places from which the castle was defended? Explain the means of defense.

Why did Master James build the well in the inner ward and construct large food-storage rooms?

WRITE   Imagine that you are giving a guided tour of this castle. Write a paragraph describing what tourists see as you enter the castle and walk through to the inner ward.

ACROSS TIME

How do Elizabeth's descriptions of England compare with the information in "Castle"?

WRITER'S WORKSHOP

Some stories use castles for their settings. Some stories have characters who travel to another time. Use these elements in a story of your own. Think of the people your main character will meet. How will they act toward your character? What exciting events will happen?

Writer's Choice   You have read about people and places from another time. Where would you go if you could travel to another time and place? Write about your ideas on the theme. Share your ideas in some way.

THEME

CROSSING BORDERS

Moving to a new country often means adapting to an entirely new way of life. The challenge of learning the customs of another culture can bring many difficult, enriching, and humorous experiences.

CONTENTS

331

PACIFIC Crossing

by Gary Soto
Illustrated by
Davy Liu

PACIFIC CROSSING

GARY SOTO

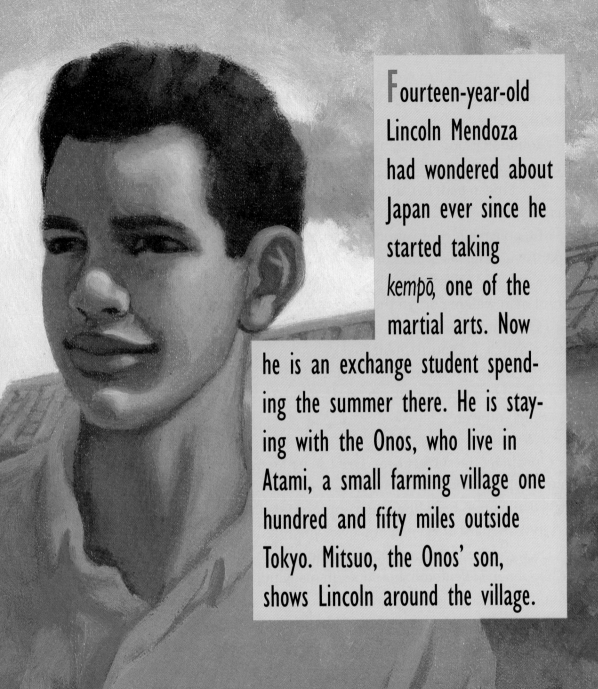

Fourteen-year-old Lincoln Mendoza had wondered about Japan ever since he started taking *kempō*, one of the martial arts. Now he is an exchange student spending the summer there. He is staying with the Onos, who live in Atami, a small farming village one hundred and fifty miles outside Tokyo. Mitsuo, the Onos' son, shows Lincoln around the village.

Mitsuo pointed to a wooden building with slat windows. "I took judo there but quit." A wind chime banged in the breeze.

"You took judo?" Lincoln said, excited. "That's bad."

"No, judo is good."

"No, I mean bad. In California, if you like something a lot, then it's bad."

Mitsuo gave Lincoln another strange look. He said, "In Japan, everyone takes judo or *kempō*. I didn't like judo. For me, it was not 'bad.' Baseball is 'bad.'" Mitsuo then pointed to a round man walking down the street. "He's Takahashi-*sensei*.[1] He's OK, but his assistant is mean. He was mean to me because I lost a match at a tournament."

"You went to tournaments? Sounds fun."

"I went to a few, but I wasn't very good."

"Sure you were."

"No, really."

Lincoln let the subject drop because he knew how sensitive he was when a defeat came up in conversation. He recalled the basketball games back home. Except for basketball at school, he had to work hard at everything, even spelling.

They watched the *sensei* open the dojo[2] with a key as large as a can opener. He entered, his shoes in his hand. The door closed behind him, and a light went on.

"I'll show you the *kempō* dojo," Mitsuo said.

"All right!" Lincoln cried.

They hurried through an alley and down three blocks, their mouths full of pumpkin seeds. When Mitsuo stopped, Lincoln nearly bumped into him.

"There," Mitsuo said, pointing.

---

[1] sensei (sen'sā): teacher
[2] dojo (dō'jō): training ground or school of martial arts

"Where?" Lincoln asked, confused. He was facing a cement driveway with a border of wild grass.

"There."

"Where?"

"There, Lincoln-kun!³"

"You mean this *driveway*?"

"Yes, they practice there and on the lawn. I think they practice at the university in winter."

Lincoln's image of a cleanly swept dojo evaporated like rain on a hot sidewalk. He was disappointed. He had come to Japan expecting to practice on tatami mats in a templelike dojo.

"They practice on concrete," he whispered.

---

³ kun (kŏon): ending to a personal name used between peers or by a superior, such as a parent, to a child

WHEN MITSUO AND Lincoln returned home, Mitsuo's father and mother were sitting with a woman on the *engawa*.[4] The woman sat erect, her face composed. All three were drinking iced tea, Mrs. Ono cooling herself with a fan that showed a picture of a baseball team.

Mitsuo gave the woman a short bow and greeted her in Japanese. Lincoln bowed, too.

---

[4] engawa (en′gä′wä): porch

"Lincoln-kun, this is Mrs. Oyama," the father said. He raised his glass, sipped, and put it down by his feet. "You and Mitsuo worked hard. The field looks tidy."

After a moment of silence, Mrs. Oyama asked, "So, Lincoln, you practice *shorinji kempō*?[5]" Her face was turned away, as if she were asking Mr. Ono.

"Yes," Lincoln answered, his back straight.

"You must be very good. You're so young and strong," Mrs. Oyama said, a smile starting at the corner of her mouth. She was still looking in the direction of Mr. Ono.

"Well, I guess so," Lincoln said, flattered, tightening his fist so that a rope of muscle showed in his forearm. He tried to hold back a smile. "I'm *sankyu*[6] rank."

"*Sankyu*. Very good for your age," Mrs. Oyama said, an eyebrow lifted. She turned to Mrs. Ono and said, "Such a strong boy."

"Oh yes, he worked so hard in the garden today," Mrs. Ono said, fanning the cool air in Lincoln's direction.

He sat straight up, his chest puffed out a little. "Well, I am pretty good. That's what Nakano-*sensei* says. I'll be a black belt when I'm fifteen."

"I'm impressed." Mrs. Oyama beamed, pressing her hands together. "I'm so happy to hear that in America we have dedicated youth."

The telephone rang in the living room. Mitsuo jumped to his feet. Lincoln started to follow, but the adults told him to stay.

"Mitsuo will answer it," Mr. Ono told Lincoln. "Lincoln-kun, what does your mother do?"

"She's sort of an artist. She has her own company." Lincoln bit his lower lip as he tried to think of what she actually did for a living. "She's a commercial artist. She does work for computer firms."

---

[5] shorinji kempō (shō'rin·jē kem'pō): a martial art
[6] sankyu (san'kyōō): brown belt

Mr. Ono shook his head, sighing, "Ah yes."

"And your father?" Mrs. Ono asked.

Lincoln had known this was coming. He had known ever since he'd boarded the jet to come to Japan that he would be asked this question. "He's a police officer," Lincoln said, not adding that he hadn't seen his father in six years. His parents had been divorced since Lincoln was seven, a hurt that had never healed.

The adults looked at each other, nodding their heads. They sipped tea and stirred the air with newspaper shaped into fans.

Mrs. Oyama rose. "I will see you tomorrow, if not sooner," she said to Lincoln and Mitsuo, who had returned from the living room. She bowed to Mr. and Mrs. Ono, thanked them for the tea, and walked down the path to the street.

While they ate fish for dinner, the Ono family helped Lincoln practice some Japanese phrases. He wanted to learn so that when he returned home he could talk in Japanese to his *kempō* instructor. So Mrs. Ono taught him some phrases. "How are you doing? Nice day. Let's eat." Her eyes shone when Lincoln said, *"Ima Atami ni sun'de imasu.* I am now living in Atami."

"You are a strong, smart boy," she said.

On the *engawa* after dinner, Mr. Ono said to Mitsuo, "Take Lincoln to the dojo. You are not too tired, are you, Lincoln-kun? It is almost eight o'clock."

"No, not at all," Lincoln said as he left the room to get his *gi*.[7] He felt good. He was ready to practice, even in a driveway.

Mr. Ono spoke to Mitsuo in Japanese, and Mitsuo turned away, almost laughing.

"What is *Chichi*[8] joking about?" Lincoln asked, smiling as well.

"He is glad you are here," Mitsuo said as he slipped on his *geta*.[9] "I'll take you to *kempō*."

---

[7] gi (gē): martial arts uniform
[8] Chichi (chē′chē): father or the speaker's father
[9] geta (ge′tä): wooden slippers

They walked four blocks in silence, and when they arrived at the driveway, Mitsuo turned away, a smile starting on his face. "I will see you in one hour. Have fun."

Puzzled at Mitsuo's smile, Lincoln watched him hurry away, *geta* ringing on the stone walk. Lincoln shrugged his shoulders as he entered the driveway with a fistful of yen, his monthly dues. On his way down the driveway, Lincoln stopped to *gasshō*—salute—to three black belts who were stretching on the lawn, sweat already soaking into the backs of their *gis*. They rose to their feet, saluted to Lincoln, and pointed to the side of the building. Lincoln went around and saw two others changing, a father and son. He changed there as well, folding his clothes neatly and placing his *geta* along the wall. He took off his watch, which glowed in the dark: 8:10.

Everyone was speaking in Japanese. No one paid Lincoln any attention as he joined the others on the lawn. He looked skyward at a plane cutting across the sky, and at that moment he wished he were on that plane.

A light lit the yard, reflecting off a small kidney-shaped pond, set among reeds and bamboo. Lincoln went and looked at the pond. He saw the reflection of his face in the murky water, rippling from long-legged water bugs.

He rejoined the others on the lawn and began stretching and practicing punches and kicks. His chest rose and fell, and his breathing became shallow. In the warm summer air, sweat was already starting to run from his body.

The *sensei* came out of the house, hands raised in a *gasshō*. She smiled and welcomed everyone as they formed two lines.

Lincoln's mouth fell open. It was Mrs. Oyama, whom he had met just before dinner—Oyama-*sensei*! He found a place at the back of the line, his face twisted with worry. Only an hour ago he had been bragging that he was *sankyu* rank, that he was as strong as any kid in the world.

After a formal salute to the spirit of *kempō*, some meditation, and warm-ups, the group finally started basic exercises. Only after basics did Oyama-*sensei* point to Lincoln, and everyone looked in his direction.

Lincoln forced a toothy smile. He hated life at that moment. He wished that he were on that plane, going back home to San Francisco. He promised himself this would be the last time he bragged.

"Lincoln, please," Oyama-*sensei* called, her outstretched hand gesturing for him to come up to the front. "Please tell us about yourself."

I'm a loudmouthed braggart, Lincoln thought; that's what I could tell you about myself.

Sweat streamed down his face, more from embarrassment than from the workout. He walked to the front, where he gave a *gasshō* and told his fellow practitioners—all eight of them—that he was from San Francisco and that he was staying with the

Ono family for the summer. When they smiled at him, he felt a little better.

They practiced *juhō*—grabs and pinning techniques—and *embu*—planned attacks. He tried his best. He didn't want these adult black belts to think he was sorry, just because he was from America and a fourteen-year-old brown belt. His punches and kicks snapped against his *gi*. His arm locks were executed quickly, but not with the ease of the adults'.

Lincoln had never worked out on grass before. In San Francisco, he had practiced on linoleum. He liked the way the grass tickled the bottoms of his feet. He also liked having the grass to cushion his falls; he fell a lot when he practiced with the advanced belts. He was thrown and twisted into painful holds, his face pressed harshly against the grass. He got up quickly when they let go, and he didn't let on that his arm felt like a drumstick being torn from the body of a chicken.

When class ended at 9:30, Oyama-*sensei* called him aside. "Lincoln-kun, you are a good boy. Strong."

"I'm not that strong," he said, this time not wanting to brag about himself. He was still warm from the workout, and his chest was rising and falling. Grass clung to his *gi* and his tousled hair.

"You are very good. In six weeks, if you practice hard, we will see about a promotion." One side of her face was hidden in the dark; the other side glowed in the porch light. Her eyes gave away nothing.

Lincoln started to walk away, but she called him back. "Lincoln-kun, you must shave your hair."

"My hair?" he asked, touching the hair around his ears.

"Yes, it must be gone."

LINCOLN CHANGED FROM his *gi* to his street clothes and was greeted by Mitsuo, who was waiting in the driveway.

"How come you didn't tell me?" Lincoln asked. "She's the *sensei*, and you didn't tell me. That was cold."

"Sorry, Lincoln, but Father wanted to make a joke. He likes you." Mitsuo thought for a moment, then asked, "What is 'cold'?"

"'Cold' is, is—I don't know how to explain it. But that was a 'cold' shot," Lincoln said as the two of them walked down the street, their *geta* ringing in unison. "Yeah, your dad is a wise guy."

"Yes, he is sometimes very wise," Mitsuo agreed.

Lincoln stopped in his tracks and was about to explain "wise guy" and the Three Stooges, but he was too tired. It had been a long day in Japan.

The stores were closed. A few cars passed in the street, silent as cats. Only a small neon light glowed in a bar window. They tiptoed over and looked inside, where men sat playing *go,* an ancient board game similar to checkers, or talking in dark corners.

"Just like California," Lincoln said.

"Really?"

"Yeah."

"My father used to come here, but he doesn't anymore. He likes it better at home."

Lincoln wanted to tell Mitsuo about his father—about his lack of a father—but didn't know how. In the United States, it was not uncommon to come from a broken home. But in Japan families all seemed to be intact—father, mother, children, all walking down the street together. In the *sentō*,[10] fathers scrubbed their children, and, in turn, the children scrubbed their fathers with all their might. It wasn't Lincoln's fault that his parents' marriage hadn't worked out. Still, at times he felt lonely and embarrassed.

---

[10] sentō (sen′tō): public bath

They walked home. Lincoln showered and then went out to the *engawa* to join Mitsuo, who was relacing his baseball mitt after having taken out some of the padding.

"This is my favorite mitt," Mitsuo said proudly. "My grandfather gave it to me."

"Nice." The night was quiet. A cat strode the thin rail of bamboo fence, his tail wavering in the moonlight. The neighbors were watching television. The vegetable garden rustled in the breeze. Lincoln felt tired but happy. He was already feeling at home.

Would you like living in another country as much as Lincoln Mendoza does? Explain your response.

What facets of the Japanese culture does Lincoln have to adjust to?

What does Lincoln do that makes him feel he is a braggart?

WRITE Write a definition for one of the expressions Lincoln uses with Mitsuo.

AWARD-WINNING
AUTHOR

WORDS FROM THE AUTHOR *Gary Soto*

Gary Soto, the son of working-class Mexican Americans, describes his growing-up life in his autobiographical writings. "We were pretty much an illiterate family. We didn't have books, and no one was encouraged to read." It was hardly the background for a writer. When he was a kid, Soto thought he might become a priest. Later, he wanted to be a barber. By the time Soto started out at community college, he thought he would major in geography. Then one day at the library, he discovered a collection of poems called *The New American Poetry*. "I thought, this is terrific. I'd like to do something like this. So I proceeded to write my own poetry, first alone, with no one's help, and then moving on to take classes at California State, Fresno."

Gary Soto has said he doesn't want to be thought of as just a Latino writer. "One of the things I would like to do is make that leap from being a Chicano writer to being simply a writer." Gary Soto has written numerous books for adults and young people and has produced several short films.

347

On the Eastern Horizon

by Hitomaro

On the Eastern horizon
Dawn glows over
The fields, and when
I look back I see
The moon setting in the West.

Name/Nombres

BY JULIA ALVAREZ

illustrations by Moses Perez

When we arrived in New York City, our names changed almost immediately. At Immigration, the officer asked my father, *Mister Elbures*, if he had anything to declare. My father shook his head, "No," and we were waved through. I was too afraid we wouldn't be let in if I corrected the man's pronunciation, but I said our name to myself, opening my mouth wide for the organ blast of the *a*, trilling my tongue for the drumroll of the *r*, *All-vah-rrr-es!* How could anyone get *Elbures* out of that orchestra of sound?

At the hotel my mother was *Missus Alburest*, and I was *little girl*, as in, "Hey, little girl, stop riding the elevator up and down. It's *not* a toy."

When we moved into our new apartment building, the super called my father, *Mister Alberase*, and the neighbors who became my mother's

friends pronounced her name, *Jew-lee-ah* instead of *Hoo-lee-ah*. I, her namesake, was known as *Hoo-lee-tah* at home. But at school, I was *Judy* or *Judith*, and once an English teacher mistook me for *Juliet*.

It took awhile to get used to my new names. I wondered if I shouldn't correct my teachers and new friends. But my mother argued that it didn't matter. "You know what your friend Shakespeare said, *'A rose by any other name would smell as sweet.'*" My family had gotten into the habit of calling any famous author "my friend" because I had begun to write poems and stories in English class.

By the time I was in high school, I was a popular kid, and it showed in my name. Friends called me *Jules* or *Hey Jude*, and once a group of troublemaking friends my mother forbid me to hang out with called me *Alcatraz*. I was *Hoo-lee-tah* only to Mami and Papi and uncles and aunts who came over to eat *sancocho*[1] on Sunday afternoons—old world folk whom I would just as soon go back to where they came from and leave me to pursue whatever mischief I wanted to in America. *JUDY ALCATRAZ:* the name on the Wanted Poster would read. Who would ever trace her to me?

My older sister had the hardest time getting an American name for

[1] sancocho: stew

herself because *Mauricia* did not translate into English. Ironically, although she had the most foreign-sounding name, she and I were the Americans in the family. We had been born in New York City when our parents had first tried immigration and then gone back "home," too homesick to stay. My mother often told the story of how she had almost changed my sister's name in the hospital.

After the delivery, Mami and some other new mothers were cooing over their new baby sons and daughters and exchanging names and weights and delivery stories. My mother was embarrassed among the Sally's and Jane's and George's and John's to reveal the rich, noisy name of *Mauricia,* so when her turn came to brag, she gave her baby's name as *Maureen.*

"Why'd ya give her an Irish name with so many pretty Spanish names to choose from?" one of the women asked.

My mother blushed and admitted her baby's real name to the group. Her mother-in-law had recently died, she apologized, and her husband had insisted that the first daughter be named after his mother, *Mauran.* My mother thought it the ugliest name she had ever heard, and she talked my father into what she believed was an improvement, a combination of *Mauran* and her own mother's name, *Felicia.*

"Her name is *Mao-ree-shee-ah,*" my mother said to the group of women.

"Why that's a beautiful name," the new mothers cried. "*Moor-ee-sha, Moor-ee-sha,*" they cooed into the pink blanket. *Moor-ee-sha,* it was when we returned to the States eleven years

later. Sometimes, American tongues found even that mispronunciation tough to say and called her *Maria* or *Marsha* or *Maudy* from her nickname *Maury*. I pitied her. What an awful name to have to transport across borders!

My little sister, Ana, had the easiest time of all. She was plain *Anne*—that is, only her name was plain, for she turned out to be the pale, blond "American beauty" in the family. The only Hispanic thing about her was the affectionate nicknames her boyfriends sometimes gave her. *Anita*, or as one goofy guy used to sing to her to the tune of the Chiquita banana advertisement, *Anita Banana*.

Later, during her college years in the late '60s, there was a push to pronounce Third World names correctly. I remember calling her long distance at her group house and a roommate answering.

"Can I speak to Ana?" I asked, pronouncing her name the American way.

"Ana?" The man's voice hesitated. "Oh! you must mean *Ah-nah*!"

Our first few years in the States, though, ethnicity was not yet "in." Those were the blond, blue-eyed, bobby sock years of junior high and high school before the '60s ushered in peasant blouses, hoop earrings, sarapes.[2] My initial desire to be known by my correct Dominican name faded. I just wanted to be Judy and merge with the Sally's and Jane's in my class. But inevitably, my accent and coloring gave me away. "So where are you from, Judy?"

"New York," I told my classmates. After all, I had been born blocks away at Columbia Presbyterian Hospital.

---

[2] sarapes: brightly colored shawls

"I mean, *originally*."

"From the Caribbean," I answered vaguely, for if I specified, no one was quite sure on what continent our island was located.

"Really? I've been to Bermuda. We went last April for spring vacation. I got the worst sunburn! So, are you from Portoriko?"

"No," I sighed. "From the Dominican Republic."

"Where's that?"

"South of Bermuda."

They were just being curious, I knew, but I burned with shame whenever they singled me out as a "foreigner," a rare, exotic friend.

"Say your name in Spanish, oh please say it!" I had made mouths drop one day by rattling off my full name, which according to Dominican custom, included my middle names, Mother's and Father's surnames for four generations back.

"Julia Altagracia Mariá Teresa Álvarez Tavares Perello Espaillat Julia Pérez Rochet González," I pronounced it slowly, a name as chaotic with sounds as a Middle Eastern bazaar or market day in a South American village.

My Dominican heritage was never more apparent than when my extended family attended school occasions. For my graduation, they all came, the whole lot of aunts and uncles and the many little cousins who snuck in without tickets. They sat in the first row in order to better understand the Americans' fast-spoken English. But how could they listen when they were constantly speaking among themselves in florid-sounding phrases, rococo consonants, rich, rhyming vowels.

Introducing them to my friends was a further trial to me. These relatives had such complicated names and there were so many of them, and their

relationships to myself were so convoluted. There was my Tía[3] Josefina, who was not really an aunt but a much older cousin. And her daughter, Aida Margarita, who was adopted, *una hija de crianza.*[4] My uncle of affection, Tío José brought my *madrina*[5] Tía Amelia and her *comadre*[6] Tía Pilar. My friends rarely had more than a "Mom and Dad" to introduce.

After the commencement ceremony my family waited outside in the parking lot while my friends and I signed yearbooks with nicknames which recalled our high school good times: "Beans" and "Pepperoni" and "Alcatraz." We hugged and cried and promised to keep in touch.

Our goodbyes went on too long. I heard my father's voice calling out across the parking lot, *"Hoo-lee-tah! Vámonos!"*[7]

Back home, my *tíos* and *tías* and *primas*, Mami and Papi, and *mis hermanas*[8] had a party for me with *sancocho* and a store-bought *pudín,*[9] inscribed with *Happy Graduation, Julie.* There were many gifts—that was a plus to a large family! I got several wallets and a suitcase with my initials and a graduation charm from my godmother and money from my uncles. The biggest gift was a portable typewriter from my parents for writing my stories and poems.

Someday, the family predicted, my name would be well-known throughout the United States. I laughed to myself, wondering which one I would go by.

---

[3] Tía, Tío: Aunt, Uncle
[4] una hija de crianza: an adopted daughter
[5] madrina: godmother
[6] comadre: woman friend

---

[7] Vámonos!: Let's go!
[8] mis hermanas: my sisters
[9] pudín: dessert

Do you agree with Julia's mother that it did not matter that Julia's friends and teachers could not pronounce her name? Explain your answer.

Julia Alvarez did not like it when people mispronounced her name. Do you think she objected to all her nicknames? Explain your answers.

WRITE Julia Alvarez tells about different versions of her name used by her family, friends, and strangers. Write a few paragraphs telling about your name. Tell about any nicknames you may have and how they originated.

354

CROSSING BORDERS

✗✗✗✗✗✗✗✗✗✗✗✗✗✗✗

What typical teenage concerns do Julia and Lincoln have? In what way are their situations a little different from those of other teenagers?

WRITER'S WORKSHOP

Imagine that you want to persuade a friend to meet Julia or Lincoln. What would you say to get your friend interested in either person? Write a persuasive paragraph telling what you would say and giving reasons that your friend would like Julia or Lincoln.

Writer's Choice   What does Crossing Borders mean to you? Choose and write about an idea that comes to mind. Think of a way to share your idea.

CONNECTIONS

MULTICULTURAL CONNECTION

AFRICAN STORYTELLERS

People around the world tell many kinds of stories in many different ways. In West Africa, storyteller-musicians known as griots tell the myths and legends of their people through song.

The griots [grē•ō′] have a long and fascinating history. In ancient times, before there were written languages in West Africa, the griots were counselors to great African kings. They memorized stories of important events and people and put those stories to music.

The griots of today maintain their link with the past. Although they no longer advise kings, they still entertain people with their story-songs rooted in African history and customs. Throughout West Africa, they can be found singing their proverbs and tales, accompanied by traditional African instruments.

Have a "World Storytelling Festival" in your class. Find a folktale from another land or a song that tells a story. Then share your story or song with a group of classmates.

ART/LANGUAGE ARTS CONNECTION

PUBLISH A BOOK

Create your own book using a favorite folktale from another land. Write the story on sheets of art paper, and add illustrations. Then make a cover for your book and fasten the pages together. Display your book at a class book fair.

SOCIAL STUDIES CONNECTION

CUSTOMS IN OTHER LANDS

With a partner, find out about life and customs in another country. Then organize your findings in a chart. Use headings such as Geography, Housing, Food, Clothing, Work, and Family Life. Add photos, drawings, and maps to your chart if you like.

Clockwise from top: Nairobi, Kenya; West African griot; father teaching daughter to read, Luxor, Egypt

UNIT FOUR 4

LIGHT MOMENTS

*Kitty started laughing.... she kept on laughing
until the tears ran down her face.*
            Walter Dean Myers

Humorous stories are enjoyed throughout
the world. From time to time, we all need
to laugh at a funny story or performance.
People who provide laughs, such as
comedian Bill Cosby or writer Betsy
Byars, have to work hard to entertain us.
As you read the selections in this unit,
remember to appreciate the people who
created these light moments.

THEMES

BOOKSHELF

JOURNAL OF A TEENAGE GENIUS

BY HELEN V. GRIFFITH

Zack, a teenage scientist, meets a girl whose family travels through time in this hilarious science fiction novel.

Award-Winning Author

HARCOURT BRACE LIBRARY BOOK

BUNNICULA

BY DEBORAH AND JAMES HOWE

Bunnicula seems like an ordinary rabbit, but his housemates begin to worry when they find vegetables drained white with two little toothmarks in them.

ALA Notable Book, Children's Choice

HARCOURT BRACE LIBRARY BOOK

MISERY GUTS

BY MORRIS GLEITZMAN

Determined to cheer up his ever-gloomy parents, Keith convinces them to close their fish-and-chips shop and move to Australia.

SKINNYBONES

BY BARBARA PARK

A natural comic, Alex Frankovitch uses humor to lighten tough situations, including the crushing defeats suffered by his baseball team.

Award-Winning Author

BINGO BROWN, GYPSY LOVER

BY BETSY BYARS

Bingo's reputation as an authority on romance is developing nicely when life throws him a curve—he's about to become a big brother!

ALA Notable Book

THEME

DOG TALES

Dogs can be cute. Dogs can be smart. But can dogs be funny? Meet Vergil, Major, and some other dogs, and decide for yourself.

CONTENTS

363

VERGIL,
THE LAID-BACK DOG

from *My Brother Louis Measures Worms*

by **Barbara Robinson**

AWARD-WINNING
AUTHOR

illustrated by **Oleana Kassian**

Mary Elizabeth
Lawson comes
from a most
unusual family.
Her brother
Louis and other
members of her
family are always getting
themselves into wacky and
unpredictable situations. In this story,
you'll read about the Lawsons' adventures
with Vergil, a very laid-back dog.

Most of Mother's relatives had animals of one kind or another, and most of the animals, according to my father, were as strange as the people they belonged to.

"I don't know," he often said, "whether they actively seek out screwy dogs and cats, or whether the dogs and cats just turn screwy after a while." He included our cat Leroy in this overall opinion, although by then Leroy was gone. He/she had produced four kittens and immediately took off for greener pastures, abandoning both us and the kittens, which my father said was completely unnatural behavior, and proved his point.

Actually there were any number of perfectly ordinary pets in the family—faithful nondescript dogs, companionable cats—but, just as good news is less dramatic than bad news and therefore less publicized, these humdrum animals were never the ones my father heard about, and the ones he *did* hear about left him forever cool to the idea of having one of his own.

Mother knew this; but, as she later said, having a dog was one thing, and having a dog come to visit for a few days was something else. So when her cousin Lloyd Otway deposited his dog Vergil on our doorstep, Mother didn't think twice about offering to keep Vergil while Lloyd went off to Milwaukee, Wisconsin, to acquire a wife.

My father said he could understand that Lloyd might find the pickings slim and overfamiliar right here at home, "—but why take off for Milwaukee?"

"Because that's where Pauline lives," Mother said. "Pauline Swavel. That's where she went back to after she and Lloyd met and fell in love. Oh, Fred, you remember Pauline!"

Obviously he didn't; but in view of the romantic circumstances involving Lloyd and Pauline Swavel, I did; and I remembered, too, that my father had been out of town that day.

"That's right, he was," Mother said. "He was in Columbus.

You were in Columbus that day, at your state convention. I know I told you about it, but you probably didn't hear me, or else you didn't listen."

"That *day*?!?" My father stared at her. "Lloyd and this Pauline met and fell in love in one day?"

"Yes," Mother said—and this was, indeed, the case: a one-day, whirlwind, love-at-first-sight affair, attended by the usual monkey puzzle of mistakes and coincidences.

Pauline Swavel, while driving through town on her way from West Virginia, was run into by Aunt Mildred, who had been distracted by the unexpected appearance in her car of Lloyd's dog Vergil.

"All of a sudden, there he was," she said. "Don't know where he came from. Just sat up in the backseat and yawned and stretched and groaned—scared me to death, and I hit the gas instead of the brake."

Vergil, equally alarmed, began to leap up and down in the car and to scramble from back to front, howling and barking. This behavior was so unnatural in Vergil—who had, at various times, slept through a fire, a burglary, and an explosion at the fertilizer plant—that Aunt Mildred lost all control, careened through a traffic light and bounced off a milk truck and into Pauline, who had pulled over to study her road map.

Pauline had taken a wrong turn somewhere north of Parkersburg and was not only completely lost but, now, involved in a traffic accident as well—with a car that seemed to her, at first glance, to be driven by a dog.

At this point Lloyd appeared. He had been delivering lawn fertilizer to Aunt Mildred, missed Vergil, and knew immediately what had happened, since it was Vergil's habit to climb into whatever car was handy and open and go to sleep.

Lloyd set out at once to find and follow Aunt Mildred— never an easy task, but a little easier this time because of all the commotion at the scene of the accident.

He arrived; retrieved Vergil; assessed the damage, which was minor; ignored Aunt Mildred (or so she said); and, on the spot, fell in love with Pauline. That Pauline should, at the very same moment, fall in love with Lloyd seemed insane to Aunt Mildred and my mother; unlikely to Louis—"Unless it was a movie," he said—and gloriously romantic to me.

"But, Lloyd," Mother said when he arrived at our house later that day, arm in arm with Pauline, to tell us the news, "isn't this awfully sudden?"

"Like a lightning bolt," Lloyd said.

"And, Pauline," Mother went on, "of course we think the world and all of Lloyd . . . but you don't even know him!"

"I feel I do," Pauline said, "after just these few hours. I've never felt so comfortable with a person, nor found anyone so easy to talk to. I figure that whatever I don't know about Lloyd, or what he doesn't know about me, will give us conversation for years. Do you believe in fate, Mrs. Lawson?"

"No, I don't," Mother said, "not when it's mixed up with Mildred and a bird dog."

"Neither do I," Pauline said, "or never did till now. But just think about it. . . . Why did I get lost and end up here? Why did Lloyd's dog get into someone else's car? Why did your sister run into me instead of someone else?"

Now, explaining it all to my father, Mother agreed that these were not mysterious events: Vergil was famous for getting into anybody's car, Aunt Mildred was famous for colliding with anybody's car, and . . . "I know all about getting lost," Mother said, "but even I know there are only two main roads north from Parkersburg, and if you miss the other one you'll end up here. But after all, they're both grown-up people—Lloyd's thirty-three years old, it's time he got married—and it wasn't as if they were going to get married that very minute. Besides, I thought it would all fizzle out. Of course, it didn't"—she smiled happily—"and now Lloyd's gone off to Milwaukee to marry Pauline."

My father eyed Vergil. "I think if I were Lloyd," he said, "I'd take that dog along with me for good luck, since he was in on the beginning of this romance."

"Well, so was Mildred," Mother said, "but she can't just go off to Milwaukee either—and you don't fool me a bit. You just don't want Vergil underfoot."

Unfortunately, because of his large and rangy size, Vergil was automatically underfoot, and he usually chose to sprawl,

full-length, in awkward places: at the top of the stairs or at the bottom of the stairs, under the dining-room table, under my father's car and, from time to time, on very warm days, in the bathtub.

The first time this happened Louis tried to make Vergil more comfortable by turning on the water; but Vergil scrambled out of the bathtub (moving faster than we had ever seen him move before) and tore all around the upstairs, barking and howling and shaking himself and spraying water everywhere.

"I think he was asleep," Louis said, "and it surprised him."

I thought so too, because Vergil was asleep most of the time . . . but when Louis tried it again, Vergil was awake and the same thing happened.

"He doesn't like the water," Mother said. "He just likes to feel the cool porcelain tub."

"So do I," my father said, "but I don't want to take turns with a big hairy dog. Isn't Lloyd back yet? He must be married by now."

"Yes," Mother said, "but they're on their honeymoon. Surely you don't begrudge them a honeymoon?"

"That depends on where they went," my father said. "They could have a very nice honeymoon between Milwaukee and here—two or three days in Chicago, maybe."

"Yes," Mother said, "they could. Listen, is that the telephone?"

"Well, hurry up and answer it. Maybe it's Lloyd."

It wasn't Lloyd. Actually, it wasn't even the telephone— Mother just made that up because she didn't want to explain that Lloyd and Pauline had gone in the opposite direction—to San Francisco—and were going to stop along the way wherever Pauline had relatives who wanted to welcome Lloyd into the family. We found out later that all these relatives lived in places like Middle Mine, Wyoming, and Clash, Nebraska, and were probably overjoyed to see anybody at all.

Of course, after two or three weeks, Mother had to admit that they weren't in Chicago and, as far as she knew, never had been. "They probably aren't even to San Francisco yet," she said. "You know how southerners are—sometimes newlywed couples visit around for months."

"But Pauline isn't a southerner, she's from Milwaukee!"

"I was giving you an example," Mother said. "It wouldn't have to be southerners. Amish people do the same thing."

"Is Pauline Amish?"

"She didn't say."

My father thought that over briefly and then shook his head. "You don't have any idea where they are, do you."

"No . . . but I do know that Lloyd is lucky, to marry into such a close and loving family."

"Lloyd is lucky," my father said, "because he was able to unload this dog on us while he tours the entire western half of the country. Oh, well," he sighed. "I'm going to take a bath—he isn't in the bathtub, is he?"

"No," Mother said, "but be careful when you come downstairs. He's asleep on the top step."

Three or four minutes later Louis and I heard the unmistakable *thump, thump, bang, thump, bang* of something or somebody falling downstairs, and went to see who or what it was.

My father heard the noise too, assumed that Mother had tripped over Vergil and came stumbling out of the bathroom with his pants half off, calling for us to get help. Mother, in the back bedroom, heard both the thumps and the cries for help, came running from that end of the house and fell over my father, who was trapped by his pants.

Meanwhile, Vergil lay at the foot of the stairs in his customary position: full-length and flat on his back—and ominously still. We thought he might be dead, and Louis got down on the floor to listen to his heart . . . which led Mother to conclude that it was Louis who had fallen *over* Vergil and then down the stairs along *with* Vergil.

"What else would I think?" she said. "Everybody on the floor in a heap." She felt responsible, though, and made my father pull on his pants and take Vergil to the animal hospital, where, as it turned out, he was well known.

"He isn't moving," Mother said. "He fell down the stairs."

"Does it all the time," the doctor told us. "This is the laziest dog in the world. He'd *rather* fall down stairs than stand up. Fell off a shed roof once. Fell out of Lloyd's truck that was loaded with fertilizer bags."

"But he isn't moving," Mother said.

"That's because he's asleep."

My father said this was the last straw—that he hadn't wanted a dog at all, and he especially didn't want a dog who was too lazy to stand up—but Mother was relieved.

"I'd hate to have Lloyd come back," she said, "and have to tell him that his dog died of injuries."

"At this rate," my father said, "his dog will die of old age before he shows up."

Vergil didn't die, but Lloyd and Pauline never did show up, either. Their car broke down in a place called Faltrey, Arkansas . . . *and we couldn't find anyone to fix it*, Lloyd wrote. *They had a garage, had a gas station, had parts and equipment, had no mechanic. The mechanic couldn't stand Arkansas, they said, and he got on his motorcycle and left. So I fixed our car and two or three other people's cars . . . and to make a long story short, they just wouldn't let us leave. And now you couldn't pay us to leave, because we love it here in Faltrey, especially Pauline. But don't worry, because we'll be back to get Vergil, the first chance we get.*

"'Yours truly, Lloyd,'" Mother finished reading. "Well, what do you know about that!"

"I know it's a long way to Arkansas," my father said, looking at Vergil.

After that we got a few postcards from Lloyd and a few letters from Pauline, who sent us a picture of the garage and a picture of their house and, eventually, a picture of their baby. All the cards and letters said they would be back for Vergil *. . . as soon as Lloyd's work lets up a little* or *as soon as we get the tomatoes in the garden* or *as soon as the baby's old enough to travel.*

My mother believed all these assurances (or said she did), and she would never admit that Vergil was anything but a temporary house guest. If anyone mentioned "your dog," she would always say, "Oh, this is Lloyd's dog. We're just keeping him for Lloyd."

In a way, my father wouldn't admit it either, because he never referred to Vergil as "our dog" or "my dog" or anything except "that dog"; but when Lloyd and Pauline finally did come back they had a sizeable family—Lloyd, Jr., was in the second grade, and the twin girls were two and a half years old—and their car was full of infant seats and baby beds and toys. My mother said the last thing they needed was Vergil. "Where would you put him?" she said.

Lloyd agreed. "I guess I just forgot how big he is. We'd better bring the truck next time."

Mother didn't mention this to my father, and in fact, Lloyd and Pauline had been gone for three days before he realized that Vergil didn't go with them, although Vergil was in plain sight, asleep, the whole time.

"You're just used to him," Mother said, "and you would miss him a lot."

"How could I possibly miss him if I haven't even noticed him for three days?"

"There!" she said. "How could any dog be less trouble!"

She was right, of course. Vergil didn't bark, or bite people, or dig up gardens, or upset trash cans, and by then we were all used to stepping over him or around him. By then, too, he was too old to climb into the bathtub; but sometimes, on very hot days, my father would lift him in—to get him out of the way, he said—and then get mad because Vergil wouldn't climb back out.

Despite Vergil's lack of interest in us, Louis and I were very fond of him. We thought of him as our dog, played with him during those brief and very occasional moments when he was awake, and whenever we had to write a paper for school about *My Best Friend*, or *My Favorite Pet*, we wrote about Vergil.

We never got very good grades on these papers because there was so little to tell, but we did share the glory when Vergil won a blue ribbon in the YMCA Pet Show. He won it for "Unusual Obedience to Command"—we commanded him to "play dead," and no dog did it better or for so long.

Which of Vergil's habits seems the most unusual to you?

How do Lloyd and Pauline first meet?

Does the family think of Vergil as their dog? Explain your answer.

Why do you think Lloyd never retrieves Vergil?

WRITE   Write your own paper on the topic "My Favorite Pet." In your paper, write a vivid description of a pet you have owned or an animal you would like to own.

Sleeping Simon

by **Deborah Chandra** • *illustrated by* **Kevin Ghiglione**

Old Simon swims
A moonlit river
On the kitchen floor—
His chin quivers.
Cold water ripples
Round his whiskers.
Closed eyes roll.

Stiff, kicking legs
Keep him from
Sinking out of sight.
A splash, a sputter,
Deep growls down under—
Dark waters foam.
Simon fights.

The river swallows Simon:
Paws, claws, tail, nose,
Gulping air, he
Wakens with a yelp—
Thumping his tail to see
Stove, chairs and door,
And sighing, slumps upon the
Friendly floor.

The
by John Ciardi
illustrated by Bernadette Lau
Dollar Dog

AWARD-WINNING POET

A dollar dog is all mixed up.

A bit of this, a bit of that.

We got ours when he was a pup

So small he slept in an old hat.

So small we borrowed a doll's beads

To make him his first collar.

Too small to see how many breeds

We got for just one dollar.

But not at all too small to see

He had an appetite.

An appetite? It seems to me

He ate up everything in sight!

The more he ate, the more we saw.

He got to be as big as two.

The more we saw, the more we knew

We had a genuine drooly-jaw,

Mishmash mongrel, all-around,

Flop-eared, bull-faced, bumble-paw,

Stub-tailed, short-haired, Biscuit Hound.

Mother
Doesn't Want
a Dog

by Judith Viorst

AWARD-WINNING
POET

Mother doesn't want a dog.
Mother says they smell,
And never sit when you say sit,
Or even when you yell.
And when you come home late at night
And there is ice and snow,
You have to go back out because
The dumb dog has to go.

Mother doesn't want a dog.
Mother says they shed,
And always let the strangers in
And bark at friends instead,
And do disgraceful things on rugs,
And track mud on the floor,
And flop upon your bed at night
And snore their doggy snore.

Mother doesn't want a dog.
She's making a mistake.
Because, more than a dog, I think
She will not want this snake.

MOJO AND THE RUSSIANS

BY WALTER DEAN MYERS

ILLUSTRATED BY CHARLES LILLY

The project at hand was teaching Major to talk. It was mainly my idea, but Kwami tried to take credit for it. We had got into this big argument about communicating with other people. Kwami said that you could communicate with anything if you knew how to. He had read this article in an old magazine where some people were teaching a monkey to talk. Now Kwami figured that a dog must be smarter than a monkey. I told him that I had learned in biology that monkeys were the next smartest things to people. He said that if monkeys were so smart how come they didn't live in apartments like dogs did. He said that he saw a program about dogs once and that some dogs got a lot of money left to them when their owners died.

"Some of those dogs are millionaires," Kwami said. "I ain't no millionaire, and I ain't never read about no monkey millionaire, either. Which is why I say that dogs is smarter than monkeys."

It didn't make a lot of book sense, but it made a lot of seeing-is-believing sense. So when I thought about trying to teach Major to talk, I knew Kwami would go for the idea. As I said, he even tried to take credit for it.

We decided to take Major up to Leslie's house to teach him how to talk. The reason we decided to take him to Leslie's house was Leslie's grandmother stayed with them, and anytime you went to her house her grandmother would always come up with sandwiches or something.

Leslie had to go up first and make sure it was okay, and Kwami had to go home and tell his mother where he would be, and Judy took Major for a short walk while she was waiting for everyone to get ready. Anthony and Wayne were playing handball, and that left me and Kitty on the stoop. Me and Kitty and the beginning of the worst day in my life. Or, if not the worst day, at least the most embarrassing moment.

Kitty had this book of word games she was doing. What you had to do was unscramble a word. Like LOTEH is HOTEL scrambled. So she was doing these and I was thinking about how she had held my hand that time in the park and how I really liked her, and it all seemed pretty nice. So I asked Kitty if she wanted a picture of me.

"A picture of you?" She turned toward me real slow.

"Yeah." I was still feeling pretty good.

"What would I want a picture of you for?" she asked.

"Well, you could put it up on your wall or something," I said.

"Oh, I see," Kitty said. She was smiling a little and so I smiled a little, too. "And we could kind of be boyfriend and girlfriend."

"Yeah, kind of."

I was just about ready to figure out what picture I was going to give her when Kitty started laughing. She dropped her book and her pencil and really started to crack up. Then she rolled off the stoop and lay on the sidewalk. I never saw anybody laugh so hard. Wayne and Anthony came over and asked me what happened, and I said I didn't know. They tried to ask Kitty but she kept on laughing until the tears ran down her face. Finally she stopped enough to get back on the stoop and then she looked over at me and started laughing again until she was really crying.

Judy got back the same time that Leslie did. They asked Kitty what she was laughing about.

"This character wants me to . . ." She slapped her leg and started laughing again.

By this time I was really feeling bad because everyone was asking me why Kitty was laughing and naturally I didn't want to tell them.

"This character . . ." Kitty started telling what had happened again and was pointing at me.

"This character wants me to be his girlfriend and hang his picture on my wall." Kitty finished just in time for more laughter to come out.

Wayne started laughing, and Anthony started laughing, and Leslie just kind of held her hand over her mouth and started giggling. I also knew that when Kwami got back I'd have to go through the whole thing all over again.

I was right. After they told him why Kitty was laughing, Kwami said, "When you people getting married, man?" Kwami and his big mouth.

Kwami put his hand on my shoulder and I pushed it off.

"Oh, I see, only Kitty can put her hand on your shoulder," he said. "I can understand that."

Then everybody started to crack up again. We started up the stairs to Leslie's house and they were still on my case. I would have liked to punch out Kwami and Kitty right then and there. I really didn't think I was good enough to beat Kwami, though—in fact, I was pretty sure that I wasn't. I had had a fight with Kitty about a year ago and it came out even, but she had gotten taller so I just tried to forget about the whole thing. At least when we started teaching Major to talk they got off me.

"The first thing we got to do," said Kwami, "is to decide what he's going to say."

"Seems to me that if he says anything he'll be just about the coolest dog in the world," Kitty said.

"'Cause he's not a puppy, see?" Kwami lifted Major's chin slightly and looked at the dog as he spoke. "If he was a puppy you could teach him to say anything because he couldn't know any better. But he knows a lot of things now, so you got to be careful. Say you try to teach him to ask for a piece of fried chicken and he don't like fried chicken. He might not say anything just because he don't like what you're trying to teach him to say, dig?"

"Suppose he don't speak English?" Wayne asked.

"Don't be dumb, Wayne. American dogs all understand American and that's what we're going to teach Major to speak." Kwami gave Wayne a mean look. "And if you come up with one more dumb statement I'm going to wait till the next time it rains and then turn your nose upside down and drown you."

"So what are we going to teach Major to say?" I asked.

"Something patriotic," Kwami said. "So he'll feel good saying it."

"How about 'Give me liberty or give me death'?"

"He might think we're trying to bump him off."

"How about 'I regret that I have only one life—'"

"There you go with that dying stuff again," said Kwami.

"All that good patriotic stuff is about being dead or how you gonna die if something don't happen." Wayne was beginning to whine. Wayne always whined when somebody got on him.

"How about 'Tip-a-canoe and Tyler too'?"

"What's that mean?"

"I don't know. But it's got to be famous 'cause we learned it in history."

"The only thing you got to be to be famous in history is dead a bunch of years."

"I have it. How about 'Don't tread on me'?"

That was the famous American saying that we decided we would teach Major. The first thing that we did was to write the words on four large pieces of paper. Then Kwami and Kitty took turns reading the words to Major as Judy held him in her arms.

"Don't," Kwami said. He looked at Major and the dog seemed to understand him.

"Tread." Major still looked at Kwami.

"On." Major's tail began to wag.

"Me." Major squirmed.

"Now comes the hard part," Kitty said.

"You meaning getting my main dog here to talk?"

"No, just getting him to try," Kitty answered. "Dogs have been treated so badly over the years that they don't even try to talk. People usually just tell them to do things like sit down, and heel, and play dead, or get off the sidewalk, and that's what they think they're supposed to be doing. We got to convince Major that he's really supposed to talk."

"Leave that to the big K," Kwami said. "Kwami Green, teacher of frogs and dogs. Kwami Green, teacher supreme. Not only will I have your frog hopping, I'll get his foot to pattin' and not only will your dog talk, he'll speak Pig Latin."

"Don't be telling us that jive, tell Major," Judy said.

Kwami knelt down in front of Major and looked him right in the eye.

"Not only can you talk if you want to, Major, but you can converse on any level on which you choose. Now, dig, watch Kwami's lips as he speaks and then you repeat after me. Don't feel self-conscious if you don't get it right the first time 'cause I got until nearly three o'clock to get you together. Now, repeat after me: Don't . . . tread . . . on . . . me."

Major just looked at Kwami and wagged his tail.

Kwami got a little closer to Major until their noses were almost touching. "Look into my eyes and believe you can talk, dog," Kwami said. "I'm not teaching you anything jive to say. I'm teaching you some good stuff. This is a famous American saying. Now, I'm going to lift my head a little so you can watch my lips. See?" Kwami lifted his head so that Major could see his lips. "Now repeat after me." Kwami moved his lips in slow, exaggerated movements as he repeated the phrase. "Don't . . . tread . . . on . . . me!"

Major barked once.

"I think he got it!" Kwami said.

"All he said was woof!"

"He's warming up," Kwami said. "Give him a little time. What's the first thing you said when you started talking, turkey? You probably couldn't even say woof.

"Don't . . . tread . . . on . . . me!"

Major got closer to Kwami and licked him on the mouth. Kwami didn't move.

"Oh, sweat!" Wayne said. "Major kissed Kwami right on the lips and Kwami didn't even move."

"I can't reject him at this crucial point, man," Kwami said, but he looked a bit uncomfortable. "That would be like leaving a kid back in kindergarten.

"Don't . . . tread . . . on . . . me!"

Major licked Kwami's face again.

"I think Major's in love with Kwami." Judy grinned.

"That's what's wrong with you people." Kwami jumped up. "Anytime you try to do something serious you people start clowning around. You don't know nothing about no psychology or nothing. I give up."

Kwami sat down on a hassock and ate one of the grilled cheese sandwiches Leslie's grandmother had made. It was obvious that he was mad.

"Don't get upset, Kwami," Kitty said. "Maybe it just takes a while. We'll try again some other time."

"He might be ready to talk now," Judy said, "and just waiting for the right time. I know a woman who had a little boy who didn't talk until he was almost seven years old and then he just started talking one day like he had been talking all along."

"That's right," Leslie added. "I've heard of that kind of thing happening myself. He may get up in the middle of the night and start talking."

"You know, I was thinking," I said. "Maybe you made more progress than you think you did."

"What do you mean?" asked Kwami.

"Well, what's the saying you were trying to teach him?"

"Don't tread on me," answered Kwami.

"Well, he didn't tread on you, did he?"

Kwami just sighed.

That night I got home and my father was all set to have one of his "meaningful" conversations with me. We had one about twice a month. He usually gets on this real calm attitude and asks me something like what I thought of the crises in South Africa, or some other good thing like that. Only, halfway through my answer, he would interrupt to tell me what he thought, and that would be the end of the conversation. I'd sit there and listen until he was satisfied, then it would be over. Sometimes, just to be different, he would start the conversation off by asking me what I did that day. Then he would tell me what I should have been doing to better myself and what he would have been doing if he had been me. Then he'd watch television until he fell asleep in his chair.

This was one of those days when he was asking about what I did during the day, so I told him about trying to teach Major to talk.

"Trying to do what?" he asked.

"Trying to teach Major to talk," I repeated.

"Okay." He nodded his head up and down, but I knew he didn't believe a word I was saying. "Major is that little blond girl's dog, isn't he?"

"Yep," I said, really enjoying the fact that he didn't know what was going on.

"Well, okay," he said, switching on the television. "I guess you know what you're doing. By the way, there's something on your dresser for you. It was pushed under the door."

On the dresser was a white envelope with my name on it. Inside the envelope was a picture of Kitty. On the back it said 'to my friend, Dean.' Things were looking up.

If this selection was made into a situation comedy on television, which character would you like to be? Explain why.

Why does Dean, the narrator, say the day begins as "the worst day in [his] life"? How do you think he feels at the end of the day?

Why do you think Kitty acts the way she does when Dean asks if she wants his picture?

What might Kwami tell his father or mother about what he did that day? Give details to show Kwami's point of view.

WRITE   Write a set of instructions that explain how to teach an animal to do something. Your instructions may be serious or humorous.

WORDS ABOUT THE AUTHOR:
WALTER DEAN MYERS

Walter Dean Myers began reading at age four at the George Bruce library branch in Harlem. By age five, he was reading the newspaper to his foster mother while she did the housework. His own mother had died before he was three.

Always self-conscious about a speech impediment, Myers spent a lot of time alone, writing. But he never thought of writing as a career. Without enough money to go to college, Myers joined the army and served in it for three years. When he left the army, Myers tried several different jobs—messenger, mail clerk, factory worker—but his ambition was to write—anything. So, when he heard about a children's book writing contest, he decided to enter a picture-book manuscript. Myers won the contest and went on to write all kinds of books—novels about urban life, mysteries, and picture books.

Though Myers has written about both Black and White characters, his most acclaimed books are about Black young adults. He portrays African Americans differently than the way they are portrayed on television: "Blacks are still portrayed in the media primarily as entertainers and athletes. These are bad role models. . . . It's an absolute lie that a child can get out of the ghetto through sports. Figure that in New York City one of the medium-sized high schools has approximately 2,000 kids. There aren't that many people who play professional basketball, baseball, and football in the country. What kids really need is a role model that says education is good."

DOG TALES

Did you think Kwami and his friends would be successful teaching Vergil new tricks? Explain your answer.

WRITER'S WORKSHOP

Imagine that you are a newspaper columnist who writes columns about pet care. List all the reasons you can think of that people should keep their dogs on leashes. Use the most persuasive reasons from your list to write a newspaper column in which you try to convince people that dogs should always be on leashes when they are outside.

Writer's Choice
These selections tell about some people and their problems with dogs. You could write about your own pet or an unusual pet. Choose an idea and write about it. Think of a way to share your writing.

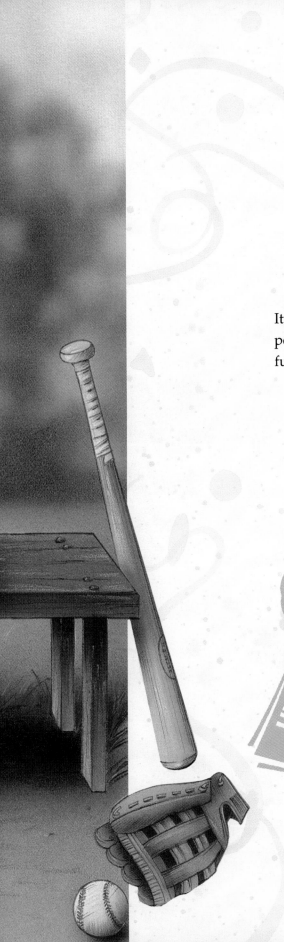

THEME

HUMOR FROM THE HEART

♥♥♥♥♥♥ ♥♥♥♥♥

It is not just out-of-the-ordinary events that make people laugh. Sometimes everyday life can be funny too.

CONTENTS

BETSY BYARS
Bingo Brown and the Language of Love
SLJ BEST BOOKS OF THE YEAR

by Betsy Byars ▼

illustrated by
Susan Melrath

Every time Bingo Brown smelled gingersnaps, he wanted to call Melissa long distance.

Actually, it was more of a burning desire than a want, Bingo decided. One minute ago he had been standing here, smiling at himself in the bathroom mirror, when without any warning he had caught a whiff of ginger. Now he had to call Melissa. Had to!

"Are you still admiring yourself?" his mom asked as she passed the door.

"Mom, come here a minute."

His mom leaned in the doorway.

"Is that a mustache on my face or what?"

"Dirt."

"Mom, you didn't even look."

"Do your lip like that."

Obediently Bingo stretched his upper lip down over his teeth.

His mom said, "Ah, yes, I was right the first time—dirt."

"Mom, it's not dirt. It's hair. There may be dirt on the hair but . . ." He leaned closer to the mirror. "I would be the first student in Roosevelt Middle School to have a mustache."

"Supper!" his dad called from the kitchen. His dad was stir-frying tonight.

"A lot of women would be thrilled to have a son with a mustache," Bingo said, "though I'll have to shave before I go to high school. You aren't allowed to have mustaches in high school."

Bingo moved away from the mirror, still watching himself. "You can't see it from here, but"—he stepped closer—"from right here, it's definitely a premature mustache."

"Bingo, supper's ready." His mother picked up a bill as she went through the living room.

Bingo followed quickly. "Hey, Dad," he said. "Notice anything different about me?"

His father turned—he was holding the wok in both hands—but before he could spy the mustache, Bingo's mom interrupted. "You will not believe the trouble I'm having with the telephone company."

Bingo's father said, "Oh?" He put down the wok and wiped his hands on his apron before taking the bill.

"Can you believe that? They're trying to tell me that somebody in this family made fifty-four dollars and twenty-nine cents worth of calls to a place called Bixby, Oklahoma."

Bingo gasped. He caught the door to keep from falling to his knees.

"Fifty-four dollars and twenty-nine cents! I told the phone company, 'Nobody in this family knows anybody in the whole state of Oklahoma, much less Bixby.' Bixby!"

Bingo said, "Mom—"

"The woman obviously did not believe me. Where does the telephone company get these idiots? I said to her, 'Are you calling me a liar?' She said, 'Now, Madame—'"

Bingo said, "Mom—"

"Wait till I'm through talking to your father, Bingo."

"This can't wait," Bingo said.

"Bingo, if it's about your invisible mustache—"

"It's n-not. I wish it were," he said, stuttering a little.

Bingo's mom sighed with impatience. Bingo knew that she got a lot of pleasure from a righteous battle with a big company and must hate his interruption. He hated it himself.

"So?" she said. "Be quick."

Bingo cleared his throat. He walked into the room in the heavy-footed way he walked in his dreams. He clutched the back of his chair for support.

"Remember Melissa—that girl that used to be in my room at school?"

"Yes, Bingo, get on with it."

"M-member I said she moved?" he was reverting back to the way he talked when he was a child.

"No, I don't, but go on."

"You have to remember! You and Dad drove me over to say good-bye! It was Grammy's birthday!"

"Yes, I remember that she moved. What about it, Bingo? Get on with it."

"Well, she m-moved to Oklahoma."

"Bixby, Oklahoma?"

Bingo nodded.

There was a long silence while his parents looked at him. The moment stretched like a rubber band. Before it snapped, Bingo cleared his throat to speak.

His mom beat him to it. "Are you telling me," she said in a voice that chilled his bones, "that you made"—she whipped the bill from his father's fingers and consulted it—"seven calls"—now she looked at him again—"for a total of"—eyes back to the bill—"fifty-four dollars and twenty-nine cents"—eyes back to him—"to this person in Bixby, Oklahoma?"

"She's not a person! She's Melissa! Anyway, Mom, you knew she had moved. I showed you the picture postcard she sent me."

"I thought she'd moved across town."

"She drew the postcard herself. I'll get it and show it to you if you don't believe me. It said, 'Greetings from Bixby, OK.' Her address was there, and her phone number.

"As soon as I got the postcard, I went into the living room. You were sitting on the sofa, studying for your real estate license. I showed you the postcard and asked you if I could call Melissa."

He was now clutching the back of the chair the way old people clutch walkers.

"My exact words were, 'Would it be all right if I called Melissa?' Your exact words were, 'Yes, but don't make a pest of yourself.' That's why the calls were so short, Mom. I didn't want to make a pest of myself!"

His mother was still looking at the bill. "I cannot believe this. Fifty-four dollars and twenty-nine cents worth of calls to Bixby, Oklahoma."

"I'm sorry, Mom. It was just a misunderstanding."

"I'll say."

"I should have explained it was long distance."

"I'll say."

Bingo's father said, "Well, it's done. Can we eat?" He glanced at the wok with a sigh. "Dinner's probably ruined."

"I don't see how you can eat when we owe the phone company fifty-four dollars and twenty-nine cents," Bingo's mother said.

"I can always eat."

"May I remind you that I have not actually gotten one single commission yet?"

"You may remind me. Now can we eat?"

In a sideways slip Bingo moved around the back of his chair and sat. He began to breathe again.

"Mom, can I ask one question?" Bingo asked, encouraged by the fact that his mother was sitting down, too.

"What?"

"Promise you won't get mad."

"I'm already furious. Just being mad would be a wonderful relief."

"Well, promise you won't get any madder."

"What is the question, Bingo?"

"Can I make one more call to Melissa? Just one? You can take it out of my allowance."

"What do you think?" she asked.

"Mom, it's important. I need to tell her why I won't be calling anymore."

"Bingo, when you put fifty-four dollars and twenty-nine cents into my hand, then we'll talk about telephone calls. Until then you are not to make any calls whatsoever. You are not to touch the telephone. Understood?"

"Understood."

"Now eat."

"I'm really not terribly hungry."

"Eat anyway."

Bingo helped himself to the stir-fry. The smell of ginger was overpowering now. It was coming from the wok! No wonder he was being driven mad. And if the mere scent of ginger had this

effect on him—it was at the moment twining around his head, pulling him like a noose toward the phone—what would the taste do to him? Would he run helplessly to the phone? Would he dial? Would he cry hoarsely to Melissa of his passion while his parents looked on in disgust?

Bingo broke off. He had promised to give up burning questions for the summer, cold turkey, but how could he do that when questions blazed like meteors across the sky of his mind? When they—

"Eat!"

Bingo put a small piece of chicken into his mouth. The taste of ginger, fortunately, did not live up to its smell.

As he swallowed, he rubbed his fingers over his upper lip. The mustache—as he had known it would be—was gone. It had come out like the groundhog, seen its shadow in the glare of his mom's anger, and done the sensible thing—made a U-turn and gone back underground.

After supper Bingo went to his room and pulled out his summer notebook. There were two headings in the notebook. One was "Trials of Today." Under that, Bingo now listed:

1. Parental misunderstanding of a mere phone bill and, more importantly, their total disregard and concern for the depth of my feeling for Melissa.

2. Disappearance of a beloved mustache and the accompanying new sensation of manliness.

3. Breaking my vow to give up burning questions for the summer.

4. Tasting ginger, which, while it did not drive me as mad as I had feared, has left me with a bad case of indigestion.

The second heading was "Triumphs of Today." Under that Bingo wrote only one word: none.

"Dear Melissa,"

Bingo lay on his Smurf sheets. He had always been able to count on a peaceful night's sleep on his Smurf sheets. But last Tuesday Billy Wentworth had come over, looked at his unmade bed, and smiled condescendingly at the Smurfs. After that, Bingo had not been easy on them.

Right now he was as uncomfortable as if he were lying on real Smurfs. However, he knew tonight was not a good time to ask his mother for more manly sheets.

He glanced at his letter and read what he had written.

"Dear Melissa,"

He retraced the comma and stared up at the ceiling.

Writing Melissa was not the same as calling her, because as soon as she heard his voice, she always said something like, "Oh, Bingo, it's you! That's exactly who I was hoping it would be."

Her voice would actually change, get warmer somehow, deeper with pleasure. Girls were fortunate to have high voices so they could deepen them so effectively. His own voice got higher when he was pleased, which wasn't a good effect at all.

If his mom only knew how it made a man feel to hear a girl's voice deepen with pleasure. He knew there was no point in trying to explain that to his mom. His mom was in no mood to understand.

After supper, he had asked her for a stamp, one measly stamp, and she had said, "I'll sell you one."

"Sell?"

"Yes, sell." She walked to the desk, tore one stamp off the roll, and held it out. Her other hand was out, too, palm up. "That'll be twenty-five cents."

"Mom!"

"One quarter, please."

Then he had to go through the indignity of borrowing a quarter from his father.

And after all that humiliation, he couldn't seem to get the letter started.

"Dear Melissa,"

He changed the comma to a semicolon.

"Dear Melissa;"

As he lay there, he thought of that terrible, heart-stopping moment when he had learned Melissa was moving.

It had been a spring day. Mr. Mark, their teacher, was back after his motorcycle accident. He walked with a cane, but there was the general feeling in the classroom that everything was back to normal at last and things would go well for the rest of the year.

Bingo was at the pencil sharpener, grinding down a pencil, admiring the April day, when Melissa stood up behind him.

Bingo had not heard the snap of pencil lead, but his pulse quickened because he thought Melissa was going to join him. He and Melissa had had pleasant, even thrilling, pencil sharpener encounters before.

He turned toward her with an encouraging smile. Melissa was standing stiffly by her desk, arms at her sides. She said, "Mr. Mark?"

"Yes, Melissa."

"May I make an announcement?"

"Can't it wait a bit? Some people are still working on their journals."

Melissa's eyes filled with tears. She started to sit down, and Mr. Mark reconsidered. "Gang, is anyone working so hard on his or her journal that their train of thought would be shattered forever by an announcement from Melissa?" His bright eyes looked them over. "Melissa, it's all yours."

"This is a personal announcement. Is that all right?"

He nodded.

Bingo's heart had moved up into his throat. As soon as he had seen the tears, he had started closing the distance between them. He and Melissa were now two feet apart, close enough so that Bingo could see her tears were getting ready to spill.

Bingo could stand tears if they stayed where they were supposed to, but if they spilled . . .

"My dad," Melissa said. She looked down at her desk and blinked her eyes. Two tears plopped onto her open journal.

Bingo gasped with concern.

"My father," she began again with brave determination, "is being transferred to Bixby, Oklahoma, and we'll be moving next month. I hope some of you will write to me. That's the end of my announcement."

Melissa sat down, but Bingo stood there. He vowed with silent fervor to write daily, and to write such letters as the post office had never seen, letters so thick postal workers would marvel at their weight. His letters would go down in postal history. Years later, an unusually thick letter would be referred to as a "Bingo letter." His letters—

"Bingo?"

"What? Oh, yes, Mr. Mark?"

"Melissa said that was the end of her announcement. I believe you might begin to think in terms of returning to your seat."

"I'm on my way."

That memory caused Bingo to pick up his pen with renewed determination.

"Well," he wrote firmly, "I guess you're surprised to be getting a letter from me instead of a call, but our telephone bill came today."

There was a knock on his window. Bingo leaped in alarm. No one had ever knocked on his window before. He was as shocked as if someone had knocked on his forehead.

He got to his feet. Whoever was doing the knocking was either incredibly stupid or incredibly impolite!

Bingo strode to the window and bent down. The reflection of his own face, frowning, was all he could see.

"Who's out there?" Bingo asked. "Didn't your mother ever teach you not to knock on—"

"It's me, Worm Brain."

Bingo swallowed the rest of his words.

"Open up."

"Oh, all right." Bingo opened the window and looked at Billy Wentworth. Billy was wearing his camouflage T-shirt. "What can I do for you?" Bingo asked.

"Why can't you talk on the phone?"

"Who says I can't?"

"Your mom. I called and asked to speak to you, and she said, 'Bingo is no longer allowed to receive calls.' Bam! She could have busted my eardrum. You being punished?"

"Unjustly," Bingo said.

"Is there any other way? What'd you do?"

"I ran up a fifty-four-dollar phone bill," Bingo said. "So, why did you knock on my window?"

"I wanted to ask you something. Well, my mom wanted me to ask you something."

"What?"

"We're going on vacation and we can't take our dog."

"Misty the poodle?" Bingo asked.

A feeling of dread began deep within Bingo's soul. Before Misty had moved next door, Bingo had not known it was possible to actually dread being stared at by a dog.

"Mom, she stares at me all the time, right into my eyes."

"That's known as eye contact," his mom had said, in her usual unconcerned way.

"And I don't know what she wants me to do. Mom, she can stare for hours. Sometimes I have to go in the house!"

"You better get used to eye contact," his mom had said. "Later on you'll be having eye contact with girls, and if you run in the house then, you've blown it."

"Yes," Billy Wentworth went on, "Misty the poodle. How many dogs you think we got, Worm Brain?"

"That's the only one I know about."

"You want to keep her?" Billy asked.

"Well, I don't know. We're probably going on vacation, too."

"Go ask your mom."

"Er, I think she's in the bathroom just—"

"No, she's in the living room. I saw her through the window."

Bingo went into the living room. "We can't keep Misty, can we?"

His mother glanced up. "The Wentworth dog? Sure, why not?"

Bingo lowered his voice. "Mom, you know I can't stand to be stared at by that dog. She—"

"You ought to be ashamed of yourself, Bingo Brown, to mind being looked at by a ten-year-old half-blind miniature poodle with kidney trouble!"

Bingo stood in silence. Up until the business of the phone bill, Bingo and his mother had been getting along unusually well. His mother had a new job selling real estate, and even though she hadn't gotten a commission yet, she was very happy.

"Tell Billy yes!" she went on forcefully. "Tell Billy we will be glad to keep the poodle. Certainly it will make up, in part, for their having to keep you last fall."

This last humiliation, being put in the category of a dog, made Bingo turn—he hoped with dignity—and start back to his room.

He went directly to Billy, at the open window. "Yes," he said. He closed the window and went back to his bed.

Well, at least he now had something to write to Melissa. "Billy Wentworth's poodle, Misty, will be spending next week with me, so this will probably be my last letter for a while. I'll have to keep an eye on her. Sincerely, but somewhat despondently, Bingo Brown"

He fumbled under the bed for his summer notebook and flipped to "Trials of Today." He wrote:

1. Continued animosity from my mother and the cruel implication that I am, socially, on the same level with a poodle.

2. Having the privacy of my bedroom invaded by an enemy agent.

3. Inability to create postal history by writing Bingo letters to Melissa.

4. Continued failure in reaching the mainstream of life.

It made Bingo feel somewhat better to have survived four trials of this magnitude, but he still had only one word to list under "Triumphs": none.

Bingo tied on his apron and looked down at the cookbook on the counter. It was open to page forty-four: chicken breasts in tarragon sauce.

Bingo cracked his knuckles, cheflike.

"Let's see," he said. Beneath his breath, he began to read the ingredients. "Chicken breasts—I have those. Onions—I have those. . . ."

In order to make up for his phone debt, Bingo had agreed to cook supper for his mom and dad for thirty-six nights. His mom had originally wanted fifty-four. "That's fair, Bingo," she had argued, "a dollar a night." But he had bargained her up to a dollar and a half.

"All right, thirty-six," she'd said finally.

This was Bingo's third supper, and he was ready for something from the spice rack. As he rummaged through the little scented tins, he caught the aroma of ginger, but with a quick glance of regret at the telephone, he continued to rummage.

"Tarragon . . . tarragon. I wonder if that's anything like oregano? Garlic . . . dill . . .

"What else do I need to do? Oven"—Bingo turned on the oven with a flourish—"three-fifty." Bingo had already learned that 350 degrees was the perfect cooking temperature. He never planned to use anything else. For example, this tarragon chicken thing called for—he checked the recipe—275, but—

The phone rang and Bingo moved sideways toward it. Bingo was now allowed to answer the phone, but he couldn't place any calls. With his eyes on the cookbook, he picked up the phone.

"Hello."

A voice said, "Could I speak to Bingo, please?"

It was a girl's voice!

Bingo was so shocked he almost dropped the phone. He had not spoken to a girl on the phone since his last call to Melissa. He did not think he would ever speak to a girl again.

Now not only was he going to speak to a girl, but it was a strange girl.

A rash of questions burned out of control in his brain. Why

was a strange girl calling him? What did she want? He was too young for magazine subscriptions, wasn't he? Could she be conducting a survey? Could it be a woman with a little girl voice wanting him to contribute to a good cause? Could it be—

"Is this Bingo?"

"Well, this is Bingo Brown," he said, emphasizing his last name.

That was quick thinking. After all, there might be other Bingos. He didn't want to proceed with the conversation only to have it end with something like, "Well, boo, I thought I was talking to Bingo Schwartznecker."

"Oh, Bingo. Hi!"

There was a faint tinge of that long-remembered deepening of pleasure. How did girls do that? Did they have two sets of vocal cords, one for everyday use and one for special occasions? Did they shift gears like a car and their motor actually—

"Bingo," she went on in a more businesslike voice, "you don't know me, but my name's Cici, with two *i*'s."

"Oh?"

Bingo's free hand had begun to twitch nervously, as if it wanted to make some sort of gesture but was unsure what the gesture should be.

Bingo put his hand firmly into his apron pocket.

"Cici Boles."

"Oh."

"I'm a good friend of Melissa's, you know? I lived next door to her. But you probably don't recognize my name because I'm not in your grade."

"Oh."

"I'm the same age as Melissa, but I started school in Georgia, and you have to already be, like, five to start kindergarten in Georgia. . . . Are you still there?"

"Yes." At least, Bingo thought, he had broken his string of *oh*s.

"Because I, like, panic when people don't answer me. I think they've gone. I think I'm talking to, you know, empty air!"

"I'm still here."

"Then answer me."

"I will."

"You're probably wondering why I called."

This time Bingo answered as quickly as a bride. "I do."

"You're going to think this is silly, Bingo, but promise you won't hang up on me."

"I promise."

Bingo switched hands, putting his telephone hand—it had started twitching now—into his pocket.

"Well, here goes. Melissa wants me to take a picture of you with my camera and send it to her. See, I knew you'd think it was silly."

Bingo breathed deeply. This was the last thing he had expected, that a girl would want to take his picture. Even his own parents never particularly wanted to take his picture, and now this! A mixed-sex photography session!

"Are you still there?" Cici asked.

"Yes."

"See, you have to answer or I panic. Like, he's gone! I am talking to empty air!"

"Actually, I was thinking."

"Oh, I never stop to do that. I just, you know, go for it. What were you thinking?"

"Er, when do you want to take this picture?"

"Would right now be too soon?"

"Right now?" Bingo bent down to check his reflection in the toaster oven.

"Yes."

Bingo reached for his apron strings. He untied them in a flourish.

"I'll need a few minutes."

"Sure."

Bingo wondered if there was any mousse in the house. He hadn't used mousse since Melissa moved. He had given it up in a sort of religious way, like for Lent.

But if he didn't use it now, Melissa might not recognize him. Worse, she might think he had gotten ugly!

"Better make that fifteen minutes," Bingo told Cici Boles.

He turned off the oven and ran for the bathroom.

As he ran, heart pumping in a way it had not pumped in months, Bingo had burning questions.

Could this mixed-sex photography session turn out to be my first Triumph of Today? Or, more likely, will it be just another Trial?

Will there be mousse?

Is a Triumph possible without mousse?

With hands that trembled, Bingo opened the medicine cabinet. "Ah," he sighed, "mousse." And he reached for the can.

Bingo was at the window, watching for Cici Boles. He was getting unhappier by the minute.

Bingo was not ready for another mixed-sex conversation. He had realized this when he was moussing his hair. He hadn't had one in such a long time that he wasn't sure he even remembered how.

Plus the fact that the only good mixed-sex conversations were those with Melissa. When you had a mixed-sex conversation with Melissa, it was like the Olympics of mixed-sex conversations.

This mixed-sex conversation might be mercifully brief.

"Smile."

"Like this?"

"Yes."

Click.

"Thank you."

"Anytime."

But still, with girls you could never tell. This Cici Boles might come up with something like, "By the way, are you doing anything Friday night?"

This thought made his heart throw itself against the wall of his chest, as if to escape.

"By the way, are you doing anything Friday night?" was exactly the kind of mixed-sex conversation he wasn't up to. Probably never would be.

He glanced at his watch. Was it too late to cancel? "Hello, Cici, this is Bingo Brown." No. No! "This is Bingo Brown's brother, and Bingo has been called out of town unexpectedly and—"

Bingo gasped. He leaned forward. A bicycle was coming down the street. There was a girl on the bike!

No, Bingo decided, putting one hand over his racing heart, this girl was much too big and too blond to be Cici. This girl was more like a high school girl—no, make that a college girl.

Bingo gasped again. There was a camera around the big blond's neck.

Bingo ran back to the kitchen so she wouldn't see him peering out the glass. When the bell rang, he walked in a brisk, businesslike manner to the door.

She said, "Well, here I am. I'm Cici."

Bingo said, "So you are."

He attempted to put his hands in his apron pockets, but his apron was back in the kitchen. He slid his hands sideways into his jeans pockets.

"I'll have to take the picture outside," Cici said, "because, you know, I don't have a flash. Is that all right?"

"Yes."

"Front or back?"

Bingo smiled slightly. "Perhaps you should take it from the front so Melissa can see my face. Otherwise, she might not recognize me."

"Oh, Bingo." Cici blinked rapidly. "I meant front yard or backyard."

"Just a little humor," Bingo mumbled.

"Oh, I get it. . . . front . . . back." With one finger—this was awkward because she had long, long nails—she pointed to her front and then her back. "Melissa told me how funny you are."

She might be as big and blond as a college girl, but that was where the similarity ended, Bingo thought. "Backyard," he said firmly.

In silence, Bingo led the way through the living room, the kitchen, past his apron and the half-skinned chicken breasts, out the back door.

"Oh, let's do it over here by the fence," Cici said. "The roses make a nice background. Melissa's the kind that couldn't care less about the background. She just wants a picture of you. I'm the kind that always likes to do my best."

Bingo stood stiffly against the rosebush, with his hands in his pockets. He said quickly, "How's this?"

"It's fine, but I'm not in focus yet."

"Go ahead and take it," he said through tight lips. He'd only

415

been smiling for a short time, but the day was so hot his teeth were dry.

"There! I've almost got it."

Why had he let this happen? Bingo wondered. Here he was with the sun in his eyes, smelling of mousse, while important chicken breasts waited to be skinned in the kitchen.

Well, he understood now man's weakness for having his picture made. He was living proof of it. The trouble with living proofs was that you actually had to become the living proof before you—

A voice from the other side of the hedge said, "Hey, Worm Brain, is that you over there?"

It was Billy Wentworth!

Bingo pulled back into the rosebush. Thorns raked his arms, but he did not feel the sting. He wanted to pull the branches around him like a blanket and disappear.

"Take it! Quick!"

"All right! Oops! Now see what you made me do! My thumb was on the lens. I got a picture of my thumb. Now we've got to start all over again."

"Hurry!"

But it was too late. Billy Wentworth, in his camouflage T-shirt, peered over the hedge. His monkey eyes landed on Bingo.

He gave a small smile, as if he had come across an enemy without any means of defense. "Here's Misty and her stuff," he said.

"In a minute," Bingo said stiffly. The main reason he had chosen the back of the house was because there was less likelihood of being spotted. Now this!

Wentworth's smile continued. "What are you taking the Worm Brain's picture for?"

"I'm doing it for a friend of mine, you know, Melissa? She wants a picture of him."

"What for?"

"I don't know. What does anybody want a picture for? To look at. Smile, Bingo."

Bingo pulled his lips back into a smile.

"Not like that. Smile like you mean it."

Bingo suddenly remembered how natural it had been to smile at Melissa. Sometimes, at night in the darkness, he had smiled just thinking of smiling at her.

"Perfect!" Cici said. "She'll love it!"

The camera clicked and Bingo started gratefully for the hedge. Without meeting Wentworth's eyes, he took Misty and her suitcase.

Cici followed. She said, "Oh, let me get one of you with the dog. This will be so precious. Hold the dog up! Oh, its face is so sweet. Could I pat it?"

Wentworth said, "Be my guest."

Cici rushed forward and scratched Misty's head with what Bingo now realized were press-on nails, some of which needed repressing.

"Oh, and it has a little suitcase for its things. Can I look in it?"

Bingo surrendered the handle of the suitcase and stood stiffly, looking over the roof of his garage.

Cici knelt and unzipped the bag—another awkward move with the press-ons. She reached inside and pulled out a squeaky rubber newspaper.

"Oh, isn't that precious? It has its own newspaper. And I can tell that it really plays with it." Cici browsed through the rest of the suitcase. "Oh, vitamins and a chew stick, and what's this in the bottom?"

"Her blanket," Billy Wentworth said.

Bingo turned in astonishment. He stared at Billy Wentworth. Billy's voice had actually deepened on those two words, "her blanket."

What was happening here?

"It's like a real baby blanket."

"It is a real baby blanket," Wentworth said. His voice was almost purring with pleasure now, like a well-tuned engine. "It was mine."

Bingo's mouth dropped open as he gaped at the faded blue square. Billy Wentworth had once been a baby!

"She doesn't have, like, you know, a basket or bed or something?"

"No, she just drags her blanket around and sleeps where she wants to."

"That's what a little neighbor of mine does! I baby-sit her. Bingo, is this darling little dog yours or"—she nodded to the face above the hedge—"his?"

"His."

"And I," the deep voice from the hedge said, "am Willy Bentworth."

Would you like to read more about Bingo Brown? Explain why or why not.

Do you think it is reasonable of Mrs. Brown to make Bingo prepare dinner as repayment for the phone bill? State an argument either for or against Mrs. Brown's decision.

What is the purpose of the photo session?

In what ways does Bingo act differently with girls than with boys? Why does his behavior seem funny?

WRITE Write a list of your own trials and triumphs of the day. Choose a day you found particularly eventful.

WORDS *from the* AUTHOR

AWARD-WINNING
AUTHOR

Betsy Byars

Betsy Byars explains how she writes and how she created the character of Bingo Brown.

When I write, I do it in longhand first. Then I put it into the word processor. I used to write eight hours a day when I was first starting out, because I needed that discipline. Sometimes when I'm writing a book, it doesn't seem like I'm writing. In the beginning, before I put down the words, I just stare into space. People may think I'm doing nothing, but I'm actually writing the book in my head. Writing is easier for me at this stage of my career, and more pleasurable. I used to resist the idea of writing sequels. But now I find I enjoy following the same characters. You know your characters, you know what they're thinking. It's a romp, really.

As far as Bingo Brown goes, the name Bingo came to me first. I was writing another book, and I was trying to think of a name for one of the characters. When Bingo popped into my mind, I thought, I don't want to waste that name on a minor character. Bingo just stuck with me. I thought of how he came to have that name—when he was being born, the doctor yelled out, "Bingo!" Finally I put aside the book I was writing. Bingo had just taken over.

I've received more mail about Bingo than any other character I've ever written about. I think kids like him because they identify with him. He's so open and vulnerable. He's really out there. Boys write and tell me they *are* Bingo. Girls enjoy Bingo, too. It gives them insight into the ways boys think. I really do enjoy writing the Bingo books because I like writing humor best.

SEVENTH GRADE

by Gary Soto
illustrated by Hector Garrido

saludo de vato: greeting

Bonjour: Hello; good day

Très bien. Parlez-vous français?: Very good. Do you speak French?

Le bateau est sur l'eau.: The boat is on the water.

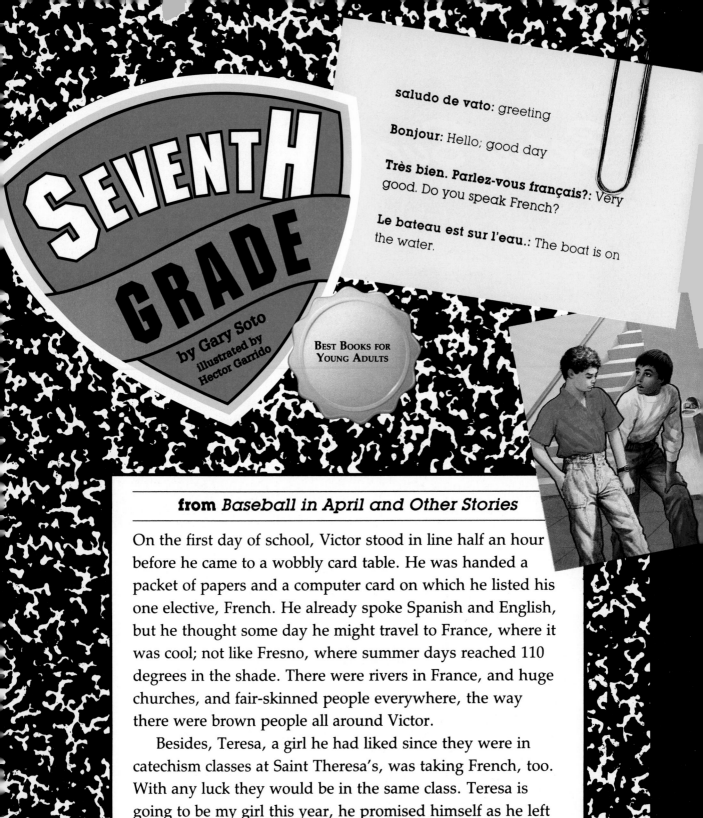

from *Baseball in April and Other Stories*

On the first day of school, Victor stood in line half an hour before he came to a wobbly card table. He was handed a packet of papers and a computer card on which he listed his one elective, French. He already spoke Spanish and English, but he thought some day he might travel to France, where it was cool; not like Fresno, where summer days reached 110 degrees in the shade. There were rivers in France, and huge churches, and fair-skinned people everywhere, the way there were brown people all around Victor.

Besides, Teresa, a girl he had liked since they were in catechism classes at Saint Theresa's, was taking French, too. With any luck they would be in the same class. Teresa is going to be my girl this year, he promised himself as he left the gym full of students in their new fall clothes. She was cute. And good at math, too, Victor thought as he walked down the hall to his homeroom. He ran into his friend, Michael Torres, by the water fountain that never turned off.

They shook hands, *raza*-style, and jerked their heads at one another in a *saludo de vato*. "How come you're making a face?" asked Victor.

"I ain't making a face, *ese*. This *is* my face." Michael said his face had changed during the summer. He had read a *GQ* magazine that his older brother borrowed from the Book Mobile and noticed that the male models all had the same look on their faces. They would stand, one arm around a beautiful woman, and *scowl*. They would sit at a pool, their rippled stomachs dark with shadow, and *scowl*. They would sit at dinner tables, cool drinks in their hands, and *scowl*.

"I think it works," Michael said. He scowled and let his upper lip quiver. His teeth showed along with the ferocity of his soul. "Belinda Reyes walked by a while ago and looked at me," he said.

Victor didn't say anything, though he thought his friend looked pretty strange. They talked about recent movies, baseball, their parents, and the horrors of picking grapes in order to buy their fall clothes. Picking grapes was like living in Siberia, except hot and more boring.

"What classes are you taking?" Michael said, scowling.

"French. How 'bout you?"

"Spanish. I ain't so good at it, even if I'm Mexican."

"I'm not either, but I'm better at it than math, that's for sure."

A tinny, three-beat bell propelled students to their homerooms. The two friends socked each other in the arm and went their ways, Victor thinking, man, that's weird. Michael thinks making a face makes him handsome.

On the way to his homeroom, Victor tried a scowl. He felt foolish, until out of the corner of his eye he saw a girl looking at him. Umm, he thought, maybe it does work. He scowled with greater conviction.

In homeroom, roll was taken, emergency cards were passed out, and they were given a bulletin to take home to their parents. The principal, Mr. Belton, spoke over the crackling loudspeaker, welcoming the students to a new year, new experiences, and new friendships. The students squirmed in their chairs and ignored him. They were anxious to go to first period. Victor sat calmly, thinking of Teresa, who sat two rows away, reading a paperback novel. This would be his lucky year. She was in his homeroom, and would probably be in his English and math classes. And, of course, French.

The bell rang for first period, and the students herded noisily through the door. Only Teresa lingered, talking with the homeroom teacher.

"So you think I should talk to Mrs. Gaines?" she asked the teacher. "She would know about ballet?"

"She would be a good bet," the teacher said. Then added, "Or the gym teacher, Mrs. Garza."

Victor lingered, keeping his head down and staring at his desk. He wanted to leave when she did so he could bump into her and say something clever.

He watched her on the sly. As she turned to leave, he stood up and hurried to the door, where he managed to catch her eye. She smiled and said, "Hi, Victor."

He smiled back and said, "Yeah, that's me." His brown face blushed. Why hadn't he said, "Hi, Teresa," or "How was your summer?" or something nice?

As Teresa walked down the hall, Victor walked the other way, looking back, admiring how gracefully she walked, one foot in front of the other. So much for being in the same class, he thought. As he trudged to English, he practiced scowling.

In English they reviewed the parts of speech. Mr. Lucas, a portly man, waddled down the aisle, asking, "What is a noun?"

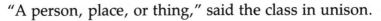

"A person, place, or thing," said the class in unison.

"Yes, now somebody give me an example of a person—you, Victor Rodriguez."

"Teresa," Victor said automatically. Some of the girls giggled. They knew he had a crush on Teresa. He felt himself blushing again.

"Correct," Mr. Lucas said. "Now provide me with a place."

Mr. Lucas called on a freckled kid who answered, "Teresa's house with a kitchen full of big brothers."

After English, Victor had math, his weakest subject. He sat in the back by the window, hoping that he would not be called on. Victor understood most of the problems, but some of the stuff looked like the teacher made it up as she went along. It was confusing, like the inside of a watch.

After math he had a fifteen-minute break, then social studies, and, finally, lunch. He bought a tuna casserole with buttered rolls, some fruit cocktail, and milk. He sat with Michael, who practiced scowling between bites.

Girls walked by and looked at him.

"See what I mean, Vic?" Michael scowled. "They love it."

"Yeah, I guess so."

They ate slowly, Victor scanning the horizon for a glimpse of Teresa. He didn't see her. She must have brought lunch, he thought, and is eating outside. Victor scraped his plate and left Michael, who was busy scowling at a girl two tables away.

The small, triangle-shaped campus bustled with students talking about their new classes. Everyone was in a sunny mood. Victor hurried to the bag lunch area, where he sat down and opened his math book. He moved his lips as if he were reading, but his mind was somewhere else. He raised his eyes slowly and looked around. No Teresa.

He lowered his eyes, pretending to study, then looked slowly to the left. No Teresa. He turned a page in the book and stared at some math problems that scared him because he knew he would have to do them eventually. He looked to the right. Still no sign of her. He stretched out lazily in an attempt to disguise his snooping.

Then he saw her. She was sitting with a girlfriend under a plum tree. Victor moved to a table near her and daydreamed about taking her to a movie. When the bell sounded, Teresa looked up, and their eyes met. She smiled sweetly and gathered her books. Her next class was French, same as Victor's.

They were among the last students to arrive in class, so all the good desks in the back had already been taken. Victor was forced to sit near the front, a few desks away from Teresa, while Mr. Bueller wrote French words on the chalkboard. The bell rang, and Mr. Bueller wiped his hands, turned to the class, and said, *"Bonjour."*

"Bonjour," braved a few students.

"Bonjour," Victor whispered. He wondered if Teresa heard him.

Mr. Bueller said that if the students studied hard, at the end of the year they could go to France and be understood by the populace.

One kid raised his hand and asked, "What's 'populace'?"

"The people, the people of France."

Mr. Bueller asked if anyone knew French. Victor raised his hand, wanting to impress Teresa. The teacher beamed and said, *"Très bien. Parlez-vous français?"*

Victor didn't know what to say. The teacher wet his lips and asked something else in French. The room grew silent. Victor felt all eyes staring at him. He tried to bluff his way out by making noises that sounded French.

"La me vava me con le grandma," he said uncertainly.

Mr. Bueller, wrinkling his face in curiosity, asked him to speak up.

Great rosebushes of red bloomed on Victor's cheeks. A river of nervous sweat ran down his palms. He felt awful. Teresa sat a few desks away, no doubt thinking he was a fool. Without looking at Mr. Bueller, Victor mumbled, "Frenchie oh wewe gee in September."

Mr. Bueller asked Victor to repeat what he had said.

"Frenchie oh wewe gee in September," Victor repeated.

Mr. Bueller understood that the boy didn't know French and turned away. He walked to the blackboard and pointed to the words on the board with his steel-edged ruler.

"*Le bateau,*" he sang.

"*Le bateau,*" the students repeated.

"*Le bateau est sur l'eau,*" he sang.

"*Le bateau est sur l'eau.*"

Victor was too weak from failure to join the class. He stared at the board and wished he had taken Spanish, not French. Better yet, he wished he could start his life over. He had never been so embarrassed. He bit his thumb until he tore off a sliver of skin.

The bell sounded for fifth period, and Victor shot out of the room, avoiding the stares of the other kids, but had to return for his math book. He looked sheepishly at the teacher, who was erasing the board, then widened his eyes in terror at Teresa who stood in front of him. "I didn't know you knew French," she said. "That was good."

Mr. Bueller looked at Victor, and Victor looked back. Oh please, don't say anything, Victor pleaded with his eyes. I'll wash your car, mow your lawn, walk your dog—anything! I'll be your best student, and I'll clean your erasers after school.

Mr. Bueller shuffled through the papers on his desk. He smiled and hummed as he sat down to work. He remembered his college years when he dated a girlfriend in borrowed cars. She thought he was rich because each time

427

he picked her up he had a different car. It was fun until he had spent all his money on her and had to write home to his parents because he was broke.

Victor couldn't stand to look at Teresa. He was sweaty with shame. "Yeah, well, I picked up a few things from movies and books and stuff like that." They left the class together. Teresa asked him if he would help her with her French.

"Sure, anytime," Victor said.

"I won't be bothering you, will I?"

"Oh no, I like being bothered."

"*Bonjour*," Teresa said, leaving him outside her next class. She smiled and pushed wisps of hair from her face.

"Yeah, right, *bonjour*," Victor said. He turned and headed to his class. The rosebushes of shame on his face became bouquets of love. Teresa is a great girl, he thought. And Mr. Bueller is a good guy.

He raced to metal shop. After metal shop there was biology, and after biology a long sprint to the public library, where he checked out three French textbooks.

He was going to like seventh grade.

Do you think Victor should have pretended to know French? Explain your answer.

What does Victor think of Michael's scowling?

What does Mr. Bueller do when he realizes that Victor doesn't know French?

Why do you think Victor will like seventh grade?

WRITE   Imagine that Teresa finds out that Victor doesn't really know French. Write a short letter from Teresa's point of view telling what she thinks and feels about Victor after discovering the truth.

HUMOR FROM THE HEART

Both Bingo and Victor become embarrassed in the classroom. How are these scenes similar? How are they different?

WRITER'S WORKSHOP

Imagine that Bingo and Victor are friends. What advice would they give each other about talking to girls? What might happen to them if they ran into a girl they knew from school? Write a short play about their meeting. Keep in mind how each character acts with girls.

Writer's Choice

What do you think of when you hear the words *humor from the heart* now that you have read Bingo's and Victor's stories? Think about your response and write about it. Read your response aloud or tell others how you feel.

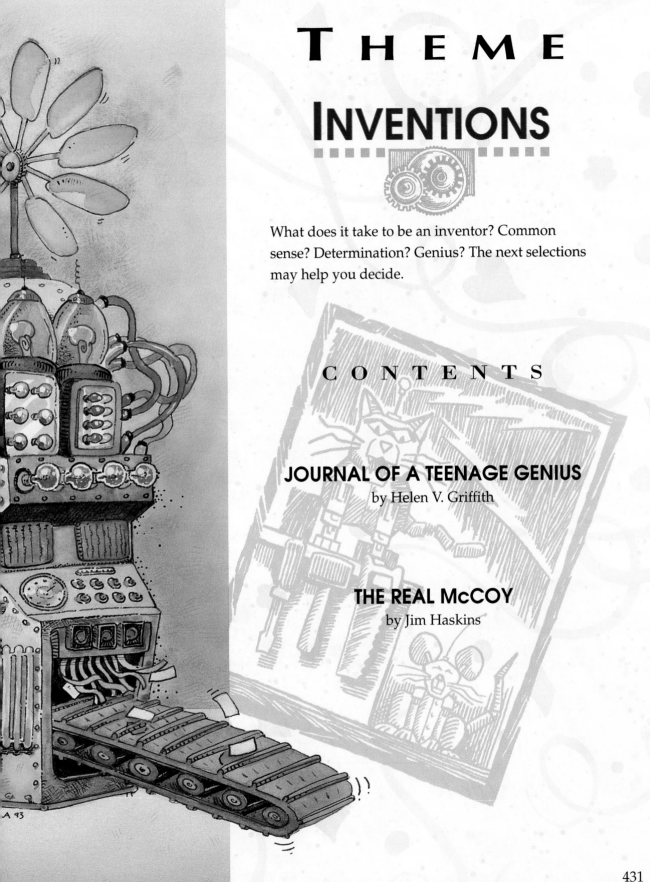

THEME

INVENTIONS

What does it take to be an inventor? Common sense? Determination? Genius? The next selections may help you decide.

CONTENTS

JOURNAL OF A

TEENAGE

GENIUS

by Helen V. Griffith

illustrated by John Ceballos

SATURDAY, AUGUST 20

9:00 A.M.

Success at last! I have achieved what nobody outside of a science-fiction novel has ever done! My place in history is secure.

In another fifteen minutes the liquid bubbling in a beaker over my Bunsen burner should reach sufficient heat for the necessary chemical change to occur, and I will have invented the formula for the transmutation of matter!

Since the dawn of science, men have attempted to discover this secret, but it took me, a young, unknown genius, to finally come up with a formula that will change one kind of metal into another. Iron into gold! Tin into silver! Wow! Mind-boggling, isn't it?

I feel that I should write my impressions of this great moment, because naturally the scientific world will be agog with curiosity about me and my work once my discovery comes to light.

First, some background. It's been a long, lonely road, and being a genius really isn't as great as you might think, mainly because nobody else takes you seriously. My mother, for instance. My mother, *especially.* She keeps saying that I don't understand what I'm doing, that it's dangerous, that I should perform my experiments in school with supervision. In other words, she talks as if I'm just an ordinary kid playing with a chemistry set.

I am working under very difficult conditions in our unequipped, poorly lit garage because my own mother has turned me out of our own basement, just because of a few minor mishaps that could happen to any scientist.

Such as the odor from one of my earlier experiments forcing us all to leave the house for the weekend. But did I complain? Even though it set me back in my work, I put up with the inconvenience and relaxed and enjoyed swimming in the motel pool.

My parents weren't such good sports, though. My mother even claimed the smell made Toodles sick. As if anything could get Toodles down. My mother worries over him as if he were a baby, and he's just a hyperactive little poodle. I think we probably would have stayed home that weekend, smell and all, if it hadn't been for Toodles.

The latest incident is the one that drove me from my basement lab, and the whole thing was Toodles's fault. He was watching me work, like the nosy little mutt he is, and just as I picked up a test tube of one of my chemical solutions, he jumped up on my leg to get a better look and I spilled the stuff right in his face.

You never heard such yelping in your life. And you never saw the mother of a teenage boy move so fast. She was down those basement stairs in about two leaps, sized up the situation in an instant, and, brushing aside my reassurances that the chemical—although irritating—was not dangerous, she stuck Toodles in the sink and turned the water on him.

After she washed him off he quit yelping and just stood there shivering and looking about half his size. I would have welcomed a quiet discussion of my mother's misunderstanding of the danger involved, but she kept saying things like, "That does it" and "This can't go on" and "That kid," so it seemed wise to defer any more explanations and to move my equipment before she did something that we would both regret.

When my journal is made public, she'll realize how wrong she was, and though I'm sorry the world has to know of her lack of foresight, still this is a factual account of the greatest scientific breakthrough of the age, and it may be an encouragement to other geniuses not to give up just because their mothers don't have faith in them or appreciate their abilities.

At this moment the solution in the beaker is bubbling away like crazy. I must record this while it is happening. It's turning wild colors and boiling and steaming and—oh, wow—it almost looks like it's going to . . .

SAME DAY

10:00 A.M.

It did. And I'm in big trouble.

I'm writing this in my room where I have come to escape a mother's wrath. She keeps saying, "You could have been injured, maybe even killed," and she's not even concerned that the greatest scientific discovery of the age just blew up.

There wasn't really that much damage, anyway. I mean, what's a broken window? The real disaster is that I failed. And my notebook with all my calculations in it is gone, destroyed in the explosion.

The work of years is now a puddle on the garage floor, and it doesn't take a genius to know that my experimenting days are over, at least around here. My father will be less than joyful when he sees the garage, and my mother is overreacting, as usual.

She must be calming down somewhat, though, because I can hear her calling her precious Toodles. If anything can cheer her up, he will.

And so, fellow scientists, I shall take this opportunity to return to the garage and see what I can salvage.

Scientists of the world, what I have to report now is going to set you all on your ears.

As I slipped into the garage I almost stumbled over a little curly-haired boy about five or six years old who was sitting all huddled up on the floor, wearing a bewildered expression and nothing else.

"Who are you?" I asked. "Are you lost or something?"

The little boy's lips started to quiver and he said, "I'm Toodles."

Being a genius, a horrible suspicion of the truth dawned on me instantly, but I said skeptically, "What do you mean, you're Toodles?" and right away the little boy started to cry out loud, and between sobs he said, "I *am* Toodles, only there's something wrong with me. I came in to look around and I found a nice puddle on the floor and I lapped it up and then I felt funny and all at once my fur was gone and I'm cold. And my nose is dry."

Well, you can imagine my amazement, not to mention my consternation, because my experiments in the transmutation of matter were not for the purpose of turning little dogs into little boys, but evidently that is just what has happened.

Some words of my mother's about danger and fooling with things I don't understand sneaked into my brain, but I pushed them out again. How could it be wrong to try to advance scientific knowledge?

Looking at Toodles, though, crying tears all over the garage floor, I saw that there was more to science than cold facts. I hadn't given any thought to what effects my experiment might have. I'd had no idea it would work on living creatures. And if there was a way to reverse the process, I hadn't discovered it yet.

And now my normally nimble brain seems to be clogged with molasses. I can't really grasp what has happened, much less predict the consequences.

All I've done so far is sneak Toodles into my room and dress him in some old stuff of mine. Everything is too big, but that can't be helped. Nobody noticed he wasn't wearing clothes when he was a furry little dog, but now it's obvious to the most casual observer.

At this moment Mom is combing the neighborhood for the dog-Toodles, while the boy-Toodles is here being his usual busybody self, only on two legs instead of four. He's having a great time going through my bureau drawers, something he wasn't able to do when he had only paws, and he seems contented enough at the moment, at least. But what am I going to do with him? How will I explain him? Without the formula to prove my story no one will believe the truth, I know that. They'll probably think I'm a kidnapper. I can see it now—like those old movies on TV—me, in a hard chair in the middle of a bare room, bright lights blinding me, harsh voices saying over and over, "Okay, talk. Where did you get the kid?" and me saying, "He's my mother's poodle."

As you can see, the situation is impossible. Not to mention that I seem to be losing my grip. I must not panic. There has to be a sane, reasonable way out of this mess.

Poor Mom. I can hear her in the yard now, calling Toodles. I know she's worr—

That was close. When Toodles heard my mother's voice, he took off down the hall like a shot, but I grabbed him and dragged him back here and we came to an understanding. I hope.

I told him that for the time being his name is Tommy, he's new in the neighborhood, and he's a *boy.* I guess he understands what I mean. He just said, "Okay," and then curled up in a ball on the floor and sighed.

My mother is calling me for lunch. This is the moment of truth. Will Toodles act the way I told him, or will he drink out of his bowl on the floor? Will Mom recognize Toodles in human form? Will she notice that the clothes he's wearing are mine? And will I break out into hysterical laughter I feel coming on?

If this is the last notation in my journal, you can draw your own conclusions.

Fellow scientists, Toodles cannot be depended on. He is not a boy, he is a two-footed poodle.

As soon as we entered the kitchen, he ran to my mother, wrapped his arms around her knees, and looked up at her adoringly with his big brown eyes.

"Why, who is this?" said my mother. "What a cute little boy."

I told her my prearranged story and felt like a rat for lying, although it wasn't totally a lie, he *was* a new kid in town. Then Mom told me about Toodles being gone and how worried she was and I felt like a *double* rat.

We got through lunch somehow, but it was touch and go, especially as Tommy showed a tendency to lap his soup and afterward asked for a biscuit. Fortunately my mother thought he meant a cookie.

After he ate his cookie he sat on the floor by my mother's chair and put his chin on her knee. With those brown eyes and that mop of curly hair he looked so much like the original Toodles that I didn't see how my mother could help but notice.

She didn't though. She just looked kind of surprised and said, "Such a friendly child. Do you go to school, Tommy?"

Toodles said, "No, but I'm smart. I can sit up, roll over, and shake hands."

Before he could demonstrate, I grabbed him by the wrist and pulled him out of the room after me, muttering something about reading him a story.

And now here I am back in my room trying to calm Toodles, who is whimpering that he is cold and that everything feels wrong.

Poor Toodles. I've really messed up his life, not to mention how bad my mother feels without her little dog. I'm beginning to think I never should have tried such a risky experiment by myself. I should have anticipated the possibility of something going wrong and been prepared for it. I should have listened to my mo—no, I won't go that far.

Enough of these recriminations. Away with this self-pity. Am I a genius or a clod? I have things to do. I have to set up a new lab somewhere. And I need a place to hide Toodles while I work on an antidote. In the meantime he stays locked in my room. I'm afraid of what he might do if he saw a cat.

Joy and euphoria! My mother is mad at me, my scientific career is at an end, my whole experiment was a flop, but I don't care. And do you know why I don't care, scientists of the world? Because Toodles is Toodles again! Yes, little curly-haired Tommy is now little curly-haired Toodles, and I've never seen a happier dog.

I was standing in the garage waiting for an inspiration when my mother came storming in wanting to know what kind of game I was playing. It seems she heard whining and scratching at my bedroom door, and when she opened it, there was Toodles, all tangled up in some old clothes. She thinks I was hiding him from her as some kind of a mixed-up joke.

I'll square things with her later, but for now I just want to sit here in my old garage-lab and appreciate my narrow escape.

Apparently the emulsion wasn't stable. The experiment was an even worse failure than I thought as first. What luck! I feel as if I've been given a second chance at life. I don't have to be a scientist. I'll be a wrestler or a cowboy. I'll be sensible. I'll throw all my scientific equipment away and sit around watching TV like everybody else.

Little Toodles just came bouncing into the garage in high spirits. I wonder if he remembers anything about his adventure. He doesn't act like it. He's playing with something he found outside, throwing it into the air pouncing on it when it lands. Hey, wait a minute—

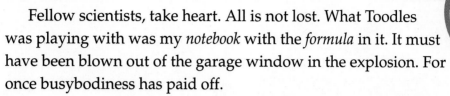
Fellow scientists, take heart. All is not lost. What Toodles was playing with was my *notebook* with the *formula* in it. It must have been blown out of the garage window in the explosion. For once busybodiness has paid off.

I can't wait to get to work. I'll set up a secret laboratory. I'll work day and night. I'll—what am I saying? Haven't I learned anything from today's experiences?

The answer to that question is—you bet I have!

I'll cool it for a while. I'll study. I'll plan. I'll listen to other scientists and try (despite my convictions to the contrary) to stop thinking I know it all.

I'll still be a genius, but I'll be a *smart* genius.

Do you think the main character is "just an ordinary kid playing with a chemistry set?" Explain your opinion.

How does Toodles look and act the same after the explosion? How is he different?

WRITE   The main character feels that no one takes him seriously. Write a journal entry about a time when you have felt misunderstood.

THE Real McCoy

NOTABLE CHILDREN'S TRADE BOOK IN SOCIAL STUDIES

outward
Dreams
Black
Inventors
and Their
Inventions
jim
haskins

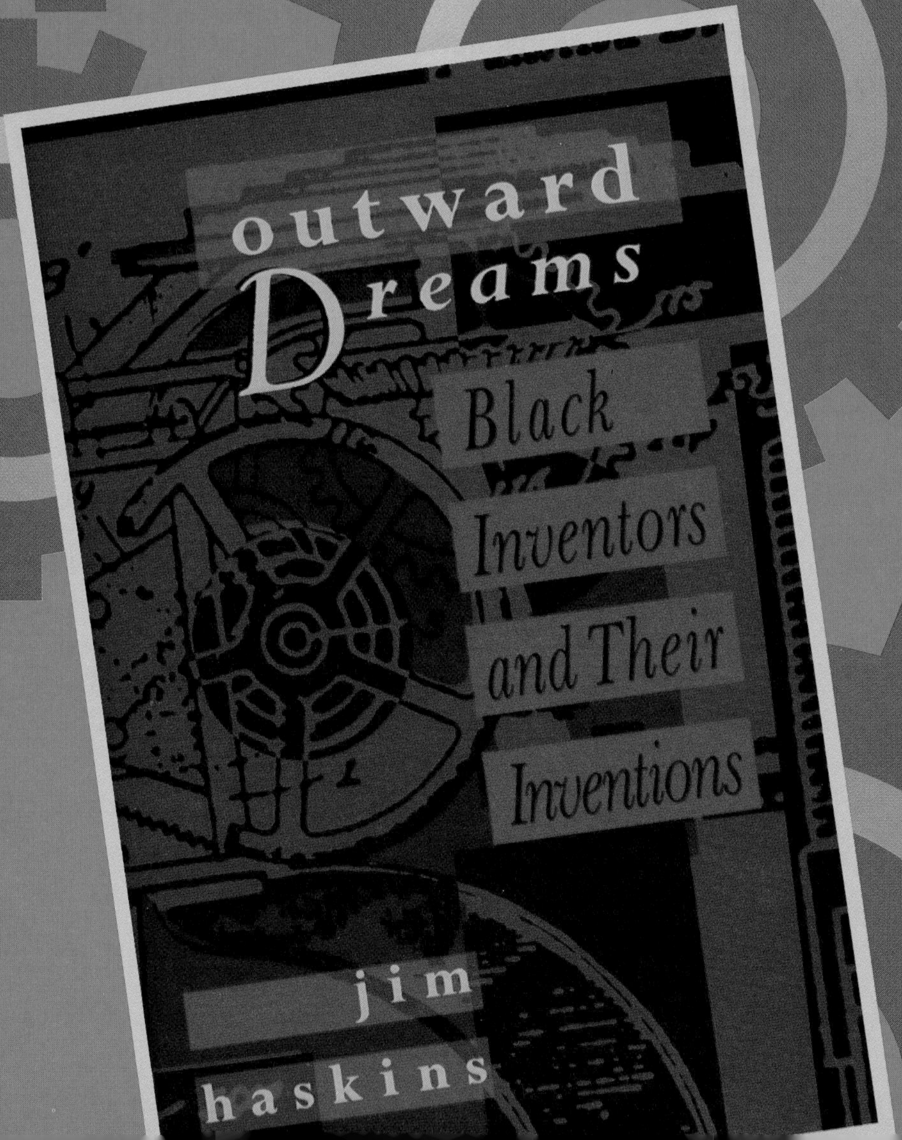

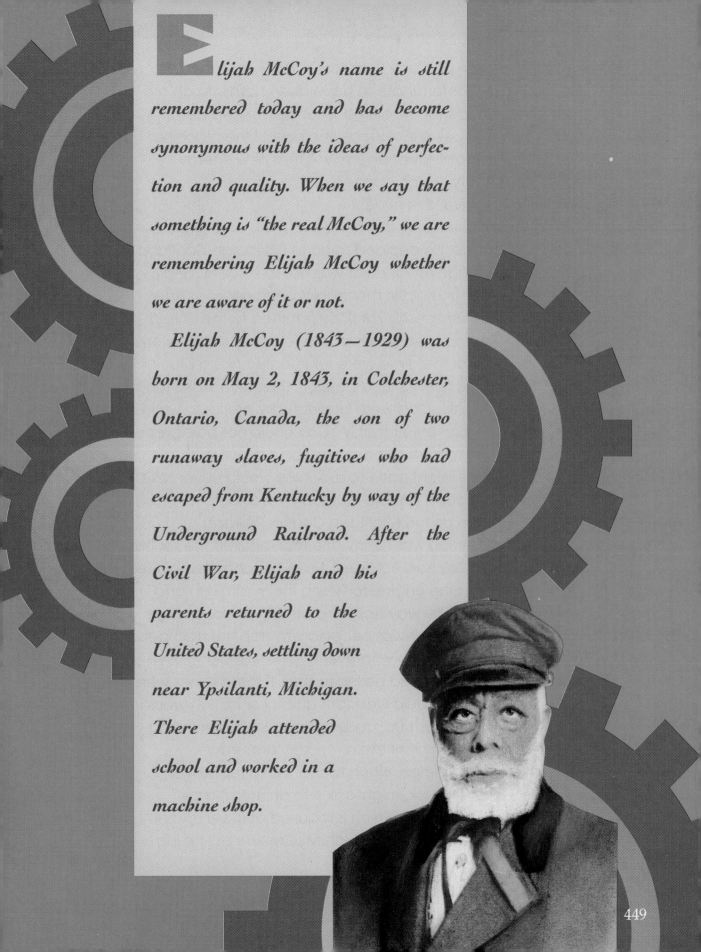

*E*lijah McCoy's name is still remembered today and has become synonymous with the ideas of perfection and quality. When we say that something is "the real McCoy," we are remembering Elijah McCoy whether we are aware of it or not.

Elijah McCoy (1843–1929) was born on May 2, 1843, in Colchester, Ontario, Canada, the son of two runaway slaves, fugitives who had escaped from Kentucky by way of the Underground Railroad. After the Civil War, Elijah and his parents returned to the United States, settling down near Ypsilanti, Michigan. There Elijah attended school and worked in a machine shop.

McCoy, even as a boy, was fascinated with machines and tools. He was fortunate to have been born into an era that suited him perfectly, a time when newer and better machines were being invented—the age of the machine. Following the footsteps of steam was that new energy source, electricity, which opened up even more opportunities for the inventive mind.

McCoy's interest only deepened with the emergence of each new device. He decided to go to Edinburgh, Scotland, where the bias against his color was not so evident, and serve an apprenticeship in mechanical engineering. After finishing his apprenticeship, McCoy returned to the United States a mechanical engineer, eager to put his skills to work. But companies at that time were reluctant to hire a black man to fill such a highly skilled position. Prejudice was strong and the myth that blacks were intellectually inferior to whites persisted. Companies felt that McCoy could not possibly be as skilled as he claimed to be and, even if he were, the white workers he might have to supervise would never take orders from a black man. The only job he was able to find was as a fireman on the Michigan Central Railroad.

The job of fireman was hardly one that required the sophisticated skills McCoy had obtained. His duties consisted of fueling the firebox of the engine to "keep the steam up" and oiling the engine. The way train and other types of engines were built meant that it was necessary to stop the train periodically—or to shut down whatever engine was being used—so the moving parts could be lubricated. If the engines were not oiled, the parts would wear out quickly or friction would cause the parts to heat up, causing fires. Hand-lubricating engines was an inefficient but necessary procedure.

Many men or women, when faced with a repetitive, essentially mindless task, might sink into an unthinking lethargy, doing only that which is required of them and no more, but this was not true of Elijah McCoy. He did his job—

oiling the engines—but that job led him to become interested in the problems of lubricating any kind of machinery that was in motion. For two years he worked on the problem on his own time in his own homemade machine shop. His initial idea was to manufacture the machines with canals cut into them with connecting devices between their various parts to distribute the oil throughout the machines while they were running. He wanted to make lubrication automatic.

Finally McCoy came up with what he called "the lubricating cup," or "drip cup." The lubricating cup was a small container filled with oil, with a stop cock to regulate the flow of oil into the parts of a moving machine. The lubricating or drip cup seemed an obvious invention, yet no one had thought of it before McCoy; it has since been described as the "key device in perfecting the overall lubrication system used in large industry today." With a drip cup installed, it was no longer necessary to shut down a machine in order to oil it, thus saving both time and money. McCoy received his patent for it on July 12, 1872.

The drip cup could be used on machinery of all types and it was quickly adopted by machine manufacturers everywhere. Of course, there were imitators, but their devices were not as effective or efficient as McCoy's. It soon became standard practice for an equipment buyer to inquire if the machine contained "the real McCoy." So commonly was this expression used that it soon spread outside the machine industry and came to have the general meaning of the "real thing," of perfection. Nowadays if someone states they want "the real McCoy," it is taken to mean that they want the genuine article, the best, not a shoddy imitation. In 1872, of course, Elijah McCoy could not foresee that his name would soon become associated with the idea of perfection. All he knew was that the thing worked and worked well on machinery of all types.

The lubrication of machinery fascinated McCoy and he continued to work in that area. In 1892 he invented and patented a number of devices for lubricating locomotive engines. These inventions were used in all western railroads and on steamers plying the Great Lakes. Eventually McCoy would invent a total of twenty-three lubricators for different kinds of equipment and, in 1920, he applied his system to air brakes on vehicles.

During his lifetime, Elijah McCoy was awarded over fifty-seven patents and became known as one of the most prolific black inventors of the nineteenth century. In addition to his patents on various kinds of lubricating systems, he also received patents for such "homey" objects as an ironing table (a forerunner of today's ironing board), a lawn sprinkler, a steam dome and a dope cup (a cup for administering medicine). He eventually founded the Elijah McCoy Manufacturing Company in Detroit, Michigan, to develop and sell his inventions.

Until his death in 1929, McCoy continued working and inventing, sometimes patenting two or three new devices a year. Today, although many may not know who he was or what he did, his name remains to remind us of the idea of quality, and the steady, ceaseless roar of machinery is a paean to his inventiveness.

What did you learn about Elijah McCoy that surprised you?

WRITE   What item would you label as a "real McCoy"? Write a paragraph describing your choice and explaining why you would give it that label.

INVENTIONS

Is the teenage genius's invention a real McCoy? Explain your answer.

WRITER'S WORKSHOP

Imagine that you must explain to someone how to operate a simple invention found in your home. Write a how-to paragraph giving step-by-step directions.

Writer's Choice
Inventions make life easier and sometimes more fun. What inventions do you like? Choose an idea about inventions and write about it. Share it with a friend.

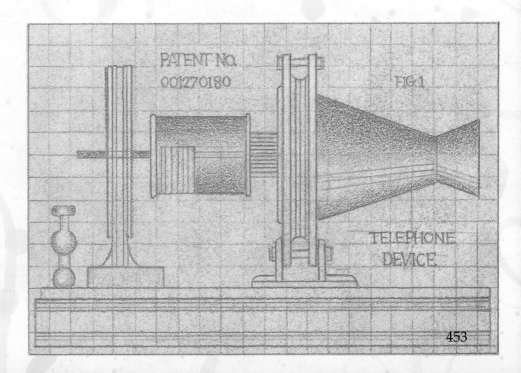

CONNECTIONS

MULTICULTURAL CONNECTION

AMERICA'S FAVORITE COMEDIAN

For over thirty years, comedian/actor/author William Henry Cosby, Jr., has brought light moments to millions of people around the world.

Raised in one of Philadelphia's poorest neighborhoods, Bill Cosby was determined to succeed. Cosby's mother, Anna, always believed in him. Later, a teacher who recognized his spark encouraged him to explore his knack for entertaining by taking roles in school plays.

While attending Temple University, where he later earned a doctorate in education, Cosby began his first professional comic appearances. By the end of 1969, he had won three Emmy Awards and had broken many racial barriers that had existed for African Americans in television.

In 1984, Bill Cosby created and began starring in the most popular situation comedy ever, "The Cosby Show," which became a smash success because it portrayed the humor and warmth of American family life so well.

Have a "Celebrity Day" in class. Find out about a favorite TV or movie legend. Bring information on his or her background and achievements to share.

454

SOCIAL STUDIES CONNECTION

BREAKING THE BARRIER

Bill Cosby broke racial barriers when he became a television star in the 1960s. Television is only one of many careers that were once closed to Blacks and others. With a partner, research entertainment, sports, or other professional careers that once excluded African Americans, Latinos, or others. Find out when these barriers were broken and by whom. Present your findings, using visual aids if possible.

LANGUAGE ARTS CONNECTION

PEOPLE ARE FUNNY

Bill Cosby's most successful comic routines, television comedies, and books are based on the idea that everyday life can be funny. With a group, write a skit about a typical day at school or in a home in your community. Use made-up names and places in your skit. Choose a director, assign roles, make simple props, and practice your skit. Perform your skit for your classmates.

UNIT FIVE 5

OCEANS

I must go down to the seas again,
To the lonely sea and the sky....
John Masefield

People have always been drawn to the sea. Some, like this poet, love the sea for its beauty, mystery, and excitement. Others, including the peoples of the Pacific islands, the Inuit, and the Eskimos, value and respect the sea because for centuries it has provided their livelihood. Develop your own appreciation as you read about the power and mystery of the earth's oceans.

THEMES

BOOKSHELF

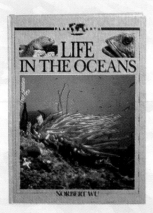

LIFE IN THE OCEANS

BY NORBERT WU

A photojournalist explores the many forms of life in the coral reefs, the kelp forest, the open sea, and the deep ocean.

Outstanding Science Trade Book for Children

HARCOURT BRACE LIBRARY BOOK

SEALS, SEA LIONS AND WALRUSES

BY DOROTHY HINSHAW PATENT

Wonderful photographs illustrate a wealth of information about these appealing animals. The book also tells how people are moving to protect them and why this is important.

Outstanding Science Trade Book for Children

HARCOURT BRACE LIBRARY BOOK

MEETING THE WHALES

BY ERICH HOYT

Will whales and humans ever communicate? Scientists study the huge brains of whales and closely observe their behaviors. Stunning photographs show whales and scientists in action.

SHADOW SHARK

BY COLIN THIELE

Twelve-year-old Joe barely escapes being killed by a huge shark called Scarface. But the hunt for Scarface off the Australian coast brings even more danger.

ALA Notable Book

EARTHQUAKES

BY SEYMOUR SIMON

This stunning book describes the destructive power of earthquakes, including the havoc they wreak by creating tremendous ocean waves.

Award-Winning Author

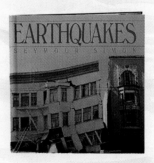

THEME

THE FROZEN OCEAN

◆◆◆◆◆◆◆ ◆ ◆◆◆◆◆◆◆

Everyone believed the gigantic ocean liner was unsinkable. Then late one evening, the *Titanic* met another titan of the sea—one even larger and more powerful. In the following selections, you'll learn how these two giants met and how the result of their tragic meeting still fascinates people today.

CONTENTS

461

Earth's Changing CLIMATE

by Roy A. Gallant

illustrated by Catherine Farley

AWARD-WINNING AUTHOR

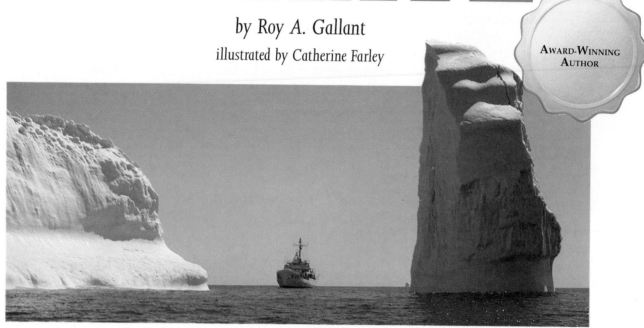

A LAND OF "PERMANENT" SNOW

Greenland is a gleaming land of snow capped with an ice sheet that began to form some 100,000 years ago. Today this ice sheet is nearly 3 kilometers (about 2 miles) thick in places. But Greenland has not always been ice-covered, nor will it always be. Each day giant chunks of ice "calve," or break, off the west coast of Greenland's ice cap and plunge into the sea as mammoth icebergs. Every year an estimated 500 cubic kilometers (125 cubic miles) of ice plunges into the frigid waters of Baffin Bay along Greenland's west coast. In only a few minutes Rink Glacier, for example, may dump 500 million tons of ice into Baffin Bay. Some of this ice forms icebergs a mile or more long and towering 100 meters (300 feet) above the water. In a very active year, from 10,000 to 15,000 icebergs may break loose from Greenland's frigid shores.

The Voyage of Iceberg X

Perhaps it was on Tuesday, June 8, 1909, that one such giant slab of ice calved off the end of one of Greenland's numerous glaciers and plunged into the dark waters near Melville Bay. A mammoth iceberg was born. Although we can compute a date for this event, no one will ever know the *exact* place or the date when this event occurred, but occur it did.

At a pace of about four kilometers (2.5 miles) a day, this small mountain of ice began drifting southward on a three-year journey that was to shock the world. First it drifted across Baffin Bay toward the east coast of Baffin Island, a journey taking about six months. Here it was caught up and moved along a little faster by the cold, southward-flowing Labrador Current, which flows down out of the Arctic Ocean. Six months later it had been carried down through the Davis Strait and into the Labrador Sea off the north coast of Newfoundland. Two years from the time it had started its journey, it was a few hundred kilometers due east of Gander, Newfoundland. By this time it had traveled a total of some 3,000 kilometers (1,800 miles). Though it had lost much of its bulk through melting, it was still a floating mountain of ice, a pilotless "ship" passively moving southward ever nearer the busy North Atlantic shipping lanes.

There we will leave our titan of ice and turn to a titan of a different sort.

The world's newest, largest, and most luxurious ocean liner sailed on her maiden voyage from Southampton, England, on April 10, 1912. She was the White Star liner *Titanic*, 274 meters (883 feet) long and displacing 66,000 tons of water. She was described as "a Victorian palace afloat." According to a London *Times* editorial, "everything had been done to make the huge vessel unsinkable, and her owners believed her to be so."

On leaving Southampton, she crossed the English Channel to France and then steered a course for Newfoundland. Aboard her were 1,315 passengers and 885 crew, although there is some confusion about these exact numbers. Her skipper was 60-year-old Edward J. Smith, a veteran of 40 years at sea. He was to retire after the *Titanic*'s maiden voyage.

For several weeks before the *Titanic* had sailed, the United States Navy's Hydrographic Office in Washington had been aware of large fields of ice drifting southward from Greenland and into the shipping lanes which the *Titanic* had now entered. The first alarm about icebergs crackled into the *Titanic*'s radio room at 9:00 A.M., Sunday, April 14: "WESTBOUND STEAMER *CARONIA* REPORTS BERGS AND FIELD ICE IN 42°N FROM 49° to 51°W APRIL 12. COMPLIMENTS." The *Titanic* was on course only a few kilometers south of that position. The ship's chief radio operator acknowledged the message. At 11:45 A.M. the *Amerika,* another liner, informed the *Titanic* it had just passed "two large icebergs" just south of the position reported by the *Caronia.* Again the *Titanic* acknowledged. At 1:42 P.M. the Greek steamer *Athenia* reported seeing icebergs directly along the *Titanic*'s course. Then at 9:40 P.M. the steamer *Mesaba* advised the *Titanic* of "much heavy pack ice and great numbers of large icebergs."

In spite of these several warnings, neither the owner of the *Titanic,* who was among the passengers, nor others on board showed much concern. They finally held to their belief that this

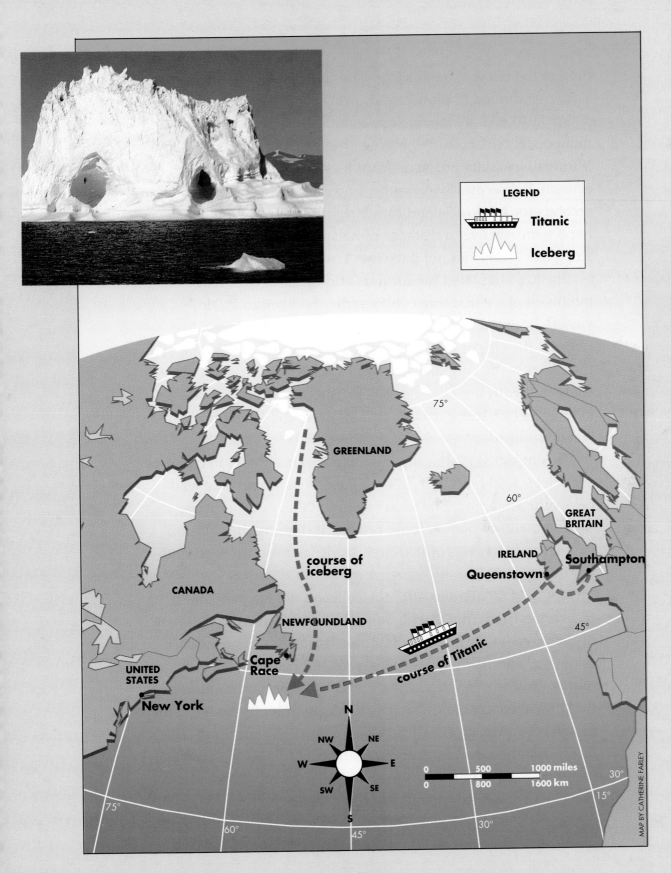

LEGEND

Titanic

Iceberg

75°

GREENLAND

60°

GREAT BRITAIN

IRELAND

Southampton

Queenstown

course of iceberg

CANADA

NEWFOUNDLAND

45°

Cape Race

course of Titanic

UNITED STATES

New York

N

NW   NE

W   E

SW   SE

S

0   500   1000 miles

0   800   1600 km

30°

15°

75°

60°

45°

30°

MAP BY CATHERINE FARLEY

465

titan of the sea was unsinkable. The night was clear and the *Titanic* continued to plow ahead, nearly at top speed.

At 11:40 P.M. a lookout sighted an iceberg dead ahead and immediately informed the bridge officer. Chief Officer William M. Murdoch instantly ordered "Hard a-starboard! Engines full astern!" But so massive was the *Titanic* that it would take 30 seconds for her to respond to full right rudder. It would also take her 4 minutes, over a distance of half a nautical mile, to come to a stop. The *Titanic* did not have that kind of time on her side.

She kept her fated rendezvous and collided with that mountain of ice that three years earlier had begun its slow voyage from the waters of Baffin Bay. Although melting had reduced the size of Iceberg X during its voyage, at the time of the collision the berg displaced an estimated 200,000 tons compared with the *Titanic*'s 66,000. The collision took place 650 kilometers (400 miles) south of Cape Race, the southern tip of Newfoundland.

The impact was almost gentle, but it was enough to cut open a 93-meter (300-foot) gash in the *Titanic*'s starboard side well below the waterline. She soon began to take on water more rapidly than her pumps could remove it. During the collision, chunks and shavings of that prehistoric ice heap tumbled onto her decks.

Not until 30 minutes after the collision did Captain Smith, recovering from utter disbelief over the seriousness of the matter, decide to radio for help. By that time it was five minutes past midnight, and many passengers were still below decks in their rooms. Several ships heard the *Titanic*'s distress calls and replied that they were on their way to her. Meanwhile, the order to man the lifeboats was given, with "women and children first." The fact is that there were not enough lifeboats for all, so sure had her owners been of her unsinkability, and many of those lifeboats launched were filled to only half their capacity.

At 2:20 A.M., Monday, April 15, the unsinkable *Titanic* slipped beneath the calm, black sea. First her bow nosed under, then for a brief moment she was poised with her stern straight up, as though in one last salute. People in lifeboats reported seeing her that way, her propellers plainly visible. Then she silently slipped beneath the calm sea to the bottom, where she remains to this day.

The *Carpathia* was first to arrive on the scene. By this time it was 3:30 A.M. and the frigid waters had claimed those unable to swim to the lifeboats helplessly standing by. Of the total of 2,201 on board the *Titanic*, 700 were saved. By the time the rescue ships had done all they could and left with the handful of survivors, all that remained was scattered debris and a small mountain of ice with a chip taken out of its side, a relic of the past formed some tens of thousands of years ago.

What interesting fact about icebergs did you learn from the selection?

Why does the author of this selection describe the iceberg as "a pilotless ship"?

Might the *Titanic*'s disaster have been avoided? Explain your answer.

Why were only 700 people from the *Titanic* saved?

WRITE Think about the feelings that people had about the *Titanic* when it sailed and after it sank. Write two headlines to show how today's newspapers would have treated each of these events.

Sea Slant

On up the sea slant,
On up the horizon,
This ship limps.

The bone of her nose fog-gray,
The heart of her sea-strong,
She came a long way,
She goes a long way.

Flying Cloud by J.E. Buttersworth, Private Collection

by Carl Sandburg

On up the horizon,
On up the sea-slant,
She limps sea-strong, fog-gray.

She is a green-lit night gray
She comes and goes in the sea fog.
Up the horizon slant she limps.

AWARD-WINNING
POET

EXPLORING THE

TITANIC

by Robert D. Ballard

How the greatest ship ever lost — was found

KEN MARSCHALL 1982

*I*n 1985, Dr. Robert D. Ballard led an expedition to find the wreck of the **Titanic**. For six weeks, a team of French researchers led by Jean-Louis Michel used advanced sonar devices to scan the ocean floor for signs of the great ship. However, their search failed to turn up any clues. Ballard's American team then took over the search, using video cameras mounted on a special underwater sled called the **Argo**. Using the research ship **Knorr** to haul such a device through the deep ocean waters was "like towing a kite on a two-and-a-half mile string," Ballard said. Time was running out. The **Knorr** would soon have to be back in port for another expedition. The **Argo** provided their best hope of finding the lost ship.

illustrated by Ken Marschall

471

Discovery

Towing *Argo* was a delicate balancing act. If the Knorr went too fast, *Argo* would lift too high off the bottom for its cameras to see anything. If the ship's speed was too slow, *Argo* might crash to the bottom. Keeping a tight balance between *Knorr* and *Argo* was very tough and very tiring work. And it went on hour after hour, day after day.

Then we had only five days left to go. The crunch had come. Suddenly the ocean seemed huge, and our doubts began to grow. Was the *Titanic* really in our carefully plotted search area? If so, surely something would have shown up on our monitor screens by now. Were we looking in the wrong place? Would we return empty-handed? I began to feel a rising panic.

In a last-ditch effort, we decided to check out a tiny portion of ocean bottom that Jean-Louis and his SAR[1] sonar system had missed because of strong currents. We headed to that spot ten miles away.

[1] SAR: The French sonar system Sonar Acoustique Remorqué [sō•när′ä•kōōs•tēk′ rə•môr•kā′], a device that locates and takes pictures of underwater objects by sending out sound waves and picking up their echoes with a microphone.

But as we began to tow *Argo* back and forth across the new search area, our hopes really began to fade. There was nothing down there. By now the routine inside our control room had become mind-numbing: hour after hour of staring at video images of flat bottom mud. On top of that, we were exhausted. The strain of it all was getting to us, and the boredom was becoming unbearable. Then, with a bad turn in the weather and only four days left, we reached our lowest point. I began to face total defeat.

Just after midnight on September 1, I went to my bunk for some rest, and the night shift led by Jean-Louis

manned their stations. About an hour into their watch, one of the team members asked the others, "What are we going to do to keep ourselves awake tonight?" All they'd seen so far was mud and more mud, endless miles of nothing. Stu Harris, who was busy flying *Argo*, didn't answer. His eyes were glued to the *Argo* video monitor.

"There's something," he said, pointing to the screen. Suddenly every member of the sleepy watch was alive and alert. No one could believe it wasn't just another false alarm, or a joke. But, no, there on the screen were clear images of things man-made. Stu yelled, "Bingo!" The control room echoed with a loud "Yeah!" from the whole team, and then wild shrieks and war-whoops. All sorts of wreckage began to stream by on the screen. Then something different appeared—something large and perfectly round. Jean-Louis checked in a book of pictures of the *Titanic*. He came across a picture of the ship's massive boilers, used to burn coal and drive the engines. He couldn't believe his eyes. He looked from book to video screen and back again. Yes, it was the same kind of boiler!

I scrambled out of my bunk when I got the news and ran to the control room. We replayed the tape of the boiler. I didn't know what to say. I turned to Jean-Louis. The look in his eyes said everything. The *Titanic* had been found. We'd been right all along. Then he said softly, "It was not luck. We earned it."

Our hunt was almost over. Somewhere very near us lay the R.M.S.[2] *Titanic*.

Word had spread throughout the ship. People were pouring into the control room. The place was becoming a madhouse. Everyone was shaking hands and hugging and slapping each other on the back.

---

[2] R.M.S.: Royal Mail Steamer

It was now almost two in the morning, very close to the exact hour of the *Titanic*'s sinking. Someone pointed to the clock on the wall. All of a sudden the room became silent.

Here at the bottom of the ocean lay not only the graveyard of a great ship, but of more than 1,500 people who had gone down with her. And we were the very first people in seventy-three years to come to this spot to pay our respects. Images from the night of the disaster—a story I now knew by heart—flashed through my mind. Out on the stern of the *Knorr*, people had started to gather for a few moments of silence in memory of those who had died on the *Titanic*. The sky was filled with stars; the sea was calm. We raised the Harland & Wolff flag, the emblem of the shipyard in Belfast, Ireland, that had built the great liner. Except for the shining moon overhead, it was just like the night when the *Titanic* had gone down. I could see her as she slipped nose first into the glassy water. Around me were the ghostly shapes of lifeboats and the piercing shouts and screams of passengers and crew freezing to death in the water.

Our little memorial service lasted about ten minutes. Then I just said, "Thank you all. Now let's get back to work."

In the short time remaining, I planned to get as many pictures of the wreck as possible. I wanted to show the world what condition the *Titanic* was in after seventy-three years on the bottom. A million questions flew through my mind. Would the ship be in one piece or broken up? Were the funnels still standing upright? Would the wooden deck be preserved in the deep salt water? And, a darker thought—would we find any remains of the people who had died that night? Photographs would give us the answers.

We started to make our first run with *Argo* over the major piece of wreckage we'd just found. But there were dangers lurking below. If *Argo* got caught in tangled wreckage, it would take a miracle to free it. It could mean the end of our mission.

As *Argo* neared the bottom, no one moved in the control room. Not a word was spoken. Now *Argo* was passing over the main hull of the *Titanic*. It was time to take a close look.

"Take it down farther. Go down to sixteen feet."

"Roger."

On the video screen, I could see the dim outline of a hull. "It's the side of the ship. She's upright!"

Suddenly, out of the gloom the Boat Deck of the ship came into view. "Keep your eyes peeled for funnels."

But there were only gaping holes where funnels had once stood. Then as we crossed over the middle of the ship, we could see the flattened outline of the bridge. Was this where Captain Smith had stood bravely to the end?

Before we knew it, *Argo* had safely passed over the wreck and back into the empty murk. We had made it safely after all. All at once the crowded control room exploded. People were whooping, hugging, and dancing around while Jean-Louis and I quietly stood there thinking about what we had just seen. We now knew that the *Titanic* had landed on the bottom upright, and that a major piece of her appeared to be intact.

I wanted to make more passes over the wreck with *Argo*, but first it was time to clear the control room. I needed my team as rested as possible for the next sixty-four hours, which was all the time we had left. "Hey, we've got too many people up. You'll all be exhausted when your watch comes up. Let's get some of you back in bed. This is a twenty-four hour operation."

During the rest of that afternoon and evening, we managed only two more *Argo* passes over the wreck because of bad weather. But we did discover to our surprise and sadness that the ship was broken in two—her stern was missing. Where the back of the ship should have been, our video images faded into a confusing mass of twisted wreckage.

By now the storm had reached its peak. We could no longer use *Argo*. For ten hours the wind howled across our rolling deck as the *Knorr* pitched and heaved in the rough sea. Well, I thought finally, if we can't use *Argo* and the video system, then we'll work with ANGUS.

ANGUS was quite like *Argo*, except that it was an older camera sled that took still photographs instead of video as it was towed over the sea floor. Our nickname for ANGUS was the "dope on a rope." Now we would bring our old friend to the rescue. After all, I had used ANGUS in rougher seas than this.

But our first runs over the wreck with ANGUS only produced blurry images. The cameras were working properly, but we had come over the wreck too high to get good pictures.

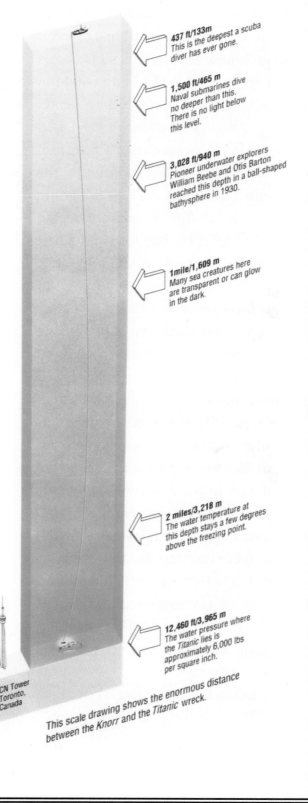

437 ft/133m
This is the deepest a scuba diver has ever gone.

1,500 ft/465 m
Naval submarines dive no deeper than this. There is no light below this level.

3,028 ft/940 m
Pioneer underwater explorers William Beebe and Otis Barton reached this depth in a ball-shaped bathysphere in 1930.

1mile/1,609 m
Many sea creatures here are transparent or can glow in the dark.

2 miles/3,218 m
The water temperature at this depth stays a few degrees above the freezing point.

12,460 ft/3,965 m
The water pressure where the *Titanic* lies is approximately 6,000 lbs per square inch.

Great Pyramid of Cheops El Gizeh, Egypt

Eiffel Tower Paris, France

Empire State Building New York, U.S.A.

Sears Tower Chicago, U.S.A.

Ostankino Tower Moscow, U.S.S.R.

CN Tower Toronto, Canada

This scale drawing shows the enormous distance between the *Knorr* and the *Titanic* wreck.

We were now down to our final hours, and I felt victory slipping away. At that moment I just wanted to go home. My leg was sore from a fall on the deck and I hadn't slept in days. We had found the *Titanic*. Wasn't that good enough? Who said we had to bring home pretty pictures?

But somehow I found the strength to continue. I was not going to leave the *Titanic* without trying one last time. We had four and a half hours left before we had to start back. The *Knorr* had to be back in port for another expedition.

I was so tired that I had to lie down or I would fall down. So I lay down in the control room and gave the commands for the last-ditch attempt. What we were about to do in these rough seas was even crazier than the risky ANGUS passes we had just made. We had to get our cameras within close range of the *Titanic*'s decks. On the surface the seas were heaving up and down at least ten to thirteen feet. That motion would travel down our 12,500 feet of cable and make ANGUS hard to control. But what the heck, it was now or never.

"Down to thirteen feet," I croaked.

"Thirteen feet? Are you crazy?" said the pilot.

"Thirteen feet," I repeated.

For the next three hours hardly a word was spoken as we made pass after hair-raising pass over the *Titanic*. One slip and ANGUS would be lost forever in the wreckage below.

Outside, the wind rattled the walls of our control room as the storm blew itself out. Then, at about six in the morning, a simple message boomed over the *Knorr*'s intercom from the captain: "You have to start up now."

Right on time, ANGUS was pulled back on deck. A few hours later, news came from our photo lab that we had good, clear photographs of the *Titanic*. We'd made it! By a whisker.

Now, finally, I went to my bunk to get some sleep. When I awoke, it was nighttime, and the good ship *Knorr* was steaming quietly and steadily to our home port.

On the clear, warm morning of September 9, 1985, as we steamed down Nantucket Sound, Massachusetts, the *Knorr* was mobbed by helicopters, small planes, and pleasure craft running circles around us and blowing their horns. News of our discovery of the *Titanic* had made headlines around the world.

Then a small boat with a welcoming party including my wife and two sons, Todd and Douglas, approached our ship. Having my family there was really important to me. They had paid a big price over the years during my long months away from home, but they'd never once complained.

As we came into port, I couldn't believe my eyes. The dock was a mass of people filling every square inch of space. There was a platform bristling with television cameras and

reporters. Banners were flying, a band was playing, schoolchildren hung on to balloons, and a cannon boomed out a salute.

What a victory welcome!

Exploring the Great Ship

With a big grin, I turned and gave the "thumbs up" sign for good luck to the crew standing on the deck of our new research ship, *Atlantis II*. In stocking feet I began to climb down the ladder inside *Alvin*, our tiny submarine. It was July 13, 1986, almost a year after our French-American expedition had first found the *Titanic* and taken photographs of her. Unfortunately, our French colleagues were not able to join us this year. I would miss my friend Jean-Louis.

We had steamed out to where the *Titanic* lay in the treacherous North Atlantic. Now it was time to take a closer look at her.

Our goal was to dive two and a half miles into the pitch-black freezing depths to where the *Titanic* lay. Then we would try to land *Alvin* on her decks. If all went well, we would be the first human beings in seventy-four years to see the legendary ship at close range.

We closed *Alvin*'s hatch, and I exchanged glances with my pilot and co-pilot as we felt our submarine gently rocking back and forth. We knew that meant we were now dangling half over the deck of *Atlantis II* and half over the water—one of the most dangerous moments of a dive. Should the sub suddenly fall, we could all get badly hurt.

But we hit the water safely. Then our lift line was released, and divers swarmed over the sub checking everything, including *Jason Junior*, or *JJ*. *JJ* was our remote-controlled underwater robot, who was attached to the outside of *Alvin* in a special garage. He operated on a long cable attached to our sub and was equipped with still and video cameras. With his help we hoped to explore inside the wreck below.

The three of us were crammed into the tiny cabin, our inner space capsule. Hemmed in by panels of instruments, we had no room to stretch out or stand up. We were like three sardines in a spherical can. It was warm and stuffy, but the ice-cold water outside would soon cool *Alvin*'s hull, both outside and inside.

Daylight began to fade into deeper and deeper blues as our sub reached its maximum descent speed of 100 feet per minute. It would take us two and a half hours to reach the bottom. There was little talking as we fell swiftly into utter darkness. Soft music played on the sub's stereo.

Suddenly, a white-tipped shark appeared outside my window and disappeared just as quickly. Sharks often swim by *Alvin* to investigate the noise. It was comforting to know that two inches of metal protected us. I remembered the time a swordfish had attacked *Alvin* and got its sword stuck in the sub.

The long fall to the bottom is usually a lulling experience. The interior gets darker and darker and begins to cool until, after less than fifteen minutes, the sub has reached a depth of 1,200 feet and total darkness. To conserve power, *Alvin*'s outside lights are left off. The only illumination inside comes from three small red lights.

But this time we had technical problems to worry about. First, we discovered that *Alvin*'s sonar had stopped working. Probably either the cold seawater or the increasing pressure had damaged it. Sonar guided us by bouncing electronic sound waves off anything in our path. Without sonar we couldn't see beyond a few yards. Our surface navigator on board *Atlantis II* would have to guide us to the *Titanic* with his sonar and our sub-to-ship telephone.

A few minutes later, at about 2,000 feet, we passed through what is known as a deep-scattering layer, because it shows up like a cloudy blur on sonar. In fact, the cloud is made up of thousands and thousands of tiny creatures that live at this depth of the ocean. Many of them glow in the dark, their small bodies exploding like fireworks as they become aware of our presence. When I first saw these creatures, they reminded me of a tiny passenger train with lighted windows passing by at night.

By the time we had passed 5,000 feet, almost one hour into our dive, it was getting cold in the sub. We put on our first layers of extra clothing. I was wearing a wool hat from my sons' hockey team to keep my head warm. During the long hours in the tiny cabin, my legs often fell asleep, and sometimes I'd get a bad cramp in my hip. At times like that, *Alvin*'s cabin was more like a torture chamber than a space capsule.

Ten minutes later, at 6,000 feet, our pilot noticed that the instrument panel was showing a saltwater leak into the battery banks that power the sub. Our time on the bottom of the ocean would have to be awfully short today. And to make things even worse, the surface navigator's sonar suddenly stopped working. That meant we were now almost completely blind.

Our lights pierced the blackness as the ocean bottom slowly emerged from the dark-green gloom below us. We'd arrived. The only trouble was, we didn't know where we were. All we could see through the portholes was our own shadow cast by *Alvin*'s lights, and some gently rolling ground covered with mud.

So close and yet so far away. The ship lay somewhere near us, probably no more than 400 feet—the length of two city blocks. But when you're more than two miles down in black murk, a few hundred feet without any guiding sonar might as well be a thousand miles.

I couldn't believe it. I'd waited thirteen long years for this moment, and now, a stone's throw away from my dream, I was trapped inside a sardine can on my hands and knees staring at nothing but mud.

Suddenly, a head-splitting alarm buzzer pierced the silence inside our tiny sub. The leak in our battery was getting to the critical point. We had very little time left if we were to get back to the surface without damaging *Alvin*. Quickly, we decided to guess where the *Titanic* might be and blindly go there in a last-ditch throw of the dice.

Alvin now gently touched the bottom with its single runner, like a one-legged skier, and we began to inch along. The shrill alarm was starting to drive us crazy, and the tension in the sub was heavy. Our time was running out fast. It was going to be a very close call if we hoped to see the *Titanic*.

Then our surface navigator called in on the telephone with the good news that his sonar was working again, and that "the *Titanic* should be about fifty yards west of us."

We turned the sub and strained our eyes to see out the portholes.

Now the bottom began to look strange. It began to slope sharply upward, as though it had been bulldozed into place. My heartbeat quickened.

"Come right," I said to the pilot. "I think I see a wall of black just on the other side of that mud mound."

Then, directly in front of us, there it was: an endless slab of rusted steel rising out of the bottom—the massive hull of the *Titanic*! I felt like a space voyager peering at an alien city wall on some empty planet. Slowly, I let out my breath; I didn't realize I had been holding it.

But one look at the fabulous wreck was all I got. Our pilot quickly dropped *Alvin*'s weights, clicked off that horrible alarm, and we went hurtling toward the surface. One moment longer on the bottom, and *Alvin*'s power system would have been in extreme danger.

All we had to show for six hours' work was a brief glimpse of the *Titanic*. But my dream had finally come true.

I was in a grim mood when I stepped out of the sub onto the deck of the *Atlantis II*. "I saw the ship for about ten seconds," I said. "But we've got a sick puppy here, and we've got to fix it." If we wanted to dive the next day, we had to take care of our growing list of technical problems. While I slept, our team of experts worked through the night to cure our sick submarine.

Luckily it was all systems go the next morning, and we were full of confidence as we began a second dive. Our goal was to check out possible landing sites for *Alvin* on the decks of the *Titanic*.

Our second view of the *Titanic* was breathtaking. As we glided soundlessly across the ocean bottom, the razor's edge of the bow loomed out of the darkness. The great ship towered above us. Suddenly it seemed to be coming right at us, about to run us over. My first reaction was that we had to get out of the way. But the *Titanic* wasn't going anywhere. As we gently brought our sub closer, we could see the bow more clearly. Both of her huge anchors were still in place. But the bow was buried more than sixty feet in mud, far too deep for anyone to pull her out of the ooze.

It looked as though the metal hull was slowly melting away. What seemed like frozen rivers of rust covered the ship's side and spread out over the ocean bottom. It was almost as if the blood of the great ship lay in pools on the ocean floor.

As *Alvin* rose in slow motion up the ghostly side of the ship, I could see our lights reflecting off the still-unbroken glass of the *Titanic*'s portholes. They made me think of cats' eyes gleaming in the dark. In places the rust formations over the portholes looked like eyelashes with tears, as though the *Titanic* were crying. I could also see a lot of reddish-brown stalactites of rust over the wreck, like long icicles. I decided to call them "rusticles." This rust turned out to be very fragile. If touched by our sub, it disappeared like a cloud of smoke.

As we rose further and began to move across the mighty forward deck, I was amazed at the sheer size of everything: giant bollards and shiny bronze capstans that were used for winding ropes and cables; the huge links of the anchor chains. When you were there on the spot, the ship was truly titanic.

I strained to get a good look at the deck's wood planking, just four feet below us. Then my heart dropped to my stomach. "It's gone!" I muttered. Most of the *Titanic*'s wooden deck had been eaten away. Millions of little wood-eating worms had done more damage than the iceberg and the salt water. I began to wonder whether the metal deck below the destroyed wood planking would support our weight when *Alvin* landed.

We would soon find out. Slowly we moved into position to make our first landing test on the forward deck just next to the fallen mast. As we made our approach, our hearts beat quickly. We knew there was a real risk of crashing through the deck. The sub settled down, making a muffled crunching noise. If the deck gave way, we'd be trapped in collapsing wreckage. But it held, and we settled firmly. That meant there was a good chance that the *Titanic*'s decks would support us at other landing sites.

We carefully lifted off and turned toward the stern. The dim outline of the ship's superstructure came into view: first B Deck, then A, finally the Boat Deck—the top deck where the bridge was located. It was here that the captain and his officers had guided the ship across the Atlantic. The wooden wheelhouse was gone, probably knocked away in the sinking. But the bronze telemotor control to which the ship's wheel had once been attached stood intact, polished to a shine by the current. We then safely tested this second landing site.

I had an eerie feeling as we glided along exploring the wreck. As I

peered through my porthole, I could easily imagine people walking along the deck and looking out the windows of the ship that I was looking into. Here I was at the bottom of the ocean looking at a kind of time capsule from history.

Suddenly, as we rose up the port side of the ship, the sub shuddered and made a clanging noise. A waterfall of rust covered our portholes. "We've hit something!" I exclaimed. "What is it?"

"I don't know," our pilot replied. "I'm backing off." Unseen overhangs are the nightmare of the deep-sub pilot. Carefully, the pilot backed away from the hull and brought us slowly upward. Then, directly in front of our forward porthole, a big lifeboat davit slid by. We had hit one of the metal arms that held the lifeboats as they were lowered. This davit was one of the two that had held boat No. 8, the boat Mrs. Straus had refused to enter that night. She was the wife of the owner of Macy's department store in New York. When she had been offered a chance to save herself in one of the lifeboats, she had turned to her husband and said, "We have been living together for many years. Where you go, I go." Calmly, the two of them had sat down on a pile of deck chairs to wait for the end.

Now, as we peered out our portholes, it seemed as if the Boat Deck were crowded with passengers. I could almost hear the cry, "Women and children first!"

We knew from the previous year's pictures that the stern had broken off the ship, so we continued back to search for the severed end of the intact bow section. Just beyond the gaping hole where the second funnel had been, the deck began to plunge down at a dangerous angle. The graceful lines of the ship disappeared in a twisted mess of torn steel plating, upturned portholes, and jumbled wreckage. We saw enough to know that the decks of the ship had collapsed in on one another like a giant accordion. With an unexpectedly strong current pushing us toward this twisted wreckage, we veered away and headed for the surface.

We made more trips down to the *Titanic*. At the end of the final dive, I knew I had visited the great ship for the last time. Two and a half hours later when we reached the surface, everybody on the *Atlantis II* prepared to head for home. Later that night there would be a party on board, but through it all I was still thinking about the *Titanic*: of the people who built her, sailed on her, and died when she went down.

Would you like to have been aboard *Alvin* when its crew explored the *Titanic*? Explain your answer.

How did the crew members confirm that the wreck was the *Titanic*?

What did Dr. Ballard and his team hope to find? Did their findings live up to their expectations?

What did Dr. Ballard mean when he said that exploring the wreckage of the *Titanic* was like looking at "a kind of time capsule from history"?

WRITE   The scientists devoted a great deal of time to discovering and exploring the *Titanic*. Do you think the expedition was worthwhile? Write a paragraph explaining your opinion.

AN INTERVIEW
WITH THE
Illustrator
KEN MARSCHALL

Ken Marschall is an artist who has spent years painting his own visions of the Titanic. *Writer Ilene Cooper spoke with him about his fascination with that great ship and about his work featured in* Exploring the Titanic.

COOPER: *You did your first painting of the* Titanic *in 1968 when you were just a teenager. What piqued your interest?*

MARSCHALL: I saw a movie about the *Titanic* on television. The story seemed like the height of fiction, yet it actually happened. The largest ship in the world on its maiden voyage. A glassy, smooth ocean. Sailors who had been at sea for twenty-five years had never seen a sea as mirror clear as it was that night. And then, out of nowhere, a rogue iceberg. Even after all these years, I'm still captivated by the story.

I'm also very interested in passenger vessels, and not just ships but trains and planes as well. The *Titanic* was like a civilization gone to sea, with restaurants, laundries, switchboards, post offices. All the human things that collectively make this beehive work are interesting to me. The size, the power, the construction, the leap forward she was in design and luxury—those were the lures.

COOPER: *Has anything else grabbed you the way the* Titanic *did?*

MARSCHALL: I worked on a book about the sinking of the *Bismarck*, but that was a naval vessel, so it did not have the same attraction for me. I also became totally wrapped up in and appreciative of the design of the *Lusitania*. I'm working on a book about the sinking of the *Andrea Doria* too. I'm also interested in ships without the disaster aspect, like the *Queen Mary*. But as far as the disaster ships go, I think I'm so interested because these wonderful ships were cheated. They didn't get to live their lives out like other ships—something as beautiful as the *Andrea Doria* or as intricate as the *Lusitania*, as magnificent as the *Titanic* on her maiden voyage, and their lives were just cut short.

THE FROZEN OCEAN

Compare the information you learned about the *Titanic* in "Earth's Changing Climate" with what you discovered in "Exploring the *Titanic*." In what ways was it helpful to gain different perspectives?

WRITER'S WORKSHOP

There is much more to learn about icebergs and the *Titanic* than what you read in these selections. Find encyclopedia articles on these topics. Then choose a narrower topic to learn about. Do research, take notes, and write a research report presenting your expert information.

Writer's Choice

What kind of animals do you think of when you hear the words *the frozen ocean*? Write about what you think living in the frozen ocean is like. Think of a way to share your response.

THEME

THE DEEP BLUE SEA

Do you wonder about the different animals that live in the ocean? You may be surprised to learn that in the depths of the vast blue seas is a cold, dark world that is home to bizarre and fascinating creatures.

CONTENTS

495

PLANET EARTH

LIFE IN THE OCEANS

OUTSTANDING
SCIENCE TRADE
BOOK

NORBERT WU

LIFE IN THE OCEANS

by Norbert Wu

THE DEEP OCEAN

With the clang of the submersible's hatch, I settled down for a long ride. There was little room to turn or move about in the small steel tube that was to take me to the bottom of the ocean. As the one passenger in the small submersible, I spent my time flat on my stomach, looking through four thick windows into the dark depths. The humidity was so high in the submersible that the windows were dripping. I heard the whir of the fans and hoped that the carbon dioxide scrubber was keeping the air clean. With a swirling of water and a splash, I began my long, dark journey to the bottom of the ocean.

A trip to the bottom of the ocean can take longer than an airplane ride across America. The steel tube I was in creaked and complained for over an hour as I dropped down deeper and deeper. Looking outside, I watched as the steep coral wall became darker and darker, until finally it gave way to exposed rock. At five hundred feet deep, the undersea landscape was covered in its eternal deep blue twilight. At this depth, not enough light is available to support the profuse covering of life that is found in surface waters. But I saw a green turtle suddenly shoot up from a crevice in the wall, as surprised to see me as I was to see it.

Descending deeper and deeper into the darkness, the craft finally touched down on a sandy bottom at one thousand feet deep. Feather stars, ancient, primitive relatives of starfish, were everywhere, sifting the water with their arms for floating food. In the lights of the sub, I saw shimmering, dancing schools of squid and small flashlight fish in the distance. Both the squid and the flashlight fish can generate their own *bioluminescent* light. Strange animals live at this depth, animals that never see sunlight, grotesque relatives of the fish up above. It was an utterly alien landscape for me.

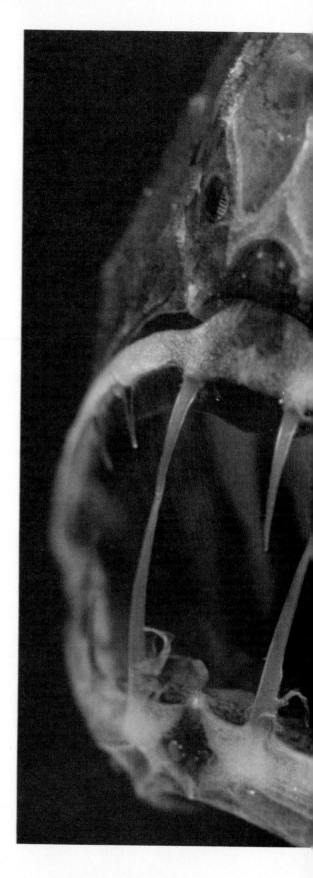

The deep-sea fangtooth (right) has a bony, hard body and tremendous fangs.

The Vast Depths

We live on a thin skin of land covering less than one-third of our planet, bathed by sunlight. Life in the upper 300 feet of the ocean is also blessed with life-giving sunlight, and we are all familiar with the richness and diversity of life off our coasts. But all of our land and ocean surface is only the paper-thin skin of a very large onion. As mentioned before, the ocean is a vast basin averaging two and one-half miles in depth. The top, biologically productive layer represents only 2.5 percent of the ocean's capacity. Humans have only recently developed the robots and submersibles that let scientists see the other 97.5 percent, and make important discoveries. Continents have been shown to drift across our planet's surface like ice cubes in a thick milkshake. Undersea canyons rivaling the Grand Canyon in size and depth have been discovered close to coastlines. Deep sea currents as strong and swift as any in shallow waters have been found everywhere, and many new species of animals have been observed.

The deep-sea swallower (right) is named for its huge, hinged mouth that opens wide to swallow prey. These fish are extremely rare and are usually found only below 5,000 feet deep. It is thought that the fish uses the light organ at the end of its tail to attract food.

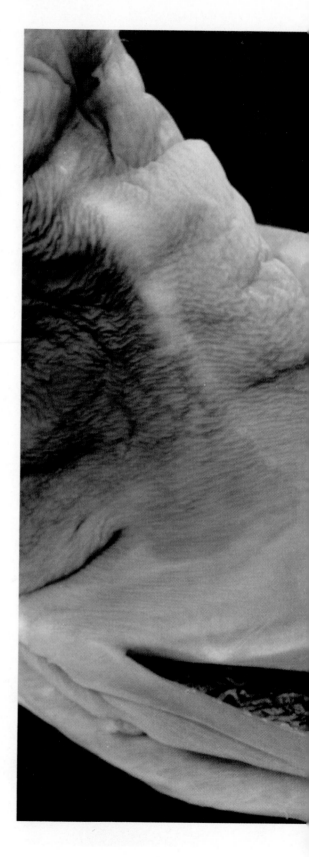

The black dragonfish (right) is a long, thin fish that uses luminous organs along its body and in front of its mouth to attract prey. Though it looks primitive, scientists consider the black dragonfish to be an advanced species.

A Cold, Black Place

At 300 feet down, the deepest scuba divers can go, there is barely enough sunlight for a plant to produce food from the energy of light (a process called photosynthesis). Water selectively filters out red light, so that only blue-green light is present. At 3,000 feet, light from the sun is almost completely gone. At such great, dark depths, the water temperatures are generally a constant, low 39 degrees F. The pressure caused by the weight of tons of water is tremendous. Living things in the deep sea have evolved many unusual features to deal with the darkness, the scarcity of food, and the high pressures of the abyss.

The Twilight Zone

Very faint levels of light may filter down to depths of 3,000 feet, and fish in this twilight zone have developed many structures to help them survive. Many animals have large, sensitive eyes, and these fish can see thirty times better in dim light than can humans. Tubular eyes allow them to judge distance and detect prey that are silhouetted against the light coming from the surface.

To avoid casting a shadow, the prey of such fish try to blend into the background. Fish merge into light from above by being transparent, by reflecting light to match the background, or by having a very low reflective surface. Larvae of deep-water fish are often transparent. Dark colors conceal well, and red colors work just as well in the depths, where all red light has been filtered out by the water. Many shrimp as well as an entire family of fish, the whalefish, are colored a brilliant red. Some fish even generate their own light, which matches the light coming from above, so they seem invisible because they do not cast a shadow. The hatchetfish possesses light organs all along the sides of its body; these emit blue-green light at the exact intensity of the light coming from the surface.

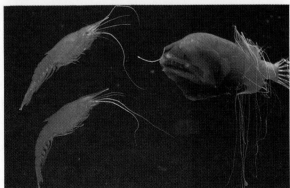

Most fish in the deep sea lay large, yolky eggs rather than huge masses of millions of tiny eggs, as most fish nearer the surface do. An example is this deep-sea anglerfish embryo (top). Deep-sea anglerfish (bottom) lure prey with a bioluminescent lure. The light is manufactured within the fish's body.

The Allure of Light

In the pitch darkness of water 3,000 feet deep, fish with fancy light sources are common, and the patterns and probable functions of these light sources are a lesson in evolution. These light sources may attract food and mates, and confuse predators. A fish may be able to identify its mate by the pattern of light organs it has. The black dragonfish can pull a black screen down to hide the light organ below its eye, and it also has a row of light cells all along its body. This fish's ability to flash these lights gives it a unique identity.

Attracting a mate with powerful displays of light is not the only function of these light organs. The female deep-sea anglerfish wriggles luminous lures to attract food; the black dragonfish has luminous barbels at the tip of its mouth, which it waves about; and the viperfish uses light organs within its mouth to lure prey right into its waiting stomach.

In an interesting turn, the *Pachystomias,* a black dragonfish, emits red light from a light organ under its eye. Since most fish in very deep waters cannot see red light,

Pachystomias is able to use this light as a sniperscope, secretly sighting and moving in on potential prey.

Living Light

In the 1970s, scientists diving at *HydroLab,* the United States' undersea habitat in the Virgin Islands of the Caribbean, were surprised to see a constellation of flickering, moving lights off the coral wall near the habitat. The lights were only noticeable on very dark nights, and they turned out to belong to a completely new family of fish called the lanterneye fish, named for a

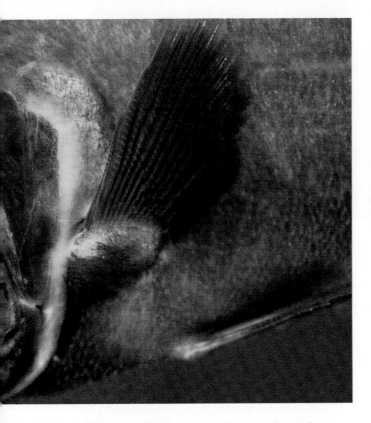

light-emitting organ beneath each eye. After hiding in caves and great depths during the day, these fish came up to shallower water on dark nights to feed on plankton. The light organ underneath each eye is filled with luminous bacteria, and these fish have developed special ways to turn the lights on and off at will. One type, *Kryptophanaron*, shuts off its light by pulling a dark piece of skin over the light organ. Other types, *Anomalops* and *Photoblepharon*, have their light organs mounted on stalks, which fit into a socket, and can be turned to block out the light.

Here (clockwise, from opposite page, top) the flashlight, or lanterneye fish, which flashes a light organ to attract mates and prey; a deep-sea anglerfish; and a viperfish.

Making the Most of a Meal

Life in the deep ocean depends on the richness of surface waters for food. The sunken bodies of large animals such as whales may provide a rare feast for scavenging fish, which can gather to a corpse in astonishing speed. Robot cameras and manned submarines have discovered frenzied schools of hagfish (eel-like, primitive fish that burrow into a fish and eat it from the inside out), isopods (large crustaceans resembling a pillbug), and even large, six-gill sharks gathered to eat bait that's been put out thousands of meters down. Food is scarce in the deep sea. Should a fish encounter a potential meal, it will likely eat it, regardless of the size. Large female anglerfish regularly take prey two or three times their own length, and black swallowers are so named for their enormously expandable stomach, which is often found filled with large prey, nearly equal in size to the hunter.

Many fish have developed long fangs and hinged mouths to catch large prey. One type of anglerfish even has teeth in the back of its throat to keep its prey from escaping as it is being swallowed. The deep-sea swallower, *Saccopharnyx*, is a serpentlike fish with an enormous head and hinged mouth that can open like a garbage truck to swallow prey. The cookie cutter shark has jaws lined with razor-sharp teeth, and many dolphins, whales, and large fish have semicircular scars from encounters with these footlong fish, which bite into their prey and twist away with a chunk of flesh.

The fish down in these depths don't get to eat very often, so they take full advantage of every opportunity.

Finding a Mate

It is difficult for any creature in these dark depths to find a suitable mate. How such isolated creatures find each other in the vast reaches of the ocean remains one of the great unsolved mysteries of deep-sea biology. For instance, anglerfish are extremely rare, although they are found in every ocean. Scientists report catching an average of only one anglerfish in two weeks of trawling, and one estimate is that there are fifteen or more males for every female. These males are much smaller than the females, and they have only one goal in life—to find and fertilize a female. The anglerfish has developed a strategy to guarantee that any meeting between sexes is fruitful. When a male encounters a female of the same species, he will attach himself to her with his mouth. Gradually, the male becomes a parasite of the female; his mouth fuses to her body, and blood vessels actually form between the couple. The male becomes little more than an attached sperm sac, about one-twentieth the size of the female. Sometimes several males are found attached to a single female, lifetime partners all.

Here (clockwise, from opposite page, top) is a deep-sea swallower; a deep-sea anglerfish; and a cookie cutter shark, its jaws lined with razor-sharp teeth suitable for tearing chunks of flesh from living whales, dolphins, and large fish.

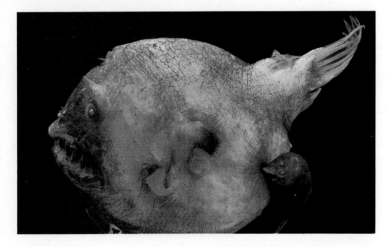

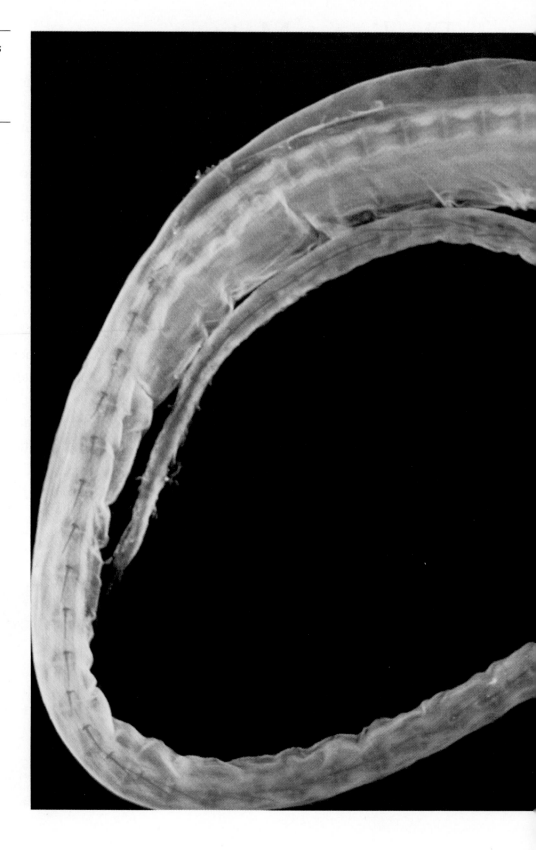

A black dragonfish has been stained to reveal the bones.

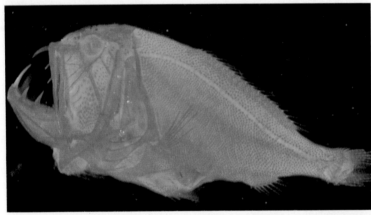

A trio of marine hatchetfish (top left); a fangtooth (bottom left); and a deep-sea anglerfish (opposite).

What was one thing you learned about the deep ocean that fascinated you?

Sunlight does not penetrate into the deep ocean. What structures on the fish that live there help them survive?

How is life more difficult for fish in the deep ocean than for fish near the surface?

What do you think the author Norbert Wu wants you to learn about the deep ocean?

WRITE Imagine that you are diving to the bottom of the ocean with Norbert Wu. What would you see? How would you feel? Write a brief paragraph about your dive.

510

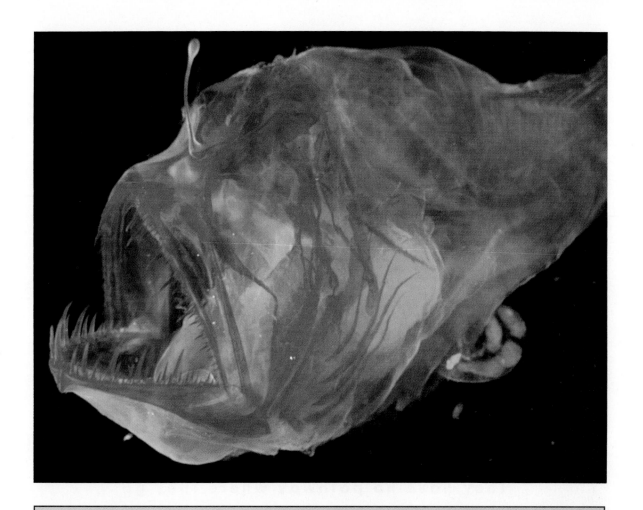

ABOUT THE PHOTOGRAPHS

None of the specimens photographed here are more than a foot long. They do look like monsters, but fortunately they are very small monsters, hardly able to threaten a photographer in a submersible exploring the ocean depths. To make the photographs more useful and interesting, the specimens in these photographs were put through acids and dyes that show the internal structure of the fish. Bones are stained red and cartilage blue.

The bizarre deep-sea fish in these photos were once thought to be extremely primitive. However, scientists now know that most animals of the deep-sea are highly advanced, and that the various species evolved in upper surface waters before heading to the deep. One indication of this is the amount of bone structure (red dye) in these fish, which is a feature of more advanced fish.

AT THE AQUARIUM

BY MAX EASTMAN

Serene the silver fishes glide,

Stern-lipped, and pale, and wonder-eyed;

As through the agèd deeps of ocean,

They glide with wan and wavy motion.

They have no pathway where they go,

They flow like water to and fro.

They watch with never-winking eyes,

They watch with staring, cold surprise,

The level people in the air,

The people peering, peering there,

Who wander also to and fro,

And know not why or where they go,

Yet have a wonder in their eyes,

Sometimes a pale and cold surprise.

THE DEEP BLUE SEA

Does the poem "At the Aquarium" reflect Norbert Wu's experiences in the deep? Explain your answer.

WRITER'S WORKSHOP

Norbert Wu describes in detail some of the unusual fish he saw near the bottom of the ocean. Choose an unusual object, plant, or animal. Study it carefully. Write a detailed description of it so that someone who has never seen it can picture it.

Writer's Choice
Think about what you have learned about the deep ocean. What do you wonder about the deep blue sea now? Write about your thoughts, and share your writing with others.

513

THEME

FOLLOWING THE WHALES

▼▼▼▼▼▼▼ 🐋 ▼▼▼▼▼▼▼

Have you ever heard the call of a baby whale or seen a bowhead whale "sky hop"? Let author Jean Craighead George take you on journeys through the undersea world. You are bound to surface with a newfound respect for the mighty whales that roam the ocean depths.

CONTENTS

515

Spring

COMES TO THE

OCEAN

ALA Notable Book

SPRING
COMES
to the OCEAN

JEAN CRAIGHEAD GEORGE

BY **JEAN CRAIGHEAD GEORGE**

ILLUSTRATED BY **JULIAN MULOCK**

Off the coast of Bandon, Washington, a gray whale surfaced. Her seven-inch-long nostrils emerged first and blew a spout of air and water fifteen feet into the air. The column swooshed with a roar that could be heard for half a mile. Having exhaled, she then inhaled, and the breath came into her lungs with a whine, like wind rushing into a tunnel. Her nostrils closed over this salty gasp. A low wall of muscle arose around the nostrils like a frown and kept the water out. She submerged.

Four seconds later, her nose, which was on the top of her head, came up again. She gave four strong blows. The waves clapped around her. She snorted at them, then headed down into the corridors of the Pacific Ocean.

The female gray whale was 43 feet long. She weighed 34 tons. She was one of a group of animals that are the largest ever to live on this earth. Like all whales she was also hostess to many small beasts. On her back and over her mountain of a belly lived thousands of barnacles. They pulled their feet in and stopped kicking food into their mouths when their great hostess surfaced to breathe. They adjusted to her rising and diving, just as we adjust to the moods of the earth as it circles the sun.

This city-block-of-an-animal plunged forward for a thousand feet. Then she surfaced and peered over the ocean. She had no language, she made no vocal sounds, but she spied now and then to make sure her kinsmen were traveling with her.

Beside her swam her son, a 20-foot baby. He had been born in January in the California Bay, and now the two of them were on their way north to the Bering Sea—a long journey of 7,000 miles.

The mother plunged down into the green spring ocean and looked around. She was following a familiar canyon wall that she knew as well as you know your own street, for she had traveled along it every year for 20 years of her life. The submarine canyon was gray and dark, and lay like a great highway up the continental shelf. The whale knew exactly where she was.

Ahead of her loomed a sand barrier. She quickened her pace for she knew she was coming to a cove. Once more she blew and looked around. She saw no other gray whales and sensed she was behind the main migration. At the sand bar she tasted the silt of Coos Bay and, because she could not feel the currents from her baby, slowed down, then stopped.

Her son was looking at a giant squid. The mother attracted his attention by crunching her wide teeth, the only sound she could make, but an effective one. The baby spurted to her side. He was eager and energetic. He whooshed friskily to the surface and peered around. He saw boats and lighthouses. This was his first trip to the summer rendezvous of the gray whales—the Bering Sea. His mother was teaching him the underwater landmarks, for in the fall he would have to travel back alone in the manner of the gray whale. Their migration was not a social affair. Each whale made the exhausting trip by itself.

The mother whale swung over the delta at the mouth of the bay and crunched her teeth again. Her son came down to her. She was taking the water from the bay in and out of her mouth. He did likewise, and the taste of the bay was forever imprinted on his senses. Each bay and cove and canyon had to be memorized in this manner, by taste, by sight, and by currents that eddied and pulled, for each was different in every inlet along the great California coast.

The mother plunged over the sand bar. The whale child followed. For a moment they lingered in the different water pressures, feeling all the details of this place with their throat grooves, the openings under their necks that were sensitive to pressures, to currents and eddies.

The mother delayed long here as if to impress this particular spot on the youngster. From here they would take out to sea, and the underwater world of the continent would be replaced by the deeps of the Pacific. From here on it would be all pressure memories. The whale child circled gently, biting the sand, filtering the water in and learning.

Then they hurried on—a thousand feet at a run. They

swam to the edge of the continental shelf.

Suddenly the whale child looked back. He whirled in panic. Coos Bay appeared different from the north. He turned and flipped back to the sand bar, tasting the salts and minerals once more, feeling the texture of the water, trying to learn well. When he was satisfied with his impressions he tailed out to meet his mother. But she was gone.

The life of the gray whale is silent for the most part, a grind on their plankton-filtering teeth, a noisy blow. Over the sea canyon walls, ticking and rasping like the beat of a tin cup on a wooden table, came the rare "distress" sound made by the clicking teeth of the baby whale.

He was lost. He surfaced, blew a great column of air and water and pulled himself skyward so high his whole chest was out. All he saw was a trawling boat harvesting the bottom-dwelling fish. He saw no mother. He glanced at the boat again. It was big, it might be a whale. He headed for it, spying tentatively as he went.

The boat was gray like his mother and covered with barnacles. Rising and blowing he came up to the object. But the whale child drew back. The wooden whale was too small, the wrong design, the wrong scent, and the water that surrounded it was not warmed by the mammal body. Oil seeped from it.

The young whale fled in terror, diving into unfamiliar hills and valleys. His eyes rolled as he searched. Schools of fish felt him on their lateral lines and wheeled away. He plunged on, but saw no sand barrier, tasted nothing familiar.

He cried into the ocean, tapping out his bleat that traveled swiftly for hundreds of yards and then faded against the coastal reefs.

As the sun went down, lopsided as it reached the horizon, the giant child circled and circled the empty waters. He spied out and looked until he was tired. Finally he slept. His flippers, once the feet of his land-walking ancestors, hung down into the sea. His tense nostrils were barely above the surface.

Two hours later the young whale awoke. His skin was cold and he turned sleepily to nurse. Then he remembered his mother was not around. He swirled in panic. He breached, head in the air, fins out. He saw the land, and knew this was where he must begin to retrace his steps. He swam south.

No adult gray whales eat on the long eight-month migration, nor do they eat in the bays where they give birth to their young and remate. No other beast can go so long without eating and still be active. Woodchucks, ground squirrels, bears feed all summer, and starve all winter; but they sleep during their starvation and do not use much energy. Not the gray whale. This beast swims constantly while starving, with the exception of the babies that nurse on the trip north.

And so, the giant whale child sucked in the ocean because he was hungry and weak. He filtered out the plankton through odd rows of baleen teeth that were more like sieves than teeth. Then he rolled southward in fear and fright.

At noon he found Coos Bay. He knew its taste. His mother had taught him this. Swimming to the familiar barrier he tapped his jaws together and called. There was no answer in all the vast ocean. The young whale drifted into the cove. It was familiar. He had been born in a cove, in the low hot waters of the California Bay where flats shone white in the dry land. The young whale spied upon the shore. It was different from his first home; there were tall trees and lush plants. The strangeness alarmed him, and he submerged for his ten minutes underwater. The bars, the shallows, the light that flickered from the sun down into the bay were comforting. But he saw no whales. There had been thousands in the bay of his birth. This was a desolate cove.

The young whale felt strong instincts pulling him, and occasionally he swam to the mouth of the bay and looked north, for gray whales work on appointments with their needs. They must give birth to calves in the protected lagoons. They must depart on schedule to travel the 7,000 miles to the only food they eat—the plankton of the Bering Sea—and they must get there on time, or they starve to death. Again in the fall they must leave on schedule in order to reach the bays in time to have their babies in the protected waters. Any interference with this timing means death to the whales.

The young whale child tapped his teeth and circled Coos Bay. He had been born in January, a magnificent male of sixteen feet. Upon his arrival in the whale world, he had been immediately nuzzled by his giant mother, who, without arms or feet with which to hug him, expressed her love by circling him. She led him to the surface to blow; then, tipping her body, she showed him where to find her milk.

The rest of the two months in the lagoon were reassuring to the young whale child. Hundreds of other whales slept and rolled with him, each one awakening instinctively before the tide went out and beached him, an event which means certain death to a whale, for they are helpless on the land. The whale child learned to tell when the tide was leaving, and how to avoid being stranded. He met other young whales, and by meeting them, knew what he was.

In March there were fewer and fewer of his kind in the bay, for the great migration had started north. Finally his mother beat her tail, crunched her teeth and led him around sand bars, over hills, and out into the sea. He stayed close to her big side. She paused beyond the bay channel to teach him the tastes and pressures of his birthplace. Then she spanked him forward to keep her schedule with the burst of spring in the Bering Sea.

The young whale felt pressures and tastes in Coos Bay similar to those he knew as an infant, and so he lingered, blowing and swirling over the bottom. By night he would swim toward the shore, and by day he would surge to the entrance, feeling the pull of his species toward the dark waters of the north. But he did not know how to go.

And so he stayed where he was.

The days passed. His mother did not return. The huge child grew weak with longing and hunger. He could not know that they had lost each other as she had spurted forward to drive a killer whale from their path. Killer whales never kill adult gray whales, but they compete for the same waters; and so to protect their rights, they molest the young. Over the eons the gray whale has learned peace by avoidance. They keep to the bottom. The killers keep to the surface.

But all life is chance. A killer whale and the whale child's mother had met, and she responded to an old instinct. She chased him. From that moment on their separation became greater as the mother moved instinctively north searching for her child in an effort to keep her schedule with June in the Bering Sea. And the child, following the instincts of the young, looked for familiar waters.

A week later the tired whale child came up to the shores of Coos Bay where people moved and boats were tied. In loneliness he watched the boats. They were almost as big as his mother. One night he nuzzled one. And close beside its purring motors he fell asleep.

But as he slept he breathed like a wind tunnel. The owner of the yacht heard the strange sound, and came out to see if a storm were brewing.

He looked down into the water and saw the young whale sleeping happily against his ship. He stared again to make sure, then paced the entire length of his deck until he came to the end of the baby. An unmistakable whale tail lay under the water. He radioed the Marine Laboratory and he radioed the Fish and Wildlife Service.

At dawn the lost whale child was a captive.

The excitement was great. During the night the men had enclosed him in a great wire fence, and they all stood and stared at him as he snapped and rolled.

Gray whales had almost become extinct in the Pacific Ocean during the whaling years in the nineteenth century, but with laws prohibiting their killing, they had increased in numbers. Nevertheless the ships and boats on the Pacific often frightened them and diverted them from keeping their precise schedules with the plankton and the bays. And these delays spelled their death.

So the scientists in Coos Bay were thrilled to be able to study a live gray whale. They measured and weighed him. They noted the movements of the whale child, they put microphones in the water to record any sounds he might make, and they watched him judge the tide and swim to the deepest pocket of the cage when it went out. They took his temperature and analyzed his blood.

To feed him they poured nutrients into the water that were similar to the nutrition in the plankton. The formula came from studies made on the stomachs of other gray whales that had washed ashore in the past. The scientists were coming to a new understanding of this remarkable beast, and they were excited.

Meanwhile the remarkable beast grew weaker and weaker, for the plankton formula was not what he needed. He needed his mother's milk. He cried at night, and eyed the men by day.

Then one night a small craft, sailing out into the ocean, was rocked by an enormous object just off the sand bar at the lighthouse. The boat was thrown off course by the swell. Its crew peered into the water to see if they had struck anything, but the sea was black. Only a trail of phosphorescent animals told them something big had passed down the channel into the bay. They gave the incident little thought, for their boat righted itself quickly and purred on out to sea.

The next morning when the scientists came to take a cardiograph of the young whale, they were distressed to find the fence crunched as if it were paper—and the whale child gone.

Far out at sea a mother whale and her son blew four times and submerged to follow green currents in the depths of the Pacific Ocean. The mother lingered to teach her son the pressure and weight of these bleak waters. She was very patient, and her child was serious and obedient.

A school of sharks circled them as they plunged over the edge of the continental shelf and thundered north, for the belly of the female bore toothlike gashes—as if raked by a wire fence.

As they followed the watery highways, known only to the gray whales, the "roadsides" were spangled with the signs of spring. Diatoms[1] bloomed, copepods[2] glittered among the diatoms, fish glimmered as they tossed their silver eggs to the sea, and clams siphoned the bright water in and out of their valves; for it was springtime in the ocean.

---

[1] diatoms [dī'ə · tomz]: any of various tiny, single-celled plants with hard cell walls found in fresh or salt water

[2] copepods [kō'pə · pädz]: any of various tiny animals having a tough outer shell and found in fresh or salt water

---

Describe one part of the story that you remember best.

In what ways does the author reveal the strong bond between the mother whale and her baby?

The mother whale teaches her baby to recognize underwater landmarks. Does this information help the baby? Explain your answer.

How does the baby whale become a captive? How does it regain its freedom?

WRITE   Do you think it was right for the scientists to capture the baby whale? Write an opinion paragraph explaining your answer.

WORDS ABOUT THE AUTHOR

Jean Craighead George

In her book *Beastly Inventions: A Surprising Investigation into How Smart Animals Really Are*, Jean George wrote about her childhood. She says that she was not a scientist like her father and her brothers, "but without knowing it at the time, I was beginning a long search for unique animals of all kinds. It was not to be as organized a quest as theirs, but rather a hopscotch trip into worlds stretching well beyond my imagination."

AWARD-WINNING
AUTHOR

527

*J*ean George was born in Washington, D.C., in 1919. Her father was an entomologist; he studied insects. Her whole family enjoyed nature and being outdoors. When she went to college, Jean George studied science and English. Later she studied art and modern dance. After she finished school, she had several jobs, all of which had to do with writing or art. She worked as a newspaper reporter, a magazine artist, and a teacher. Then she became an editor and reporter for *Reader's Digest* magazine. Her experiences at the *Reader's Digest* gave her many ideas for her work as an author and illustrator.

Jean George's specialty is writing about nature and natural history, and she writes both books and magazine articles about nature and animal life. Her first books, which she wrote as her three children were growing up, were animal stories for children. At first she wrote and illustrated all her books by herself, but after writing *Summer of the Falcon* in 1962, she decided to have other illustrators do the pictures for her books.

To get ready for her writing, Jean George studies and travels, spending time in libraries and museums. She explores places like the Colorado River or the sea ice off Alaska and takes notes on what she sees. Doing such extensive research is a difficult job, but she makes good use of her work. She typically uses what she has learned about a subject to write both a nonfiction magazine article and a fiction book for young people.

When Jean George writes, she mixes natural history with good stories. Sometimes her stories are about the customs and backgrounds of people from different parts of the world. Although most of her books are written for and are usually about young people, she has written one or two books for adults. Her most famous book is *My Side of the Mountain*, which is about a boy who spends a winter surviving alone in the woods. Paramount Pictures made the story into a movie in 1969. Her own favorite, however, is *Spring Comes to the Ocean*, which she wrote in 1965. The American Library Association liked the book too. It put *Spring Comes to the Ocean* on its list of Notable Children's Books.

Jean George doesn't like to repeat the subjects she writes about. She has written about many things, including animals, nature, weather, cities, and regions of the earth. In 1982 she wrote her autobiography. She has even written a cookbook.

Whatever she writes, one thing is always the same: Jean George keeps searching. Even though she has learned a lot about nature and the world around her, she knows there is always more to discover.

illustrated by Wayne McLoughlin

530

WATER SKY

Jean Craighead George

• • •

Weir Amaogak is among the last of the old Eskimo whale hunters. In his time, the number of whales passing by the Alaskan coast has dropped sharply because commercial whaling ships have taken too many. The giant bowhead whales are endangered to such an extent that the Eskimos are now limited by the government to catching just a few each year. The Eskimo people believe in taking from the ocean only what they need to survive. They depend on the whales for food, shelter, and fuel for their fires.

Weir is on his way to the camp of another hunter, Vincent Ologak. Weir and Vincent share the Eskimo belief that whales give themselves to the hunters. The two men believe that a bowhead will soon present itself to them.

OUTSTANDING
SCIENCE TRADE
BOOK

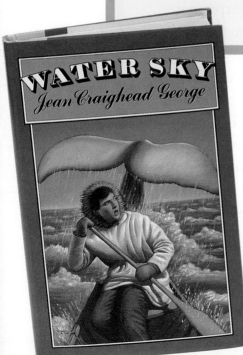

Iñupiat words in Water Sky

agviQ (ahg′ vik): bowhead whale
aiviQ (eye′ vik): walrus
Ataata (ah · ta′ ta): grandfather
boyer (boi′ yər): boy
Iñupiat (in · you′ pea · it): Eskimo people and language
Nukik (noo′ kik): "strength"
piayaaq agviQ (pie · ya · ahk′ ahg′ vik): a young whale
umiaq (oom′ me · ak): a boat made of animal skins

Weir Amaogak was somewhere in the white barrens between Wainwright and Barrow, humming as he pulled his graceful basket sled with a borrowed snow machine. He was coming along the coast on his way to join the Vincent Ologak crew. He glanced back to check on his thirteen-year-old grand-daughter, Ukpik. She was tucked in the furs on the old-style sled Weir had made of bent willow limbs from the foot of the Brooks Range. She sat with her feet straight out like a sitting bear's. Her nose and eyes peeked out of her blowing wolverine ruff. Weir Amaogak smiled to see his favorite person in all the world riding through the ice-bound wilderness with him. This was the second time he had taken her whaling, and he was glowing with thoughts of whales and this helpful grandchild.

Ukpik sat on a box that held Weir's harpoon, whale lance, ice saws and block and tackle. The harpooner had spent three weeks cleaning, sharpening and oiling the equipment out of respect for the whale. Everything must be perfect for the perfect animal.

Weir Amaogak was the last traditional harpooner. He used a harpoon to which was attached a pre-white-man sealskin float. When the harpoon was embedded in the whale, the float brought the animal to the surface and slowed it down so Weir could take it mercifully and honorably with his lance. He did not use the modern harpoon and shoulder gun that are equipped with bombs, for Weir did not use modern equipment. He used his old and primitive tools, his own knowledge of the anatomy of whales and his strength. He never missed.

He was also one of the last Eskimos in the Arctic to own a dog team. He had borrowed a friend's snow

machine for this trip, leaving his lively huskies at home out of consideration for his beloved friend Vincent Ologak. Dogs require a lot of food, and Vincent was no longer wealthy.

Also on the sled were survival supplies. The harpooner traveled his Arctic homeland with a stove, pots, food, gun, ammunition and skins. He carried these in the summer and winter, on five-hundred-mile trips as well as on two-mile excursions. He was alive because he took the same precautions his ancestors had taken when they traveled—he carried a home with him. No modern technology, which had changed so much of the North Slope and Eskimo life, could change the weather at the top of the world. As far as Weir was concerned, it was as dangerous and unpredictable as it had been when the Eskimos had migrated to the Arctic twenty thousand years ago.

Weir drove at a steady pace on the smooth ice along the beach. He noted the caribou on the land, the eider ducks out over the ice and, here and there, the graceful little Arctic foxes. This was a dangerous time for the foxes. It was spring, and they were anticipating the gray landscape of summer. Their fur was changing from white to gray. This, together with their black eyes and noses, made them more visible to enemies on the white snow and ice.

Weir checked on Ukpik again, and this time she pointed to her mouth to say she was hungry. Gladly he slowed down and stopped. He had been driving

for many hours and was ready for a rest. He reached into a skin bag, brought out the paniqtaq—dried fish and seal meat—and carried it to her.

"How much longer?" she asked.

"Less than half a sleep to go."

She slid off the sled, stretched her arms and hopped up and down to exercise her legs and toes. Ukpik was a petite young lady whose small nose and large black eyes gave her the wondrous look of natchiagruk, the baby seal. Her skin was like golden silk, and her red cheeks knotted into little apples when she smiled. Ukpik was very beautiful.

Ukpik means snowy owl in Iñupiat. Although her English name was Patsy, she preferred to be called Little Owl.

Little Owl was studying her native tongue in school. She also studied English, mathematics and American and English history, and took a course in corporate law. This was in preparation for her dual way of life as an American citizen and an Eskimo. The native villages of Alaska are incorporated. They invest their percentage of the oil taken on their land and spend the profits on their people. Schoolchildren are given a hundred dollars apiece by the North Slope School District to invest in their own school corporations. The children make and sell Eskimo doughnuts, charge for dances and invest the money they raise. Some graduate and manage the village corporations. Little Owl enjoyed her complicated education and was an excellent student.

She sat down on the snow machine beside Weir to finish her seal meat.

"What is Vincent Ologak's new apprentice like, Ataata?" she asked her grandfather.

"The what?"

"The new boyer, Vincent Ologak's relative from the outside? I heard you talking to Bertha about him."

"The new boyer. Yes, yes, that would interest you. I am getting old. Let me see, Bertha says he has not so much Eskimo in him and that he is very strong."

"Oh, Ataata, that's not what I'm asking. Did she say he was handsome? How old is he?"

"He is young. He is a piayaaq agviQ—a whale who has just left his mother."

"I mean how many years, silly Ataata."

"So young that his blubber is soft, like a young whale's."

She stopped pursuing that subject. "Do you think he'll be angry with me?"

"Be angry with you? Why would he be?"

"Because I will be paddling the umiaq with you when you go out to harpoon the whale."

"Yes, I want you. You are a strong paddler. But why should the boyer care?"

"Well, don't you think a boyer from the lower forty-eight would resent that? Me, a girl, in the boat and him in the kitchen?"

"Oh, he will be in the boat all right. Vincent Ologak says Nukik, the whale, will give himself to this boy."

"Vincent Ologak said that?" Her eyes widened. "Then it must be so."

Weir Amaogak pushed back his parka hood to better see the frozen ocean. A thick cap of silver-gray hair tumbled around his face and neck. Bold lines ran from his nose to the corners of his mouth, calling attention to his broad full lips. The half-moon eyes were permanently squinted from a lifetime of watching the ice and the wildlife. He blew on his bare hands and studied the horizon.

"Water sky, Ukpik," he said. "Want to ride out and see if the whales are passing through that lead?"

"I love to watch whales."

"The second wave of whales is late. Maybe we can learn something."

Weir Amaogak unhitched the sled. Little Owl swung onto the backseat of the snow machine and hugged her grandfather around the waist. They started out across the land-fast shore ice that forms in coves and is smoother than the open-sea ice. In a short distance the ice roughened, and Weir was bumping the machine through valleys and over pressure ridges beyond the cove. The water sky grew darker and darker until it hung like a rainstorm above them.

"We are here," Weir said, pulling around a blue-green ice mound and stopping beside a lake of open water in the continent of ice.

"Whale puddle," he said of the lake.

Its edges sparkled with a covering of thin clear ice that was forming in the calm. Weir studied the open water in the middle of the puddle while Little Owl observed the shores.

"AiviQ," she said, pointing to a monstrous brown walrus sitting like a pompous king on the edge of the whale puddle. His ivory tusks, which came down to the middle of his chest, were blunted by years of fighting bulls for his harem. The light gleamed on the wire-thick whiskers that jutted out of his puffy lips. He stared stone faced at Little Owl.

"Is he giving himself to us?" Ukpik asked. "He sits so still."

Weir did not answer. He was concentrating on the new ice near the east end of the whale puddle. Ukpik turned back to the walrus.

"Go home, aiviQ," she called. "We do not need you."

"Whale!" whispered Weir, pointing to a black slick at the far end of the lake. "AgviQ—see him?"

The slick moved and the black blowhole of an enormous whale lifted into the air.

Whoosssfff. The giant shot a geyser into the sun. Although Weir and Ukpik had seen hundreds and hundreds of whales, they watched as if this were their very first—in awed silence.

The whale went under, came up, breathed out and in, went under again. He did this seven times, then he sounded—dived deep and stayed down for thirteen minutes.

The thin ice that had formed in front of Weir and Little Owl buckled up into a huge air-filled dome. A whale could be seen inside it taking a breath. Weir dropped onto his stomach. Little Owl lay down beside him. They waited. The whale vanished.

Presently it blew in the open water, then lifted itself up until its twenty-foot head was in view. It turned one eye on the man and the girl. Thrashing its flukes, it rose yet higher.

"Sky hopping!" Weir whispered. "That's higher than a breach. The whale is excited." Little Owl held her breath. The giant was no more than thirty feet away and as big as the Wainwright church. The profile of its mouth curved up, then down, and ended just below its thoughtful eye. Water poured out between the rows of baleen in the great smile. It stood on end for a long moment, then threw itself onto the new ice and shattered it. Pieces shot out in all directions like glass spears. They tinkled as they fell back. Green and purple waves rolled up from the fall, breaking more ice. The whale spiraled onto its belly and, with a graceful twist, put its head in the water. Its back came into view. A flipper whirled and the tail stock, which seems too narrow for the bowhead bulk, curved above the water. Slowly the huge flukes lifted. They were white.

"Nukik!" Weir said softly.

A chill ran down Little Owl's spine. The leviathan was, indeed, looking for someone. She had seen his humanlike eye scanning Weir, then herself. The intelligence behind it had been dissatisfied or perhaps not interested. Nukik, she knew in her heart, was searching for Vincent Ologak's camp and the boyer. The white teachers at school did not believe whales gave themselves to people.

Another whale surfaced and blew far out in the whale puddle, and close at hand a female with a baby at her side came up to breathe. The mother lifted her youngster to the surface with a flipper. He took a breath, peered around and saw Little Owl. He lifted his head higher and wiggled his long gray-blue body, as if he knew another youngster when he saw one. Little Owl clapped her mittens over her mouth to keep from crying out in glee. The baby splashed and waved its flippers; then the mother scooped him up and dove with him. They left whale tracks, great swathes of smooth water on the surface outlined with turbulent bubbles.

"Oh, Ataata," Little Owl whispered. "I wish I could swim under the water with them. We land creatures can never really know the whales—only their blowholes and tails."

"Perhaps I can help you, Little Owl," Weir said, getting to his feet. "I sometimes feel that I am part whale. Sit down, little granddaughter. I will tell you what Nukik is doing.

"The water where he swims is green. Spears of gold light come down from the top of the water. They are the glowing lamps that lead Nukik to air. He looks for these bright guides that tell him where the leads are when he travels under the ice. It is pretty in Nukik's world. Fish flash around him, the ice shines, the kelp on the bottom of the sea dances and reaches up to him.

"The mother and baby have followed Nukik to the east end of the puddle. They are resting now." Weir sat very still, waiting for Nukik to do something else.

"Nukik is leading them under the ice."

Seven minutes passed without Weir speaking.

"Nukik has found a crack in the ice beyond the puddle, and the mother and baby are breathing there. They hang at the surface. They are comfortable and safe.

"Nukik is listening to the ice and current. He learns from the screeching of ice against ice that the leads are closed for miles and miles ahead. He and his pod of friends and relatives cannot travel their ancestral route along the shore." Weir suddenly smiled.

"Close your eyes, Little Owl. Can you see Nukik? He is very big and very fat. His head is slightly pointed. White scars mark his black skin. He is pocked with many holes and bumps. He is an old whale.

"He must be my age, Little Owl. Whales are like people. They have a long childhood, and like people they don't have babies until they are in their teens. They grow wise and old like us, and some, like some people, become good leaders. Nukik is one of these.

"And like us, whales grow old and die. Nukik's life is run. He is ready to complete the cycle and live again in our spirits and our bodies." Weir's voice was reverent and low.

"Much of this knowledge I know from my father and grandfather, who learned it from their fathers and grandfathers as far back as there have been Eskimo whalers. And I have added some new knowledge of my own."

"The whales must know about the Eskimos," Little Owl said. "Do you think, Ataata?"

"They probably know a lot about us," answered Weir. "And they probably know individual Eskimos as we know individual whales. I have seen Nukik of the white fluke many times. I am sure he knows me. One spring I saw him off Point Hope, when I harpooned for Ernie Fellow. Nukik waved a flipper. Last spring I saw him when I was with Vincent Ologak. He sky hopped for us, but he would not give himself to us. We were not the person he was looking for."

Weir stopped talking and read the sun as if it were a clock in the sky. He started the snow machine and drove back to the sled. Little Owl did not get on it.

"Don't go yet, Ataata," she said. "Nukik and

his friends are in trouble. Please tell me what he is doing now."

Life in the Arctic cannot be rushed, as every Eskimo knows, so Weir sat down. Passing on knowledge to the young is the most important thing an elder can do, and Weir took his responsibilities seriously.

He closed his eyes.

"Nukik has left the mother and baby resting in the crack. He pumps his whole body up and down and swims under the pack ice. He is watching for the lamps in the gloom. He sees only purple darkness, and far behind him the glow of the whale puddle like a moonrise under the sea."

Little Owl felt as if she were under the water at last. She closed her eyes.

"Now Nukik uses his senses. He hears the cracks and tastes the air pockets. They taste of sun. He finds an area where there are many cracks.

"Ahead is a mountain range of pack ice that reaches almost down to the ocean floor. It is jagged in some places, smooth in others. It is yellow and blue and green. The water pressure tells Nukik that the barrier goes on and on. The baby cannot dive deep enough to get under it or hold its breath long enough to find the air pockets.

"Nukik takes his kind of compass reading on this location. He photographs the shapes on his brain and notes the taste of the water. He returns to his pod and leads them to the breathing cracks under the pack ice. Now he returns to the mother and baby."

Apparently there was a lull in the events in the ocean, for Weir was silent. Little Owl thought of a question while they waited.

"Where did Nukik come from?" she asked.

"In the winter Nukik and his pod live with the sun in a secret place in the Bering Sea. Almost two weeks ago the lengthening day and the warming waters told them it was time to migrate to their summer home. They swam east with the second wave of a thousand or more whales.

"The first wave is made up of adolescents and young adults. They left the Bering Sea in early April and are now in their summering grounds. The third wave, of assorted sizes and ages, will pass Barrow in late May and early June.

"Nukik's wave is made up of mothers, their babies and youngsters, pregnant females and old whales like himself. Why the whales break up into these waves is known only to the whales.

"Nukik's wave swam until they came to the Bering Straits. There they were stopped by an ice jam that blocked the narrow pass.

"They were delayed many days. Finally, the sun warmed the water, the ice jam melted and floated away and Nukik and his pod continued. They swam past the Point Hope whalers without giving themselves. They swam by the Wainwright whalers without giving themselves and were stopped today by that wall of pack ice. So happily we came upon them." Weir's eyes opened and closed again. "Nukik is active."

"What is he doing now, Ataata?"

"He is circling the mother and baby. He slows down, for he hears something. He listens. A walrus is calling; his voice sounds like a church bell ringing underwater. The walrus is on his way to the bottom to dig in the mud for clams. Seals are whistling like chirruping birds. One shoots up from the depths, passes Nukik and pops up into her blue iglu. But now he is not listening for walrus and seals.

"Nukik usually pays attention to the seals. They feed on the fish that feed on the plankton. By joining the seals he finds the plankton.

"He also listens for the chirps of the beluga whales. They, too, eat the fish that feed on the plankton. But these voices do not interest him now." Weir cocked his head to one side, and the creases in his dark face smoothed as he concentrated.

"Nukik is listening for the voice of a bowhead, a deep lugubrious moo. He heard it once. He knows who it is, and the whale's call is urgent."

Little Owl clasped her hands together.

"Ataata, what is happening?"

"Nukik is back to the whale puddle. He finds the whale. She is a pregnant female. Nukik sounds, swims toward her and with grace breaches and looks around.

"There is no midwife or attendant with the female. Whales need help with their newborns. A friend usually lifts the baby to air as soon as it is born and while the mother recovers.

"Most whales are born in the water, but this mother throws her tail up on a thick piece of new ice. Her abdomen contracts with great force. Nukik sky hops, rising to the base of his tail stock. The female gives a long, low moo and delivers a fifteen-foot baby onto the ice."

"A baby whale has been born? Ataata, how lovely." Little Owl leaned closer, for Weir's eyes were scrunched tight and his voice was low.

"The infant snorts air, and the mother gently nudges him into the sea with her tail. She holds him up on her flipper to breathe. She lets him sink. She lifts him up. She lets him sink. At last the baby has learned the rhythm of breathing. Nukik swims quietly up to the little whale.

"He noses his granddaughter affectionately."

"Ataata, Ataata." Little Owl clapped her hands. "Nukik has a granddaughter. She will be good to him and love him." Weir squeezed Little Owl's hands and got to his feet. He glanced at the sun, then back at his granddaughter.

"Nukik will not lead his pod on. They will swim east without him. Nukik will stay with his daughter and granddaughter and the other mother and baby. He will teach them about the sea. He will breach and splash for them.

"And then, when the shore leads open again, Nukik will lead them to Vincent Ologak's camp. There he will leave them forever."

Would you like to live as Little Owl does? Why or why not?

How do you know Weir respects whales?

In what ways does Little Owl live in two worlds?

WRITE   In a short poem, show your feelings about an animal that is special to you.

FOLLOWING THE WHALES

In "Water Sky," Little Owl says, "We land creatures can never really know the whales—only their blowholes and tails." How do the two selections support or disprove this statement?

WRITER'S WORKSHOP

Think of an animal you have observed or read about. Choose one of the animal's unusual features, such as the cheetah's speed or the dolphin's appearance of smiling. Write an imaginative story about how that animal got its special feature.

Writer's Choice
By reading these selections, you followed whales. Now it is your chance to write about them. What do you want to say? Choose an idea, write about it, and share your writing in some way.

CONNECTIONS

MULTICULTURAL CONNECTION

LIFE IN THE SOUTH SEAS

Long ago, the people of the South Seas sailed the Pacific Ocean in giant canoes. They traveled great distances and settled thousands of islands, including Hawaii. Today these islands are known as Oceania. The 25,000 islands in Oceania are very small, and only a few thousand are inhabited.

Hawaii is a state of the United States. It is the only state that was once an independent monarchy. The last monarch was Queen Liliuokalani [li•lē•ə•wō•kə•län′ē], the only woman ever to rule Hawaii. Liliuokalani tried to maintain the independence of her people. However, in 1893 she agreed to give up her throne to protect her people from threats by foreign businesses. Queen Liliuokalani is remembered today for her bravery and her struggle to keep Hawaii from being taken over by foreign settlers.

Have a "South Seas Day" in class. Bring pictures or examples of South Seas island life and culture, and share them with classmates. Discuss what life might be like on a South Seas island.

Queen Liliuokalani

SCIENCE CONNECTION

ISLAND ENVIRONMENT

There are two main types of islands in the South Pacific: high islands and low islands. Research the origins and features of each type, and share this information with your classmates.

SOCIAL STUDIES/ART CONNECTION

ISLAND CHART

With a partner, find out about one of the islands or island groups in Oceania. Make a chart and list your findings. Display your chart, and be prepared to answer questions from your classmates.

UNIT SIX

OTHER PLACES

When people from places all over the world come to live in the United States, they enrich our nation with the ideas and values of their own cultures. Individuals from all groups, such as Chinese-born architect I. M. Pei, have made fine contributions to our country. Journeying to a faraway place and adjusting to a new way of life can be a difficult and trying experience. As you read the next selections, think about how having courage and a willingness to take risks helps people adapt to new environments and develop friendships with people of different worlds.

THEMES

BOOKSHELF

HELLO, MY NAME IS SCRAMBLED EGGS

BY JAMIE GILSON

Harvey Trumble and his family are temporarily hosting the Nguyens, who have recently arrived from Vietnam. Harvey's attempts to westernize their son Tuan prove comical as both boys learn a lesson in literal and figurative language appreciation.

Award-Winning Author

HARCOURT BRACE LIBRARY BOOK

TAKING SIDES

BY GARY SOTO

When Lincoln moves from the barrio to a white suburb, he worries about playing basketball against his former teammates in the big game.

Award-Winning Author

HARCOURT BRACE LIBRARY BOOK

NEIGHBORHOOD ODES

BY GARY SOTO

This collection of poetry celebrates the rich diversity of Mexican-American life in a modern California community.

Notable Children's Trade Book in the Field of Social Studies

EL GÜERO

BY ELIZABETH BORTON DE TREVIÑO

When his father is jailed under false charges, a young Mexican boy must travel a great distance to seek help.

Notable Children's Trade Book in the Field of Social Studies

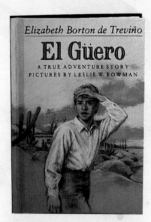

HOANG ANH: A VIETNAMESE-AMERICAN BOY

BY DIANE HOYT-GOLDSMITH

Hoang Anh, a young Vietnamese immigrant, describes his boyhood in the United States and tells how he keeps the customs and traditions of his native Vietnam.

Notable Children's Trade Book in the Field of Social Studies

T H E M E

QUIET COURAGE

What would you do if you found yourself stranded on an island, completely alone in a hostile environment? Read about a young girl in that situation who finds the courage to survive on her own and come to terms with her enemies.

C O N T E N T S

ISLAND OF THE BLUE DOLPHINS

BY
SCOTT O'DELL

ILLUSTRATED BY
LORI LOHSTOETTER

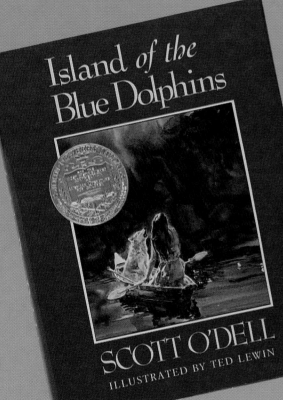

Island of the
Blue Dolphins

SCOTT O'DELL
ILLUSTRATED BY TED LEWIN

In the early 1800s, Karana, a Native American girl, lived with her tribe on an island off the coast of California. Aleut hunters attacked the tribe, killing most of the men. Fearful of another attack, Karana and the other remaining villagers boarded a rescue ship bound for the mainland. When Karana discovered her young brother had accidentally been left behind, she dove off the ship and swam back to the island. Two days later, Karana's brother was killed by a pack of wild dogs, and she was left totally alone.

THERE HAD been wild dogs on the Island of the Blue Dolphins as long as I remember, but after the Aleuts had slain most of the men of our tribe and their dogs had left to join the others, the pack became much bolder. It spent the nights running through the village and during the day was never far off. It was then that we made plans to get rid of them, but the ship came and everyone left Ghalas-at.

I am sure that the pack grew bolder because of their leader, the big one with the thick fur around his neck and the yellow eyes.

I had never seen this dog before the Aleuts came and no one else had, so he must have come with them and been left behind when they sailed away. He was a much larger dog than any of ours, which besides have short hair and brown eyes. I was sure that he was an Aleut dog.

Already I had killed five of the pack, but there were many left, more than in the beginning, for some had been born in the meantime. The young dogs were even wilder than the old ones.

I first went to the hill near the cave when the pack was away and collected armloads of brush which I placed near the mouth of their lair. Then I waited until the pack was in the cave. It went there early in the morning to sleep after it had spent the night prowling. I took with me the big bow and five arrows and two of the spears. I went quietly, circling around the mouth of the cave and came up to it from the side. There I left all of my weapons except one spear.

I set fire to the brush and pushed it into the cave. If the wild dogs heard me, there was no sound from them. Nearby was a ledge of rock which I climbed, taking my weapons with me.

The fire burned high. Some of the smoke trailed out over the hill, but much of it stayed in the cave. Soon the pack would have to leave. I did not hope to kill more than five of them because I had only that many arrows, but if the leader was one of the five I would be satisfied. It might be wiser if I waited and saved all my arrows for him, and this I decided to do.

None of the dogs appeared before the fire died. Then three ran out and away. Seven more followed and a long time afterwards a like number. There were many more still left in the cave.

The leader came next. Unlike the others, he did not run away. He jumped over the ashes and stood at the mouth of the cave, sniffing the air. I was so close to him that I could see his nose quivering, but he did not see me until I raised my bow. Fortunately I did not frighten him.

He stood facing me, his front legs spread as if he were ready to spring, his yellow eyes narrowed to slits. The arrow struck him in the chest. He turned away from me, took one step and fell. I sent another arrow toward him which went wide.

At this time three more dogs trotted out of the cave. I used the last of my arrows and killed two of them.

Carrying both of the spears, I climbed down from the ledge and went through the brush to the place where the leader had fallen. He was not there. While I had been shooting at the other dogs, he had gone. He could not have gone far because of his wound, but though I looked everywhere, around the ledge where I had been standing and in front of the cave, I did not find him.

I waited for a long time and then went inside the cave. It was deep, but I could see clearly.

Far back in a corner was the half-eaten carcass of a fox. Beside it was a black dog with four gray pups. One of the pups came slowly toward me, a round ball of fur that I could have held in my hand. I wanted to hold it, but the mother leaped to her feet and bared her teeth. I raised my spear as I backed out of the cave, yet I did not use it. The wounded leader was not there.

Night was coming and I left the cave, going along the foot of the hill that led to the cliff. I had not gone far on this trail that the wild dogs used when I saw the broken shaft of an arrow. It had been gnawed off near the tip and I knew it was from the arrow which had wounded the leader.

Farther on I saw his tracks in the dust. They were uneven as if he were traveling slowly. I followed them toward the cliff, but finally lost them in the darkness.

The next day and the next it rained and I did not go to look for him. I spent those days making more arrows, and on the third day, with these arrows and my spear, I went out along the trail the wild dogs had made to and from my house.

There were no tracks after the rain, but I followed the trail to the pile of rocks where I had seen them before. On the far side of the rocks I found the big gray dog. He had the broken arrow in his chest and he was lying with one of his legs under him.

He was about ten paces from me so I could see him clearly. I was sure that he was dead, but I lifted the spear and took good aim at him. Just as I was about to throw the spear, he raised his head a little from the earth and then let it drop.

This surprised me greatly and I stood there for a while not knowing what to do, whether to use the spear or my bow. I was used to animals playing dead until they suddenly turned on you or ran away.

563

The spear was the better of the two weapons at this distance, but I could not use it as well as the other, so I climbed onto the rocks where I could see him if he ran. I placed my feet carefully. I had a second arrow ready should I need it. I fitted an arrow and pulled back the string, aiming at his head.

Why I did not send the arrow I cannot say. I stood on the rock with the bow pulled back and my hand would not let it go. The big dog lay there and did not move and this may be the reason. If he had gotten up I would have killed him. I stood there for a long time looking down at him and then I climbed off the rocks.

He did not move when I went up to him, nor could I see him breathing until I was very close. The head of the arrow was in his chest and the broken shaft was covered with blood. The thick fur around his neck was matted from the rain.

I do not think that he knew I was picking him up, for his body was limp, as if he were dead. He was very heavy and the only way I could lift him was by kneeling and putting his legs around my shoulders.

In this manner, stopping to rest when I was tired, I carried him to the headland.

I could not get through the opening under the fence, so I cut the bindings and lifted out two of the whale ribs and thus took him into the house. He did not look at me or raise his head when I laid him on the floor, but his mouth was open and he was breathing.

The arrow had a small point, which was fortunate, and came out easily though it had gone deep. He did not move while I did this, nor afterwards as I cleaned the wound with a peeled stick from a coral bush. This bush has poisonous berries, yet its wood often heals wounds that nothing else will.

I had not gathered food for many days and the baskets were empty, so I left water for the dog and, after mending the fence, went down to the sea. I had no thought that he would live and I did not care.

All day I was among the rocks gathering shellfish and only once did I think of the wounded dog, my enemy, lying there in the house, and then to wonder why I had not killed him.

He was still alive when I got back, though he had not moved from the place where I had left him. Again I cleaned the wound with a coral twig. I then lifted his head and put water in his mouth, which he swallowed. This was the first time that he had looked at me since the time I had found him on the trail. His eyes were sunken and they looked out at me from far back in his head.

Before I went to sleep I gave him more water. In the morning I left food for him when I went down to the sea, and when I came home he had eaten it. He was lying in the corner, watching me. While I made a fire and cooked my supper, he watched me. His yellow eyes followed me wherever I moved.

That night I slept on the rock, for I was afraid of him, and at dawn as I went out I left the hole under the fence open so he could go. But he was there when I got back, lying in the sun with his head on his paws. I had speared two fish, which I cooked for my supper. Since he was very thin, I gave him one of them, and after he had eaten it he came over and lay down by the fire, watching me with his yellow eyes that were very narrow and slanted up at the corners.

Four nights I slept on the rock, and every morning I left the hole under the fence open so he could leave. Each day I speared a fish for him and when I got home he was always at the fence waiting for it. He would not take the fish from me so I had to put it on the ground. Once I held out my hand to him, but at this he backed away and showed his teeth.

On the fourth day when I came back from the rocks early he was not there at the fence waiting. A strange feeling came over me. Always before when I returned, I had hoped that he would be gone. But now as I crawled under the fence I did not feel the same.

I called out, "Dog, Dog," for I had no other name for him.

I ran toward the house, calling it. He was inside. He was just getting to his feet, stretching himself and yawning. He looked first at the fish I carried and then at me and moved his tail.

That night I stayed in the house. Before I fell asleep I thought of a name for him, for I could not call him Dog. The name I thought of was Rontu, which means in our language Fox Eyes.

Karana made a choice about the wild dog. Would you have made the same choice? Explain your answer.

How did Karana's feelings toward the dog change during the story? How did you know she had a change of heart?

Do you think Karana is brave? Explain your answer.

WRITE Make a list of things she should do for the dog. Then list things the dog might do for Karana.

Words About the Author:

SCOTT O'DELL

Scott O'Dell moved around a lot when he was growing up. There was San Pedro, which is a part of Los Angeles. And Rattlesnake Island, across the bay from San Pedro, where he lived in a house on stilts.

In 1960, when O'Dell began to write *Island of the Blue Dolphins,* his first book for young people, he remembered those early years on Rattlesnake Island. He and other boys his age used logs as canoes and paddled with their hands around the bay, exploring the surrounding islands. Karana, the heroine of the novel, is based on a Mexican girl

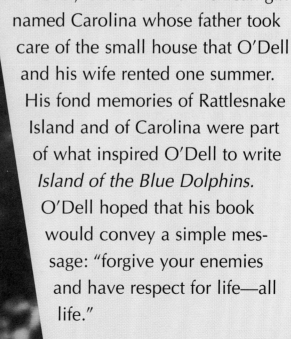

named Carolina whose father took care of the small house that O'Dell and his wife rented one summer. His fond memories of Rattlesnake Island and of Carolina were part of what inspired O'Dell to write *Island of the Blue Dolphins.* O'Dell hoped that his book would convey a simple message: "forgive your enemies and have respect for life—all life."

A Song of Greatness

When I hear the old men
Telling of heroes,
Telling of great deeds
Of ancient days,
When I hear them telling,
Then I think within me
I too am one of these.

When I hear the people
Praising great ones,
Then I know that I too
Shall be esteemed,
I too when my time comes
Shall do mightily.

A Chippewa Indian song
(transcribed by Mary Austin)

QUIET COURAGE

In what ways could Karana identify with "A Song of Greatness"?

WRITER'S WORKSHOP

Karana is alone on her island home. Imagine how you would feel if you were Karana. Write a poem to express your feelings. Try to use comparisons to show how you feel.

Writer's Choice

What does the theme Quiet Courage bring to mind now that you have read the selections? Think of some ideas, choose one, and write about it. Share your writing with others.

England

Puerto

Jamaica

ITAL

Vietnam

THEME

A NEW HOME

Language helps us communicate, but what happens when we meet a language we don't know? A language barrier is a challenge to the people in the following selections.

CONTENTS

573

The Vietnamese IN AMERICA

by Paul Rutledge

Immigrants have been coming to the United States since early in its history. Among the most recent groups of immigrants are people from Vietnam, a country in Southeast Asia.

Almost every aspect of daily life changes for Vietnamese refugees who settle in the United States. Attitudes toward the family, methods of education, language, even as common a matter as shopping for food—all these can be sources of culture shock for the Vietnamese. Their backgrounds, habits, and ways of everyday life are sometimes the opposite of American customs, and trying to blend the old ways with the new may cause the refugees bewilderment, pain, and conflict.

FAMILY

The Vietnamese family is under a great deal of pressure in trying to adjust to the American way of life. In the United States, a family usually consists of father, mother, and children. In Vietnam, a family is an extended one that includes the parents and the younger children, grandparents, married children, aunts, uncles, and a variety of other relatives. In some cases, all the members of an extended family live in the same house.

The family is the center of Vietnamese society, and it is the responsibility of every member to help the family survive. But the size of an extended Vietnamese family can make it difficult to find housing in America. Families want to establish themselves as close units but often cannot find adjacent housing large enough to accommodate 20 or 30 relatives.

In the Vietnamese culture, the older a person is, the more he or she is respected. Young people are always expected to seek the advice of older persons within the family. Children are taught to listen to and accept the decisions of their elders. In the traditional American family, however, individual members are more independent. In the United States, children are taught and advised by their parents in a less structured way.

When young Vietnamese refugees become friends with young Americans and see the more informal relationships between them and their families, the Vietnamese are likely to want the same kind of independence—something their Vietnamese parents find difficult to accept.

EDUCATION

The Vietnamese culture places a high value on education. As persons of knowledge, teachers are considered some of the most important members of society.

Before the Europeans entered Vietnam, the Confucian system of education dominated the country. This system was based on memorization. People could memorize large amounts of material and then take exams in which they quoted the memorized material. If they passed, they could improve their employment and social standing. Anyone —farmer or aristocrat—could take the exams.

During the French colonial period[1] in Vietnam, public schools were built, and education was emphasized. Teachers in these schools were considered role models as well as instructors, and children were reluctant to question their statements. Discipline was an important part of the educational system.

When they attend American schools, refugee children may find a conflict between Vietnamese methods of education and those used in the United States. In Vietnam, children listen to, and learn from, the teacher, who is always correct. In America, students learn from the teacher but are also taught to think for themselves. Many Vietnamese children find this difficult to do. They will always agree with everything the teacher says because to do otherwise would show great disrespect.

Some other aspects of U.S. education are unfamiliar to Vietnamese students. Activities such as individual research, classroom debates, learning by doing, and group projects are new and strange to them. Despite these differences, many young Vietnamese have adapted well to American education and are making good grades.

---

[1] French colonial period: the period during which Vietnam was governed by France—from 1883 to 1945

LANGUAGE

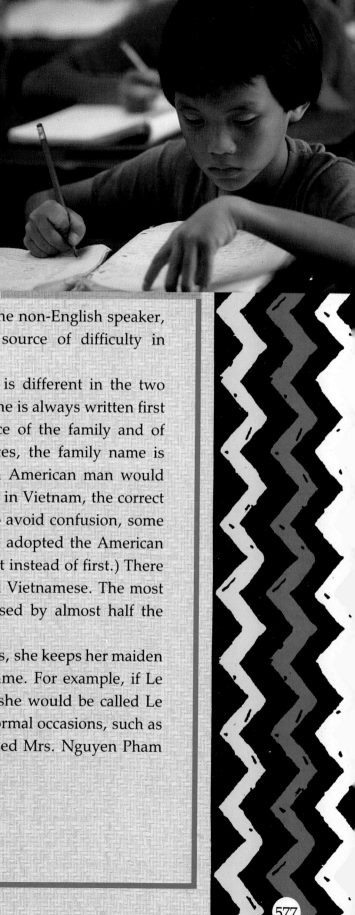

One of the most necessary, but also one of the hardest, tasks for a new refugee is learning the English language. The Vietnamese language contains six basic tones, and the sound of each word is part of the meaning of the word. English, which is not tonal, uses one word to mean many things. For the non-English speaker, this can be very confusing and a source of difficulty in attempting to learn English.

Even the way names are written is different in the two languages. In Vietnam, the family name is always written first in order to emphasize the importance of the family and of one's inheritance. In the United States, the family name is usually written last. For instance, an American man would write his name John Michael Doe, but in Vietnam, the correct form would be Doe John Michael. (To avoid confusion, some Vietnamese in the United States have adopted the American system and put their family names last instead of first.) There are only about 30 family names for all Vietnamese. The most common one is Nguyen, which is used by almost half the population.

When a Vietnamese woman marries, she keeps her maiden name and also uses her husband's name. For example, if Le Thi Ba married Nguyen Pham Binh, she would be called Le Thi Ba in informal situations, but on formal occasions, such as during a ceremony, she would be called Mrs. Nguyen Pham Binh.

C U S T O M S

The basic customs of Vietnamese life have been handed down from generation to generation just as American customs have been. There are many differences between the habits and attitudes of the two cultures.

Respect is very important to Vietnamese people. When greeting others, the Vietnamese bow their heads to show respect and honor. It takes some time for newly arrived refugees to get used to a casual "Hi" or "Hello" from people they pass on the street. In Vietnam, it is polite to look away when speaking to someone and rude to look directly at the person. This is exactly the opposite of behavior in the United States and often causes misunderstandings. Refugees are accused of being rude and unfriendly because they apparently ignore those speaking directly to them.

Even something as simple as color can be the source of conflict for the refugees. In Vietnam, the color white represents death. For the Vietnamese who enter an American hospital for the first time, seeing the white sheets and doctors and nurses dressed in white may convince them they are going to die.

Many of the practical aspects of life in the United States demand an adjustment by Vietnamese people. For example, the American transportation system presents a challenge, particularly for those used to living in farming areas. In Vietnam, walking and riding a bike were the most common forms of travel. Certainly not every family had a car. In the United States, the Vietnamese must cope with buses, subways, trains, airplanes, and especially cars.

Learning to drive is very difficult for older refugees, who are fearful of the heavy traffic and fast speeds in large U.S. cities. The younger generation, however, has fallen in love with American cars, and this causes some conflict in Vietnamese families. The parents feel that the car is breaking up the family, that the teenagers are always driving off by themselves or with friends when they should be spending time with relatives.

The ways in which food is prepared and even packaged can be confusing to recent arrivals. Fast-food hamburgers, pizza, and fried chicken are new to the refugees. In fact, the Vietnamese are not used to eating such greasily prepared items and usually do not like fried food at first.

Even the cans, boxes, and jars in American supermarkets can cause misunderstanding. One Vietnamese family in a large city spent several hours in a grocery looking at all the items. They were confused because they thought that the picture on each can and box showed what was inside the container. The family's young daughter was understandably frightened by a box of cereal with a monster pictured on it. These people would buy nothing but the fresh vegetables they could see and touch. Experience eventually made them more comfortable shopping for food American style.

Although Vietnamese immigrants want to learn as much as possible about American culture and to adapt to American life, most of them also want to keep the customs and language of their homeland alive. Like many earlier groups of immigrants, their goal is to become Americans without losing their ethnic identity.

What did you find out about the Vietnamese culture that you think is important in understanding the Vietnamese people? Explain why you feel this is important.

What are some of the differences between the American and Vietnamese cultures?

Compare the education a child in Vietnam receives with the education you are receiving. How do they differ and how are they similar?

WRITE Write an opinion paragraph convincing others of the importance of learning about different cultures.

Foreign Student

by Barbara B. Robinson
illustrated by Kevin Ghiglione

In September she appeared
   row three, seat seven,
   heavy pleated skirt,
   plastic purse, tidy notepad,
there she sat,
silent,
straight from Taipei,
and she bowed
when I entered the room.
A model student
I noticed,
   though she walked
   alone through the halls,
every assignment neat,
on time, complete,
and she'd listen
when I talked.

But now it's May
and Si Lan
is called Lani.
She strides in with Noriyo and
Lynne
and Natividad.
She wears slacks.
Her gear is crammed
into a macrame
shoulder sack.
And she chatters with Pete
during class
and
I'm glad.

Hello,

MY NAME IS SCRAMBLED EGGS

BY JAMIE GILSON

Harvey and Julia Trumble's family is hosting a family of Vietnamese refugees who have just arrived in America. Harvey knows it will be tough for the Nguyens to feel at home in their new country, so he takes on the responsibility of teaching young Tuan Nguyen everything he needs to know about American life. Harvey also wants to help Tuan make friends with the right people—and to keep him away from people like Quint Calkins, the class know-it-all. Right away, Harvey realizes that learning a new language is likely to be Tuan's biggest obstacle.

"Harvey, come look!" Julia called from the top of the third-floor steps. "They sleep funny."

"Quiet," I whispered and leaped the stairs two at a time to shush her. "Quiet, or they won't sleep at all." Still, it was the middle of Sunday afternoon, and they'd been up there almost twenty-four hours. The trip must really have zonked them out.

"Look at *that*," she whispered back and pointed into Pete's room.

illustrated by Bernadette Lau

AWARD-WINNING
AUTHOR

The door was open and I could see inside. It wasn't true they slept funny. They were sleeping like people do, all curled up. It was *where* they were sleeping that was funny. They were all in Pete's bedroom, but they weren't in bed. They'd taken the bedspreads off and put them on the floor, and that's where they were sleeping. I'd only slept on the floor at sleepovers, but it never worked out too good. When I woke up in the morning, I always had a crick in my neck.

"Julia!" I pulled her away from the door. "Don't be nosy." And I headed her back down the steps. On the way, though, I coughed a little, hoping to wake the kid up. We had work to do.

When Tuan came downstairs about an hour later, he was a lot hungrier for food than for facts. He ate two apples from the bushel in the kitchen, some of the big bowl of rice Mom had made special, and a whole lot of beef stew. I would never have thought that using a fork could be so hard. Just watching him made me nervous. And I wondered how anybody could possibly eat all those slippery little grains of rice with sticks.

Right after he ate, I steered him down to the basement to meet Felix, trusty computer. I'd decided it was time for Felix to teach him some new words. The first one would be *marble.* My dad had dug out a wrinkled leather pouch of his old marbles and given them to me so I'd have something in common with the kid. I mean, it wasn't as though I could shoot marbles or anything like that. My dad said it was an old American sport, but since I wasn't an old American, I didn't play it. Anyway, I opened the bag and dug out a big yellow one with tiny bubbles in it and gave it to the kid. He looked it over but didn't remember what it was called.

"Marble," I said, and typed it out on Felix. "What is it called in Vietnamese?"

He typed DANH-BI. "Need mark through *d* and over *n,*" he told me, but the computer couldn't handle that. "Say, '*dańh-bi.*'"

It was hard to say. It didn't fit my mouth, and so I only tried once. He started to hand the marble back. "Keep it," I said, holding my hands behind my back. "Keep it." He put it on the workbench.

Pete's bike was leaning up against the wall, in storage till he came home.

BICYCLE, I typed out on Felix and, giving the handlebars a pat, said it out loud.

So did the kid. "Bi-cyc-le."

"Close," I told him.

XE-DAP, he typed. "And mark through . . ." He pointed at the *d*. "*Bicycle* is *xe-dap.*"

"Shut up?" I asked. That's sure what it sounded like.

"Close," he said.

"Do you know what *shut up* means?"

"*Shut up*? No. What means *shut up*?"

"It means 'be quiet.'" I put my finger in front of my lips and said, "Shhhhhhhhhh." He nodded. "Shut up!" I yelled.

"You talk loud to ask be quiet?"

"Right. *Shut up!* That's the way to say it," I shouted.

"*Shut up!*" he yelled back, laughing.

"You boys all right down there?" Mom called down the steps.

"Fine," I told her. "We're OK."

"What means *OK*?" he asked.

"*OK* means 'good,' 'terrific.' *OK* is basic. *OK* is the best. We'll have Felix tell you 'OK' every time you get a word right, OK?"

"OK."

We sat there for a long time with me teaching him words like *follow*. First I marched around behind him. "I *follow* you." Then I got in front of him and made him say, "I *follow* you." I was the leader. He was my follower. We did verbs like *throw* and *hide* and *laugh* and *vomit.* After we'd both acted them out, I'd write them into the computer. And Tuan would write in the Vietnamese word so he'd remember what the English one meant. Input, output. Input, output. It was terrific. We were working on *hiccup* when Mom called down the steps again.

"Harvey, you've got company. It's almost ten o'clock, though, just about time for bed."

"Tuan just barely got up," I told her, "and he's got lots of work to do. Who's there?"

"Quint the Quintessential," he called down grandly.

Big deal, I thought. "Enter," I said, though, since nothing was likely to stop him. He took the steps slow and heavy, waving and grinning. I turned back to the computer.

"Hi, there, Zilch," he said. "Having a good time with your new toy?"

"The computer's not all that new," I told him, punching a few keys casually.

"I wasn't talking about the computer." He grinned, and leaning with his mouth close to my ear, he whispered, "Uncovering the mysteries of the Orient?"

"No!" I pushed him away with my shoulder. "I'm teaching Tuan English."

He gave the kid a big hello like he was his biggest admirer and then circled around behind him and rolled his eyes at me. "So, why bother?" he asked.

"He's got to learn it. He starts school Friday, the end of this week. With us."

"You're kidding. Our *class*?"

"Why not? He's twelve. Mom says it's fixed so he can be with me."

Quint laughed through his nose. "He doesn't know his elbow from an escalator and he's going to be in the same class with *me*? Gifted old me? He ought to be in Julia's room."

Tuan was working on the words we'd programmed. OK, Felix printed, turning on his computer charm. OK, TUAN. The kid glanced at Quint, who clapped his hands, yelled, "OK!" and nodded as if the kid had just won the Nobel Peace Prize.

Tuan turned back to the computer, smiling. Quint rolled his eyes again.

"You *are* good," he said to Tuan, as Felix went OK once again.

The kid beamed back.

"Will you teach me marbles?" Quint asked him.

"Teach?" He turned away from the computer. "*Teach* you?"

"Right." Quint picked up my yellow marble from the counter. "Will you teach me how?"

"Yes." Tuan grinned at him. "OK."

"Tomorrow?" Quint was trying to take my kid away from me. That's what he was trying to do. He handed Tuan the marble *I'd* given him just ten minutes before. "My uncle wants to ask the kid some questions," he whispered to me, like we were both in on some big joke. "Wayne knows a lot of words in Vietnamese. He wants to look him over."

"Sorry. Tuan's busy with important stuff tomorrow and Tuesday and Wednesday and Thursday, and he starts school Friday."

"After school Friday it is, then. You come to my house Friday," Quint told the kid. "OK?"

"I've got to work after school Friday," I told him.

"I didn't ask you," Quint explained like I was a little kid who'd begged to tag along to a party. "OK?" he said to Tuan again.

"OK! Marbles." You'd have thought the president had invited him to breakfast at the White House, he was so pleased.

"See you around." Quint took the stairs two at a time, slamming the basement door so we'd have something to remember him by.

When the place had stopped shaking, I said to the kid, patiently and slowly, "You don't want to go to Quint's."

"Yes," he said, smiling broadly, "I go to him house."

"*His* house."

"His house. He is . . . Quint?"

"Yes, he's Quint, all right."

"Quint is OK. Right way to use OK?"

"Right," I said. But I sure didn't mean it.

"Hello, my name is jelly," Julia said, staring at the name tag stuck to a jar on the kitchen table. She'd guessed wrong. It said, HELLO, MY NAME IS JAM. Tossing her stuffed owl Zachary onto her chair, Julia climbed on top of him, leaned back, and stared up.

"Hello, my name is Ceiling. Is that right?" I nodded. "I can read *ceiling*! Maybe they'll let me skip first grade." She craned her neck to look at the sign again. "Are you sure that says *ceiling*? Mrs. Broderick says the snake sound, *Ssssssssssssssssss*, is *S*. Silly Sally Ceiling. See, it's got to be wrong."

"Ceiling," Tuan said automatically, copying it into a small notebook I'd given him. NEW WORDS, I'd printed on the cover. He was eating breakfast and hadn't noticed that one yet.

"Remember '*I* before *E* except after *C*,'" I told him as he wrote. He blinked at me.

I'd got the name tags from this huge stack left over from a party of Mom's where nobody wore them. The tags had little red wavy borders with HELLO, MY NAME IS printed on the front and sticky stuff on the back. I'd written about a hundred names of things on them. Then I'd matched them up, sticking them on the sugar bowl, the doors, floors, apples, toilet, computer, boot box. Every day after I came home from school, I'd take the kid around naming things for him. The house was beginning to look like a first-grade workbook.

"Hello, my name is Butter Dish," Julia said. "Harvey, make one for Zachary. He's jealous."

"That tag better not leave a mark on the ceiling," Dad told me, wiping his mouth with his napkin. "And the day you lay one on my scrambled eggs, you've had it."

Actually, I *had* made a Scrambled Eggs label, but I'd decided it would slide off, and so I'd just stuck it in my back pocket.

"Your father is absolutely right," Mom said. "If there's anything that flusters me, it's eggs that try to get too friendly. More toast, Tuan?"

He shook his head and leaned over his scrambled eggs with a fork, watching me closely as I ate. He waited a long time before picking up the bacon with his fingers as I did, making sure that's how Dad ate his, too. His grandmother sat by herself at the end of the table. He called her Ba Noi, which means, he said, "your father's mother." A white wool shawl Mom had found for her was tucked tightly around her like a cocoon. She was not having scrambled eggs for breakfast, but broth with noodles in it, first drinking the broth and then eating the noodles with chopsticks she'd brought with her.

"Get Tuan to school on time, now," Dad called, barreling out the back door. Then Ba Noi spoke. She said something to Tuan—low, fast, and kind of sharp. Tuan answered her quietly, glancing around at us and then down at his feet.

"Is something wrong?" Mom asked him. "May we help?"

The kid shook his head and took a deep breath. I wondered if he was trying to think what to say or how to say it. "Ba Noi say I not . . . look good for school," he whispered.

He looked good to me. I'd told him what to wear—faded jeans, a striped T-shirt, and the red, white, and blue tennis shoes Mom had bought him the day before. Perfect.

"Tell her I say it's *very* American."

"She want me *very* Vietnamese . . . blue pants. . . ." He sliced across his leg with his hand to show he meant the short ones he'd worn when he arrived.

I laughed. "You dress like that and everybody'll think you're weird. Besides, in this weather you'd die of terminal goose bumps." I knew he hadn't understood that. "Cold," I said, shaking myself with a shiver. "Short pants are for summer."

"Hello, my name is Clock," Julia announced. "We're going to be late."

Tuan spoke again to his grandmother. She still did not look pleased. But we waved good-bye to her and to Mom and hurried off. Tuan was smiling as if he liked looking very American.

On the way, we worked on tree names and street names. I named. He repeated. Once we got to school, I showed him the water fountain, the john, and the trophy case. People kept saying, "Hi," and so I taught him a few of the kids' names, too. It was an educational experience.

Finally, I got him to the principal's office. Mr. Saine was on the phone when I poked my head in. ". . . will deal with that matter immediately," he told the phone, motioning us to come on in.

Mr. Saine stood up, way up. I mean, he must be six-five. Tuan came about to his belt.

"Hi," Tuan said, holding out his hand when Mr. Saine came over to greet us.

"Why, hello, young man." Mr. Saine shook his hand, looking pleased by good manners and all that. "I've been expecting you. How's his English?" he asked me, his voice lowered.

"I'm teaching him," I said.

"Good, fine." He sat back in his chair and started looking through some papers. "First you take him to homeroom. And after that we'll line up some diagnostic tests to see where square one should be, since there aren't any transcripts. Understood?"

I nodded. The kid smiled, understanding nothing. I could read the look by now. Mr. Saine shuffled through a stack of papers on his desk. "Reverend Zito tells me your name is . . ." He clamped his hands together, took a deep breath, and pronounced it all wrong.

And that was when I got the idea. If the kid really did want to be an American and to be one fast, the name Tuan Nguyen wouldn't do. It wouldn't do any more than short pants on a cold day. You put that name in lights or across a headline and people would get it wrong almost every time.

"He's just decided to change it. The name you've got isn't right. It *used* to be Tuan Nguyen. But now he's going to be . . ."

I tossed the sounds around in my head a few times until his name turned, without any problem at all, into . . . "Tom. His first name is Tom." Mr. Saine glanced at Tuan/Tom, who smiled and nodded, but clearly understood not a word. Mr. Saine wrote down Thomas. I took a breath, and before I let it out, had the whole thing. From Nguyen to Gwen to Win, easy as that. "Win. His full American name is Tom Win. W-I-N." I felt like an artist painting a brand-new picture.

"And a fine name it is, too," Mr. Saine said loudly to the kid, who was still staring blankly into our fog of too-fast words. *"Welcome to Pittsfield and Pittsfield Junior High School, Tom Win!"* His voice made the trophies on the shelf vibrate.

"Thank you." Tuan smiled politely. "Shut up," he said, a little louder.

Mr. Saine's jaw dropped open. So did mine. The room turned suddenly still, as if somebody had vacuumed out all the sound. My knees felt like rubber bands. Mr. Saine's face was gray.

Tuan kept smiling, though he did look uneasy.

"I . . . I . . . I . . ." I stuttered, my voice turned high like I'd just swallowed a balloonful of helium. "I think . . . I think . . . See, I told him, I taught him, that 'shut up' means 'be quiet.' I think"—I swallowed hard because my throat had become a desert—"he means you don't have to shout. A lot of people have been shouting at him, thinking it will help him understand. And it *doesn't* help, really. I taught him 'shut up' because it sounds a lot like Vietnamese bicycles." Mr. Saine's frown deepened. "He means to be polite. He learns fast. I even *told* him to say it loud, I—"

"All right, Harvey," Mr. Saine interrupted me, still looking grim. His face was flushed. "I'll accept that." He said it, but I wasn't sure he meant it. "It's late," he said, using his normal voice. "Give these papers to your homeroom teacher, and, Harvey"—he took a deep breath—"*re*-explain 'shut up.'"

"Good night," the kid said, beaming.

We hurried out of the office toward homeroom, Tuan looking so cheerful I started to laugh out loud. He was positively the only kid in the whole school, in the whole world, maybe, who could get away with saying "shut up" to Mr. Saine. I was laughing, but my knees wobbled as I walked.

"Oh, by the way," I told Tuan as we reached the homeroom door, "your new American name is Tom." I stopped, opened my notebook, and wrote it down. "Tom," I repeated. "You."

"Tuan," he said. "Me."

"You have a new name, Tom Win. It's a terrific name. I made it up myself. I wish it was mine. I mean, like, it goes more with jeans and tennis shoes than the old one did. When you hit a homer at the bottom of the ninth with the bases loaded, they'll say, 'Win wins!' Tom Win," I repeated slowly. "The American you."

He stopped and thought about it. "Ba Noi say no. Father say no." The last bell rang.

"Do you want to be American or don't you?"

He nodded. "But Ba Noi say . . ."

"OK, then, just at school. Tom Win at school. Tuan Nguyen in the privacy of your own home. Ba Noi won't have to know. To her and your dad you'll stay Tuan. No kidding, could I be Vietnamese and have a name like Harvey Trumble?"

He laughed and shook his head. "OK," he said. "Tom Win is me."

I rushed him into homeroom, a new kid.

The class, most all of them in their seats by now, looked up from what they were doing and stared at us.

"Uh, Miss Schwalbach," I said, handing her the papers Mr. Saine had given me, "this is the new Vietnamese boy we've been talking about, only he's changed his name. It's . . . uh . . . Tom Win. Mr. Saine says after homeroom he's supposed to go to the office for tests."

"Of course." She beamed at him. "So it's to be Tom Win?"

He glanced at me. "Yes," he told her. He held his hand out, and she shook it.

"We're glad you're here, Tom. People," she told the class, "I want you to be sure to welcome Tom Win cordially."

"That's not what I heard him called." Quint tilted back in his chair.

"Goes to show you don't know everything," I said very casual, like of course *I* did. "He's called Tom Win," I announced to the class. My kid, named by me.

Miss Schwalbach motioned to an empty place in the front row. "Sit here, Tom."

He sat. Tom Win sat. He could host a game show with a name like that.

When the bell rang for first period, I delivered the kid to the office. Even though I said good-bye and wished him good luck, I was certain they'd be calling me out of science or language arts to help him with the tests. The morning went by without a messenger, though, and I guessed they'd given up on him or something. So I was really surprised when I got to the cafeteria at lunch and there he was, still smiling, sitting with Suzanna, eating a hamburger layered with pickles, mustard, and catsup.

"I just explained that hamburger isn't made out of ham." Suzanna popped a french fry in her mouth.

"It is cow," Tom told me. "It is good." He took another bite.

"Did the whole family change their names?" She drew a smiley face in a pool of catsup with her last fry.

"Not yet." That might take some doing. We'd break it to them slowly. It was going to be some trick keeping the Tom/Tuans straight. The kid had this double identity like a spy. If only I could change my name, too. Tom Win would have suited me fine. "How'd it go?" I asked him. "Were the tests hard?"

He took a gulp of chocolate milk and blinked at the taste, licking his upper lip. "Words hard, Harvey. Numbers . . . weird."

That was a word I'd taught him by making faces. _Weird_. He liked it, but I guess it was like _shut up_. He didn't know what it meant. Numbers are a lot of things—like impossible. Weird, though, they're not.

But Mr. Tandy, our math teacher, sounded like he thought so, too. "A little strange," he said when class started. He smiled at Tom, who had finished his tests in time to come to the last class of the day. "Yes, class, you'd think that math was math the whole world over, but there are differences. I talked to our remarkable new student, Tom Win, this morning as he was taking some tests, and he suggested that some of our ways with numbers were unusual. I thought I'd check it out with the rest of you."

The kid looked at the floor, embarrassed.

"Tom, go to the chalkboard. And Quint, you too, just to demonstrate the differences."

Quint, wearing his fabulous-me face, brought the kid with him to the board. They both took pieces of chalk and, when Mr. Tandy told them to, wrote down 675 divided by 15. Quint's problem looked normal: $15\overline{)675}$. When he finished doing the problem, he looked over at the kid, who already had the answer. "Bizarre," he said. Mr. Tandy grinned. The kid had written, very neatly:

$$\begin{array}{c|c} 675 & 15 \\ 075 & 45 \end{array}$$

"Why'd he do it like that?" Quint asked, cocking his head. He shrugged. "I could have done it in my head."

"I expect he could have too, but that, of course, is not the point." Mr. Tandy was annoyed with him. "Now, both of you, write down twenty-five dollars."

Quint scribbled out $25.00 as fast as he could. Nobody was going to outrace him.

Carefully, the kid wrote: 25$00.

"More bizarre," Quint said, and everybody had to agree.

"You boys can sit down." I never saw Mr. Tandy quite so pleased. He grinned like everybody had gotten the extra-credit question right, or something equally miraculous. "And in Vietnam, when two thousand is written down it's . . ." Glancing first to the ceiling, where he always looks for approval, he wrote on the board 2.000. "There's a *point* after the thousand. On the other hand, they use a decimal *comma*. Thusly." He wrote 1,52. "Anybody think of a reason why one system is any better than the other, aside from the fact that you're used to it?"

Nobody raised a hand. He chuckled. "Neither can I. Isn't that fascinating!"

Quint rolled his eyes. "Knocks me out," he said sarcastically. A few kids giggled. Mr. Tandy laughed mildly, too. He knows not everybody is as crazy about math as he is. But he could afford to laugh. He was passing out a pop quiz. Aaarg.

"So, will this test count?" Caroline asked.

"Pieces of paper can't count. But I certainly hope you can. Any other questions?"

"Yes." Caroline sighed. "Do we have to take it?"

"You're wasting our time, Caroline."

All the time in the world wouldn't help. I knew I should have studied the night before instead of helping the kid learn English. We'd fooled around at Felix for a couple of hours, watched a little TV, sung with the commercials. I scratched on.

When Mr. Tandy said, "Exchange papers, please," a mass groan swelled out over the desks. I wasn't finished. A lot of kids weren't. The story problem was quicksand sucking me under.

Quint had already turned his paper over on his desk so no one could cheat from it. He was cleaning his fingernails with a toothpick.

Suzanna grabbed the kid's paper quick before I could. How she thought she was going to read it, I couldn't imagine. "What do I do about the commas and points?" she asked.

"If everything else is OK, grade them right. He'll get the knack of the mechanics soon enough."

"That's not fair," Quint complained.

Mr. Tandy started down the row, asking kids for answers and talking about problems.

"So, what do I do when Quint's decimal point's wrong?" Caroline asked. "Because one *is*."

"Mark it wrong. He knows better." Quint leaned over to look, not believing it.

When we got to the last problem, Suzanna raised her hand excitedly and said, "Tuan . . . or Tom, whatever, got them all right. He did most of the marks our way. But he skipped the story problem."

"Terrific! Tom? The story problem?" Mr. Tandy pointed to it.

"I cannot read it."

Mr. Tandy looked at the ceiling again with a smile. He'd found another math person. Big deal. "I think it's *remarkable* that he's adjusted so quickly. Suzanna, mark the paper one hundred percent. And a big A. It ought to give him a real boost. He'll be able to read the story problems as well as you can before long."

"That isn't fair," I said. "If it's wrong, it's wrong. He's got to learn that." *I'd* gotten it wrong. And half the other problems too. There's such a thing as being too nice. I didn't want my kid spoiled. Besides, he'd kept me from studying. And he'd had all day Wednesday and Thursday to look at the books I'd brought him from school. He couldn't read most of the stuff, and so he'd probably spent all his time on the math I'd told him we were doing. He'd been *studying*. Hours probably. He didn't have anything else to do with me gone. "No fair," I said again.

Quint, who'd been looking pretty mad himself, suddenly crossed his arms and tilted his chair back. "Oh, forget it. He's no real hotshot," he said to me. "But he's no Zilch either." Then he looked at me funny. "*You* didn't teach him that stuff, did you?"

I smiled, genius in disguise.

"Your problem," Mr. Tandy said to the class, "is that you're not reading carefully enough. You're not following directions. I want you all to read that story problem over tonight and then to work it correctly."

Caroline opened her assignment notebook. It was plastered with puffy and smelly stickers. "Tonight's Friday," she said. "That's T.G.I.F."

"As good a night as any. Do this as part of your weekend homework. You *must* learn to follow directions." He chopped the air with his hand to pound out every single syllable. "Fol-low the di-rec-tions!"

Tom Win stood up at once. All heads turned to him. He turned his to me. What did he think he was doing? "Harvey?" he asked me.

I shrugged and stared down at the field of initials scratched on my desk. I didn't know what he was getting at. He was embarrassing me, standing there all by himself saying, "Harvey?"

"Where," he asked Mr. Tandy, "where is . . . Directions . . . so I can follow him?"

The bell rang, but even though it was Friday, the kids stayed in their seats and laughed out loud. He was a big joke to them. A hundred percent in math, and he thought it was time for Follow the Leader. And they weren't just laughing at *him.* I could feel it in the hairs on the back of my neck. They knew he was mine. They were laughing at me, too.

But when I looked up again, Quint had already gathered the kid up and was heading him out the door.

"Marbles," Tom Win called, holding up his bag of them. "Good night."

Quint waved. "This foreign person may be more interesting than I thought. I'll find out if my uncle is right. Anyway, your clone," he said, "has flown."

I couldn't possibly have followed them, even though *follow* seemed to be the word of the day. I'd have been late for work. But, I decided, the kid seems to be pretty smart. He'll figure Quint out in a hurry. It'll be good for him. I headed off, whistling.

After reading about the Trumble family's experience, do you think you would or would not enjoy hosting a family from another country? Explain your answer.

How does Harvey help Tuan learn the names of objects around the house?

Is learning a new language Tuan's only obstacle? Explain your answer.

Do you think Harvey has a right to consider Tuan *his* kid?

WRITE   Write a brief set of instructions telling how to help someone feel at home in a new place and learn a new language.

A NEW HOME

Does "The Vietnamese in America" reflect the experiences of Si Lan and Tom Win? Explain your answer.

WRITER'S WORKSHOP

Imagine that Tom Win wants to order some clothes to wear to school. Write a business letter in which he asks for clothing that most American students wear.

Writer's Choice

The selections describe people adjusting to new homes. What comes to mind when you think about a new home? Write a poem or story about what you think. Respond in your own way. Then find someone with whom you can share your writing.

THEME

RIDING THE SEAS

Crossing the mighty, rolling Atlantic Ocean in an eighteenth-century sailing ship would be an adventure for anyone. You will read about a girl whose adventure on the high seas changes her life.

CONTENTS

In 1832, after years of attending school in England, thirteen-year-old Charlotte is crossing the Atlantic Ocean to rejoin her family in Providence, Rhode Island. She is sailing aboard the

The True Confessions of
Charlotte Doyle
BY AVI
ILLUSTRATIONS BY PETE HARRITOS

Seahawk, a freight-carrying brig run by Captain Andrew Jaggery, a man with a reputation for being harsh with his crew. When Charlotte learns that the crew plans to take over the ship, she warns the captain and spoils their plot. But Captain Jaggery doles out such extreme punishment that Charlotte realizes she was wrong to tip him off. Now she wonders how to regain the trust of the crew.

NEWBERY HONOR
BOSTON GLOBE-
HORN BOOK AWARD
SLJ BEST BOOKS OF
THE YEAR

The True
Confessions of
CHARLOTTE
DOYLE
a novel by
AVI

That night I remained in my cabin. I couldn't eat. Now and again I slept, but never for long. There were times I fell on my knees to pray for forgiveness. But it was from the crew as much as God that I sought pardon. If only I could make restitution, if only I could convince the men that I accepted my responsibility.

Close to dawn an idea began to form, at first only an echo of something Fisk had said. But the mere thought of it was appalling and I kept pushing it away. Yet again and again it flooded back, overwhelming all other notions.

At last I heaved myself off the bed, and from under it brought out the canvas seaman's garments Zachariah had made for me. Some roaches skittered away. I held the wrinkled clothing up and looked at its crude shape, its mean design. The feel of the crude cloth made me falter.

I closed my eyes. My heart was beating painfully as if I were in some great danger. No, I could not. It was too awful. Yet I told myself I *must* accept my responsibility so as to prove to those men that it had been my head that was wrong, not my heart. Slowly, fearfully, I made myself take off my shoes, my stockings, my apron, at last my dress and linen.

With fumbling, nervous hands I put on the seaman's clothing. The trousers and shirt felt stiff, heavy, like some skin not my own. My bare toes curled upon the wooden floor.

I stood some while to question my heart. Zachariah's words to Fisk, that I was the "very soul of justice" echoed within me.

I stepped out of my cabin and crept through the steerage. It was dawn. To the distant east, I could see the thinnest edge of sun. All else remained dark. I moved to the galley, praying I would meet no one before I reached it. For once my prayers were answered. I was not noticed. And Fisk was working at the stove.

I paused at the doorway. "Mr. Fisk," I whispered.

He straightened up, turned, saw me. I had, at least, the satisfaction of his surprise.

"I've come," I managed to say, "to be one of the crew."

For a second time I stood in the forecastle. The room was as dark and mean as when I'd first seen it. Now, however, I stood as a petitioner in sailor's garb. A glum Fisk was at my side. It hadn't been easy to convince him I was in earnest about becoming one of the crew. Even when he begrudged a willingness to believe in my sincerity he warned that agreement from the rest of the men would be improbable. He insisted I lay the matter before them immediately.

So it was that three men from Mr. Hollybrass's watch, Grimes, Dillingham, and Foley, were the next to hear my plea. As Fisk had foretold, they were contemplating me and my proposal with very little evidence of favor.

"I do mean it," I said, finding boldness with repetition, "I want to be the replacement for Mr. Johnson."

"You're a girl," Dillingham spat out contemptuously.

"A *pretty* girl," Foley put in. It was not meant as a compliment. "Takes more than canvas britches to hide that."

"And a gentlewoman," was Grimes's addition, as though that was the final evidence of my essential uselessness.

"I want to show that I stand with you," I pleaded. "That I made a mistake."

"A mistake!" Foley snapped. "Two able-bodied men have died!"

"Besides," Dillingham agreed, "you'll bring more trouble than good."

"You can teach me," I offered.

"God's fist," Grimes cried. "She thinks this a school!"

"And the captain," Foley asked. "What'll he say?"

"He wants nothing to do with me," I replied.

"That's what he *says*. But you were his darling girl, Miss Doyle. We takes you in and he'll want you back again. Where will that put us?"

613

So it went, round and round. While the men made objections, while I struggled to answer them, Fisk said nothing.

Though I tried to keep my head up, my eyes steady, it was not easy. They looked at me as if I were some loathsome *thing*. At the same time, the more objections they made, the more determined I was to prove myself.

"See here, Miss Doyle," Dillingham concluded, "it's no simple matter. Understand, you sign on to the articles, so to speak, and you *are* on. No bolting to safe harbors at the first blow or when an ill word is flung your way. You're a hand or you're not a hand, and it won't go easy, that's all that can ever be promised."

"I know," I said.

"Hold out *your* hands," he demanded.

Fisk nudged me. I held them out, palms up.

Foley peered over them. "Like bloody cream," he said with disgust. "Touch mine!" he insisted and extended his. Gingerly, I touched one of them. His skin was like rough leather.

"That's the hands you'd get, miss. Like an animal. Is that what you want!"

"I don't care," I said stoutly.

Finally it was Dillingham who said, "And are you willing to take your place in the rigging too? Fair weather or foul?"

That made me pause.

Fisk caught the hesitation. "Answer," he prompted.

"Yes," I said boldly.

They exchanged glances. Then Foley asked, "What do the others think?"

Fisk shook his head and sighed. "No doubt they'll speak the same."

Suddenly Grimes said, "Here's what I say: let her climb to the royal yard. If she does it and comes down whole, and *still* is willing to serve, then I say let her sign and be like the rest of us."

"And do whatever she's called on to do!"

"No less!"

With no more than grunts the men seemed to agree among themselves. They turned toward me.

"*Now* what does Miss Doyle say?" Grimes demanded.

I swallowed hard, but all the same I gave yet another "Yes."

Foley came to his feet. "All right then. I'll go caucus the others." Out he went.

Fisk and I retreated to the galley while I waited for word. During that time he questioned me regarding my determination.

"Miss Doyle," he pressed, "you have agreed to climb to the top of the royal yard. Do you know that's the highest sail on the main mast? One hundred and thirty feet up. You can reach it only two ways. You can shimmy up the mast itself. Or you can climb the shrouds, using the ratlines for your ladder."

I nodded as if I fully grasped what he was saying. The truth was I didn't even wish to listen. I just wanted to get past the test.

"And Miss Doyle," he went on, "if you slip and fall you'll be lucky to drop into the sea and drown quickly. No mortal could pluck you out fast enough to save you. Do you understand that?"

I swallowed hard but nodded. "Yes."

"Because if you're *not* lucky you'll crash to the deck. Fall that way and you'll either maim or kill yourself by breaking your neck. Still certain?"

"Yes," I repeated, though somewhat more softly.

"I'll give you this," he said with a look that seemed a mix of admiration and contempt, "Zachariah was right. You're as steady a girl as ever I've met."

Foley soon returned. "We're agreed," he announced. "Not a one stands in favor of your signing on, Miss Doyle. Not with what you are. We're all agreed to that. But if you climb as high as the royal yard and make it down whole, and if you still want to sign on, you can come as equal. You'll get no more from us, Miss Doyle, but no less either."

Fisk looked at me for my answer.

"I understand," I said.

"All right then," Foley said. "The captain's still in his cabin and not likely to come out till five bells. You can do it now."

"Now!" I quailed.

"Now before never."

So it was that the four men escorted me onto the deck. There I found that the rest of the crew had already gathered.

Having fully committed myself, I was overwhelmed by my audacity. The masts had always seemed tall, of course, but never so tall as they did at that moment. When I reached the deck and looked up my courage all but crumbled. My stomach turned. My legs grew weak.

Not that it mattered. Fisk escorted me to the mast as though I were being led to die at the stake. He seemed as grim as I.

To grasp fully what I'd undertaken to do, know again that the height of the mainmast towered one hundred and thirty feet from the deck. This mast was, in fact, three great rounded lengths of wood, trees, in truth, affixed one to the end of the other. Further, it supported four levels of sails, each of which bore a different name. In order, bottom to top, these were called the main yard, topsail, topgallant, and finally royal yard.

My task was to climb to the top of the royal yard. And come down. In one piece. If I succeeded I'd gain the opportunity of making the climb fifty times a day.

As if reading my terrified thoughts Fisk inquired gravely, "How will you go, Miss Doyle! Up the mast or on the ratlines!"

Once again I looked up. I could not possibly climb the mast directly. The stays and shrouds with their ratlines would serve me better.

"Ratlines," I replied softly.

"Then up you go."

I will confess it, at that moment my nerves failed. I found myself unable to move. With thudding heart I looked frantically around. The members of the crew, arranged in a crescent, were standing like death's own jury.

It was Barlow who called out, "A blessing goes with you, Miss Doyle."

To which Ewing added, "And this advice, Miss Doyle. Keep your eyes steady on the ropes. Don't you look down. Or up."

For the first time I sensed that some of them at least wanted me to succeed. The realization gave me courage.

With halting steps and shallow breath, I approached the rail only to pause when I reached it. I could hear a small inner voice crying, "Don't! Don't!"

But it was also then that I heard Dillingham snicker, "She'll not have the stomach."

I reached up, grasped the lowest deadeye, and hauled myself atop the rail. That much I had done before. Now, I maneuvered to the outside so that I would be leaning *into* the rigging and could even rest on it.

Once again I looked at the crew, *down* at them, I should say. They were staring up with blank expressions.

Recollecting Ewing's advice, I shifted my eyes and focused them on the ropes before me. Then, reaching as high as I could into one of the middle shrouds, and grabbing a ratline, I began to climb.

The ratlines were set about sixteen inches one above the other, so that the steps I had to take were wide for me. I needed to pull as much with arms as climb with legs. But line by line I did go up, as if ascending an enormous ladder.

After I had risen some seventeen feet I realized I'd made a great mistake. The rigging stood in sets, each going to a different level of the mast. I could have taken one that stretched directly to the top. Instead I had chosen a line which went only to the first trestletree, to the top of the lower mast.

For a moment I considered backing down and starting afresh. I stole a quick glance below. The crew's faces were turned up toward me. I understood that they would take the smallest movement down as retreat. I had to continue.

And so I did.

Now I was climbing inside the lank gray-white sails, ascending, as it were, into a bank of dead clouds.

Beyond the sails lay the sea, slate-gray and ever rolling. Though the water looked calm, I could feel the slow pitch and roll it caused in the ship. I realized suddenly how much harder this climb would be if the wind were blowing and we were well underway. The mere thought made the palms of my hands grow damp.

Up I continued till I reached the main yard. Here I snatched another glance at the sea, and was startled to see how much bigger it had grown. Indeed, the more I saw of it the *more* there was. In contrast, the *Seahawk* struck me as having suddenly grown smaller. The more I saw of *her,* the *less* she was!

I glanced aloft. To climb higher I now had to edge myself out upon the trestletree and then once again move up the next set of ratlines as I'd done before. But at twice the height!

Wrapping one arm around the mast—even up here it was too big to reach around completely—I grasped one of the stays and edged out. At the same moment the ship dipped, the world seemed to twist and tilt down. My stomach lurched. My heart pounded. My head swam. In spite of myself I closed my eyes. I all but slipped, saving myself only by a sudden grasp of a line before the ship yawed the opposite way. I felt sicker yet. With ever-waning strength I clung on for dearest life. Now the full folly of what I was attempting burst upon me with grotesque reality. It had been not only stupid, but suicidal. I would never come down alive!

And yet I had to climb. This was my restitution.

When the ship was steady again, I grasped the furthest rigging, first with one hand, then the other, and dragged myself higher. I was heading for the topsail, fifteen feet further up.

Pressing myself as close as possible into the rigging, I continued to strain upward, squeezing the ropes so tightly my hands cramped. I even tried curling my toes about the ratlines.

At last I reached the topsail spar, but discovered it was impossible to rest there. The only place to pause was three *times* higher than the distance I'd just come, at the trestletree just below the topgallant spar.

By now every muscle in my body ached. My head felt light, my heart an anvil. My hands were on fire, the soles of my feet raw. Time and again I was forced to halt, pressing my face against the rigging with eyes closed. Then, in spite of what I'd been warned not to do, I opened them and peered down. The *Seahawk* was like a wooden toy. The sea looked greater still.

I made myself glance up. Oh, so far to go! How I forced myself to move I am not sure. But the thought of backing down now was just as frightening. Knowing only that I could not stay still, I crept upward, ratline by ratline, taking what seemed to be forever with each rise until I finally reached the level just below the topgallant spar.

A seasoned sailor would have needed two minutes to reach this point. I had needed thirty!

Though I felt the constant roll of the ship, I had to rest there. What seemed like little movement on deck became, up high, wild swings and turns through treacherous air.

I gagged, forced my stomach down, drew breath, and looked out. Though I didn't think it possible, the ocean appeared to have grown greater yet. And when I looked down, the upturned faces of the crew appeared like so many tiny bugs.

There were twenty-five or so more feet to climb. Once again I grasped the rigging and hauled myself up.

This final climb was torture. With every upward pull the swaying of the ship seemed to increase. Even when not moving myself, I was flying through the air in wild, wide gyrations. The horizon kept shifting, tilting, dropping. I was increasingly dizzy, nauseous, terrified, certain that with every next moment I would slip and fall to death. I paused again and again, my eyes on the rigging inches from my face, gasping and praying as I had never prayed before. My one hope was that, nearer to heaven now, I could make my desperation heard!

Inch by inch I continued up. Half an inch! Quarter inches! But then at last with trembling fingers, I touched the spar of the royal yard. I had reached the top.

Once there I endeavored to rest again. But there the metronome motion of the mast was at its most extreme, the *Seahawk* turning, tossing, swaying as if trying to shake me off—like a dog throwing droplets of water from its back. And when I looked beyond I saw a sea that was infinity itself, ready, eager to swallow me whole.

I had to get back down.

As hard as it was to climb up, it was, to my horror, harder returning. On the ascent I could see where I was going. Edging down I had to grope blindly with my feet. Sometimes I tried to look. But when I did the sight of the void below was so sickening, I was forced to close my eyes.

Each groping step downward was a nightmare. Most times my foot found only air. Then, as if to mock my terror, a small breeze at last sprang up. Sails began to fill and snap, puffing in and out, at times smothering me. The tossing of the ship grew—if that were possible— more extreme.

Down I crept, past the topgallant where I paused briefly on the trestletree, then down along the longest stretch, toward the mainyard. It was there I fell.

I was searching with my left foot for the next ratline. When I found a hold and started to put my weight upon it, my foot, slipping on the slick tar surface, shot forward. The suddenness of it made me lose my grip. I tumbled backward, but in such a way that my legs became entangled in the lines. There I hung, *head downward.*

I screamed, tried to grab something. But I couldn't. I clutched madly at nothing, till my hand brushed against a dangling rope. I grabbed for it, missed, and grabbed again. Using all my strength, I levered myself up and, wrapping my arms into the lines, made a veritable knot of myself, mast, and rigging. Oh, how I wept! my entire body shaking and trembling as though it would break apart.

When my breathing became somewhat normal, I managed to untangle first one arm, then my legs. I was free.

I continued down. By the time I reached the mainyard I was numb and whimpering again, tears coursing from my eyes.

I moved to the shrouds I'd climbed, and edged myself past the lowest of the sails.

As I emerged from under it, the crew gave out a great "Huzzah!"

Oh, how my heart swelled with exaltation!

Finally, when I'd reached close to the very end, Barlow stepped forward, beaming, his arms uplifted. "Jump!" he called. "Jump!"

But now, determined to do it myself, I shook my head. Indeed, in the end I dropped down on my own two India-rubber legs—and tumbled to the deck.

No sooner did I land than the crew gave me another "Huzzah!" With joyous heart I staggered to my feet. Only then did I see Captain Jaggery push through the knot of men and come to stand before me.

There I stood. Behind me the semicircle of the crew seemed to recoil from the man and from Mr. Hollybrass, who appeared not far behind.

"Miss Doyle," the captain said with barely suppressed fury. "What is the meaning of this?"

I stood mute. How could I explain to *him?* Besides, there were no words left within me. I had gone through too many transformations of mood and spirit within the last twenty-four hours.

When I remained silent he demanded, "Why are you dressed in this scandalous fashion? Answer me!" The angrier he became, the darker grew the color of the welt on his face. "Who gave you permission to climb into the rigging?"

I backed up a step and said, "I . . . I have joined the crew."

Unable to comprehend my words Captain Jaggery remained staring fixedly at me. Then gradually he did understand. His face flushed red. His fists clenched.

"Miss Doyle," he said between gritted teeth, "you will go to your cabin, remove these obscene garments and put on your proper dress. You are causing a disruption. I will not allow it."

But when I continued to stand there—unmoving, making no response—he suddenly shouted, "Did you not hear me? Get to your cabin!"

"I won't," I blurted out. "I'm no longer a passenger. I'm with them." So saying, I stepped back until I sensed the men around me.

The captain glared at the crew. "And you," he sneered. "I suppose you'd have her?"

The response of the men was silence.

The captain seemed unsure what to do.

"Mr. Hollybrass!" he barked finally.

"Waiting your orders, sir."

The captain flushed again. He shifted his attention back to me. "Your father, Miss Doyle," he declared, ". . . he would not allow this."

"I think I know my father—an officer in the company who owns this ship, and your employer—better than you," I said. "He *would* approve of my reasons."

627

The captain's uncertainty grew. At last he replied, "Very well, Miss Doyle, if you do not assume your proper attire this instant, if you insist upon playing these games, you shall not be given the opportunity to change your mind. If crew you are, crew you shall remain. I promise, I shall drive you as I choose."

"I don't care what you do!" I threw back at him.

The captain turned to the first mate. "Mr. Hollybrass, remove Miss Doyle's belongings from her cabin. Let her take her place in the forecastle with the crew. Put her down as *Mister* Doyle and list *Miss* Doyle in the log as lost. From this point on I expect to see that *he* works with the rest." With that, he disappeared into the steerage.

No sooner had he done so than the crew—though not Mr. Hollybrass—let out another raucous cheer!

In just such a fashion did I become a full-fledged crew member of the *Seahawk.* Whatever grievous errors I had made before—in thwarting the mutiny led by Cranick and in causing the resulting cruelty toward Zachariah—the sailors appeared to accept my change of heart and position without reservation. They saw my desire to become a crew member not only as atonement, but as a stinging rebuff to Captain Jaggery. Once I had showed myself willing to do what they did—by climbing the rigging—once they saw me stand up to Jaggery, an intense apprenticeship commenced. And for it the crewmen became my teachers. They helped me, worked with me, guided me past the mortal dangers that lurked in every task. In this they were far more patient with all my repeated errors than those teachers at the Barrington School for Better Girls when there was nothing to learn but penmanship, spelling, and the ancient authors of morality.

You may believe me too when I say that I shirked no work. Even if I'd wanted to, it was clear from the start that shirking would not be allowed. I pounded oakum into the deck. I scraped the hull. I stood watch as dawn blessed the sea and as the moon cut the midnight sky. I tossed the line to measure the depths of the sea. I took my turn at the wheel. I swabbed the deck and tarred the rigging, spliced ropes and tied knots. My mess was shared with the crew. And I went aloft.

Indeed, that first journey to the top of the mainmast was but the prelude to many daily climbs. Of course, after that first there were always others who went along with me. High above the sea, my crewmates taught me to work with one hand—the other *must* hold on—to dangle over spars, to reef sails, to edge along the walk ropes. So I came to work every sail, at every hour of the day.

If you were a member of the crew, would you let Charlotte join? Explain your answer.

Explain in detail what Charlotte Doyle has to do to join the crew.

Why does Charlotte want to join the crew? What do her actions tell you about her character?

Compare how Charlotte looks and acts at the beginning of the story with the way she looks and acts at the end.

WRITE Charlotte says that her head, not her heart, was wrong when she warned the captain. Write a paragraph explaining what you think she meant.

Words About the Author:

Avi

Every book Avi writes is different. For example, he has published *S.O.R. Losers*, a funny, contemporary novel, *The True Confessions of Charlotte Doyle*, an historical adventure, and *Nothing But the Truth*, a story told through letters, newspaper articles, dialogues, and diary entries. When asked why all his books are so different from one another, Avi replies, "You know there are lots of ways to tell a story. To me that's just fun."

Avi was born in New York City in 1937. He comes from a family of writers and has always been around books. At first, he tried writing plays and novels for adults, but he didn't have much success. "Only when my own kids came into my life did I start to write for young people," Avi says. "Writing for kids has been at the center of my life ever since."

The True Confessions of Charlotte Doyle is Avi's twenty-third book. Although it won many awards, some critics said the book had an improbable ending. Avi responded in his *Boston Globe-Horn Book* Award acceptance speech: "I am deeply grateful for the award you have given me today. But I hope you will understand me when I tell you that if the 'improbable' life I wrote lives in someone's heart as a life *possible*, then I have already been given the greatest gift a writer can receive."

Tides

by Rachel Field

AWARD-WINNING
AUTHOR

The tide is high! The tide is high!
The shiny waves go marching by
Past ledge and shallow and weedy reach
Up the long gray lengths of shingle beach;
Like an army storming height on height
With green-blue armor and banners white
On, on they charge to the farthest line
Of scattered seaweed brown and fine—
So far, then, grumbling, back creep they,
And the tide has turned for another day.

The tide is low! The tide is low!
Weed-decked and gaunt the ledges show
With mussel shells in blues and blacks
And barnacles along their backs.
Now kelp shines like mahogany
And every rock pool brims with sea
To make a little looking glass
For sky and clouds and birds that pass.

Painting by John Rewald Seurat
Le Bec du Hoc, Grandcamp. 1885
Courtesy, Harry N. Abrams, Inc., New York
Northeaster, 1895

RIDING THE SEAS

How is the ocean as Charlotte experiences it different from the ocean as described in "Tides"?

WRITER'S WORKSHOP

Think about a time when your feelings changed about something as Charlotte's change about the crew. Describe your feelings before and after the change took place.

Writer's Choice
Riding the seas meant adventure for Charlotte Doyle. What does it mean to you? Write about what you think of the theme. Choose some way to share your writing.

CONNECTIONS

MULTICULTURAL CONNECTION

BUILDING A DREAM

Nearly 2 million people immigrate to the United States yearly, seeking a new home and a new life. In return, many immigrants make valuable contributions to American life.

As Chinese-born architect Ieoh Ming (I. M.) Pei watched many new buildings rise in Canton in the 1920s and 1930s, he became interested in architecture. In 1954, Pei became an American citizen and, soon after, began his own architectural firm. The building of the east wing of the National Gallery of Art in Washington, D.C., challenged Pei's ingenuity and problem-solving skills. Pei's firm also designed the National Center for Atmospheric Research in Colorado and the glass pyramid at the Louvre museum in Paris.

Despite his preference for classical music, Pei was selected in 1987 to design the Rock and Roll Hall of Fame in Cleveland, Ohio.

I. M. Pei has worked with a sense of understanding and responsibility and has given the world some of its most interesting architecture.

Hold an "Immigrant Day" in class. With a group, find out why and how one immigrant group came to the United States. Share your findings with your classmates in a creative way, such as a skit or a mural.

I.M. Pei, architect

SOCIAL STUDIES CONNECTION

IMMIGRANT HALL OF FAME

Research an immigrant who contributed to American society. Examples include Elizabeth Blackwell, Mikhail Baryshnikov, Arnold Schwarzenegger, and Claude McKay.

Find answers to these questions:

- What country did the immigrant leave? Why?
- What obstacles did he or she face?
- How has the person made a difference?

Find or draw a picture of the immigrant you chose. Make up an award that recognizes his or her achievements. Make an "Immigrant Wall of Fame" display on a classroom wall or bulletin board. Invite other classes to view your display.

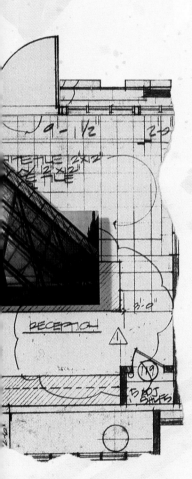

MATH CONNECTION

CIRCULAR REASONING

Make a circle graph from the information below about the regions of origin of immigrants in the early 1900s.

- Northern and Western Europe — 39.6%
- Asia — 2.75%
- Southern and Eastern Europe — 49.6%
- Latin America — 2.4%
- North America — 5.4%
- Other — .25%

Write four word problems based on the graph, and exchange them with a partner. After you answer the questions, use an almanac to find out the regions of origin of immigrants in the 1990s. Work with your partner to use the information to make another circle graph. What differences do you notice in the two graphs? Why do you think they are so different?

GLOSSARY

The **pronunciation** of each word in this glossary is shown by a phonetic respelling in brackets; for example, [dis′ri·gärd′]. An accent mark (′) follows the syllable with the most stress: [in·koun′tər]. A secondary, or lighter, accent mark (′) follows a syllable with less stress: [an′ti·dōt′]. The key to other pronunciation symbols is below. You will find a shortened version of this key on alternate pages of the glossary.

Pronunciation Key*

a	add, map	m	move, seem	u	up, done
ā	ace, rate	n	nice, tin	û(r)	burn, term
â(r)	care, air	ng	ring, song	yo͞o	fuse, few
ä	palm, father	o	odd, hot	v	vain, eve
b	bat, rub	ō	open, so	w	win, away
ch	check, catch	ô	order, jaw	y	yet, yearn
d	dog, rod	oi	oil, boy	z	zest, muse
e	end, pet	ou	pout, now	zh	vision, pleasure
ē	equal, tree	o͝o	took, full	ə	the schwa, an
f	fit, half	o͞o	pool, food		unstressed vowel
g	go, log	p	pit, stop		representing the
h	hope, hate	r	run, poor		sound spelled
i	it, give	s	see, pass		a in *above*
ī	ice, write	sh	sure, rush		e in *sicken*
j	joy, ledge	t	talk, sit		i in *possible*
k	cool, take	th	thin, both		o in *melon*
l	look, rule	t̶h̶	this, bathe		u in *circus*

*Adapted entries, the Pronunciation Key, and the Short Key that appear on the following pages are reprinted from *HBJ School Dictionary*. Copyright © 1990 by Harcourt Brace & Company. Reprinted by permission of Harcourt Brace & Company.

A

a·byss [ə·bis'] *n.* A bottomless
space, as a crack in the earth.

ac·com·mo·date [ə·kom'ə·dāt'] *v.*
To hold or house comfortably: **We
rented a larger apartment to**
accommodate **our growing
family.** *syn.* fit

ac·knowl·edge [ak·nol'ij] *v.*
ac·knowl·edged,
ac·knowl·edg·ing To indicate
that one has received something.

ad·ja·cent [ə·jā'sənt] *adj.* Close by;
next to: **Miguel and Gus lived in**
adjacent **homes, and one was
always running next door to see
the other.** *syn.* nearby

ad·o·les·cent [ad'ə·les'ənt] *n.*
A person or an animal who is no
longer a child but is not yet an
adult: **The students in high
school are** *adolescents.*

ad·ver·si·ty [ad·vûr'sə·tē] *n.* Great
misfortune or trouble: **Family
members help each other get
through times of** *adversity.*
syn. hardship

af·fec·tion·ate·ly
[ə·fek'shən·it·lē] *adv.* In a way
that shows love or kindness. *syn.*
lovingly

a·ghast [ə·gast'] *adj.* Shocked or
horrified: **We were** *aghast* **at such
rude behavior.**

am·u·let [am'yə·lit] *n.* A charm
worn to keep away evil or bad
luck: **People in ancient Egypt
believed that wearing** *amulets*
would keep them safe.

an·i·mos·i·ty [an'ə·mos'ə·tē] *n.*
Hatred: **Because he had been
bitten once, Oscar felt nothing but** *animosity* **toward
dogs.**

an·tag·o·nism [an·tag'ə·niz'əm] *n.*
Opposition to each other:
Antagonism **had existed for years
between the two countries.**

an·tic·i·pate [an·tis'ə·pāt'] *v.*
an·tic·i·pat·ed, an·tic·i·pat·ing
To look forward to something.
syn. expect

an·ti·dote [an'ti·dōt'] *n.* Anything
that counteracts or removes the
effects of a poison or disease: **The
doctor gave an** *antidote* **to the
snakebite victim.**

anx·ious [angk'shəs] *adj.* Nervous
or worried: **The shy girl felt**
anxious **about going to a new
school.** *syn.* uneasy

ap·prox·i·mate [ə·prok'sə·mit] *adj.*
Almost exact, correct, or like: **The
class made guesses about the**
approximate **number of beans
in the jar.**

ar·chae·ol·o·gist [är'kē·ol'ə·jist] *n.*
A person who studies past cul-
tures, usually by examining
ancient artifacts.

a·ris·to·crat [ə·ris'tə·krat'] *n.* A
person of inherited high rank; an
upper-class person: **In that
nation, an** *aristocrat* **had more
wealth and power than someone
of the middle class.** *syn.* patrician

as·cend [ə·send'] *v.* **as·cend·ed,
as·cend·ing** To go upward: **The
children carefully** *ascended* **the
steep staircase.** *syn.* rise

as·pect [as'pekt] *n.* A part, an angle,
or an appearance of something.

as·sess [ə·ses'] *v.* **as·sessed,
as·sess·ing** To look at and figure
out. *syn.* evaluate

as·sur·ance [ə·shŏŏr'əns] *n.*
Something a person says to keep
someone else from worrying.

B

ba·leen [bə·lēn'] *n.* Whalebone,
which is a flexible material hanging
from the upper jaw of some types
of whales: **A whale's** *baleen* **sepa-
rates seawater from the tiny plants
and animals the whale eats.**

archaeologist

affectionately

ban·ish [ban′ish] *v.* **ban·ished, ban·ish·ing** To force to leave a country or place: **He was *banished* from the country because he spoke out against the king.**

bar·na·cle [bär′nə·kəl] *n.* A shellfish that attaches itself to objects or other animals: **When the sailor turned the boat over to clean it, he noticed that its bottom was covered with *barnacles*.**

be·grudge [bi·gruj′] *v.* To envy someone because of something he or she has: **Don't *begrudge* him his success—he worked hard for it.**

bel·lig·er·ent·ly [bə·lij′ər·ənt·lē] *adv.* In an argumentative or challenging manner.

bi·zarre [bi·zär′] *adj.* Odd or unusual: **We were puzzled by the stranger's *bizarre* behavior.** *syns.* strange, weird

bus·tle [bus′(ə)l] *v.* **bus·tled, bus·tling** To move around with excitement: **The students *bustled* around the stage, getting ready for the next act of the play.**

C

cap·stan [kap′stən] *n.* A large spool on a ship's deck that cables or ropes are wound around: **Teams of sailors worked together to turn the *capstans* and wind the heavy cables around them.**

car·cass [kär′kəs] *n.* The dead body of an animal: **The vultures picked at the rabbit *carcass* by the roadside.**

car·ou·sel [kar′ə·sel′] *n.* A merry-go-round: **The wooden horses moved up and down as the *carousel* turned.**

cas·u·al·ly [kazh′oo·əl·ē] *adv.* Done offhandedly or without thinking. *syn.* informally

ca·tas·tro·phe [kə·tas′trə·fē] *n.* A sudden great disaster: **The famous Chicago Fire was an enormous *catastrophe* because it cost so many lives and destroyed so much property.** *syns.* calamity, misfortune, cataclysm

cat·e·chism [kat′ə·kiz′əm] *adj.* Relating to religious education: **Some students attend *catechism* classes at church one afternoon a week.**

chant [chant] *n.* A simple, rhythmic melody sung or shouted: **The monks joined together to sing *chants* after their evening meal.** *syn.* song

cir·cum·stance [sûr′kəm·stans′] *n.* Surrounding condition or situation: **The *circumstances* at his mother's house made it impossible for us to talk there in private.** *syn.* context

claus·tro·pho·bi·a [klôs′trə·fō′bē·ə] *n.* Fear of being in a small or enclosed place: **Her *claustrophobia* kept her from using the small walk-in closet in her bedroom.**

co·in·ci·dence [kō·in′sə·dəns] *n.* An unlikely event; the appearance of two things at the same place or time.

com·mend [kə·mend′] *v.* **com·mend·ed, com·mend·ing** To speak highly of: **The teacher *commended* the pupils on their homework.** *syn.* praise

com·po·sure [kəm·pō′zhər] *n.* Calmness: **She never loses her *composure*, even in a dangerous situation.** *syn.* self-control

com·pre·hend [kom′pri·hend′] *v.* **com·pre·hend·ed, com·pre·hend·ing** To understand: **I had trouble *comprehending* that difficult book.** *syn.* grasp

con·cil·i·a·to·ry [kən·sil′ē·ə·tôr′ē] *adj.* In a soothing or peacemaking manner: **The salesclerk spoke to the angry customer in a *conciliatory* tone and soon calmed him down.**

belligerently Today we use *belligerently* to describe any hostile or threatening way of acting. The Latin ancestor of this word—*bellum gerere*—was military. It meant "to wage war." If individuals or nations behave *belligerently*, watch out! They may be angry enough to go to war.

capstan

carousel

a	add	o͞o	took
ā	ace	o͞o	pool
â	care	u	up
ä	palm	û	burn
e	end	yo͞o	fuse
ē	equal	oi	oil
i	it	ou	pout
ī	ice	ng	ring
o	odd	th	thin
ō	open	th	this
ô	order	zh	vision

ə = { a in *above*   e in *sicken*
      i in *possible*
      o in *melon*   u in *circus*

cordially When you welcome a friend *cordially*, you are doing so in a warm and sincere way. You are acting from your heart. In fact, *cordially* goes back to the Latin word *cor*, meaning "heart." If you are in *accord* with someone, you agree with him or her. Your hearts are together. When there is *discord* between you, your hearts are far apart. The prefix *ac-* has the sense of "to" or "toward," and *dis-* means "away."

cordially

diagnostic This word and its relatives *diagnose*, *diagnosis*, and *diagnostician* go back to the ancient Greek *dia*, "between," and *gignoskein*, "to know." A doctor who knows the differences between diseases is a *diagnostician*. Incidentally, the English word *know* and the Greek *gignoskein* both come from the same ancient word *gno*, "to know."

con·de·scend·ing·ly [kon′di·sen′ding·lē] *adv.* In a way that looks down on something or someone. *syns.* arrogantly, patronizingly

con·se·quence [kon′sə·kwens′] *n.* A result or effect: **Consider the *consequences* of your acts.**

con·serve [kən·sûrv′] *v.* To save: **Hiroshi sat quietly by the track because he wanted to *conserve* his energy for the relay race.** *syns.* preserve, protect

con·sul·ta·tion [kon′səl·tā′shən] *n.* A meeting to discuss ideas or get advice: **Maria held a *consultation* with her lawyer to discuss her rights in the dispute.** *syn.* conference

con·tor·tion [kən·tôr′shən] *n.* The act of twisting: **We were amazed by the *contortions* of the acrobats.**

con·verse [kən·vûrs′] *v.* To have a conversation with someone. *syns.* speak, talk

con·vic·tion [kən·vik′shən] *n.* Strong belief in something.

cor·dial·ly [kôr′jəl·ē] *adv.* With friendliness and sincerity: **Smiling with delight, Mr. Cortez greeted his guests *cordially*.** *syns.* warmly, heartily

cour·ti·er [kôr′tē·ər] *n.* A member of a ruler's court: **The Queen called for all the *courtiers* to meet the visiting prince.**

cru·cial [krōō′shəl] *adj.* Extremely important. *syns.* key, significant

D

dav·it [dav′it] *n.* One of two cranes on the side of a ship, used for lowering and raising smaller boats: **One *davit* did not let out the cable, so we could not lower the lifeboat into the water.**

ded·i·cat·ed [ded′ə·kāt′id] *adj.* Set apart for or devoted to a special purpose: **The *dedicated* teacher spent many hours preparing her lessons.**

de·ject·ed·ly [di·jek′tid·lē] *adv.* In a downcast or depressed manner. *syn.* unhappily

de·scent [di·sent′] *n.* The act of going or coming down to a lower point.

des·o·late [des′ə·lit] *adj.* Lonely; without any people. *syns.* deserted, remote

des·per·a·tion [des′pə·rā′shən] *n.* A state of great need or helplessness leading to reckless behavior: **The child was overcome by a sense of *desperation* when he couldn't find his mother.** *syns.* terror, hopelessness

de·spon·dent·ly [di·spon′dənt·lē] *adv.* In a discouraged way. *syn.* despairingly

des·ti·ny [des′tə·nē] *n.* An unavoidable outcome. *syn.* fate

di·ag·nos·tic [dī′əg·nos′tik] *adj.* Having to do with analyzing or evaluating a condition or situation: **The *diagnostic* exam helped the school determine which grade the new student belonged in.**

dis·dain·ful·ly [dis·dān′fəl·ē] *adv.* In a scornful or disgusted manner. *syn.* contemptuously

dis·re·gard [dis′ri·gärd′] *n.* Lack of concern: **Miguel did not vote in the election because he had a *disregard* for politics.**

dis·rup·tion [dis·rup′shən] *n.* The act of breaking up: **The loud sound caused a *disruption* to the class.** *syn.* interruption

di·ver·si·ty [di·vûr′sə·tē] *n.* Being unlike: **Our class is interesting because of the *diversity* of ideas.** *syn.* difference

di·vert [di·vûrt′] *v.* **di·vert·ed, di·vert·ing** To throw someone off his or her planned course. *syn.* distract

dol·drums [dōl'drəmz *or* dol'drəmz] *n.* A bored or inactive state of mind. *syns.* dullness, listlessness

dom·i·nate [dom'ə·nāt'] *v.* **dom·i·nat·ed, dom·i·nat·ing** To control or have power over.

dou·blet [dub'lit] *n.* A tight-fitting jacket with or without sleeves: **A *doublet* was worn as commonly by a man in the fifteenth century as a suit jacket is worn today.**

du·bi·ous·ly [d(y)oo̅'bē·əs·lē] *adv.* With doubt or suspicion: **Brett looked at Meg *dubiously* when she claimed she spoke seven languages.** *syns.* doubtfully, questioningly

E

ed·i·ble [ed'ə·bəl] *adj.* Fit to be eaten. *syns.* eatable, palatable, appetizing

ef·fu·sive [i·fyoo̅'siv] *adj.* Gushing with emotion or enthusiasm.

e·lec·tive [i·lek'tiv] *n.* A course that a student may or may not choose to take.

e·lec·tro·cute [i·lek'trə·kyoot'] *v.* **e·lec·tro·cut·ed, e·lec·tro·cut·ing** To execute or kill with a charge of electricity.

em·bed [im·bed'] *v.* **em·bed·ded, em·bed·ding** To enclose something in a material of which it may eventually become a part: **The tiles were so deeply *embedded* in the concrete of the patio that we could not free them.** *syn.* implant

e·mit [i·mit'] *v.* **e·mit·ted, e·mit·ting** To give or send out, usually light or sound.

em·pha·size [em'fə·sīz'] *v.* **em·pha·sized, em·pha·siz·ing** To point out or call attention to: **We *emphasized* our team spirit by wearing the school colors.** *syns.* accentuate, stress

en·coun·ter [in·koun'tər] *n.* An unexpected meeting.

en·hance [in·hans'] *v.* **en·hanced, en·hanc·ing** To add to: **Good grooming *enhances* good looks.** *syn.* increase

e·on [ē'ən *or* ē'on] *n.* An extremely long time; hundreds of thousands of years: **Dinosaurs lived *eons* ago.**

ep·i·sode [ep'ə·sōd'] *n.* Any incident or event that is part of something continuous: **Mrs. Freeman told about an *episode* in the author's life.**

er·ror [er'ər] *n.* Something done, said, or believed incorrectly: **I made an addition *error* on the math test.** *syn.* mistake

etch [ech] *v.* **etched, etch·ing** To engrave a pattern or image: **The artist *etched* the image of her mother's face into the stone.**

e·ter·nal [i·tûr'nəl] *adj.* Having no beginning or end; lasting forever: **The wait to see the doctor seemed *eternal*.** *syn.* endless

eth·nic [eth'nik] *adj.* Belonging to a specific group of people who share the same language and culture. *syn.* cultural

e·ven·tu·al·ly [i·ven'choo̅·əl·ē] *adv.* At some point in the future. *syn.* ultimately

ex·ag·ger·at·ed [ig·zaj'ə·rāt'əd] *adj.* Larger than life or reality; much more than is real or possible.

ex·as·per·at·ed [ig·zas'pə·rāt'əd] *adj.* Very irritated or annoyed. *syn.* frustrated

ex·cur·sion [ik·skûr'zhən] *n.* A short trip or journey, usually for pleasure: **Harry and his cousin often went on *excursions* to the park for picnics.** *syn.* outing

ex·hort [ig·zôrt'] *v.* **ex·hort·ed, ex·hort·ing** To advise or urge earnestly: **The coach *exhorted* the team to play better.**

embed

ethnic

exaggerate In Latin, *agger* means "heap" or "pile." A person who *exaggerates* something really "piles it on" by making it seem more than it is. Sometimes people who *exaggerate* their troubles are said to "make mountains out of molehills."

a	add	oo̅	took
ā	ace	oo̅	pool
â	care	u	up
ä	palm	û	burn
e	end	yoo̅	fuse
ē	equal	oi	oil
i	it	ou	pout
ī	ice	ng	ring
o	odd	th	thin
ō	open	th	this
ô	order	zh	vision

ə = { a in *above*, e in *sicken*, i in *possible*, o in *melon*, u in *circus* }

F

fal·ter [fôl′tər] *v.* **fal·tered, fal·ter·ing** To hesitate or seem uncertain: **When he gave his speech without** *faltering* **once, he was glad he had practiced.**

fa·vor·a·ble [fā′vər·ə·bəl] *adj.* Helping: **A** *favorable* **wind made the boat move faster.**

fe·roc·i·ty [fə·ros′ə·tē] *n.* Fierceness. *syn.* savagery

fidg·et [fij′it] *v.* To stir about in an impatient, nervous, or restless way: **Children often** *fidget* **on rainy days.**

fit·ful·ly [fit′fə·lē] *adv.* In a way that ceases from time to time: **The noise outside caused her to sleep** *fitfully.* *syn.* unsteadily

flus·ter [flus′tər] *v.* To confuse or make upset.

for·bid·ding [fər·bid′ing] *adj.* Unfriendly and frightening. *syns.* repellent, intimidating

fore·sight [fôr′sīt′] *n.* The act or power of foreseeing or looking ahead: **Shondra had the** *foresight* **to study her notes before the test.**

frig·id [frij′id] *adj.* Extremely cold.

frus·tra·tion [frus·trā′shən] *n.* Anger or impatience at wasted effort or ineffectiveness. *syn.* exasperation

hieroglyphics

G

gar·ish [gâr′ish] *adj.* Too showy or bright: **The** *garish* **sign brought in many customers.** *syn.* gaudy

glint [glint] *v.* **glint·ed, glint·ing** To gleam or flash: **The shining metal** *glinted* **in the sunlight.**

gro·tesque [grō·tesk′] *adj.* Distorted or very strange or ugly in appearance or style: **The hyena is a** *grotesque* **animal.**

H

harsh·ly [härsh′lē] *adv.* In a way that is grating, rough, or unpleasant to the senses: **The** *harshly* **blowing winds made us go inside quickly.**

head·land [hed′lənd] *n.* A point of high land extending out into water: **From the** *headland,* **Janet could see sailboats on almost every side.**

hearth·fire [härth′fīr′] *n.* A fire in a fireplace or hearth: **We stood near the burning logs and warmed ourselves by the** *hearthfire.*

her·o·ine [her′ō·in] *n.* A girl or woman who is known for acts of courage and intelligence: **Everyone called her a** *heroine* **after she rescued the drowning child.**

hi·er·o·glyph·ics [hī′ər·ə·glif′iks *or* hī′rə·glif′iks] *n.* A written language of pictures and symbols, such as that used by the ancient Egyptians: **The explorer was able to read the** *hieroglyphics* **carved into the walls of the Egyptian tomb.**

horde [hôrd] *n.* A great crowd: **A** *horde* **of people attended the state fair.**

hum·drum [hum′drum′] *adj.* Dull and boring: **Kim could not sit through the entire** *humdrum* **television show.**

hy·per·ac·tive [hī′pər·ak′tiv] *adj.* Overly active: **The** *hyperactive* **child had trouble sitting still until the movie began.**

hys·te·ri·a [his·tir′ē·ə *or* his·ter′ē·ə] *n.* A state of uncontrolled excitement or emotion: **He was overcome by** *hysteria* **when he learned that his daughter had been in an accident.** *syn.* frenzy

I

il·lu·mi·na·tion [i·lōō′mə·nā′shən] *n.* Lighting; an amount of light.

im·pe·ri·ous [im·pir′ē·əs] *adj.* Proud and haughty: **The cat gave us an** *imperious* **look as it sat like a queen on the chair.** *syns.* arrogant, domineering

im·pli·ca·tion [im′plə·kā′shən] *n.* Something that is hinted at but not directly said: **The** *implication* **was that she did not want to go to the party, though she clearly did not want to say so.**

im·pres·sion [im·presh′ən] *n.* A feeling or idea: **Even though George was polite to the guests, I had the** *impression* **that he would rather be alone.** *syn.* perception

im·prob·a·ble [im·prob′ə·bəl] *adj.* Not likely: **The teacher didn't believe Mary's** *improbable* **excuse for not completing her homework.** *syn.* unlikely

in·ci·dent [in′sə·dənt] *n.* An event, often one of little importance: **He gave a long, boring account, including each** *incident* **of his trip to the store.**

in·ci·sive [in·sī′siv] *adj.* Sharp: **Her** *incisive* **wit kept everyone at the table laughing through the entire meal.** *syns.* keen, penetrating

in·con·se·quen·tial [in·kon′sə·kwen′shəl] *adj.* Unimportant: **Matthew crossed out** *inconsequential* **details as he prepared his report.** *syn.* minor

in·crim·i·nate [in·krim′ə·nāt′] *v.* **in·crim·i·nat·ed, in·crim·i·nat·ing** To declare or show to be guilty: **The fingerprints at the scene of the crime** *incriminated* **the suspect.**

in·dig·nant·ly [in·dig′nənt·lē] *adv.* With anger at something unjust or untrue: **The audience shouted** *indignantly* **at the speaker's lies.**

in·for·mal [in·fôr′məl] *adj.* On a relaxed or friendly basis: **I often have** *informal* **talks in the hallway with my English teacher.** *syn.* casual

in·her·i·tance [in·her′ə·təns] *n.* Something passed on through family or received from a parent or an ancestor: **This house was left to us as part of our** *inheritance* **when our father died.**

in·tact [in·takt′] *adj.* Whole or without any damage.

J

jeer [jir] *v.* **jeered, jeer·ing** To make fun of with insulting words: **The crowd** *jeered* **the opposing team when their star player missed the foul shot.** *syns.* ridicule, mock

L

leg·en·dar·y [lej′ən·der′ē] *adj.* Famous: **The** *legendary* **pyramids attract visitors from all over the world.**

le·vi·a·than [lə·vī′ə·thən] *n.* A huge animal or thing: **The great white shark is a** *leviathan* **that frightens many deep-sea divers.**

lu·gu·bri·ous [lōō·gōō′brē·əs] *adj.* Full of sadness: **The lost, hungry dog let out a** *lugubrious* **howl.** *syn.* mournful

leviathan

a	add	o͝o	took
ā	ace	o͞o	pool
â	care	u	up
ä	palm	û	burn
e	end	yo͞o	fuse
ē	equal	oi	oil
i	it	ou	pout
ī	ice	ng	ring
o	odd	th	thin
ō	open	t͟h	this
ô	order	zh	vision

ə = { a in *above*, e in *sicken*, i in *possible*, o in *melon*, u in *circus* }

luminous

lu·mi·nous [lōō′mə·nəs] *adj.* Full of light: **The** *luminous* **waves shone in the moonlight.** *syn.* glowing

M

mag·ni·tude [mag′nə·t(y)ōōd′] *n.* Great importance.

main·te·nance [mān′tə·nəns] *n.* Means of support: **A beautiful garden requires routine** *maintenance.*

ma·jes·ti·cal·ly [mə·jes′tik·lē] *adv.* In a way that shows great dignity: **The eagle circled the mountain-top** *majestically.* *syn.* royally

mar·tyr [mär′tər] *n.* A person who suffers a great deal: **He felt strongly enough to be a** *martyr* **for the cause.**

mas·sive [mas′iv] *adj.* Very large and heavy. *syns.* bulky, huge

meas·ly [mēz′lē] *adj.* Not having much worth: **When Cathy looked in the cookie jar, all she found were a few** *measly* **crumbs.** *syn.* meager

med·i·tate [med′ə·tāt′] *v.* To think deeply and quietly: **She sat down to** *meditate* **about how to thank her aunt for the special gift.** *syn.* contemplate

med·i·ta·tion [med′ə·tā′shən] *n.* The act or process of thinking deeply: **Quiet** *meditation* **helps me relax after a rough day.** *syns.* contemplation, reflection

mes·mer·ized [mez′mə·rīzd′] *adj.* Hypnotized: **We sat** *mesmerized* **by the beautiful song.**

mo·men·tum [mō·men′təm] *n.* The force of a moving body. *syn.* force

mo·not·o·nous [mə·not′ə·nəs] *adj.* Unchanging or boringly repetitive. *syn.* tedious

monotonous A voice that doesn't change in tone is a monotone. *Monos* is the Greek word for "single." Listening to someone who speaks in a monotone is difficult. In fact, it is downright boring! So *monotonous* has come to refer to anything that bores us because it is always the same.

N

nau·ti·cal [nô′ti·kəl] *adj.* Having to do with the sea: **The** *nautical* **mile, which is longer than the standard mile, is used to measure the length of a ship's journey.**

no·bil·i·ty [nō·bil′ə·tē] *n.* People of noble birth with inherited titles or rank; those possessing fine qualities: **Although she was not born into the** *nobility,* **her intelligence and generosity made her noble.** *syn.* aristocracy

non·de·script [non′də·skript′] *adj.* Not special or distinctive: **Her shoes were so** *nondescript* **that I don't remember anything about them.** *syns.* common, ordinary

O

ob·vi·ous [ob′vē·əs] *adj.* Clear or easy to see or understand: **It was** *obvious* **that the student hadn't read the assignment after the teacher asked him a few questions.** *syns.* evident, visible

oc·cu·pa·tion [ok′yə·pā′shən] *n.* Forced military takeover and possession.

om·i·nous·ly [om′ə·nəs·lē] *adv.* In a way that points to something bad or frightening: **The clouds gathered** *ominously* **before the storm.** *syn.* threateningly

op·ti·mis·tic [op′tə·mis′tik] *adj.* Full of hope and cheerfulness: **My mother is** *optimistic* **that she will get a job soon.**

or·tho·pe·dist [ôr′thə·pē′dist] *n.* A doctor who specializes in treating bones and joints: **The** *orthopedist* **put a cast on my broken leg.**

o·ver·whelm [ō′vər·(h)welm′] *v.*
o·ver·whelmed,
o·ver·whelm·ing To overcome
completely: **The long assignment**
overwhelmed **Jason.**

P

pa·le·on·tol·o·gist
[pā′lē·on·tol′ə·jist] *n.* A person
who studies ancient forms of life,
usually by looking at fossils: **The**
paleontologist **carefully exam-**
ined the fossil skull of a small
dinosaur.

pan·de·mo·ni·um
[pan′·də·mō′nē·əm] *n.* Great dis-
order and uproar: *Pandemonium*
erupted when the election results
were announced.

pa·py·rus [pə·pī′rəs] *n.* A kind
of paper made from the papyrus
plant and used by the ancient
Egyptians, Greeks, and Romans:
The ancient manuscript was writ-
ten on *papyrus.*

pe·des·tri·an [pə·des′trē·ən] *n.* A
person walking or traveling on
foot: **The young bicyclist almost**
ran into two *pedestrians* **who**
were walking slowly along the
path through the park.

per·spec·tive [pər·spek′tiv] *n.* A
way of seeing the relative importance of things: **Studying world**
history has given me a new
perspective **on the events of**
today. *syn.* outlook

pit·i·ful [pit′i′fəl] *adj.* Arousing
sympathy: **My sister gave a**
pitiful **look when she was told**
she couldn't go.

plank·ton [plangk′tən] *n.* Tiny
animals and plants that float in
water but cannot swim: **Many**
fish and other sea animals eat
plankton **as the major part of**
their diet.

port [pôrt] *n.* A place where ships
arrive and depart: **Frank always**
enjoyed going to the *port* **to**
watch the ships coming in. *syn.*
harbor

po·ten·tial [pə·ten′chəl] *adj.*
Possible, but not yet actual: **The**
storm posed a *potential* **danger.**

prac·ti·cal [prak′ti·kəl] *adj.* Having
to do with actual use or practice
rather than theories or ideas: **She**
learned theories in class, but
gained *practical* **experience on**
the job.

prat·tle [prat′(ə)l] *n.* Talk that is not
important: **Part of the school**
council president's speech was
about serious issues, but another
part was just silly *prattle* **about**
table tennis and video games.
syn. foolishness

pre·cau·tion·ar·y
[pri·kô′shən·er′ē] *adj.* Serving
to prevent or avoid harm:
Fastening your seat belt is a good
precautionary **measure.** *syn.*
preventative

pre·cious [presh′əs] *adj.* Highly valued: **The pirates discovered gold**
coins and *precious* **jewels in the**
treasure chest.

pre·cise [pri·sīs′] *adj.* Carefully
planned or exact. *syn.* accurate

prej·u·dice [prej′o͞o·dis] *n.* An
unfair opinion or judgment
formed in advance of or without
examination of the available facts:
My parents had a *prejudice*
against the new song even before
they heard it.

prim·i·tive [prim′ə·tiv] *adj.* Old-
fashioned or not advanced. *syns.*
archaic, crude

pro·cras·ti·nate [prō·kras′tə·nāt′]
v. **pro·cras·ti·nat·ed,**
pro·cras·ti·nat·ing To avoid or
put off until later.

pro·mo·tion [prə·mō′shən] *n.*
Advancement in rank or grade:
My mother received a *promotion*
in her job.

paleontologist

procrastinate Do you
ever *procrastinate*, or put
off until the future something that you should do
right now? Everybody
does, and so did the
ancient Romans. They had
a word for it—*procras-*
tinare. It was formed from
pro, "forward," and *cras*,
"tomorrow."

a	add	o͝o	took
ā	ace	o͞o	pool
â	care	u	up
ä	palm	û	burn
e	end	yo͞o	fuse
ē	equal	oi	oil
i	it	ou	pout
ī	ice	ng	ring
o	odd	th	thin
ō	open	th	this
ô	order	zh	vision

ə = { a in *above*   e in *sicken*
      i in *possible*
      o in *melon*   u in *circus*

rendezvous This word for a planned meeting or joining of forces comes from a command in French. *Rendez vous* means "present yourself." Don't be late for a *rendezvous*!

pub·lic·i·ty [pub·lis′ə·tē] *n.* Any information intended to bring a person or thing to the attention of the public: **That story was released to get** *publicity.*

pulse [puls] *n.* The rhythmical beating of the arteries resulting from the contractions of the heart: **She checked the** *pulse* **of the runners before and after the race.**

Q

quin·tes·sen·tial [kwin′tə·sen′shəl] *adj.* Possessing the purest or most essential part or quality of something: **Fans of jazz think that it is the** *quintessential* **form of music.**

quiv·er [kwiv′ər] *v.* **quiv·ered, quiv·er·ing** To make a slight trembling motion; vibrate: **The old dog was so cold from being left outside that his nose began to** *quiver.*

R

receptionist

ra·tion [rash′ən *or* rā′shən] *v.* **ra·tioned, ra·tion·ing** To control the distribution of something scarce.

re·as·sure [rē′ə·shoŏr′] *v.* To free from doubt or fear: **Mrs. Allen tried to** *reassure* **the frightened boy by telling him that nothing would harm him.** *syns.* console, encourage

re·cep·tion·ist [ri·sep′shə·nist] *n.* A person employed in an office to answer the telephone and greet people.

re·lent [ri·lent′] *v.* To become less severe and more gentle and cooperative. *syn.* slacken

rel·ic [rel′ik] *n.* Something remaining from a past culture or time period. *syn.* artifact

re·mark·a·ble [ri·mär′kə·bəl] *adj.* Worthy of notice: **The pilot was known all over the country for her** *remarkable* **airplane stunts.** *syn.* extraordinary

ren·dez·vous [rän′dā·voŏ′] *n.* A planned meeting.

re·sis·tance [ri·zis′təns] *n.* A group of people fighting to oppose a military invasion.

re·trieve [ri·trēv′] *v.* **re·trieved, re·triev·ing** To get something back. *syns.* recover, regain

re·vert [ri·vûrt′] *v.* **re·vert·ed, re·vert·ing** To go back to a previous condition or attitude.

right·eous [rī′chəs] *adj.* Being exactly right according to rules or principles: **The coach knew the rules so well that he felt** *righteous* **in arguing with the umpire about the play.**

ri·val [rī′vəl] *v.* **ri·valed, ri·val·ing** To try to outdo or defeat: **The teams** *rivaled* **each other for the championship.**

S

sar·cas·ti·cal·ly [sär·kas′tik·lē] *adv.* In a way that makes fun of someone; with mocking insincerity. *syns.* jokingly, tauntingly

scape·goat [skāp′gōt′] *n.* A person, group, or animal made to bear the blame for the errors of others: **When the team lost the game, they made Jennifer the** *scapegoat.*

seg·ment [seg′mənt] *n.* A part cut off or divided from the rest of something: **One** *segment* **of the audience seemed to enjoy the show.** *syn.* section

self·con·scious [self′kon′shəs] *adj.* Feeling embarrassed because people are watching.

sen·si·tive [sen′sə·tiv] *adj.* Capable of feeling, reacting, or appreciating quickly or easily: The ear is *sensitive* to sound.

se·rene [si·rēn′] *adj.* Peaceful; tranquil; unruffled: The *serene* mood was shattered when a motorcycle roared through. *syn.* calm

sig·nif·i·cant [sig·nif′ə·kənt] *adj.* Important or noteworthy: I have noticed a *significant* difference in my health since I started exercising.

skep·ti·cal·ly [skep′tik·lē] *adv.* In a way that shows question or doubt: He opened the box and looked *skeptically* at the 1,500 pieces of the puzzle.

slain [slān] *v.* Killed, especially by violent means: Bethanne likes to read fantastic stories about fire-breathing dragons who are *slain* by brave knights.

spec·ta·tor [spek′tā·tər] *n.* A person who watches an event: I enjoy being a *spectator* at an exciting game like basketball.

star·board [stär′bərd] *n.* The right, in nautical language; the right-hand side of a ship when one is on board facing the front: The captain shouted the command to turn the ship to the right—"Hard a-*starboard*!"

stench [stench] *n.* A foul odor: The *stench* alerted us that the garbage hadn't been taken out. *syn.* stink

stra·te·gic [strə·tē′jik] *adj.* Of or having to do with careful planning: A *strategic* move at the beginning helped him win the chess game.

strick·en [strik′ən] *adj.* Strongly affected or overcome: She was *stricken* with the disease at an early age.

sub·merge [səb·mûrj′] *v.* **sub·merged, sub·merg·ing** To go underwater: Chiang *submerged* herself in the cool water of the lake.

sub·side [səb·sīd′] *v.* **sub·sid·ed, sub·sid·ing** To become less violent or intense: After my anger had *subsided*, I was able to apologize. *syns.* lessen, calm

suf·fi·cient [sə·fish′ənt] *adj.* Equal to what is needed: Do you have *sufficient* money to go to the movies? *syns.* enough, adequate

su·per·vi·sion [soo′pər·vizh′ən] *n.* Direction or control: The day care center had adequate *supervision* for the children. *syns.* regulation, management

sup·press [sə·pres′] *v.* **sup·pressed, sup·press·ing** To put down or end: I had to *suppress* my anger at her rudeness. *syn.* crush

sur·geon [sûr′jən] *n.* A doctor whose practice is largely limited to the repair or removal of diseased or injured organs or parts of the body: The *surgeon* prepared to operate on the patient.

sus·pense [sə·spens′] *n.* A state or condition of uncertainty and intense curiosity: The storyteller held us in *suspense* by not revealing the secret until the very end.

T

tact·ful·ly [takt′fəl·ē] *adv.* In a manner that does not offend or hurt others: She declined his invitation to dinner so *tactfully* that his feelings were not hurt. *syns.* skillfully, gracefully

ten·ta·tive·ly [ten′tə·tiv·lē] *adv.* Cautiously or with hesitation: Aiko walked *tentatively* along the wall of the dark room, feeling for the light switch. *syn.* reluctantly

surgeon

a	add	oo	took
ā	ace	oo	pool
â	care	u	up
ä	palm	û	burn
e	end	yoo	fuse
ē	equal	oi	oil
i	it	ou	pout
ī	ice	ng	ring
o	odd	th	thin
ō	open	th	this
ô	order	zh	vision

ə = { a in *above*   e in *sicken*
 i in *possible*
 o in *melon*   u in *circus*

tex·ture [teks′chər] *n.* The feel of something's surface: **The *texture* of the cloth was rough and prickly.**

to·nal [tō′nəl] *adj.* Of or having to do with tones, pitches, or certain sounds: **In *tonal* languages the same word can have different meanings, depending on the pitch at which it is spoken.**

tor·ture [tôr′chər] *n.* Great mental or physical suffering: **For a week I suffered the *torture* of not knowing my test grade.**

trans·fixed [trans·fikst′] *adj.* Motionless, as with horror or fear: **We were *transfixed* when we saw the tornado in the distance.**

trans·for·ma·tion [trans·fər·mā′shən] *n.* A big change in appearance, character, condition, or form: **We were surprised at the *transformation* of Ricky's mood.**

trans·par·ent [trans·pâr′ənt] *adj.* Easily seen through: **The *transparent* walls let the sunlight in.** *syn.* clear

tread [tred] *v.* To step on: **The worker put a barrier around the sidewalk so that no one would *tread* on the wet cement.** *syn.* trample

tur·bu·lent [tûr′byə·lənt] *adj.* Disturbed or moving around a great deal: **As the storm clouds darkened, the sea became *turbulent* and rocked the ship.** *syn.* tumultuous

turbulent

U

u·nique [yoo·nēk′] *adj.* Being the only one of its type: **Each person in this world has a *unique* personality.** *syn.* singular

u·ni·son [yoo′nə·sən] *n.* Agreement in pitch, as among two or more voices or instruments: **The class sang the song in *unison*.**

un·wav·er·ing [un·wā′və·ring] *adj.* Not faltering or failing: **No matter what trouble the boy got into, his mother's love was *unwavering*.** *syns.* steady, constant

ut·ter [ut′ər] *adj.* Complete: **The politician felt *utter* joy when she won the election.** *syn.* total

V

van·tage [van′tij] *n.* A position of superiority or advantage: **From this *vantage*, we can see for miles.**

vir·tu·al·ly [vûr′choo·əl·lē] *adv.* For the most part: **Virtually everyone applauded after he sang.**

vul·ner·a·ble [vul′nər·ə·bəl] *adj.* Capable of being hurt, injured, or wounded: **The young bird was *vulnerable* without its mother nearby.**

W

war·i·ly [wâr′ə·lē′] *adv.* In a watchful and suspicious way: **We eyed the stranger *warily*.** *syns.* carefully, cautiously

wea·ry [wir′ē] *v.* **wea·ried, wea·ry·ing** To make tired, discontented, or bored: **I fell asleep because his endless talking *wearied* me.**

wrath [rath] *n.* Great or violent anger: **We suffered the *wrath* of the terrible hurricane.** *syn.* rage

INDEX OF
TITLES AND AUTHORS

Page numbers in light type refer to biographical information.

Acknowledgments continued

HarperCollins Publishers: From *Spring Comes to the Ocean* by Jean Craighead George, cover illustration by John Wilson. Text and cover illustration copyright © 1965 by Jean Craighead George. From *Water Sky* by Jean Craighead George. Text and cover illustration copyright © 1987 by Jean Craighead George. "Vergil, the Laid-back Dog" from *My Brother Louis Measures Worms* by Barbara Robinson. Text copyright © 1988 by Barbara Robinson. Cover illustration by John Suh from *Shadow Shark* by Colin Thiele. Illustration © 1988 by John Suh. "Silent Bianca" from *The Girl Who Cried Flowers and Other Tales* by Jane Yolen. Text copyright © 1974 by Jane Yolen.

Holiday House, Inc.: Cover photograph from *The Wright Brothers: How They Invented the Airplane* by Russell Freedman. Photograph courtesy of The Smithsonian Institution. Cover photograph by Lawrence Migdale from *Hoang Anh: A Vietnamese-American Boy* by Diane Hoyt-Goldsmith. Photograph copyright © 1992 by Lawrence Migdale.

Houghton Mifflin Company: "A Song of Greatness" from *The Children Sing in the Far West* by Mary Austin. Text copyright 1928 by Mary Austin, text © renewed 1956 by Kenneth M. Chapman and Mary C. Wheelwright. From *Number the Stars* by Lois Lowry. Text and cover photograph copyright © 1989 by Lois Lowry. From *The One Hundredth Thing About Caroline* by Lois Lowry, cover illustration by Diane de Groat. Text copyright © 1983 by Lois Lowry; illustration copyright © 1983 by Diane de Groat. From *Castle* by David Macaulay. Copyright © 1977 by David Macaulay. From *Island of the Blue Dolphins* by Scott O'Dell. cover illustration by Ted Lewin. Text copyright © 1960, renewed 1988 by Scott O'Dell; cover illustration copyright © 1990 by Ted Lewin.

Alfred A. Knopf, Inc.: From *James and the Giant Peach* by Roald Dahl, cover illustration by Nancy Ekholm Burkert. Text and cover illustration copyright © 1961 by Roald Dahl; copyright renewed 1989 by Roald Dahl. Cover illustration by Rob Sauber from *Skinnybones* by Barbara Park. Illustration copyright © 1982 by Rob Sauber.

Deborah Nourse Lattimore: Cover illustration by Deborah Nourse Lattimore from *Detectives in Togas* by Henry Winterfield.

Lerner Publications, 241 First Avenue North, Minneapolis, MN 55401: From pp. 42–51 in *The Vietnamese in America* by Paul Rutledge. Text copyright 1973 by Lerner Publications.

Little, Brown and Company: "Books Fall Open" from *One at a Time* by David McCord. Text copyright © 1965, 1966 by David McCord. Cover illustration by Holly Meade from *All Day Long* by David McCord. From *Maniac Magee* by Jerry Spinelli, cover photograph by Carol Palmer. Text and cover photograph copyright © 1990 by Jerry Spinelli. From *Life in the Oceans* by Norbert Wu. Copyright © 1991 by Tern Enterprise, Inc.

Lothrop, Lee & Shepard Books, a division of William Morrow & Company, Inc.: From *Hello, My Name Is Scrambled Eggs* by Jamie Gilson, cover illustration by John Wallner. Text copyright © 1985 by Jamie Gilson; Cover illustration copyright © 1985 by John Wallner.

Macmillan Publishing Company: From *Zeely* by Virginia Hamilton, cover illustration by Symeon Shimin. Text copyright © 1967 by Virginia Hamilton; illustration copyright © 1967 by Macmillan Publishing Company.

Margaret K. McElderry Books, a division of Macmillan Publishing Company: Cover illustration by Kinuko Craft from *A Jar of Dreams* by Yoshiko Uchida. Copyright © 1981 by Yoshiko Uchida.

Alan Mazzetti: Cover illustration by Alan Mazzetti from *Taking Sides* by Gary Soto.

Mendola Ltd.: Cover illustration by Carol Newsom from *Bingo Brown and the Language of Love* by Betsy Byars.

The Millbrook Press: Cover photograph from *Colin Powell: Straight to the Top* by Rose Blue and Corinne J. Naden. Cover photograph courtesy of Gamma-Liaison; camouflage courtesy of Ginger Giles.

Morrow Junior Books, a division of William Morrow & Company, Inc.: Cover photograph from *Earthquakes* by Seymour Simon. Cover photograph courtesy of The Image Bank/Garry Gay.

National Council of Teachers of English: "Foreign Student" by Barbara B. Robinson from *English Journal*, May 1976. Text copyright 1976 by the National Council of Teachers of English.

New Directions Publishing Corp.: Poem XXI (Retitled: "On the Eastern Horizon") from *One Hundred More Poems from the Japanese* by Kenneth Rexroth. Text copyright © 1974, 1976 by Kenneth Rexroth.

Orchard Books, New York: From *The True Confessions of Charlotte Doyle* by Avi, cover illustration by Ruth E. Murray. Text copyright © 1990 by Avi; cover illustration copyright © 1990 by Ruth E. Murray.

Puffin Books, a division of Penguin Books USA Inc.: Cover illustration by Lino Saffioti from *The Summer of the Swans* by Betsy Byars. Illustration copyright © 1991 by Lino Saffioti.

G. P. Putnam's Sons: From pp. 7–38 in *UFOs, ETs & Visitors from Space* (Retitled: "The UFO Question") by Melvin Berger. Text copyright © 1988 by Melvin Berger.

R studio T: Cover design by R studio T from *Outward Dreams: Black Inventors and Their Inventions* by Jim Haskins. © R studio T, New York.

Random House, Inc.: From *The Phantom Tollbooth* by Norton Juster, illustrated by Jules Feiffer. Text copyright © 1961 by Norton Juster; text copyright renewed 1989 by Norton Juster. Illustrations copyright © 1961 by Jules Feiffer; illustrations copyright renewed 1989 by Jules Feiffer.

Goro Sasaki: Cover illustration by Goro Sasaki from *Pacific Crossing* by Gary Soto.

Scholastic, Inc.: From *Exploring the Titanic* by Robert D. Ballard. Text copyright © 1988 by Ballard & Family. A Scholastic/Madison Press Book.

The Rod Serling Trust: "The Monsters Are Due On Maple Street" by Rod Serling. Text © 1960 by Rod Serling; text © 1988 by Carolyn Serling, Jodi Serling and Anne Serling.

Sniffen Court Books: From pp. 18–23 in *Behind the Sealed Door: The Discovery of the Tomb and Treasures of Tutankhamun* by Irene and Laurence Swinburne. Text copyright © 1977 by Sniffen Court Books.

Viking Penguin, a division of Penguin Books USA Inc.: From *Bingo Brown and the Language of Love* by Betsy Byars. Text copyright © 1989 by Betsy Byars. Cover illustration by Carol Newsom from *Bingo Brown: Gypsy Lover* by Betsy Byars. Illustration copyright © 1990 by Carol Newsom. From pp. 64–72 in *Mojo and the Russians* by Walter Dean Myers. Text copyright © 1977 by Walter Dean Myers.

Walker and Company, 435 Hudson Street, New York, NY 10014: From *Outward Dreams: Black Inventors and Their Inventions* (Retitled: "The Real McCoy") by Jim Haskins. Text copyright © 1992 by Jim Haskins.